Psychoeducational Assessment and Report Writing

Stefan C. Dombrowski

Psychoeducational Assessment and Report Writing

 Springer

Stefan C. Dombrowski
Rider University School Psychology Program
Lawrenceville, NJ, USA

ISBN 978-1-4939-1910-9   ISBN 978-1-4939-1911-6 (eBook)
DOI 10.1007/978-1-4939-1911-6
Springer New York Heidelberg Dordrecht London

Library of Congress Control Number: 2014951198

Printed on acid-free paper

Springer is part of Springer Science+Business Media (www.springer.com)

Preface

This book is designed to help graduate students in school and clinical child psychology acquire the needed knowledge and necessary skill set to evaluate students (K-12) and write effective psychoeducational assessment reports. Psychoeducational assessment reports, most of which are conducted by psychologists working in a school setting, are by far the most prevalent form of child psychological evaluation. The lack of availability of a training text on psychoeducational assessment and report writing makes this book a useful resource that fills a needed gap in the literature. Existing texts are too broad, offering simultaneous guidance on clinical assessment, psychoeducational assessment, adult assessment, and preschool assessment. The contents of these sources are primarily geared toward students (or practitioners) who seek to work in a private practice, university clinic, or hospital setting and span all age ranges (infant through geriatric). None of the existing books provide sufficient coverage of the process of psychoeducational assessment and report writing particularly in relation to the IDEA/state special education classifications for which psychologists in the schools will become responsible: learning disabilities, emotional disturbance, autism, intellectual disabilities, and other health impairment.

Unlike other volumes, this book presents an approach to assessment and report writing that may be readily adopted by trainers in school and clinical child psychology, understood by professionals and parents alike, and effectively utilized by IEP teams. The book casts a narrow net, seeking to offer specific guidance on the practice of psychoeducational assessment and report writing for school-aged children. Because no other books sufficiently focus on this topic, this text portends to become a useful resource for instructors in school and clinical child psychology who teach coursework on the evaluation of children. It will also be useful to graduate students in those disciplines as well as early career psychologists who wish for a refresher to their knowledge base.

The book comprises four sections. The first section furnishes a general overview of the process of psychoeducational assessment and report writing. The second section offers a section-by-section report writing discussion (e.g., Reason for Referral; Assessment Methods and Sources of Data; Assessment Results; Conceptualization and Classification; Summary and Recommendations) with a chapter devoted to each major report component. The third section furnishes general guidance regarding the psychoeducational evaluation of major IDEA classification categories (e.g., LD, ED, autism, OHI, and intellectual disability). It also presents sample reports for those categories in an appendix at the end of each chapter. The final section discusses miscellaneous legal, ethical, and professional issues including practical guidance on the process of oral reporting.

Objectives

Geared toward graduate students in school and clinical child psychology, but also useful as a refresher for practicing child psychologists, this book seeks to accomplish the following objectives:

1. Offer a comprehensive, practical resource that may be useful to instructors and graduate students in school and clinical child psychology on the process of conducting comprehensive psychoeducational assessments, writing reports, and furnishing feedback to parents.
2. Offer specific guidance on gathering information and data on the child via interviewing, rating forms, classroom observations, and developmental history questionnaires.
3. Offer a section-by-section detailed discussion of each psychoeducational report component including identifying information, referral reason, assessment methods and sources of data, assessment results, conceptualization and classification, and summary and recommendations.
4. Offer a structured approach to the provision of feedback to parents, caregivers, and teachers.
5. Offer a discussion of ethical, practical, legal, and empirical considerations when engaging in psychoeducational assessment, report writing, and oral reporting.

As a resource for graduate students, this text assumes that students already have a sufficient grasp of standard written English. Therefore, it will not review basic writing principles. If writing is generally an area of weakness then remediation is strongly suggested. This text will not cover functional behavioral assessment (FBA). An FBA may be an important adjunct to the psychoeducational report but the topic is covered adequately in other texts on this topic. It will also not cover the assessment of children's intelligence including reviews of specific cognitive ability instruments. This topic is adequately covered in existing texts. Instead, this book restricts its focus to the psychoeducational assessment of children in kindergarten through 12th grade. It does not extend its gaze downward to infant and preschool assessment nor upward to college, adult, and geriatric assessment. Additionally, the book does not discuss neuropsychological, vocational, or forensic assessment.

It approaches the practice of assessment from a psychoeducational, rather than clinical, perspective although there is overlap between the two approaches particularly when the psychoeducational assessment is conducted in a clinic, university, private practice, or hospital setting. The distinction between psychoeducational and psychological assessment and report writing is covered in the first chapter of this book.

The Book's Genesis

This book was born out of my own need for a teaching text for the training of graduate students in school and clinical child psychology on the processes and principles of psychoeducational assessment and report writing in the school-aged child. There are several available resources on children's assessment and diagnosis, but none that specifically worked well for my purposes. There are even fewer texts that present real-world examples of comprehensive psychoeducational reports within a specifically delineated report writing framework. I have endeavored to accomplish this task and hope that you find that it augments your understanding of the process of psychoeducational assessment, report writing, and oral reporting.

Cherry Hill, NJ, USA   Stefan C. Dombrowski

Acknowledgments

This book is dedicated to the past, present, and future graduate students in School Psychology at Rider University. Without your insightful questioning over the years this book would not have come to fruition. I also express continued appreciation to Judy Jones and Garth Haller at Springer. This is now my third book with Springer and the process of publishing with them has been enjoyable.

I also dedicate this book to my wife, Debbie; my two amazing little boys (Maxwell, age 9, and Henry, age 7); my nephew, Kevin; and my father.

S.C.D.

Contents

Part II   Section-by-Section Report Writing Guidance

Part IV   Oral Reporting and Miscellaneous Topics in Psychoeducational Assessment and Report Writing

Part I
Overview of the Psychoeducational Assessment and Report Writing Process

Chapter 1
Purpose of Psychoeducational Assessment and Report Writing

1.1 Definition and Purpose of Psychoeducational Assessment

It is important to define psychoeduational assessment and distinguish it from psychological assessment. The term psychoeducational assessment may be defined as a type of assessment that is used to understand an individual's cognitive, academic, social, emotional, behavioral, communicative, and adaptive functioning within an educational setting. Psychoeducational assessment may extend downward to the preschool age time period or upward to the college and adult time period. The majority of psychoeducational assessments are conducted on the kindergarten to grade 12 populations. Psychoeducational assessment addresses whether the child is eligible for services and what those services might look like in a school setting. It places primary emphasis upon impairment that occurs in the educational setting rather than in environments outside of the educational context that is customary in clinical classification. Psychoeducational assessment frequently involves an evaluation of a child's learning and academic needs. However, it can also include the evaluation of intellectual, behavioral, social, emotional, communication, and adaptive areas if those areas are suspected to adversely impact educational functioning. As a result, individuals conducting psychoeducational evaluations must have a thorough understanding of what may be considered clinical conditions. This includes but is not limited to autism spectrum disorders, schizophrenia, Attention-Deficit/ Hyperactivity Disorder (ADHD), disorders of mood (e.g., anxiety, depression, bipolar), disorders of conduct, and medical conditions that may come to bear on educational functioning. Keep in mind, however, that IDEA, not DSM, drives classification decisions in U.S. schools so respective state special education classification categories should be referenced.

Psychoeducational assessment is distinguished from psychological assessment by its narrower scope and focus on an individual's (i.e., children's) functioning in an educational setting. Psychological assessment is broader and may address questions of custody in divorce proceedings, fitness to stand trial, qualification for social

© Springer Science+Business Media New York 2015
S.C. Dombrowski, *Psychoeducational Assessment and Report Writing*,
DOI 10.1007/978-1-4939-1911-6_1

security benefits, or qualification for additional support and services under a diagnosis of intellectual disability. Psychoeducational assessment deals primarily with educationally based classification and services. The vast majority of psycho-educational assessments are conducted on primary school (K to 12) populations although psychoeducational evaluations may also be conducted in university settings. Within the USA, questions typically addressed include whether a child qualifies for additional support under a specific IDEA classification and what school-based accommodations and services are appropriate. The focus is on how the suspected disability impacts the child's educational functioning within a school setting and what recommendations are appropriate to support the child's educational functioning.

1.2 Who Conducts Psychoeducational Assessments?

Although precise data is unavailable, it is likely safe to assume that psychologists working in the schools conduct the vast majority of psychoeducational evaluations. These psychologists (i.e., masters, Ed.S., or doctoral level) are employed by the school district and receive their school psychologist certification most commonly through a state department of education. The school psychologist may also be a licensed psychologist who can "hang up a shingle" and work in private practice. However, in most states with few exceptions (e.g., Wyoming) only certified school psychologists may be employed by a school district for purpose of completing a psychoeducational evaluation.

Licensed psychologists working in private practice may also be involved in the completion of psychoeducational reports. Many times parents seeking questions about their child's functioning may wish to obtain an outside opinion. In these instances, and for a cost, the outside psychologist may be able to devote the time and energy to completing a thorough evaluation. Of course, the parent should be warned that the outside psychological/psychoeducational evaluation must be considered, but need not be accepted, by the receiving school district. The outside psychoeducational evaluation may provide valuable information but it sometimes lacks alignment with the customs and nuances of psychoeducational evaluations written by psychologists in the schools. This may limit the utility of such evaluations for classification and educational planning within the school.

For graduate students in clinical child psychology who may wish to pursue a private psychoeducational evaluation practice this book will be useful. At times, a parent or legal guardian may wish to challenge the results of the school-based evaluation. When this occurs, the legal guardian is permitted to obtain an Independent Educational Evaluation (IEE). An IEE is generally high stakes and anxiety-evoking because it could involve a due process hearing or litigation. However, if psychologists follow the guidance within this book then the potential due process hearing is likely to be less contentious because assessment will be comprehensive and the subsequent report thorough, well-organized, and of high quality.

1.3   Psychoeducational Versus Psychological Assessment and Report Writing

Psychoeducational assessment and report writing has areas of overlap and distinction from psychological assessment report writing.

Similarities

- Assesses most domains of functioning including cognitive, academic, social, emotional, behavioral, and adaptive functioning.
- The report structure and format are similar.
- The approach to conceptualizing and classifying/diagnosing is data-driven and evidenced based.
- Uses many of the same norm-referenced assessment instruments.

Differences

- Psychoeducational assessment may not fully present the results of an evaluation of family functioning because of concerns over family privacy issues. A psychological assessment may evaluate family functioning more fully.
- The bulk of psychoeducational assessments occur within the kindergarten to grade 12 time period. Psychological assessment spans the life span from infant to geriatric.
- To determine a classification, psychoeducational assessment primarily determines whether there has been an adverse impact on children's educational functioning whereas psychological assessment will investigate for an impact on social, vocational, and relational functioning.
- Psychoeducational assessment generally stays away from personality assessment and projective measures (e.g., Rorschach). Psychological assessment will investigate more fully personality dimensions and may utilize projective measures.
- Psychological assessment encompasses forensic evaluation including child custody, child welfare, criminal cases, and other forensic matters.
- Psychological assessment usually involves a licensed psychologist. In the US school setting, psychoeducational assessment may be conducted by master's level or educational specialist (Ed.S.) practitioners.
- Psychoeducational assessment includes observations of children in vivo (i.e., in the classroom or school setting) whereas psychological assessment generally uses a clinic-based assessment setting observation.
- Psychological assessment may provide interview results from a wider range of individuals (i.e., collateral contacts). Psychoeducational assessment generally only gathers interview data on students, parents, teachers, teacher's aides, and professionals who provide direct support to the child.
- In the USA, psychological assessment utilizes the DSM or ICD to make classification decisions whereas psychoeducational assessment uses IDEA for classification decisions. The DSM is used in Canada for both psychological and psychoeducational assessment.

1.4   Feedback Conference

Students learning how to furnish feedback to parents/legal guardians regarding a psychoeducational assessment are best served by a structured framework. The provision of feedback requires practice to improve in this area. The purpose of the feedback conference is to convey the report's contents and conclusion in as clear and concise manner as possible. As close to the beginning of a report conference as possible, it is important to furnish a summary of your classification conclusion (i.e., whether the child was found eligible for special education support). Otherwise, the parent or caregiver may anxiously anticipate this discussion and may not hear anything that is discussed until you present your opinion on classification.

Of course, the assumption that the process will unfold as planned is naïve. The oral feedback session will generally unfold smoothly, but there are times when it will not. For instance, let's take the example of an oral feedback session preceding an IEP meeting that did not go as planned. Sometimes parents will appear unexpectedly with a special education advocate who will raise questions about the report and its conclusions. (This should not be misconstrued to suggest that the presence of a special education advocate automatically makes the meeting contentious). This may feel unnerving for even the most veteran psychologist but it need not be if the psychologist assumes a collaborative approach. To assist with the provision of oral feedback, the chapter on oral reporting will offer guidance for various feedback scenarios. This includes the unexpected response, the caregiver who may be in denial, and the appreciative caregiver.

1.5   Conclusion

The practice of psychoeducational assessment and report writing is complex and draws upon multiple skill sets to arrive at a quality written report. The process of psychoeducational assessment and report writing are intertwined and serve the purpose of understanding a child's specific intellectual, academic, behavioral, and social-emotional needs. Additional details on the practice of psychoeducational assessment and report writing will be discussed throughout this book.

Chapter 2
The Psychoeducational Assessment Process

2.1 Overview

What follows is an overview of the psychoeducational assessment process for children and adolescents. The assessment of children and adolescents requires a specialized skill set that may be introduced through reading a book on the topic, but you will need actual experience with the process to become an expert in it (although expertise is illusive, if ever attained). As you progress through your practica, clinic, and internship you will become increasing competent and self-assured in the psychoeducational evaluation process.

Within this chapter, the overarching framework of the psychoeducational assessment process will be presented followed by general and specific guidance. The comprehensive psychoeducational evaluation process requires that you use data-based decision-making and gather multiple sources of data via many methods of assessment. In some respects, you are undertaking psychological detective work, attempting to uncover as much information as possible about a child to permit you to confidently make an informed, data-based decision.

2.2 Steps in the Psychoeducational Assessment Process

There are generalized steps in the psychoeducational assessment process that should be undertaken.

1. *Obtain signed consent prior to starting the assessment.*

This is a critically important step which should not be overlooked. Do not begin the assessment process until you have signed consent from a legal guardian. When both parents are considered legal guardians in the case of divorce or separation then it is legally permitted to begin the process with just one party's consent particularly if it

© Springer Science+Business Media New York 2015
S.C. Dombrowski, *Psychoeducational Assessment and Report Writing*,
DOI 10.1007/978-1-4939-1911-6_2

serves in the best interests of the child. Of course, a good practice would be to obtain signed consent from both legal guardians in this case.

2. *Gather and review relevant educational, medical and psychological records.*

Consistent with the requirement to gather information from multiple sources of data, you should gather relevant educational, medical, and psychological records from the child. This may include information from the following sources:

- Child's therapist
- Pediatrician
- Report cards
- Prior psychological reports
- Functional behavioral assessments
- Behavior intervention plans
- Behavioral write-ups
- Section 504 plans
- IEP documents

Once these documents are collected, you will need to review them and then reconcile with additional information that will be collected during your interview with parents, teachers, and other caregivers involved with the child. For instance, perhaps your collection and review of medical records will reveal a medical condition that better accounts for the child's symptoms of autism or intellectual disability. Or perhaps your review of behavioral write-ups identifies a particular environment or pattern wherein the child is experiencing difficulties (e.g., transition between recess and lunch). This type of information (among others) is something that will need to be sorted out.

3. *Observe the child, conduct interviews, and gather rating forms and questionnaires.*

You will need to observe the child in the classroom and school setting. You will also need to observe the child during the testing session in accord with Chap. 4. If a developmental history questionnaire (i.e., see Child Development Questionnaire (CDQ); Dombrowski, 2014; Chapter 2) or behavior rating forms (e.g., BASC-2) are distributed then these should be collected and reviewed. Additionally, it will be important to interview legal guardians and other collateral contacts (i.e., teachers, support staff, behavioral specialists) to ascertain their perspective regarding the child's functioning across all domain areas (cognitive, academic, behavioral, social, emotional, communication, and adaptive).

4. *Engage in norm-referenced, informal, and curriculum-based assessment.*

Evaluate the child's cognitive, academic, behavioral, social-emotional, and adaptive functioning using a variety of norm-referenced and informal measures. You also need to observe the child during the testing session and interview the child. The interviewing of the child may occur following the testing session. Testing requires a specific skill set that is described in a later section of this chapter. Interviewing is discussed in Chap. 3 while observing the child is discussed in Chap. 4.

5. *Integrate, conceptualize, classify and recommend.*

Following scoring of standardized and informal assessment instruments, and gathering of relevant background, interview and observational data from multiple techniques and informants (e.g., child, parents, teachers), you must integrate the information collected. Integration of data sources is a necessary prerequisite to writing the conceptualization, classification, and recommendations section of a psychoeducational report. In short, I like to use an acronym—ICCR—to refer to this process. It stands for integrate, conceptualize, classify and recommend.

(I)ntegrate
(C)onceptualize
(C)lassify
(R)ecommend

Detailed guidelines for integrating salient information and writing the conceptualization, classification and recommendation section of the report is offered in Chap. 9.

6. *Furnish feedback during an in-person meeting.*

This is often called a feedback session or report conference. It may only be with the parent. This is common in a clinic-based approach (and sometimes a school setting) or it is more likely in the presence of the multidisciplinary team. Please see Chap. 18 for the discussion regarding the provision of oral feedback.

Now that you have been introduced to a general framework for psychoeducational assessment, I would like to discuss additional aspects regarding the process of conducting a comprehensive assessment. This includes how to work with children, a brief overview of how to observe the child, and the nuances of administering standardized tests.

2.3   Working with Children

It is likely that you are pursuing a degree in school or clinical child psychology because you enjoy working with children (or you think you do). These dispositional traits are necessary but insufficient. The next step will be for you to gain experience working directly with children or indirectly by observing how others work with them. If you are in your first year of a graduate program in school or clinical child psychology then you would be well served by observing other experienced practitioners who work with children. I recommend shadowing an experienced psychologist who engages in the assessment of children. I also recommend observing the classroom of a veteran elementary and middle school teacher (i.e., one with greater than 10 years of experience). These individuals have an extensive repertoire of skills for effective management and support of children's behavior. These observational experiences will get you only so far. Equally valuable would be for you to gain direct work experience with children and adolescents. Some of you may already have had this experience whether through coaching a sport, working at a summer camp, teaching in the classroom, working at a daycare, counseling children, working as a babysitter, having your own children, or even being an older sibling. These experiences will give you greater insight into, and practice with, working with children, but that is still not enough. The assessment of children requires complex clinical skills and a hefty dose of practice. Research suggests that you will not fully develop your expertise until 7–10 years into your role as a school or clinical child psychologist (Ericcson & Smith, 1991).

2.4   Observing the Child

The classroom and school observation is an important component of the psychoeducational evaluation. Research supports the incremental validity of classroom and test session observations (McConaughy et al., 2010). Chapter 4 discusses a framework for various observations in the classroom and school setting. An observation should be conducted prior to meeting the child to avoid the Hawthorne Effect. The Hawthorne Effect is a phenomenon where individuals being observed behave differently, often more favorably, then when not being observed. A second observation occurs during the testing session itself. Be mindful, again, that within session validity is limited (Glutting, Oakland, & McDermott, 1989). Children often behave in a more compliant way upon first meeting clinicians or even act out when they normally are well behaved in another setting.

2.5   The Testing Environment and the Test Session

A large amount of your time will be spent in direct contact with the child collecting assessment data via formal standardized testing or informal assessment. This will require the consideration of several issues.

2.5.1   Establish a Working, Not a Therapeutic, Relationship with the Child

The assessment process requires a working relationship, not a therapeutic relationship. Nonetheless, the same processes and skills involved in establishing a therapeutic relationship will come to bare. Your initial contact with the child is important. You should greet the child sincerely and with a smile. If the child is younger or of smaller stature, then you should squat down to meet the child at his or her eye level. Keep in mind cultural considerations when using this approach as some children from diverse cultural backgrounds may be apprehensive about returning the eye contact of the examiner. Ask the child what he or she prefers to be called. Be cautious about using affected, high pitched speech. It is reasonable to use an elevated tone of voice with very young children, but children who are of school age may respond better to enthusiasm (e.g., "It is very nice to meet you Jacob. I've been looking forward to working with you" as opposed to "Hi! How are you? Are you ready for some funsie onesie?"). This affected style with children over age 7 will seem just as odd to the child as it does to the adult. Additionally, you will need to be cautious about being overly loud and assertive. This may serve to intimidate a timorous child. Your body language is also important. Generally, you should not overcrowd a child's space or tower over a child. This can be intimidating to anyone let alone a child.

While considering the above recommendations, you ought to avoid spending a protracted time attempting to establish a working relationship with the child. Your goal is a working relationship where you can quickly, efficiently, validly and reliably ascertain the information you need from the child. You are less concerned about rapport building than you would be if you were in a counseling relationship with the child.

2.5.2   *Take Advantage of the Honeymoon Effect*

Generally speaking, you have a window of opportunity when first meeting children where they will be on their best behavior. The chances are good that even children with significant behavioral difficulties will behave well upon first meeting you. Take advantage of this and begin the testing process quickly.

2.5.3   *The Room Layout*

The room where you evaluate the child should be free from distractions such as noise, smells, toys, and other tangibles that may distract or be of interest to the child. It is also important to have an appropriately sized table and chairs. Some school districts may not have adequate space. For example I have been asked to evaluate children in two locations that are worth noting: (1) Next to the music room with thin walls and (2) in the Janitor's office next to the cafeteria. I will first describe the music room's poor conditions. The room where I was conducting the testing was situated adjacent to the music room. It was spacious, had comfortable chairs and a table. For the first 30 min, the room seemed ideal. It was away from the noise of the main hallway and well lighted and ventilated. The problems began approximately mid-way through a working memory test on a measure of cognitive ability. The music teacher played the piano as the rest of the class sang the song, "Little Teapot." Unfortunately, the walls did not block the music and spoiled the memory test. We had to relocate to another room. This location was clearly inappropriate as it was not free from noisy distractions. The second location was not ideal, but it was acceptable. The testing was conducted during off cafeteria hours in a janitorial alcove. There weren't any distractions and the location was quiet, so the location, while not aesthetically appealing, sufficed as it suffer from foul smells. Of course, the ideal environment would be a separate office with a table, chairs and the ability to close the door to block out external distractions. You may not always have that ideal location but you do need a quiet location free from noise and distractions. If not, you may jeopardize the validity of the testing session.

2.5.4   How to Start the Testing Session

You will need to be brief, direct and honest. Discuss the rationale for testing and then move directly to administration. Many of the tests of cognitive ability have their own suggested introductions to the test. I like to use the following to introduce the overall process as I walk the child down the hall to the testing room (or when I take the child to the clinic office).

> Today we are going to do a number of activities. Some are like puzzles and games while others are like school. I think you may have fun with some of these activities. They will be used to better understand how you think and learn. I may also ask you questions about your friend's and behavior at school. Do you have any questions?

After providing this introduction and briefly addressing any questions the child might have then it is time to start the testing session.

2.5.5   Examiner Anxiety

Oftentimes, neophyte examiners will feel a degree of anxiety about their skills in administering standardized assessment instruments. In fact, I have observed the occasion where a child attains a low score on an instrument and the examiner attributes this score to an error with his or her administration. While it is accurate that new examiners make scoring errors (Mrazik, Janzen, Dombrowski, Barford, & Krawchuk, 2012) examiners should not necessarily misattribute examinee errors to administration problems. When standardized procedures are assiduously followed and protocol scoring errors are minimized then it is more likely that the obtained score reveals the level of the examinee's ability rather than a presumed error in the examiner's administration.

2.5.6   Be Well Prepared and Adhere to Standardized Directions

Students in training (and any psychologist acquiring skills with a new instrument) need to rehearse thoroughly prior to administering an instrument. The time to practice a new assessment instrument should not be when you administer to a child who needs an evaluation. This would be in violation of Test Standards and could jeopardize the validity of the scores. For this reason, students should practice thoroughly the instruments that they will be using. Similarly, you will need to vigorously adhere to standardized directions. This eliminates a high degree of the construct irrelevant variance associated with the test. Departure from either of these strictures is contra-indicated and suggests that a norm-referenced score should not be computed.

2.5.7   Triple Check Protocol Scoring

I cannot tell you how many times I have encountered scoring errors in the protocols of examiners. A red flag sometimes may be an unusually high or low score on a subtest or an index area. However, variability in subtest scores should not be construed to mean that the administrator made an error. But it should trigger the need to thoroughly scrutinize your scoring.

2.5.8   Breaks, Encouragement and Questions

Younger children may need a break to stretch and get a drink of water. You will need to use your judgment when offering breaks. I would not ask a child every 15 min whether he or she requires a break; otherwise, your testing session may extend for hours if not days. More reticent children may be acquiescent and require a predetermined break. Younger children may also require a bathroom break and may need to be prompted about this. More assertive and verbally impulsive children sometimes frequently ask for a break. During these situations, you may need to redirect the child back to the testing session.

Some more active and garrulous children may ask a significant amount of questions and get drawn off task. You would be wise to avoid engaging in frequent responding to questions of the child and instead prompt the child to remain on task. Much of standardized testing requires that the psychologist avoid praising correctness of response. This may have an awkward feel to the child and is different from what is experienced within the classroom where teachers tend to offer effusive feedback and praise. As a result, a younger child may become discouraged or feel like your transaction with him or her somewhat strange. (It actually is a bit awkward to put on a poker face and avoid offering whether the child answered correctly.) When

I get the sense that a child is beginning to feel uneasy or lacking in confidence from providing an answer and not receiving feedback, I am reminded to offer effusive praise of effort. Another option that I sometimes use to circumvent frustration and upset is to use the following statement:

> I really appreciate how hard you are working. I can see that you are wondering how you are doing on this test. This is not important. What is important is that you just try your best. I cannot give you answers or tell you whether your answer is correct. You only need to try your best.

The combination of this statement and frequent praise of effort often serves to alleviate any sense of frustration or anxiety faced by the child.

2.5.9 Debrief the Testing Process

At the end of the testing process, you should praise the child for his or her hard work. For younger children, it is a good idea to offer a selection of stickers from which the child may choose. Most children appreciate this end of testing reward. You should also mention to the child the next steps in the process which will include the production of a written report and a discussion of the report with his or her caregivers. This brings closure to the testing process for the child.

2.6 Conclusion

Within this chapter, you were introduced to the nuances of the psychoeducational assessment process. This chapter serves as a general framework and there are additional skills that will need to be attained. Chapter 3 discusses interviewing and gathering of additional sources of data including rating forms, records, and background information. Chapter 4 furnishes an overview of how to conduct an observation. The remaining chapters in the book discuss report writing including integrating information, writing a report, and providing oral feedback. Additional ethical, legal and practical issues are discussed in Chaps. 18 and 19.

References

Dombrowski, S. C. (2014). *Child development questionnaire*. Unpublished Document.
Ericcson, K. A., & Smith, J. (1991). *Toward a general theory of expertise: Prospects and limits.* Cambridge, MA: Cambridge University Press.
Glutting, J. J., Oakland, T., & McDermott, P. A. (1989). Observing child behavior during testing: Constructs, validity, and situation generality. *Journal of School Psychology, 27*, 155–164.

McConaughy, S. H., Harder, V. S., Antshel, K. M., Gordon, M., Eiraldi, R., & Dumenci, L. (2010). Incremental validity of test session and classroom observations in a multimethod assessment of attention deficit/hyperactivity disorder. *Journal of Clinical Child Adolescent Psychology, 39*, 650–666. doi:10.1080/15374416.2010.501287.

Mrazik, M., Janzen, T. M., Dombrowski, S. C., Barford, S. W., & Krawchuk, L. L. (2012). Administration and scoring errors of graduate students learning the WISC-IV: Issues and controversies. *Canadian Journal of School Psychology, 27*, 279–290.

Chapter 3
Interviewing and Gathering Data

3.1 Introduction

The ultimate goal of conducting an assessment is to be able to understand a child's functioning, offer a classification decision, and then make intervention and other recommendations that support and improve the child's functioning. This chapter contains two sections. Presented first will be a discussion of interviewing key stakeholders in the child's life including teachers and parents. This will be followed by a discussion of the process of collecting relevant background information including prior psychological reports, medical records, IEP documents, grade reports, and any additional pertinent sources. A comprehensive child development questionnaire (CDQ; Dombrowski, 2014) will be presented and is a useful option for gathering information regarding children's background and development.

3.2 Interviewing

The purpose of conducting an interview with a child, parent, teacher or other individual is to gather information about the child to help better understand the child's functioning. Along with other methods of assessment and sources of information, data gathered from interviews serve to assist in conceptualizing a child's functioning, making a classification decision, and recommending intervention strategies and accommodations that will improve the child's functioning. Interviewing, like other methods of assessment, serves to furnish data regarding a child.

There are three main approaches to interviewing: structured, semi-structured, and informal. The informal approach is constructivist in nature and allows the process to unfold based upon responses provided by the interviewee. It might begin

© Springer Science+Business Media New York 2015   17
S.C. Dombrowski, *Psychoeducational Assessment and Report Writing*,
DOI 10.1007/978-1-4939-1911-6_3

with a question such as "Tell me why this assessment is being conducted?" Follow-up questions are then offered depending upon responses provided. The benefit to an informal approach is to be able to branch off on lines of inquiry based upon the response offered. Structured interviewing, by contrast, requires a series of detailed questions from which the examiner may not deviate. A semi-structured interview has a theme of questions that need to be addressed, but permits the clinician to deviate and explore a topic more fully with the caregivers. Unfortunately, the availability of structured and semi-structured interview formats for teachers and psychoeducational assessment is unavailable (Frick, Barry, & Kamphaus, 2005; Loeber, Green, Lahey, & Stouthamer-Loeber, 1991)

The structured interview has the highest degree of validity and reliability, but requires the greatest time commitment (60–90 min) (Silverman & Ollendick, 2005). A structured interviewing style is straightforward (and perhaps easiest for an inexperienced clinician), but it can be quite time consuming depending upon the structured interview selected. Structured interviewing requires the clinician to ask a series of questions of caregivers (e.g., parents, teachers, counselors) despite the question's relevance to the referral question or diagnostic issue. For instance, a parent may be asked questions about the child's ability to participate in activities of daily living even though the child has solid cognitive abilities and the referral question was about the child's mathematical understanding. This approach casts a wide net seeking to be as comprehensive as possible and to leave no stone unturned. The structured interview process often uses instruments such as the DISC-IV (Shaffer, Fisher, Lucas, Dulcan, & Schwab-Stone, 2000), which is linked to DSM diagnostic criteria and is intensely comprehensive. Structured and semi-structured interview formats are available, but they are geared toward clinical (e.g., DSM) diagnoses. Structured and semi-structured interview formats based upon DSM diagnostic categories can certainly be helpful for exploration of emotional and behavioral conditions that may not be assessed on behavior rating scales, but keep in mind that psychoeducational classifications within the school are not based on the DSM, but rather on IDEA classification categories. A structured or semi-structured clinical interview may have its place if one is considering an OHI (via ADHD) or autism spectrum classification, or when attempting to rule out social maladjustment from emotional disturbance, but IDEA/state special education classification criteria supersedes DSM diagnostic criteria when determining special education eligibility (Zirkel, 2011).

3.3 Psychoeducational Interview Format

Because there is a lack of structured or semi-structured interview formats for the psychoeducational evaluation of children, I would like to offer the following semi-structured format for interviewing caregivers and teachers regarding a child's functioning. A format for interviewing students is also presented.

3.3.1 Caregiver/Parent Format

Introductory Statement to Caregiver

I am conducting the evaluation of your child. As part of this process, I would like to speak to you about your child's progress at school to ascertain your perspective regarding your child's functioning in the academic, behavioral, social, emotional arena, as well as your child's areas of strength and areas of need. First, I would like to ask you why your child is being evaluated? What do you think is the purpose of the evaluation?

Academic Functioning

I would next like to inquire about your child's progress at school.
Please describe his or her grades in each class?
Does your child struggle with any academic subjects? Please explain.
Please describe your child's progress in reading? Do you know your child's guided reading level?
Please describe your child's progress in writing?
What is your child's handwriting like?
Please describe your child's progress in spelling?
Please describe your child's progress in mathematics?
What are your child's areas of academic strength and areas of academic need?

Behavioral and Social-Emotional Functioning

The approach to the interview will depend upon the child's referral issue. Additional, more specific questioning may be necessary if the child has a disorder or condition that might make the child eligible under autism, emotional disturbance, or other health impairments. Otherwise, the following list of questions is a good start to the interview process.

Please describe your child's behavioral functioning at school.
What are your child's strengths and areas of interest?
Does your child participate in any activities or have any hobbies?
Does your child follow classroom and teacher rules?
Does your child get into trouble at school? If so, for what?
How does your child respond to teacher and staff requests to follow rules?
How does your child get along with peers at school?
Describe your child's mood.
Does your child seem anxious, depressed or worried?
Does your child have anger issues?
Does your child have friends at school?

(continued)

Does your child ever indicate that he or she hears voices or sees things that other people do not?
Does your child believe that they are someone or something they are not?
Does your child ever state a desire to hurt him or herself?
Does your child ever state that he or she wishes he or she were dead?
Does your child have an outside classification from a doctor or a psychologist?

Is your child taking medication? If so, what type of medication (name, dosage, when started)?

Adaptive Functioning

Questioning a parent about adaptive functioning is particularly relevant if the child is suspected of struggling with an intellectual disability or an autism spectrum disorder. Of course, a norm-referenced instrument such as the Vineland-2 or ABAS-II would also be necessary in these cases. When interviewing a parent, caregiver, or teacher, you will need to inquire about the child's functioning in the conceptual, communication and social domains. Also inquire about sensory responses, gross and fine motor skills and stereotyped behaviors. Because of the range of adaptive tasks across the developmental spectrum, I would recommend that you place primary reliance on a norm-referenced adaptive behavior scale to gain insight into a child's adaptive functioning. The following brief questions along with a broad-band behavior rating scale could serve as a screener to determine whether you should move to a comprehensive interview of adaptive functioning.

Does your child struggle with everyday activities such as brushing teeth, tying shoelaces, getting dressed, toileting, and eating?
Does your child struggle with keeping clean and bathing?
Can your child find his or her way around school without assistance?
Does your child understand the difference between dangerous and safe situations?
Does your child have difficulty communicating with other children and adults?
Does your child struggle when playing with other children? Does he or she show interest in playing with other children? When your child plays with other children, does he or she interact with or just play alongside them?
Does your child display any repetitive activities, interests or actions?

Supplemental Caregiver Interview Questions

It would be optimal for caregivers to complete a structured developmental history questionnaire such as the *Child Development Questionnaire* (CDQ, Dombrowski, 2014) prior to an interview. However, this may not be practical in all cases. The questionnaire may not be returned or time constraints make it more practical to just go through sections of the CDQ with caregivers. If time constraints preclude the completion of each component of the CDQ, then it will be important at a minimum to collect information regarding a child's familial, prenatal, perinatal, early development, medical, recreational, behavioral, and educational history. The caregiver interview will not necessarily be as detailed as the child development questionnaire but the following may suffice if a questionnaire cannot be completed or is not returned by the caregiver. This information will be added to the caregiver interview described at the beginning of this chapter.

Parental and Family History
1. Who provides primary caregiving for child?
2. Is there a family history of learning or mental health issues?
3. Are there family medical issues?

Prenatal, Perinatal, and Early Childhood History
1. Were there any issues during pregnancy with this child?
2. Were there any complications during delivery?
3. Was the child born early or with low birthweight?
4. Did the child stay in the neonatal intensive care unit (NICU) following delivery?
5. Was the pregnancy healthy or were there illnesses during pregnancy?
6. Did you child experience colic?

Early Childhood Development
1. Were there any issues with your child's early development (i.e., crawling, walking, talking, learning to count or read)?
2. Did your child attend daycare or preschool and were there any concerns expressed while in attendance?

Medical History
1. Are your child's vision and hearing intact?
2. Does your child have a history of head trauma or concussions?
3. Does your child have a history of illness?
4. Does your child take any medications?
5. Has your child experienced any infections and other illness?

Strength-Based Questions

What are some activities your child likes to participate in?
What is your child good at?
What hobbies does your child enjoy? Does your child play any sports or musical instruments?
What are some positives about your child?

3.3.2 Teacher Format

Introductory Statement to Teacher
I am conducting an evaluation of your student. As part of this process, I would like to speak to you about the student's progress at school in the academic, behavioral, social, emotional, and adaptive arena, as well as the student's areas of strength and areas of need.

Academic Functioning

I would like to inquire about your student's progress at school. Please describe his or her grades in your class?
Does this student struggle with any academic subject? Please explain.
Please describe this student's progress in reading? What is the student's guided reading level?
Please describe this student's progress in writing?
What is the student's handwriting like?
Please describe this student's progress in spelling?
Please describe this student's progress in mathematics?
What are the student's areas of academic strength and areas of academic need?

Behavioral and Social-Emotional Functioning

The approach to the interview will be dependent upon the child's referral issue. More specific questioning may be necessary if the child has a specific disorder or condition that might make the child eligible under autism, emotional disturbance or other health impaired. In the meantime, here is a list of questions that are appropriate for ascertaining a sense of the student's social, emotional, and behavioral functioning.

Please describe this student's behavioral functioning at school.
Does this student follow classroom and teacher rules?
Does this student get into trouble at school? If so, for what?
How does the student respond to teacher and staff requests to follow rules?
How does the student get along with peers at school?
Describe this student's work habits?
Describe the student's homework completion and quality.
Describe this student's mood.
Does the student seem anxious, depressed, or worried?
Does the student have anger issues?
Does the student have friends at school?
Does the student ever indicate that he or she hears voices or sees things that other people do not?

(continued)

Does the student believe that they are someone or something they are not?
Does the student ever state a desire to hurt him or herself?
Does the student ever state that he or she wishes he were dead?
Does the student have an outside classification from a doctor or a psychologist?
Are you aware of whether the student is taking medication? If so, what type
of medication (name, dosage, when started)?

Adaptive Functioning

Questioning a teacher about adaptive functioning is particularly relevant if the child
is suspected of struggling with an intellectual disability or an autism spectrum disorder. Of course, a norm-referenced instrument such as the Vineland and ABAS
would be necessary in these cases.

Does the student struggle with everyday activities such as brushing teeth,
tying shoelaces, getting dressed, toileting, and eating?
Does the student struggle with keeping clean and bathing?
Can the student find his or her way around school without assistance?
Does the student understand the difference between dangerous and safe
situations?
Does the student have difficulty communicating with other children and
adults?
Does the student struggle when playing with other children? Does he or she
show interest in playing with other children? When the student plays with
other children does the student play alongside or engage with the other
students?
Does the student display any repetitive activities, interests or actions?

Strength-Based Questions

What are some activities the student likes to participate in?
What is the student good at?
What hobbies does the child have? Does the child play any sports or musical
instruments?
What are some positives about the child?

3.3.3 Student Interview Format

When conducting a psychoeducational assessment it is critically important to interview the child or adolescent. Younger children may be acquiescent (i.e., be agreeable
and rarely furnish what they think you would disagree with) or less capable of being
insightful about their functioning. When this occurs, the younger child will perceive

his progress favorably. Starting at around fourth grade children gain greater insight into their internal functioning and are able to compare their abilities with other children. From that age forward, you may be able to ascertain greater insight into their self-perception of academic, behavioral, and social-emotional functioning. Still, the question remains as to how much emphasis should be placed upon an interview with a child. Some children report positive feelings despite facing severe struggles.

Introductory Statement

I would like to talk to you about how you like school, think you are doing in school, and about your thoughts and feelings.

General Questions About School

How do you like attending the Smith Public School? What is your favorite part of school? What do you like the least? How are you doing in school [or each of your classes for older students?] Do you have any difficult with any subjects at school?

Academic Functioning

I'd next like to inquire about your progress at school.
Do you struggle with any academic subject? Please explain.
How are you doing in reading? Do you know your guided reading level?
How are you doing in writing?
How are you doing in spelling?
How are you doing in mathematics?
Do you need any help with any of your subjects?
Describe your reading, writing and mathematics skills? Have you ever received extra support for difficulties?
What are your grades in each of your classes? [Question for older students]

Behavioral and Social-Emotional Functioning

I would now like to talk about your behavior and friendships at school.
How are you with following classroom and teacher rules?
Do you get into trouble at school? If so, for what?
Do you have friends at school? If so, do you get along with them?
What do you like to do with friends?
Do you have any fears or worries?
Do you ever feel down or very sad? If so, about what?
Do you have temper or anger control problems?
Do you ever hear voices or see things that other people do not?
Are you taking any medication? If so, for what?

Strength-Based Questions

What are some activities you like to do?
What are you good at?
What do people say you are good at?
Do you have any hobbies or play any sports or musical instruments?

Suspected ADHD

The questions below are directly linked to ADHD symptoms from the DSM5 and revised to make more readable and in the form of a question for the interviewer.

Introductory statement:

"I'm now going to ask you some detailed questions about the child's activity, attention and focus."

Inattention

(a) Does the child struggle with giving close attention to details or making careless mistakes in schoolwork, work, or other activities. In other words, does your child overlook or miss details? When your child completes work, is it accurately completed?

(b) Does your child have difficulty sustaining attention in tasks or play activities? Does your child have difficulty remaining focused during classroom activities, conversations, or when reading?

(c) Does your child not seem to listen when spoken to directly? Does your child's mind seem elsewhere, even in the absence of any obvious distraction?

(d) Does your child often not follow through on instructions and fail to finish schoolwork or chores? Does your child start a task but quickly lose focus and become easily sidetracked?

(e) Does your child often have difficulty organizing tasks and activities? Does your child have difficulty managing tasks sequentially? Does your child have difficulty keeping materials and belongings in order? Is your child's work messy and disorganized? Does your child have poor time management? Does your child fail to meet deadlines?

(f) Does your child avoid, dislike, or is reluctant to engage in tasks that require sustained mental effort such as schoolwork or homework? (For older adolescents this may include tasks such as preparing reports, completing forms, or reviewing lengthy papers).

(g) Does your child often lose things needed for tasks and activities (e.g., school materials, pencils, books, tools, wallets, keys, paperwork, eyeglasses, or mobile devices)?

(h) Is your child often easily distracted by extraneous stimuli? (For older adolescents this may include unrelated thoughts.)

(i) Is your child often forgetful in daily activities (e.g., chores, running errands)? For older adolescents this may include returning calls, paying bills, keeping appointments.)

Hyperactivity and Impulsivity

(a) Does your child often fidgets with hands or feet or squirms in seat?
(b) Does your child often leave his or her seat in situations when remaining seated is expected (e.g., leaves his or her place in the classroom or in other situations that require remaining seated)?
(c) Does your child often run about or climb in situations where it is inappropriate. (In adolescents this may be limited to feeling restless).
(d) Is your child often unable to play or engage in leisure activities quietly?
(e) Is your child often "on the go" or often acts as if "driven by a motor"? Is your child unable or uncomfortable being still for an extended time, such as in restaurants?
(f) Does your child often talk excessively?
(g) Does your child often blurts out answers before questions have been completed (e.g., completes people's sentences and "jumps the gun" in conversations, cannot wait for next turn in conversation)?
(h) Does your child often have trouble waiting his or her turn (e.g., while waiting in line).

Source: Adapted from the DSM-5, American Psychiatric Association (2013).

Suspected Autism

The questions below are aligned with symptoms from the DSM 5 regarding autism spectrum disorder and revised to make more readable and in the form of a question for the interviewer.

Introductory statement:

"I'm now going to ask you some detailed questions about the child's socialization, communication and behavior."

Social Communication and Social Interaction

The diagnostic criteria require persistent deficits in social communication and social interaction across multiple contexts, as manifested by the following, currently or by history (examples are illustrative, not exhaustive):

1. Does your child experience deficits in social-emotional reciprocity? In other words, does your child struggle with normal back-and-forth conversation? Does your child struggle with entering into social situations? Does your child struggle with or fail to share interests and emotions? Does your child fail to mirror the emotions of others? Does your child struggle with initiating or responding to social interactions.
2. Does your child experience deficits in nonverbal communicative behaviors used for social interaction, ranging, for example, from poorly integrated

verbal and nonverbal communication; to abnormalities in eye contact and body language or deficits in understanding and use of gestures; to a total lack of facial expressions and nonverbal communication.

3. Does your child struggle with developing, maintaining, and understanding relationships. For example, does your child experience difficulties with adjusting behavior to suit various social contexts, sharing imaginative play or in making friends. Does your child display a lack of interest in peers.

Restricted, repetitive patterns of behavior, interests, or activities

Requires at least two of the following, currently or by history (examples are illustrative, not exhaustive):

1. Does your child display stereotyped or repetitive motor movements, use of objects, or speech (e.g., simple motor stereotypies, lining up toys or flipping objects, echolalia, idiosyncratic phrases).

2. Does your child insist on sameness or demonstrate an inflexible adherence to routines, or ritualized patterns or verbal nonverbal behavior (e.g., extreme distress at small changes, difficulties with transitions, rigid thinking patterns, greeting rituals, need to take same route or eat food every day)?

3. Does your child have highly restricted, fixated interests that are abnormal in intensity or focus (e.g., strong attachment to or preoccupation with unusual objects, excessively circumscribed or perseverative interest).

4. Is your child hyper or hyporeactive to sensory input or unusual interests in sensory aspects of the environment (e.g., apparent indifference to pain/temperature, adverse response to specific sounds or textures, excessive smelling or touching of objects, visual fascination with lights or movement)?

Source: Adapted from the DSM-5, American Psychiatric Association (2013).

Oppositional Defiant Disorder

The questions below are aligned with symptoms from the DSM 5 regarding oppositional defiant disorder and revised to make more readable and in the form of a question for the interviewer.

Introductory statement:

"I'm now going to ask you some detailed questions about the child's behavior and ability to listen to those in authority including parents and teachers."

Angry/Irritable Mood

1. Does the child often lose his or her temper?
2. Is the child often touchy or easily annoyed?
3. Is the child often angry and resentful?

Argumentative/Defiant Behavior

4. Does the child often argue with authority figures or with adults
5. Does the child often actively defy or refuse to comply with requests from authority figures or with rules?
6. Does the child deliberately annoy others?
7. Does the child often blame others for his or her mistakes or misbehavior?

Vindictiveness

8. Has the child been spiteful or vindictive at least twice with the past 6 months?

Source: Adapted from the DSM-5, American Psychiatric Association (2013).

Disruptive Mood Dysregulation Disorder
The questions below are aligned with symptoms from the DSM 5 regarding disruptive mood dysregulation disorder and revised to make more readable and in the form of a question for the interviewer.

Introductory statement:

"I'm now going to ask you some detailed questions about the child's behavior and ability to modulate his or her anger."

1. Does the child experience severe recurrent temper outburst manifested verbally (e.g., verbal rages) and/or behavioral (e.g., physical aggression toward people or property) that are grossly out of proportion in intensity or duration to the situation or provocation?
2. Are the temper outbursts are inconsistent with developmental level?
3. Do the temper outbursts occur, on average, three or more times per week?
4. Is the child's mood between temper outbursts is persistently irritable or angry most of the day, nearly every day, and is observable by others (e.g., parents, teachers, peers)?

Decision for Psychologists

5. Are criteria 1–4 are present in at least two of three settings (i.e., at home, at school, with peers)? Is the behavior severe in at least one of these?
6. The diagnosis should not be made for the first time before age 6 years or after age 16 years.
7. By history or observation, the age or onset of criteria 1–5 is before age 10 years.
8. There has never been a distinct period lasting more than 1 day during which the full symptom criteria, except for duration, for a manic or hypomanic episode have been met.

   Note: Developmentally appropriate mood elevation, such as occurs in the context of a highly positive event or its anticipation, should not be considered as a symptom of mania or hypomania.

9. The behaviors do not occur exclusively during an episode of major depressive disorder and are not better explained by another mental disorder (e.g., autism spectrum disorder, posttraumatic stress disorder, separation anxiety disorder, persistent depressive disorder [dysthymia].

10. The symptoms are not attributable to the physiological effects of a substance or to another medical or neurological condition.

Source: Adapted from the DSM-5, American Psychiatric Association (2013).

3.3.4   Interview Format for Mental Health Conditions that Might Impact Educational Functioning

If the child has received an outside diagnosis of autism, ADHD, schizophrenia, or a mood disorder, or if there is suspicion that any of the above symptoms associated with these diagnoses may have an adverse impact upon educational functioning that may result in an ED, OHI, or autism classification then questions from either a structured interview or directly from the DSM-5 may assist with a special education classification decision. Keep in mind, however, that you are not arriving at a DSM classification but rather a special education classification so be cautious about placing primary emphasis on instruments or interview procedures with specific linkage to DSM. There is not necessarily a one-to-one correspondence between a special education classification and a DSM classification.

Questions from either the DSM or a structured interview may be used to assist you in arriving at your special education classification decision. In Canada, practitioners do not have to concern themselves with IDEA classification categories and should instead reference the DSM. In Canada, or in a US clinic-based setting that offers and DSM classification, the use of a structured or semi-structured interview format is recommended so long as the evaluation also considers pertinent IDEA classification categories.

The following will present commonly experienced disorders of childhood—ADHD, ODD, Disruptive Mood Dysregulation Disorder, and Autism Spectrum—with their associated DSM diagnostic criteria rephrased in the form of an interview question for the caregiver or teacher. Endorsement of sufficient items may be indicative of eligibility for special education so long as educational impairment can be documented. This approach to interviewing may be used with other possible disorders of childhood including schizophrenia, bipolar disorder, and depression. All relevant psychological disorders of childhood discussed within the DSM-5 are not listed below. Instead, I have listed a sampling of commonly experienced psychological disorders of youth and demonstrate how to implement a structured/semi-structured interview with direct linkage to the DSM. I am including several frequently observed psychological disorders of childhood as examples. This approach can be used with any of the DSM disorders with which a child might struggle.

There are additional childhood psychological disorders which could contribute to a child's eligibility for a special education-based classification including Major Depressive Disorder, Selective Mutism and Generalized Anxiety Disorder. This list discussed above is not exhaustive. Rather, it is meant to be illustrative and serve as a guide for interviewing caregivers and teachers.

3.4   Gathering Background and Additional Data

Information about a child may be collected via structured developmental history questionnaires, direct questioning of caregivers, teachers and related personnel, review of records, and via distribution and collection of rating forms. This section will discuss these additional data sources.

3.4.1   Structured Developmental History Questionnaires

For the graduate student in school and clinical child psychology, it is recommended that a structured developmental history questionnaire be used to gather information about a child's prenatal, perinatal, early childhood history, and medical, educational, and family history. There are several questionnaires that are appropriate for such purposes including the BASC-2 *Structured Developmental History* (Reynolds & Kamphaus 2004) and a new, very comprehensive one that has recently been created called the *Child Development Questionnaire* (*CDQ*; Dombrowski, 2014). The *CDQ* is available from Dr. Dombrowski free of charge to purchasers of this book. When completed, structured developmental history questionnaires can provide valuable information about a past and present functioning.

3.4.2   Child Development Questionnaire (CDQ)

The CDQ is presented below and available to purchasers of this book who may contact the author via email for a copy. The CDQ is one of the more comprehensive structured child developmental history questionnaires available in the marketplace.

Child Development Questionnaire (CDQ)

STEFAN C. DOMBROWSKI, PH.D.

Demographic Information

Child's Name: _____

Date: _____

Sex:

☐ Male

☐ Female

☐ Transgender

Grade: _____

Date of Birth: _____

Race/Ethnicity: (Please select all at that apply)

☐ White

☐ Black or African-American

☐ Native Hawaiian or Pacific Islander

☐ Asian

☐ Hispanic or Latino

☐ Native American or Native Alaskan

☐ Other: _____

Primary Language(s) spoken in home:

_____

Preferred language? _____

English a Second Language:

☐ Yes or

☐ No?

Describe: _____

Name of Person Completing Form: ____

_____

Relationship to Child:

☐ Biological parent

☐ Stepparent

☐ Grandparent

☐ Foster Parent

☐ Aunt/Uncle Other _____

Address: _____

Mobile Phone: _____

Home Phone: _____

Work Phone: _____

Reason for Evaluation: _____

_____

At what age did you first become concerned? _____

What are your concerns about your child? (Check all that apply)

☐ Language/Speech/Communication

☐ Cognitive/learning development

☐ Emotional development

☐ Medical

☐ Motor development

☐ Behavior problems

☐ School performance

Child Development Questionnaire (CDQ)

Stefan C. Dombrowski, Ph.D.

Parental Information

Mother's Name: _____
Age: _____
Highest Grade Level Completed:
☐ 9th grade
☐ High School
☐ Some College
☐ Associates Degree
☐ Bachelor's
☐ Master's or Juris Doctor
☐ Doctorate (M.D., Ph.D., DDS, DVM)
Schools Attended: _____
Occupation _____
Primary Language: _____
Secondary Language: _____

Father's Name: _____
Age: _____
Highest Grade Level Completed:
☐ 9th grade
☐ High School
☐ Some College
☐ Associates Degree
☐ Bachelor's
☐ Master's or Juris Doctor
☐ Doctorate (M.D., Ph.D., DDS, DVM)
Schools Attended: _____
Occupation _____
Primary Language: _____
Secondary Language: _____

Family Constellation

Where and with whom does the child reside? _____

Are parents

☐ Together

☐ Separated

Individuals living with child:

Name	Age	Sex	Relationship to Child

Child Development Questionnaire (CDQ)

STEFAN C. DOMBROWSKI, PH.D.

Child Strengths, Interests and Hobbies

What are the child's strengths? _____

What are the child's interests and hobbies? _____

With what activities is the child involved? _____

Prenatal History

Number of prior pregnancies _____

Was Mom under doctor's care during pregnancy? _____ If so, how many visits? _____

Was the pregnancy _____

☐ Planned

☐ Planned with preconception counseling
☐ Unplanned

Experience of any of the following during pregnancy:

☐ Difficulty getting pregnant with this child?

Fertility treatment? Yes or No   Describe:

Multiple Fetuses during pregnancy? Yes or No Describe:

Infection(s) during Pregnancy: (Please select all that apply)

☐ Influenza

☐ Fever

☐ Measles

☐ Chicken Pox

☐ Herpes

☐ HIV

☐ Other Sexually Transmitted Infections

☐ Other Infection

Need for bedrest?

☐ Yes

☐ No

How long? _____

Hospitalization during pregnancy:

☐ Yes

☐ No

Why? _____

Maternal injury during pregnancy?

☐ Yes

☐ No

Premature rupture of membranes?

☐ Yes

Substance Use during Pregnancy

☐ Alcohol: Frequency: _____

☐ Cocaine: Frequency: _____

☐ Marijuana: Frequency: _____

☐ Heroin: Frequency: _____

☐ Other: Frequency: _____

Child Development Questionnaire (CDQ)

STEFAN C. DOMBROWSKI, PH.D.

Cigarettes Used During Pregnancy?

☐ Yes

☐ No

Frequency: _____

Prescription Medication (s) taken during pregnancy?

☐ Yes

☐ No

Describe: _____

During pregnancy, mother had

☐ High blood pressure

☐ Diabetes

☐ Sexually Transmitted Infection

☐ Measles

Abnormal Ultrasound:

☐ Yes

☐ No

Explain: _____

Abnormal tests during pregnancy:

☐ Yes

☐ No

Explain: _____

Stress during Pregnancy:

☐ Yes

☐ No

Explain: _____

Other pregnancy problems:

☐ Yes

☐ No

Explain: _____

Perinatal

Age of Mother at birth of child: _____

Age of Father at Birth of the child: _____

Length of Pregnancy: _____ Weeks: _____

Birthweight _____ lbs _____ oz

Length at birth: _____ inches

Labor Length: _____ Hours

Delivery Type:

☐ Vaginal

☐ C-section

☐ Breech

Delivery Type (Continued)

☐ Forceps

☐ Vacuum used

Antibiotics given during labor?

☐ Yes

☐ No

Any placental issues?

☐ Yes

☐ No

Child Development Questionnaire (CDQ)

STEFAN C. DOMBROWSKI, PH.D.

Did the baby experience any of the following:

☐ Jaundice

☐ Apnea

☐ Bilirubin Lights

☐ Reflux

☐ NICU stay

☐ Blood problems

☐ Breathing Problems

☐ Tube feeding

☐ Need for ventilator

☐ Low oxygen

☐ Infection

☐ Feeding/Sucking problems

☐ Intraventricular hemorrhage (bleeding in the brain):

Medication (s) given to baby:

Early Developmental History

Breastfed

☐ Yes

☐ No

Until What age? _____

Overall baby was

☐ Easy

☐ Moderate

☐ Difficult

Early Developmental Milestones

(Check and include comments, if appropriate)

Gross Motor	Normal	Abnormal
Turn over	☐	☐
Sit alone	☐	☐
Crawl	☐	☐

Gross Motor	Normal	Abnormal
Pull to stand	☐	☐
Walk alone	☐	☐
Climb up stairs	☐	☐
Walk	☐	☐
Run	☐	☐
Hop	☐	☐
Pedal tricycle	☐	☐
Ride Two wheel bike	☐	☐
Throwing	☐	☐
Catching	☐	☐

Fine Motor	Normal	Abnormal
Reach for Objects	☐	☐
Zippers & buttons	☐	☐
Pincer grasp	☐	☐
Uses spoon	☐	☐
Removes clothing	☐	☐
Feeds with fingers	☐	☐
Hold cup	☐	☐
Prints name	☐	☐
Draws picture	☐	☐

Child Development Questionnaire (CDQ)

STEFAN C. DOMBROWSKI, PH.D.

	Normal	Abnormal			Normal	Abnormal
Tie Shoes	☐	☐	Holds conversation		☐	☐

Language/Social	Normal	Abnormal
Smiles at others	☐	☐
Coo	☐	☐
Laugh	☐	☐
Babble	☐	☐
Wave bye-bye	☐	☐
Say mama/dada	☐	☐
Says first word	☐	☐
Point to object	☐	☐
Follow command with gesture	☐	☐
States name	☐	☐
Uses complete sentences	☐	☐

Language/Social	Normal	Abnormal
Loss of language	☐	☐
Share emotion	☐	☐

Toilet trained

☐ Yes

☐ No

Age: _____

☐ Urine: _____ Daytime _____ At night:

☐ Stool: _____ Daytime _____ At night:

☐ Problems toileting?

Explain: _____

Behavioral and Temperamental History

Temperament

Activity Level:	☐ Normal	☐ High	☐ Low
Mood:	☐ Normal	☐ Happy	☐ Sad
Task Persistence	☐ High	☐ Medium	☐ Low
Irritability	☐ Low	☐ Average	☐ High
Fearfulness	☐ Low	☐ Average	☐ High
Shyness	☐ Low	☐ Average	☐ High
Adaptable/Flexible	☐ Low	☐ Average	☐ High

Sociability and Play

Does or did your child (check all that apply):

☐ Ignore children   ☐ Initiate play   ☐ Observe them   ☐ Parallel play

☐ Join play   ☐ Intrude on play   ☐ Prefer adults   ☐ Play alone

Child Development Questionnaire (CDQ)

STEFAN C. DOMBROWSKI, PH.D.

Sports/Hobbies/Interests

Describe your child's hobbies, sports and interests?

_____

Has there been a decrease in interest in participating in these activities recently?

_____

Behavior

Does your child have difficulty with any of the following (currently or past)

☐ Colic   ☐ Obsessions/Compulsions   ☐ Sleeping (too little or too much)
☐ Eating   ☐ Unusual Interests   ☐ Temper Tantrums
☐ Head banging   ☐ Unusual body movements   ☐ Hitting others
☐ Biting   ☐ Forgetfulness   ☐ Distractibility
☐ Attention span   ☐ Concentration   ☐ Hyperactivity
☐ Task completion   ☐ Trouble with Peers   ☐ Fears
☐ Stealing   ☐ Destructiveness   ☐ Fighting
☐ Anxiety   ☐ Need for same routine   ☐ Involvement with law
☐ Irritability   ☐ Rituals   ☐ Trouble with siblings
☐ Impulsivity   ☐ Fire setting   ☐ Self-stimulation
☐ Excessive crying   ☐ Failure to thrive   ☐ Separating from parents
☐ Sensory issues   ☐ Overreactivity to problems ☐ Meeting new people
☐ Calming down   ☐ Unhappiness   ☐ Needs parental supervision
☐ Smoke   ☐ Drink alcohol   ☐ Use illicit substances

Comments:_____

Parenting Style

How do you deal with behavioral issues? (Check all that apply)

☐ Ignoring   ☐ Explaining   ☐ Scolding
☐ Spanking   ☐ Send child to room/Time out ☐ Removal of privileges

Child Development Questionnaire (CDQ)

STEFAN C. DOMBROWSKI, PH.D.

☐ Reinforcement   ☐ Other: _____

Educational History

Attend daycare/preschool? ☐ Yes ☐ No   At what age? _____

Attend Kindergarten? ☐ Yes ☐ No   At what age? _____

Any problems in daycare/preschool or kindergarten? ☐ Yes ☐ No

Explain: _____

_____

_____

Does your child or did your child receive any of the following services:	When	Frequency	Service Provider
Early intervention			
Feeding therapy			
Physical therapy			
Occupational therapy			
Speech therapy			
Behavior therapy			
Other			

Elementary/Middle School/High School

	Check if applicable	Explain
Ever change schools?		
Repeated a grade?		
Skipped a grade?		
Difficulty with Reading?		
Difficulty with Math?		
Difficulty with writing?		
Receives poor grades?		
Been tested for special		

Child Development Questionnaire (CDQ)

STEFAN C. DOMBROWSKI, PH.D.

education?		
Frequent absences?		

Medical History

	Normal	Abnormal	Comments
Head, eyes, ears, nose, throat			
Vision Screening (Date: _____)			
Hearing Screening (Date: _____)			
Heart			
Lungs			
Kidney			
Stomach/Intestinal/Constipation			
Reflux			
Asthma			
Feeding Issues			
Eczema/Skin issues			
Seizures			
Muscles			
Cerebral Palsy			
Joints/Bones			
Nervous system			
Exposure to toxins (lead; cigarette smoke; mold)			
Sleeping/Snoring			
Nutrition/Diet			
Other			

Celiac ☐ Yes ☐ No   Allergies ☐ Yes ☐ No   Explain: _____

Immunizations up to date   ☐ Yes ☐ No   Explain: _____

Diagnosed with any medical or genetic conditions? ☐ Yes ☐ No

Explain: _____

Is the child a picky eater?

Explain: _____

Hospitalizations

Date: _____   Reason _____

Date: _____   Reason _____

Child Development Questionnaire (CDQ)

STEFAN C. DOMBROWSKI, PH.D.

Date: _____   Reason _____

Medications

Name _____   Dose _____

Frequency _____

Family History

Condition	Biological Father's Side	Biological Mother's Side	Sibling
ADHD			
Learning Disabilities			
Speech Problems			
Autism Spectrum Disorder			
Cognitive Delays			
Suicide			
Bipolar Disorder			
Anxiety			
Depression			
Birth Defects			
Genetic Disorders			
Seizures			
Substance Abuse			
Obsessive Compulsive Disorder			
Tics/Tourette's			
Thyroid Disorders			
Behavior Problems			
Contact with law			
Medications for Mental Health			
Other			

Additional Remarks/Comments:

3.4.3   Ascertaining Additional Background Information

In addition to the interview questions and developmental history noted above, there are additional sources of data that will need to be collected about a child. Information from rating forms and records are particularly important and need to be collected.

1. Educational and Behavioral Records at School

   - Report cards
   - State administered standardized test results (e.g., Iowa Test of Basic Skills; New Jersey Ask; PSSAs)
   - Curriculum-based assessments
   - School discipline records
   - Guided reading evaluations
   - Writing samples and other portfolios of the student's work

2. Prior Psychological and Functional Behavioral Assessment Reports—These reports contain important data such as previous norm-referenced and functional evaluation data that will be relevant to your report, serving as a source of base-line data and furnishing additional insight into the child's functioning.

3. Other Professionals Reports—This may include reports from the speech-language pathologist, the counselor, the physical and occupational therapist, and the behavior analyst.

4. IEP Document—If available, the prior IEP should be reviewed to determine what domains are targeted for intervention and whether the child has been making progress toward goals and objectives stated within the IEP.

5. Medical Records—This may contain information not furnished by caregivers including data regarding a child's hearing, vision, and infection history; whether the child has experienced any head trauma; and information on the child's early developmental history.

6. Rating Forms—These are often of a standardized nature including broad (e.g., BASC-2) and narrow (e.g., Beck Depression Inventory) band rating forms. This is not the place to discuss how to administer and score such instruments, but only to indicate that they are vitally important to the psychoeducational report. Rating forms should be distributed to parents, teachers, and the student.

3.5   Conclusion

After collection of the numerous sources of information described in this chapter, you will be one step closer to integrating this information with other data sources. Review and integration of the sources of data is a necessary process when attempting to conceptualize a child's cognitive, academic, behavioral, social, emotional, and adaptive functioning. These important processes are explained in forthcoming chapters of this book.

References

American Psychiatric Association. (2013). *Diagnostic and statistical manual of mental disorders* (5th ed.). Arlington, VA: American Psychiatric Publishing.

Dombrowski, S. C. (2014). *Child development questionnaire.* Cherry Hill, NJ: Stefan C. Dombrowski Publishers.

Frick, P. J., Barry, C. T., & Kamphaus, R. W. (2005). *Clinical assessment of child adolescent personality and behavior* (3rd ed.). New York, NY: Springer.

Loeber, R., Green, S. M., Lahey, B. B., & Stouthamer-Loeber, M. (1991). Differences and similarities between children, mothers, and teachers as informants on disruptive child behavior. *Journal of Abnormal Child Psychology, 19*, 75–95.

Reynolds, C. R., & Kamphaus, R. W. (2004). *Behavior assessment system for children* (2nd ed.). San Antonio, TX: Pearson.

Shaffer, D., Fisher, P., Lucas, C. P., Dulcan, M. K., & Schwab-Stone, M. E. (2000). *NLMH diagnostic interview schedule for children version, IV IMH (DISC-IV): Description.*

Silverman, W. K., & Ollendick, T. H. (2005). Evidence-based assessment of anxiety and its disorders in children and adolescents. *Journal of Clinical Child and Adolescent Psychology, 34*, 380–411.

Zirkel, P. (2011). The role of DSM in case law. *Communique, 39.* Retrieved May 20, 2014 from: http://www.nasponline.org/publications/cq/39/5/RoleofDSM.aspx

Chapter 4
Observing the Child

by Karen L. Gischlar

4.1 Introduction

According to the Individuals with Disabilities Education Improvement Act of 2004, when a child has been referred for a special education evaluation, he must be observed by a member of the evaluation team in the general education setting. This mandate is reflected in practice, as a survey of school psychologists revealed that observation of students is the most frequent assessment method utilized. In fact, school psychologists reported conducting more than 15 observations per month via this survey (Wilson & Reschly, 1996). Direct observation of the student's performance in the classroom is used to screen students, assess emotional and behavioral problems, evaluate the classroom environment in the design of interventions, and monitor student performance and progress (Volpe, DiPerna, Hintze, & Shapiro, 2005). Observational data may be either qualitative (e.g., anecdotal recording) or quantitative (e.g., frequency count) in nature (National Joint Committee on Learning Disabilities [NJCLD], 2011) and aid in verifying teacher report of an academic or behavioral problem (Shapiro & Clemens, 2005).

Observation of the student should occur after the teacher interview, when the referral problem has been identified. This enables the observer to determine which instructional periods and settings are most relevant to the referral (Shapiro, 2011a). For example, if the teacher reported during the interview that the student was having difficulty with reading, the practitioner should observe during the reading instructional period and during other times when the student has the opportunity to read. Observations should also be conducted across different instructional arrangements, such as large and small group settings, to determine discrepancies in performance (Shapiro, 2011a). Ideally, multiple observations of the student across settings and time should be conducted (NJCLD, 2011), as a child's behavior is apt to vary from day to day (McConaughy & Ritter, 2002).

© Springer Science+Business Media New York 2015

S.C. Dombrowski, *Psychoeducational Assessment and Report Writing*,
DOI 10.1007/978-1-4939-1911-6_4

Generally, there are two approaches to direct observation of student behavior, naturalistic and systematic. Naturalistic observation involves the anecdotal recording of all behaviors occurring, with no behavioral target predefined (Shapiro, Benson, Clemens, & Gischlar, 2011). Systematic direct observation (SDO), on the other hand, is conducted under standardized procedures and entails the recording and measurement of specific behaviors that are operationally defined prior to observation (Shapiro et al., 2011). These two approaches are described in greater detail within this chapter, which also includes a review of commercially available structured observation codes. Further, this chapter offers recommendations for reporting and sample narratives and tables.

4.2   Types of Observation

4.2.1   Naturalistic Observation

Naturalistic observation is the most frequently used type of direct observation in the schools, most likely due to its minimal training requirements and facility (Hintze, Volpe, & Shapiro, 2008). When conducting a naturalistic observation, the practitioner chronologically records behavioral events in the natural setting (e.g., classroom, playground) as they occur. The following section describes two types of naturalistic observation, the anecdotal recording and the antecedent-behavior-consequence chart, both of which are commonly used in the schools.

4.2.1.1   Anecdotal Recording

Often times during observation an anecdotal record is kept, which includes a description of the student's behaviors, discriminative stimuli, and the context in which the behaviors occurred. Interpretation is limited to a descriptive account, with little inference drawn (Hintze et al., 2008). In fact, the practitioner is cautioned not to "over-interpret" data from anecdotal observations, as they are not standardized and generally are not evaluated with respect to the psychometric properties (i.e., reliability and validity) that other assessment methods are (Hintze, 2005). As such, these sorts of observations should not be used in high-stakes decision making (Hintze et al., 2008), but rather to confirm existence of a problem, operationally define target behaviors, develop future observation procedures, and identify antecedents and consequences to behavior (Skinner, Rhymer, & McDaniel, 2000).

Following is a sample anecdotal report for a naturalistic observation of a 3rd grade student, Chloe, who engages in problematic behaviors in her classroom, as reported by her teacher Mrs. Dancer.

Chloe was observed by the school psychologist in Mrs. Dancer's general education 3rd grade classroom on January 20, 2014 from 1:00 p.m. until 2:00 p.m. during the social studies lesson. There were 16 children and one teacher present in the room. The desks were arranged in four groups of four and there was a carpeted area at the front of the room with an easel and a large chair. The room was colorfully decorated with posters that included both academic material (e.g., parts of speech, multiplication table) and behavioral expectations (e.g., listen when others are speaking). The lesson observed focused on maps and was the first in a unit.

At the start of the observation, students had just entered the room from recess and the teacher allowed them to get drinks from the fountain at the back of the classroom before taking a seat on the carpet. As students waited for all to be seated, they spoke to one another. Chloe sat in between two other girls and was laughing and talking with them until the teacher sat in the large chair. The teacher signaled for quiet and the students turned their attention toward her. At 1:05 p.m., the teacher began to read the children's book "Mapping Penny's World" (Leedy, 2003), which is a component of the social studies curriculum. As the teacher read, Chloe was observed whispering in the ear of the girl to the right of her. When this student did not respond, Chloe ceased talking and looked toward the teacher. She sat quietly and still for the remainder of the story.

After the story, the teacher asked questions of the students. Chloe was observed to call out three times during this component of the lesson, which lasted from approximately 1:20 p.m. until 1:26 p.m. After the first two call-outs, the teacher put her finger to her lips and called upon other students. After the third call-out, the teacher reminded Chloe of the classroom rule for raising a hand. Chloe smiled and raised her hand. The teacher called upon her and allowed Chloe to provide a response to the question.

After discussion of the book, the teacher explained that the students would be working with their table mates to "find treasure" with a map. Chloe appeared excited and began to call out questions about the "treasure." The teacher ignored her first three questions and continued to speak. Upon the fourth question, the teacher stopped her instruction to speak with Chloe individually. After this discussion, the teacher resumed giving directions and Chloe sat quietly looking at the carpet. At 1:31 p.m., the children were dismissed by groups with their maps to hunt for the "treasure." Each group was assigned a certain colored box to find. They were instructed to return to the carpet when they had found the appropriate box.

By 1:31 p.m., all groups were quietly reseated on the carpet. For the next 3 min, the teacher allowed the groups to share where they had found their boxes and what was inside—stickers. After the students had the opportunity to share, the teacher called their attention to the book that she had read earlier.

(continued)

They reviewed the maps, then the teacher explained that each group would work at their desks to make a map of the classroom. At 1:58 p.m., she dismissed the students to their desks, where each group found a large piece of paper and markers that the teacher had left while students searched for "treasure." During the group work period, Chloe called the teacher twice to her desk to look at her group's work. She was also observed on one other occasion out of her seat speaking with another group. When directed by the teacher, Chloe promptly returned to her seat to resume work. At 1:58 p.m., the teacher announced that students needed to put away materials in preparation for the science lesson and that they would be allotted time to finish on the following day. The observation ended as students were cleaning up materials.

4.2.1.2   A-B-C Recording

Antecedent–Behavior–Consequence (A-B-C) recording is a second type of naturalistic observation that frequently occurs in the schools, especially as a component of functional behavioral assessment (FBA). A-B-C observation involves the recording of antecedents, behaviors, and consequences that are subsequently analyzed to determine the relationships between behaviors and the environment (Eckert, Martens, & Di Gennaro, 2005). Antecedents are the conditions that precede a behavior, whereas consequent events occur contingent upon production of the behavior (Gresham, Watson, & Skinner, 2001). A popular method for completing an A-B-C observation is to use a recording schedule that includes three columns, one for each of the three conditions—antecedents, behaviors, consequences. Typically, the observer records the behavior in the middle column first, followed by the antecedents and consequences for each of the behaviors. Because many behaviors will occur during an observation, only those behaviors of clinical importance are usually recorded (Hintze et al., 2008).

As with anecdotal recordings of behavior, data collected via the A-B-C system are descriptive in nature and, thus, causality between events should not be assumed. That is, it is impossible to differentiate events that are contiguous with, contingent upon, or dependent on behavior (Eckert et al., 2005). To increase the accuracy of A-B-C data in the FBA process, Eckert et al. (2005) suggest computing conditional probabilities for target behaviors that occur with moderate to high frequency, then constructing graphs. Such diagrams illustrate whether antecedents and consequences are more likely to occur with a behavior, or in its absence (Eckert et al., 2005), and bolster the functional hypothesis statement.

The chart below provides a sample A-B-C recording for Chloe, Mrs. Dancer's 3rd grade student. The observation took place during a social studies lesson on maps.

Student: Chloe
Date: January 20, 2014
Subject: Social Studies
Time: 1:00–2:00
Observer: Mr. Singer, School Psychologist

Time	Antecedent	Behavior	Consequence
1:22 p.m.	Circle, teacher reading story	Calls out answer to teacher question	Teacher places her finger to her lips and calls upon another student
1:25 p.m.	Circle, teacher reading story	Calls out answer to teacher question	Teacher stops lesson and addresses Chloe individually to remind her of classroom rules
1:28 p.m.	Circle, teacher giving direction for assignment	Calls out question about the assignment	Teacher ignores and continues to speak
1:31 p.m.	Circle, teacher giving direction for assignment	Calls out question about the assignment	Teacher stops instructing to address Chloe individually and remind her of classroom rules

4.2.2 Systematic Direct Observation

Systematic direct observation (SDO) involves the recording and measurement of specific, operationalized behaviors. An operational definition is based on the shape or topography and describes the behavior in narrow terms, so that occurrence can be verified (Skinner et al., 2000). For example, the term "aggressive behavior" is broad and may lead to inconsistencies in recording. The operational definition "hitting or kicking other students" helps to clarify when an occurrence of the target behavior should be recorded (Skinner et al., 2000). SDO of predefined behaviors is conducted under standardized conditions; scoring and summary of data also are standardized, which limits variability among observers (Shapiro et al., 2011) and improves reliability of the recordings. Further, the use of SDO enables replication, unlike anecdotal recording, which is filtered through the perceptual lens of the observer. Because SDO is standardized, it can be used across time and even across observers. Replication allows for goal setting and the tracking of progress toward goals (Shapiro & Clemens, 2005). The following section describes different forms of SDO, example situations of when each system might be used, and sample data collection forms.

4.2.2.1 Event Recording

One method that can be used to quantify behavior is event recording, which involves drawing a tally mark each time the predefined behavior is exhibited. Event recording is best used for discrete behaviors, which are those that have a clearly discernible beginning and end (Shapiro & Clemens, 2005). For example, this system might lend itself well to Mrs. Dancer's student, Chloe, as our anecdotal and A-B-C recordings suggested that she primarily engages in two problematic behaviors, calling out and extraneous talking. For purposes of this example, "calling out" is defined as "responding without raising a hand and/or waiting to be asked for a response." The chart below represents frequency data for Chloe. Each hash mark represents one occurrence of "calling out" as previously defined.

Student: Chloe
Date: Week of January 20–24, 2014
Behavior: Calling out—responding without raising a hand and/or waiting to be asked for a response
Observer: Mr. Singer, School Psychologist

Subject	Time	January 20	January 21	January 22	January 23	January 24
Morning Meeting	9:00–9:15	////	//	##// ///	////	///
Language Arts	9:15–10:45	//		//		/
Mathematics	10:45–12:00		/	//	/	/
Social Studies	1:00–2:00	##/ //	///	###/ ///	///	##/ //
Science	2:00–3:00	/		//		
Health	3:00–3:30	/		//		/

Although the frequency count above indicates that Chloe is calling out in class, greater information can be gained by calculating the behavior's rate. The rate takes into account the amount of time during which the behavior was observed. Without knowing the timeframe, the data are less meaningful (Shapiro & Clemens, 2005). For example, the chart indicates that Chloe called out eight times during the morning meeting period on January 22 and eight times during the social studies period on the same day. However, these data cannot be directly compared because the morning meeting period was 15 min long, whereas the social studies period was 60 min. The rate is calculated by dividing the number of behavioral occurrences by the number of minutes observed (Shapiro & Clemens, 2005). Thus, in our example, on January 22 the rate of Chloe's behavior was 0.53 per minute (approximately once every 2 min) during morning meeting and 0.13 per minute (approximately once every 7.5 min) during social studies. Although the frequency was the same, the rate indicates that calling out was a bigger problem for Chloe during morning meeting on January 22 than it was during social studies. The data can be further analyzed for trends, including subject areas and days of the week during which the highest and lowest rates of the behavior tend to occur.

4.2.2.2   Duration Recording

In some cases, the length of time a behavior lasts may be more important than the frequency with which it occurs (Skinner et al., 2000). For example, a student may get out of his seat only twice during the 45 min instructional period, but if those instances occur for 7 and 8 consecutive minutes respectively, one third of the period is lost. To collect duration data, the observer needs a timing device, such as a stopwatch. During the observation, the timing device is started as soon as the student begins the behavior and is stopped when he ceases to engage (Skinner et al., 2000). Without resetting the device, the observer begins timing again on the next occurrence and continues this pattern until the observation session is complete; the total time is then recorded. To determine the percentage of time the student engaged in the behavior during the observation period, divide the number of minutes the behavior was observed by the number of minutes in the observation, then multiply by 100 (Shapiro & Clemens, 2005).

As example, Mrs. Dancer is concerned with the amount of time that Chloe spends talking with her classmates, rather than engaged in the social studies lesson. The problem, "extraneous talking," is operationally defined as "speaking with classmates about topics not related to instruction and without permission." The following chart represents duration data collected during the social studies period.

Student: Chloe
Date: Week of January 20–24, 2014
Subject: Social Studies
Time: 1:00–2:00
Behavior: Extraneous talking—speaking with classmates about topics not related to instruction and without permission
Observer: Mr. Singer, School Psychologist

Date	Duration of behavior (min)	Percentage of time (%)
January 20	7.5	13
January 21	3	5
January 22	9.5	16
January 23	12	20
January 24	4	7

4.2.2.3 Latency Recording

Latency recording involves measuring the amount of time that elapses between the onset of a stimulus or signal, such as a verbal directive, and the start of the desired behavior (Hintze et al., 2008). To employ latency recording, both the stimulus and the target behavior must have discrete beginnings. As with duration recording, the observer uses a stopwatch. Timing begins immediately after the signal or stimulus is elicited and stops at the instant the behavior of interest is initiated (Hintze et al, 2008). In Chloe's case, Mrs. Dancer might be concerned with how long it takes the student to cease talking and begin work after teacher direction is given. The observer collecting latency data would begin timing upon the teacher direction, "Complete page 56 in your social studies book." and stop timing the instant that Chloe complied and began to work on the assignment.

4.2.3   Time Sampling Procedures

Event, duration, and latency data recording all require the observer to record every instance of the behavior, which can be difficult for behaviors that occur with high frequency (Shapiro & Clemens, 2005) or those that are more continuous than discrete (Skinner et al., 2000). Furthermore, these systems prevent the observer from recording other pertinent behaviors that may be occurring during the session (Shapiro & Clemens, 2005). To address these issues, the practitioner may want to employ a time sampling procedure. Within a time sampling system, the observation session is divided into smaller, equal units of time and behavior is recorded during specific intervals (Skinner et al., 2000). Because every instance of the behavior is not recorded, these systems provide an estimate of the behavior (Whitcomb & Merrell, 2013).

There are three methods for collecting time sampling data that can be employed— momentary time sampling, whole interval time sampling, and partial interval time sampling. For each of these three procedures the observer will need a recording sheet or device with intervals marked and a method for cuing the intervals (Skinner et al., 2000). The recording sheet could contain a number for each interval. When observing, the practitioner would put a slash through a number to indicate that the behavior was observed during that interval and leave it blank if it was not (Skinner et al., 2000). To cue the intervals, a special timing device should be used. Use of a clock or watch with a second hand is discouraged because it will likely decrease reliability and validity of the observation, as the practitioner attempts to observe both child and the timing device. Rather, it is more efficient to use a timing device such as a vibrating watch or audio-cued system that alerts the observer to record behavior (Whitcomb & Merrell, 2013). Audio-cue files are freely available on the Internet from websites such as Intervention Central (http://www.interventioncentral.org/free-audio-monitoring-tapes).

4.2.3.1   Momentary Time Sampling

Momentary time sampling involves recording the target behavior only if it occurs at a specified moment (Skinner et al., 2000). Prior to the observation, the practitioner should have operationally defined the behavior and developed an interval recording system. During the session, the observer would look at the student on the cue (e.g., audio, vibrating watch cue) and record presence of the behavior only if it occurred at the time of the cue. During the remainder of the interval, the observer could record other behaviors or events, such as the antecedents and consequences (Skinner et al., 2000). However, if the target behavior occurs at any time other than the start of the interval, it should not be recorded in this system (Hintze et al., 2008).

As an example, a momentary time sampling system with an audio cue could be used to record the calling out behavior of our demonstration student Chloe. The observer might divide a 15-min observation period into 5-s intervals, for a total of

180 intervals. On the cue every 5 s, the observer would look to see if Chloe were calling out, as defined previously. If Chloe were to call out on the audio tone, the observer would mark an occurrence. However, if Chloe called out at any other time during the interval, no occurrence would be recorded. In other words, the behavior would need to occur as the tone is sounding.

Because the behavior is not recorded continuously when using momentary time sampling, it should be used for behaviors that occur at a high frequency (Skinner et al., 2000). Otherwise, this type of system could result in behaviors being under-reported. Furthermore, the observer should somehow indicate on the recording form if there was a missed opportunity to observe. For example, if the teacher or another student walked between the target student and the observer on the cue occluding the observer's vision, this should be noted on the recording sheet (Skinner et al., 2000). It is important to distinguish lack of opportunity to observe from nonoccurrence of the behavior in describing it as accurately as possible.

4.2.3.2 Partial Interval Time Sampling

Partial interval time sampling works well for behaviors that occur at moderate to high rates or that are of inconsistent duration (Shapiro & Clemens, 2005). As with momentary time sampling, the target behavior should be operationally defined and an interval recording system designed prior to observation. Within this system, a behavior is recorded as occurring if it is observed during any part of the interval. Therefore, whether a behavior begins before the interval is cued and continues, or begins after the interval is cued, an occurrence is recorded. If multiple occurrences of the behavior occur during the same interval, it is only scored as if the behavior presented once (Hintze et al., 2008).

A partial-interval time sampling system could be employed with our demonstration student Chloe for her "extraneous talking" behavior. For example, the observer could divide a 15-min observation period into ninety 10-s intervals. He or she would then watch to see if Chloe engaged in the predefined target behavior at any time during each 10 s interval. An occurrence could be slashed by marking the interval number, whereas a nonoccurrence would result in no mark. Again, it would be important to indicate somehow if an opportunity to observe was missed, perhaps by circling the number.

A concern with partial-interval recording systems is that they tend to overestimate the actual occurrence of the behavior, especially if it is somewhat continuous (Hintze et al., 2008; Shapiro & Clemens, 2005). If we consider Chloe, she might be engaged in the "extraneous talking" target behavior for only 3 s of the 10 s interval, but occurrence of the behavior would be recorded for the full interval. Or if Chloe began to speak at the end of one interval and continued briefly into the next, both intervals would be scored for occurrence. However, a benefit to using a partial-interval system is that it enables the observer to monitor and score multiple behaviors during the same interval (Shapiro & Clemens, 2005). For example, we could observe both of Chloe's target behaviors with this system. If she were to speak with a classmate and/or call out at any time during a given interval, both behaviors could easily be recorded when employing partial-interval recording.

4.2.3.3   Whole Interval Time Sampling

Whole interval time sampling is best used for behaviors that are continuous or with intervals of short duration because it requires a behavior to be present for an entire interval (Hintze et al., 2008). In other words, the target behavior must occur continuously for the full interval in order to be marked as an occurrence. For example, the observer might divide a 15-min observation period into 180 intervals of 5-s each. During each interval where the behavior presented continuously for 5-s, occurrence would be recorded.

A system such as this could be used to record the "extraneous talking" behaviors of our demonstration student Chloe. However, it is important to note that whole interval time sampling can underestimate the occurrence of behaviors (Hintze et al., 2008). Consider the use of a 5-s interval when observing Chloe. If she were to talk for the full 5-s, an occurrence would be marked. However, if she talked for 3-s, occurrence during that interval would not be recorded. Thus, it is possible for her to have engaged in many more instances of the target behavior than will be reflected in the data. For this reason, it is suggested that the observer keep the interval duration brief (Skinner et al., 2000).

4.2.4   Observation of Comparison Students

Comparison peer data provide information about the degree of discrepancy between the target child's behavior and the expected levels of behavior for students in the classroom, which aids in problem verification (Shapiro, 2011a) and the establishment of empirical goals (Skinner et al., 2000). Peer data can be collected either through simultaneous or discontinuous recording (Skinner et al., 2000). Simultaneous data can be collected on one or more peer comparisons when a momentary time sampling system is employed. Because momentary time sampling requires the observer to record the behavior for the target student on the interval, the rest of the interval can be devoted to observation of peer behavior. This type of system is best utilized when students are in close proximity to one another in the physical setting (Skinner et al., 2000).

If the observer is using a whole-interval system to record the behavior of the referred student, simultaneous recording of peers is not recommended; whole-interval recording requires the practitioner to observe the target student for the entire interval. Observing more than one child at the same time might result in data that are less than accurate (Shapiro, 2011a). In this case, discontinuous recording of peers would be appropriate. In a discontinuous system, the practitioner would designate certain intervals during which to observe the peer (Skinner et al, 2000). For example, the observer could record behavior of a peer comparison student, rather than the target student, every fifth interval (Shapiro, 2011a). In a system such as this, the observer could record data for comparison student 1 during the 5th interval, for comparison student 2 during the 10th interval, and for comparison student 3 during the 15th interval; the cycle would then be repeated by observing comparison student 1 during the 20th interval (Skinner et al., 2000).

Prior to conducting a peer comparison observation, the practitioner will need to decide which peers to select. One approach is to ask the teacher to identify a few students whose behavior is "average" or "typical" for her classroom (Shapiro & Clemens, 2005). If using this method, the observer should be careful to ensure that the teacher has not selected the best behaved or most poorly behaved students. The goal of peer observation is to supply a normative base or benchmark to which to compare the target student's behavior in problem verification (Shapiro & Clemens, 2005).

To avoid bias in teacher judgment of students, the observer could randomly select peers to observe, such as those sitting in close proximity to the student of interest (Shapiro, 2011a). However, this method of selection also may present problems. The practitioner may not be aware of the characteristics of the selected peers and may inadvertently choose students who are not considered "typical" in the classroom. Whichever method is used to identify comparison peers, peer comparison provides a method for problem verification and the establishment of intervention goals and is a recommended practice.

4.2.5 Analogue Observation

Analog observation involves the use of controlled situations that simulate particular environments or circumstances of concern (Knoff, 2002) and reflect how a student might behave in the natural environment (Hintze, Stoner, & Bull, 2000). Typically, a hypothetical situation is designed to mimic the real-life environment in which the target behavior usually occurs, with the assumption that there will be some degree of similarity between the student's behavior in the contrived setting and his behavior in the natural environment. Analogue observation has utility for tracking multiple behaviors simultaneously and accommodating variability across behavioral domains (Mori & Armendariz, 2001). School-based applications involve enactment and role play procedures, paper-and-pencil techniques, audiotape, or videotape procedures (Hintze et al., 2000).

Enactment exercises require the student to respond to contrived situations that are artificially arranged to mirror the natural setting (Hintze et al., 2000). For example, for a student having problems on the bus, the practitioner may set up lines of chairs to mimic the seating arrangement on a bus and observe children as they naturally interact. Conversely, role playing involves scripted behavior (Hintze et al., 2000). For example, the practitioner may want to assess the social skills of a child by asking him to approach another child to play during recess. During an enactment, the behavior of a student is free, but is clearly defined during role play. The third analogue method, paper and pencil, requires the student to respond to a stimulus presented in written format, either through writing, speaking, or displaying a physical behavior (Hintze et al., 2000). For example, the practitioner may present a situation in which a child is experiencing a problem with a friend and ask the target student to give a written or oral response. Finally, audiotape and videotape analogues require the student to listen to or view a situation and respond. Although analogue observations may have utility for behaviors that are situation specific, they are not without limitation. Their application requires expertise and time (Stichter, 2001). Certainly, analogue assessment should not be employed without proper training and supervision.

4.2.6 Observation of Permanent Products

A permanent product is the tangible outcome of a student behavior (Steege & Watson, 2009). A block pattern, the number of math problems completed, and the number of words written on a page all can be considered permanent products. An advantage to utilizing such is that the practitioner need not be present to observe the behavior, yet still has a record of its occurrence. This can save time and circumvent issues with scheduling. A drawback to this procedure, however, lies in certifying authenticity. For example, it can be difficult to determine whether a student completed a task alone, or with support (Steege & Watson, 2009). Observation of permanent products is perhaps best used along with direct observation of student behavior.

4.2.7 Observation Systems

4.2.7.1 Behavior Assessment System for Children (BASC-2)

The BASC-2 (Reynolds & Kamphaus, 2004) is a multidimensional system used to evaluate the behavior and self-perceptions of children and young adults between the ages of 2- and 25-years. It includes the following components which can be used individually, or in any combination: (a) parent and teacher rating scales; (b) self-report scale; (c) a structured developmental history recording form; and (d) a form for recording and classifying behavior from direct classroom observations. The Student Observation System (SOS) is designed for use by the practitioner in diagnosis, treatment planning, and for monitoring the effects of intervention and includes the following behavior domains: (a) Response to Teacher/Lesson; (b) Peer Interaction; (c) Work on School Subjects; and (d) Transition Movement (Reynolds & Kamphaus, 2004).

The SOS is designed to be used across multiple 15-min observations. To use the system, the observer needs both the recording form and a timing device. The form is divided into three sections. Part A includes a list of 65 specific behaviors across

13 categories. This list provides a reference for the observation session, but also serves as a checklist that is to be completed after the session. Part B is used to document the 15-min observation. During the observation, the observer records student behavior across thirty observations. Specifically, each observation occurs for 3-s at the end of each 30-s interval. During the 3-s interval, the observer should place a checkmark in the corresponding box for each class of behaviors exhibited by the student; specific examples for the classes are included on Part A of the form. At the end of the observation period, the observer tallies occurrences across classes in Part B, then retrospectively completes Part A by noting whether specific behaviors were not observed, sometimes observed, or frequently observed. Additionally, within Part A the observer should indicate whether the behavior was disruptive to instruction. Part C includes space for the observer to record the teacher's interaction with the student during the observation. This section also is completed retrospectively and requires the observer to record information regarding the teacher's physical position in the classroom and attempts to change the student's behavior (Reynolds & Kamphaus, 2004).

The SOS is designed to provide information about the types of behavior being displayed and their frequency and level of disruption. To aid in defining the problem, the system can also be used to collect peer comparison data or to develop local norms (Reynolds & Kamphaus, 2004). The SOS is available in both paper-and-pencil and digital formats. Although the SOS appears easy to use and requires minimal training, it should be noted that the manual provides limited information about the reliability and validity of the system. It is unknown to what extent the SOS code categories correlate with clinical criteria in the identification of disorders. Furthermore, no norms are offered to allow for norm-referenced interpretation of scores (Frick, Barry, & Kamphaus, 2005). These limitations suggest that although the SOS may have utility in defining and monitoring behavior problems, caution should be used in the interpretation of results for high stakes decisions, such as diagnoses and classification for special education services.

4.2.7.2 Behavioral Observation of Students in Schools (BOSS)

The BOSS (Shapiro, 2011a) is an observation code that can be used to confirm or disconfirm teacher judgment of a problem, determine the severity of a behavior problem, and provide a baseline against which to measure the success of an intervention (Shapiro, 2011a). The system measures two types of engaged time, active and passive, and three classes of off-task behaviors, verbal, motor, and passive. In addition to collecting these data on the target student, the observer also records data on peer-comparison students and the teacher's instruction. To conduct an observation with the BOSS, the practitioner needs a recording form (see Shapiro, 2011b) and a cuing device, such as a digital recorder or vibrating watch, to mark intervals. Use of a stopwatch is not recommended because such would require the observer to look frequently at the watch, which could result in inaccurate data recording (Shapiro, 2011a).

The recording form for the BOSS (Shapiro, 2011a) includes a section for identifying information. In addition to personal information for the student, the practitioner should note the academic subject, type of activity (e.g., worksheets, silent reading), and instructional situation observed. Within this system, there are codes for the four most common types of instructional situations: (a) ISW:TPsnt (individual seatwork, teacher present), which indicates that the student was observed engaged in an individual seatwork activity as the teacher circulated the room checking assignments or worked with individual students; (b) ISW:TSmGp (individual seatwork, teacher working with a small group of students), which indicates that the teacher worked with a small group of students as the target student engaged in individual seatwork apart from the group; (c) SmGp:Tled (small group led by the teacher), which indicates that the target student was part of the small group directly taught by the teacher; and (d) LgGp:Tled (large group led by the teacher), which indicates that the target student was part of a large group during which at least half of the class was taught by the teacher (Shapiro, 2011a). If the instructional situation does not fit any of these codes (e.g., learning centers or cooperative groups), the observer should indicate this with a note on the recording form. Furthermore, during an observation, the instructional arrangement may change. If a change occurs during the session, this should be indicated on the form at the interval during which it occurred; the observer can circle the interval number and make a notation (Shapiro, 2011a).

Generally, an observation with the BOSS is conducted for at least a 15-min period (Shapiro, 2011a). If 15-s intervals are used, each 15-min session requires one recording form. Under the information section previously described, is the section of the form wherein behaviors are recorded. The left-hand column lists the behaviors to be observed, while the top row lists the intervals. Every fifth interval is shaded gray, indicating that it is designated for peer comparison and teacher directed instruction data. Momentary time sampling is employed while observing the student for active and passive engaged time, whereas partial interval recording is used while observing off-task motor, verbal, and passive behaviors. Likewise, teacher directed instruction is observed via a partial interval system (Shapiro, 2011a).

The BOSS manual clearly defines all classes of behaviors (Shapiro, 2011b). For example, at the instant each interval is cued (momentary time sampling), the observer is to score the occurrence or non-occurrence of active engaged time (AET) or passive engaged time (PET). Both AET and PET require the student to be on task. Examples of AET include writing, responding to a question, and reading aloud. Examples of PET include reading silently, listening to the teacher or a peer speak, and looking at the blackboard during instruction. During the remainder of the interval, the observer notes whether the student engaged in any off-task behaviors, including motor (OFT-M, e.g., rocking in chair, out of seat, or playing with pencil), verbal (OFT-V, e.g., making noise, talking to a peer off-topic), and passive (OFT-P, e.g., staring out the window). This same system is employed for observation of a peer student every fifth interval. Additionally, during that same interval, the teacher is observed for direct instruction, which includes lecturing to the class or modeling a skill (Shapiro, 2011b).

Once data are collected, the manual instructs the user how to calculate percentages and interpret the data. It should be noted that there is also an electronic version of the BOSS available for handheld devices (Pearson, Inc., 2013). The BOSS is relatively easy to learn (Hintze et al., 2008) and use of the electronic version simplifies the process even further by eliminating the need to manage the recording form, timing device, and clip board during the observation and by performing the calculations afterward (Shapiro, 2011a).

Following is a suggested format for reporting BOSS (Shapiro, 2011a) data for our example student, Chloe, for one observation. In practice, it would prove beneficial to conduct multiple observations with the BOSS, which would enable the observer to detect patterns in student behavior.

Chloe was observed during the social studies period on January 21, 2014 with the Behavioral Observation of Students in Schools (BOSS), a structured observation code. The BOSS enables the observer to record occurrences of both on-task and off-task behavior for the referred student, as well as peer comparison and teacher directed instruction data, which aids in problem definition. During the 30-min observation, there were 16 children and one teacher present in the room. Student desks were arranged in four groups of four and there was a carpeted area at the front of the room with an easel and a large chair. The room was colorfully decorated with posters that included both academic material (e.g., parts of speech, multiplication table) and behavioral expectations (e.g., listen when others are speaking). During the portion of the lesson observed, students were seated at their desks completing a small group task that required them to take turns reading aloud from the social studies text. Once finished reading within their small groups, students worked together to answer the questions at the end of the selection and then made a poster, as directed by the teacher. During the activity, the teacher circulated from group to group and offered assistance when necessary.

Percentage of observed intervals		
Behavior	Chloe (96 intervals)	Peer comparison (24 intervals)
Active engagement	39 %	76 %
Passive engagement	22 %	20 %
Off-task motor	19 %	3 %
Off-task verbal	23 %	5 %
Off-task passive	9 %	–
Teacher-directed instruction	79 %	–

During the observation session, Chloe was observed across ninety-six 15-s intervals, whereas peer comparison students were observed across 24 intervals, as was teacher instruction. During observed intervals, Chloe was either actively (39 %) or passively (22 %) engaged, for a total engagement time of 61 %. Active engaged time (AET) includes tasks such as writing in a workbook or reading aloud, whereas passive engaged time (PET) refers to activities such as reading silently or listening to a lecture. Chloe was either actively or passively engaged during fewer observed intervals than her peers (AET = 76 %; PET = 20 %; total engaged time = 96 %). It should be noted that Chloe was observed to be on task more often during those intervals when students were reading, than when they were working on the poster.

Chloe was observed to be engaged in off-task motor (OFT-M) behaviors such as getting out of her seat and playing with materials during 19 % of observed intervals, whereas peer comparison students engaged in OFT-M behaviors for only 3 % of observed intervals. Likewise, Chloe engaged in more off-task verbal (OFT-V) behavior, such as talking off topic and humming, than did her peers. OFT-V behaviors were recorded during 23 % of the observed intervals for Chloe and during 5 % of observed intervals for her peers. Finally, Chloe engaged in off-task passive (OFT-P) behaviors such as staring out the window or looking around the room during 9 % of the intervals, whereas her peers were not observed engaging in OFT-P behaviors. The BOSS data suggest that Chloe engaged in higher levels of off-task behaviors and was less engaged than her peers during this social studies lesson, despite the high level of teacher-directed instruction (TDI = 79 %).

4.3   How Many Observations Are Enough?

Typically, classroom observations are conducted for brief periods of time with the hope that a representative sample of behavior will be captured. From this sampling, generalities about the student's behavior are made (Tiger, Miller, Mevers, Mintz, Scheithauer, & Alvarez, 2013). However, there currently is no standard regarding the frequency and duration of observation sessions necessary to obtain a representative sample of behavior. Although the questions of frequency and length of observation have been examined in the literature, research studies may be difficult to translate into a heuristic for school-based practitioners. To address this issue, Tiger et al. (2013) designed a study to evaluate more closely the nature of observations conducted in the natural classroom environment.

Tiger et al. (2013) utilized duration recording methods in consecutive 10-minute sessions to observe the behavior of three referred students. The authors then culled 10-, 20-, 30-, and 60-min observation sessions from the complete record and compared those data to the daily mean of behavioral occurrences to assess their accuracy. The findings suggested that when there was low behavioral variability, the briefer observations were more representative of the overall levels, than when there was more variability in behavior. In fact, even 60-min observations did not capture the true levels of behavior when variability was high (Tiger et al., 2013). Tiger et al. (2013) concluded that the variability in the behavior is more relevant than its absolute level and suggested that the practitioner might attempt to control for variability in behavior by identifying the environmental variables that impact performance and then holding those variables constant. Implementing this type of structure might help to minimize the number of observations sessions achieve stability.

Relative to the behavioral representativeness of direct observation of its psychometric properties. Other evaluation methods, such as inte........... ...... achievement tests and behavior rating scales, are expected to meet standards for reliability and validity, but the same is not true of direct observation as utilized in practice (Hintze, 2005). To address this shortcoming, Hintze (2005) has proposed a series of quality indicators that the practitioner can apply when developing an observation system or when selecting a commercially available system for use. These seven indicators include: (a) internal consistency reliability, which indicates that the observation is of sufficient length to sample occurrence and nonoccurrence of the behavior accurately; (b) test-retest reliability, which means that multiple observations are conducted to ensure consistency of behavior over time; (c) interobserver agreement, which pertains to the extent to which independent observers agree on the occurrence and nonoccurrence of behavior with and across observation sessions; (d) content validity, which indicates that operational and response definitions accurately describe the behavior of interest; (e) concurrent and convergent validity, which speaks to the level of agreement between data garnered from direct observations and other assessment information (e.g., rating scales and interviews); (f) predictive validity, which indicates how accurately observational data predicts behavior in future situations; and (g) sensitivity to change, which pertains to how observational data change as a function of environmental manipulations and/or to developmental changes in the child over time (Hintze, 2005). Use of indicators such as these helps to ensure that the direct observation system employed is psychometrically sound and produces reliable, useful outcomes (Hintze, 2005).

4.4   Observation of Student Behavior during Administration of Standardized Assessments

In addition to the naturalistic environment, the practitioner also may have the opportunity to observe the student during the administration of standardized assessments, such as intelligence and achievement tests. During this time, the psychologist will want to note any individual or situational variables that might influence performance (McGrew & Flanagan, 1998). For example if the student was highly distractible and inattentive during the testing session, his score may not accurately reflect his or her level of the trait being measured (i.e., his performance would be underestimated). It is important in the interpretation of scores to note when an administration might not truly portray the individual's abilities ((McGrew & Flanagan, 1998).

Furthermore, observation during the administration of tests can provide additional information about the student in terms of the referral problem. There are opportunities for the examiner to observe areas such as language abilities, motor coordination, problem solving, persistence to task, response to feedback, frustration, and impulsiveness (Flanagan & Kaufman, 2009). These observations may aid in interpretation of results, but might also suggest further areas for evaluation and are important to the assessment process.

4.5 Hawthorne and Halo Effects

Over 80 years ago, the results of the Hawthorne studies demonstrated that measurements of behavior in controlled studies were altered by the participants' knowledge of being in an experiment. This phenomenon came to be known as the Hawthorne Effect and it has been suggested that it may extend beyond experimental behavior (Adair, 1984). For example, it is possible that a student's behavior could be altered in the classroom or during an assessment session by the very fact that he is being observed. Furthermore, in the classroom setting the presence of an observer might also impact the nature of the student and teacher relationship (Mercatoris & Craighead, 1974), or even the level of integrity at which a teacher implements instruction (Gresham, MacMillan, Beebe-Frankenberger, & Bocian, 2000). One way to limit this reactivity is to observe the student prior to meeting him during the evaluation process and to conduct multiple observation sessions to increase the validity of findings.

Another phenomenon that may impact observations of the child is known as the halo effect. The halo effect, or error, occurs when the rater's overall impression strongly influences the rating of a specific attribute (Murphy, Jako, & Anhalt, 1993). For example, it has been demonstrated that when a child is identified as being "impulsive," the teacher tends to rate other problematic behaviors such as restlessness, poor concentration, and poor sociability as present, even if such cannot be verified by other sources (Abikoff, Courtney, Pelham, & Koplewicz, 1993). The halo effect is important for the practitioner to keep in mind, as previous behavioral reports or knowledge of a diagnosis (e.g., Attention Deficit Hyperactivity Disorder) may impact the observation and overall impressions of a student.

4.6 Summary

School psychologists and other education professionals frequently observe children in the classroom and other school settings when a behavior or learning problem has been suspected. Observation of the student is an integral component of a multi-method evaluation and can be used in the screening, assessment, and monitoring of student performance. There are two primary types of observation, naturalistic and systematic. Naturalistic observation entails the recording of behavioral events in the natural setting, whereas systematic observation involves the recording and measurement of specific, operationalized behaviors. Practitioners are encouraged to employ both methods in conducting multiple observations of student behavior and to evaluate their systems for reliability and validity, which enhances their utility in the decision making process.

References

Abikoff, H., Courtney, M., Pelham, W. E., Jr., & Koplewicz, H. S. (1993). Teachers' ratings of disruptive behaviors: The influence of halo effects. *Journal of Abnormal Child Psychology, 21*, 519–533.

Adair, J. G. (1984). The Hawthorne effect: A reconsideration of the methodological artifact. *Journal of Applied Psychology, 69*, 334–345.

Eckert, T. L., Martens, B. K., & Di Gennaro, F. D. (2005). Describing antecedent-behavior-consequence relations using conditional probabilities and the general operant contingency space: A preliminary investigation. *School Psychology Review, 34*, 520–528.

Flanagan, D. P., & Kaufman, A. S. (2009). *Essentials of WISC-IV assessment* (2nd ed.). Hoboken, NJ: John Wiley & Sons.

Frick, P. J., Barry, C. T., & Kamphaus, R. W. (2005). *Clinical assessment of child and adolescent personality and behavior* (3rd ed.). New York, NY: Springer.

Gresham, F. M., MacMillan, D. L., Beebe-Frankenberger, M. E., & Bocian, K. M. (2000). Treatment integrity in learning disabilities intervention research: Do we really know how treatments are implemented? *Learning Disabilities Research & Practice, 15*, 198–205.

Gresham, F. M., Watson, T. S., & Skinner, C. H. (2001). Functional behavioral assessment: Principles, procedures, and future directions. *School Psychology Review, 30*, 156–172.

Hintze, J. M. (2005). Psychometrics of direct observation. *School Psychology Review, 34*, 507.

Hintze, J. M., Stoner, G., & Bull, M. H. (2000). Analogue assessment: Emotional/behavioral problems. In E. S. Shapiro & T. R. Kratochwill (Eds.), *Conducting school-based assessments of child and adolescent behavior* (p. 519). New York, NY: The Guilford Press.

Hintze, J. M., Volpe, R. J., & Shapiro, E. S. (2008). Best practices in the systematic direct observation of student behavior. In A. Thomas & J. Grimes (Eds.), *Best practices in school psychology* (5th ed., Vol. 2, pp. 319–335). Bethesda, MD: National Association of School Psychologists.

Individuals With Disabilities Education Act, 20U.S.C. § 1400 (2004).

Knoff, H. M. (2002). Best practices in personality assessment. In A. Thomas & J. Grimes (Eds.), *Best practices in school psychology, vol. 2* (4th ed., pp. 1303–1320). Bethesda, MD: National Association of School Psychologists.

Leedy, L. (2003). Mapping Penny's world. New York, NY: Henry Holt & Co.

McConaughy, S. H., & Ritter, D. R. (2002). Best practices in multidimensional assessment of emotional or behavioral disorders. In A. Thomas & J. Grimes (Eds.), *Best practices in school psychology, vol. 2* (4th ed., pp. 1303–1320). Bethesda, MD: National Association of School Psychologists.

McGrew, K. S., & Flanagan, D. P. (1998). *The intelligence test desk reference*. Needham Heights, MA: Allyn & Bacon.

Mercatoris, M., & Craighead, W. E. (1974). Effects of nonparticipant observation teacher and pupil classroom behavior. *Journal of Educational Psychology, 66*, 512–519.

Mori, L. T., & Armendariz, G. M. (2001). Analogue assessment of child behavior problems. *Psychological Assessment, 13*, 36–45.

Murphy, K. R., Jako, R. A., & Anhalt, R. L. (1993). Nature and consequences of halo error: A critical analysis. *Journal of Applied Psychology, 78*, 218–225.

National Joint Committee on Learning Disabilities. (2011). Comprehensive assessment and evaluation of students with learning disabilities. *Learning Disability Quarterly, 34*, 3–16.

Pearson, Inc. (2013). *BOSS user's guide*. Bloomington, MN: Author. Retrieved on February 7, 2014 from http://images.pearsonclinical.com/images/Assets/BOSS/BOSS_UsersGuide.pdf

Reynolds, C. R., & Kamphaus, R. W. (2004). *The behavior assessment system for children manual* (2nd ed.). Circle Pines, MN: AGS.

Shapiro, E. S. (2011a). *Academic skills problems* (4th ed.). New York, NY: The Guilford Press.

Shapiro, E. S. (2011b). *Academic skills problems workbook* (4th ed.). New York, NY: The Guilford Press.

Shapiro, E. S., Benson, J. L., Clemens, N. H., & Gischlar, K. L. (2011). Academic assessment. In M. Bray & T. Kehle (Eds.), *Oxford handbook of school psychology*. New York, NY: Oxford University Press.

Shapiro, E. S., & Clemens, N. H. (2005). Conducting systematic direct classroom observations to define school-related problems. In R. Brown-Chidsey (Ed.), *Assessment for intervention: A problem-solving approach*. New York, NY: The Guilford Press.

Skinner, C. H., Rhymer, K. N., & McDaniel, E. C. (2000). Naturalistic direct observation in educational settings. In E. S. Shapiro & T. R. Kratochwill (Eds.), *Conducting school-based assessments of child and adolescent behavior*. New York, NY: The Guilford Press.

Steege, M. W., & Watson, T. S. (2009). *Conducting school-based functional behavioral assessments: A practitioner's guide* (2nd ed.). New York, NY: The Guilford Press.

Stichter, J. P. (2001). Functional analysis: The use of analogues in applied settings. *Focus on Autism and Other Developmental Disabilities, 16*, 232–239.

Tiger, J. H., Miller, S. J., Mevers, J. L., Mintz, J. C., Scheithauer, M. C., & Alvarez, J. (2013). On the representativeness of behavior observation samples in classrooms. *Journal of Applied Behavior Analysis, 46*, 424–435.

Volpe, R. J., DiPerna, J. C., Hintze, J. M., & Shapiro, E. S. (2005). Observing students in classroom settings: A review of seven coding schemes. *School Psychology Review, 34*, 454–474.

Whitcomb, S., & Merrell, K. W. (2013). *Behavioral, social, and emotional assessment of children and adolescents* (4th ed.). New York, NY: Routledge.

Wilson, M. S., & Reschly, D. J. (1996). Assessment in school psychology training and practice. *School Psychology Review, 25*, 9–23.

Chapter 5
General Guidelines on Report Writing

5.1 Overview

Chapter 5 offers a general discussion of psychoeducational assessment reporting writing guidelines. This chapter offers a panoramic perspective with more specific guidance provided in Chaps. 6–10. Specific conceptual issues to improve report writing will be presented.

5.2 Structure of the Psychoeducational Report

A psychoeducational report has several components. The following table presents a broad overview of the contents including the generalized structure of a report.

Title
Identifying Information
Referral question
Assessment methods and background information
Assessment results
- Cognitive and academic
- Behavioral and social emotional
- Adaptive

(continued)

© Springer Science+Business Media New York 2015
S.C. Dombrowski, *Psychoeducational Assessment and Report Writing*,
DOI 10.1007/978-1-4939-1911-6_5

(continued)

- Interview results
  - Student
  - Parent/caregiver
  - Teacher
  - Other personnel
- Observations

  - Classroom-based
  - School-based
  - Testing-based

Conceptualization and classification (or diagnostic impressions)
Summary and recommendations

Forthcoming chapters will discuss each of these report components in greater detail. The purpose of psychoeducational assessment and report writing is to gather information about a child and convey that information so that parents, teachers, and other caregivers will be able to help the child succeed (Blau, 1991). A second purpose of the report is to determine whether the child receives specially designed instruction (i.e., special education support) and to provide guidance as to how those supports are to be furnished. The report should be structured to appropriately convey this information.

5.3 Conceptual Issues in Psychoeducational Report Writing

Graduate students in school and clinical child psychology need to be mindful of selected report writing pitfalls and best practices. Some of these are addressed below. This listing is by no means exhaustive, but it will furnish the reader with a pathway for addressing commonly encountered report writing issues.

5.3.1 Address Referral Questions

The exclusion of referral questions within a report is considered by most texts and articles on report writing to be poor practice (Ownby, 1997; Tallent, 1993; Watkins, 2014; Weiner, 1985, 1987). All reports, whether psychological or psychoeducational, should contain referral questions that need to be addressed by the report (Brenner, 2003). This will help to focus the report and assure that issues of concern are addressed by the psychologist.

5.3.2 Avoid Making Predictive and Etiological Statements

Research within psychology is often associative, not causative, and therefore quasi-experimental. This makes the provision of predictive and etiological statements extremely difficult. The public and even the courts may seek simple, categorical descriptions of behavior. This is sometimes offered by health care providers, so the public and even the courts may come to expect a similar response style from the psychologist. For instance, when a child is taken to the pediatrician for a persistent sore throat the caregiver may wish to have strep ruled out by the pediatrician. The medical community has tools for such purpose and can determine etiology through the use of a rapid strep test and a culture-based strep test. In these situations the physician offers a direct causation for the sore throat and a specific intervention (e.g., antibiotics) to resolve the issue. A definitive test may be able to determine etiology (e.g., child has sore throat because of the streptococcus bacteria). With psychology, such definitive tools may not be as readily available and the psychologist must be left to infer possible causation. But this should be done extremely cautiously and only after exhaustive research and consideration, if it is done at all. As an example, suppose a child scores at the seventh percentile on a measure of cognitive ability. This same child was born at 31 weeks gestation. Although there is an association between reduced cognitive ability scores and gestational age (see Martin & Dombrowski, 2008), it would be inappropriate to conclude that the child's prematurity caused the reduced cognitive ability scores. There may be other similarly plausible explanations that are responsible for the IQ test score decrement.

As with the provision of etiological statements, it is inappropriate to make predictive statements about a child's functioning. One cannot state with certainty that a child who scores in the gifted range on an IQ test will be destined for an Ivy League education with a prosperous career on Wall Street. Nor can we conclude that the child with severe learning disabilities will ever attend college. Psychologists must be genuine in their statements of abilities and disabilities about children, but must make such statements tentatively based upon the empirical evidence. Of course, when we make such tentative statements, we are talking probabilities. There are always individuals who defy group level statistics. Do not dismiss group level statistics, however, in a Pollyanna fashion (Matlin & Gawron, 1979), but also do not be overly pessimistic in your conceptualization of a child.

5.3.3 Make a Classification Decision and Stand by It

Do not be timid when making a classification decision. You need to offer a classification, discuss your rationale for it, and stand by your decision. Of course, your decision should be predicated upon solid data and sound clinical judgment. Similarly, you need to rule out additional classifications and state why you ruled them out. Express your classification decision-making clearly, use data-based decision making, and then stand by your decision.

5.3.4   Rule Out Other Classifications and State Why You Ruled Them Out

A corollary to making a classification decision and sticking by it is to discuss the other classifications you considered and why they are not as appropriate as the one you decided upon. The classification decision is not as straightforward as it might appear at the outset. There are times when you weighed the data and decided upon one classification over another. In these circumstances you should state why you arrived at your decision and ruled-out the other.

5.3.5   Use Multiple Sources of Data and Methods of Assessment to Support Decision-Making

Gone are the days of using a single method of assessment (e.g., the WISC, Bender or Draw-A-Person) to infer that a child has an emotional disturbance or behavioral issue. Here are the days that require multiple sources of data to inform decision-making via an iterative problem-solving process. When multiple sources of information converge then we can be confident in a decision made about a child. These sources of data may include norm-referenced assessment, functional assessment, interview results, observations, and review of records as supported by clinical judgment.

5.3.6   Eisegesis

Eisegesis is the interpretation of data from a report in such a way that it introduces one's own presuppositions, agendas, or biases into and onto the report (Kamphaus, 2001; Tallent, 1993). Generally, this will entail overlooking the data and research evidence and instead applying one's own interpretation schema to the interpretation of the data. Tallent (1993) suggests that selected clinicians' reports can even be identified by the type of judgments that they superimpose upon the data. This is poor practice and should be eschewed.

5.3.7   Be Wary of Using Computer Generated Reports

Errors abound and mistakes are made when computer generated reports are freely relied upon. Be cautious about the practice of cutting and pasting computer generated reports. This is poor practice and should be avoided. Butcher et al. (2004) suggests that nearly half of all computer generated narrative may be inaccurate.

For this reason, the apparently sophisticated, well-written, and reliable computer generated interpretation and narrative should not supplant clinical judgment. It might be tempting to incorporate narrative from computer generated reports. Many programs incorporate computer scoring and interpretive statements in an organized format similar to what can be found in a psychological report. However, Michaels (2006) notes that simply cutting and pasting may be in violation of ethical principles.

While acknowledging some of these limitations, Lictenberger (2006) points out benefits of using computer generated reports. She notes that there is potential to reduce errors in clinical judgment (e.g., relying on data collected early or late in the evaluation; judgments influenced by information already collected; attending to information most readily available or recalled) so there may certainly be a place for computer assisted assessment and report writing. However, it should receive an ancillary emphasis and relied upon cautiously.

5.3.8 Sparingly Use Pedantic Psychobabble

Your report should be written at an accessible level to most parents/caregivers. You should avoid using psychology jargon and overly ornate language and terminology (Harvey, 1997, 2006; Watkins, 2014) whenever possible. Instead write concisely and in terms understandable to most readers. For example, you should avoid a sentence like the following:

Jack display of anhedonic traits likely emanate from ego dystonic features related to a chaotic home life and rearing by a borderline caregiver.

Instead, indicate the following:

Jack reported feeling sad and depressed. He explained that his parents are divorcing and this has been quite upsetting for him.

This second sentence is superior in that it uses more accessible language and avoids making etiological statements.

Although you are to use psychology jargon sparingly, please keep in mind that this guideline is not to be rigidly adhered to in all circumstances. Certain words or phrases cannot be adequately expressed parsimoniously without the use of a psychological term. In some situations it will be necessary to use psychology terminology. For instance, when describing a child with autism spectrum disorder who repeats a word or phrase over and over, it may be more parsimonious to indicate that the child displays echolalia (i.e., repeats the phrase "Hi Jack" after hearing it). Of course, you should provide an example of what you mean by echolalia. But it may be necessary to use this term as an example of how a child meets criteria for an autism spectrum classification. I also understand that this raises the possibility that neophyte psychologists will misinterpret what I am trying to convey and may be more apt to write using complex psychological terms. This would be inappropriate.

5.3.9   Avoid Big Words and Write Parsimoniously

This is similar to the above admonition about avoiding the use of psychology jargon. Do not write to impress. Unusually ornate language will obfuscate meaning and obscure the message in your report. Write clearly and succinctly and use accessible language (Shively & Smith, 1969). If a word conveys meaning more precisely and parsimoniously then by all means use that word. However, be cautious about using an extravagant word unless it enhances meaning or clarity.

Harvey (1997; 2006) and others (e.g., Wedding, 1984) conducted studies regarding the readability of psychological reports and found that they were beyond the level of most parents, the majority of whom read at about an 11th grade level. Harvey noted that the reports were rated at a readability level of anywhere from the 15th to the 17th grade! When these reports were revised to a more readable 6th grade reading level they were viewed much more positively and were better able to be understood even among highly educated parents. It is not entirely known why psychologists write using jargon and highly technical terms. It is suspected that this is done because we tend to write for other colleagues or our supervisors (Shectman, 1979). However, it is important to write at a level that is accessible to parents and other stakeholder's in the school.

5.3.10   Address the Positive

Much of psychological and psychoeducational report writing is focused on identifying areas of deficit and psychopathology (Brenner & Holzberg, 2000; Tallent, 1993). This is the nature of report writing where access to services is predicated upon a classification of psychopathology. When writing psychoeducational reports, it will be important to emphasize positive features of a child's background and functioning (Michaels, 2006; Rhee, Furlong, Turner, & Harari, 2001; Snyder et al., 2006). The inclusion of positive aspects of a child's functioning and a discussion of the child's resiliency is important to caregivers who intuitively understand that their children are not defined by a simplistic label.

5.3.11   Write Useful, Concrete Recommendations

The recommendation section within a psychoeducational report is arguably the most important section (Brenner, 2003). It offers parents, teachers, and others a way forward for the child. A recommendation that merely reiterates the concerns posed in the referral questions is generally less meaningful. For instance, if a child were referred for reading difficulties, and is found to struggle in this area, then resist a generic recommendation that suggests need for reading difficulties. Instead, provide more detailed, concrete, and empirically based guidance regarding how a specific deficit in reading will be remediated. In studies asking parents, teachers, and other personnel what they wished to gain from a report the response is invariably recommendations on how to intervene or treat the difficulty (Musman, 1964; Salvagno & Teglasi, 1987; Tidwell & Wetter, 1978; Witt, Moe, Gutkin, & Andrews, 1984).

5.4 Stylistic Issues in Psychoeducational Assessment Report Writing

5.4.1 Report Length

Specific guidance in the literature is unavailable about optimal report length (Groth-Marnat & Horvath, 2006; Tallent, 1993). There is not general threshold for report length that is considered appropriate. More is not always better. Emphasize the presentation of important information that helps to conceptualize the child's functioning, classify the child, and understand the child. Do not include information just to fill space. Clarity is more important than report length (Wiener & Kohler, 1986). Favor parsimony over superfluity.

5.4.2 Revise Once, Revise Twice, Revise Thrice, and Then Revise Once More

The importance of revising your report cannot be emphasized enough. Keep in mind that a psychoeducational report written for public school districts in the USA is a legal document that becomes part of a student's educational records. This means that the report may be read by numerous stakeholders including other psychological professionals, teachers, physicians, caregivers, and even attorneys and judges. For this reason, an error free report is critical. One suggestion would be to write your report, put it down for 3 days, and then return to it on the fourth day. Obviously, time may be of the essence particularly with the IDEA mandated 60 day threshold, but the pressure to meet the 60-day deadline (or that prescribed by your state) should be balanced with the need for an error-free report. In the long run an error-laden report can pose greater problems than being out-of-compliance with the 60 day deadline. Save yourself considerable embarrassment and revise your report repeatedly.

5.4.3 Avoid Pronoun Mistakes

A rookie mistake that continues to plague veteran report writers involves mismatched pronouns. This emanates from the use of the search and replace button in word processing programs. For instance, suppose you use a prior report as a template from which to write a new report. The prior report was based upon a female but you miss changing the /she/ to a /he/ in a few places. This is embarrassing and the psychologist needs to be vigilant about this type of flagrant error. For example, the following sentence is problematic:

> Rick scored in the 50th percentile on a measure of cognitive ability. This instrument evaluates her ability to reason and solve problems.

This error not only degrades the quality of the report, but undermines the credibility of the psychologist writing the report.

5.4.4 Use Headings and Subheadings Freely

The liberal use of headings and subheadings with underlined, bolded, and italics formatting is an effective way to organize your report. Without the use of such an organizational approach, the report may feel overwhelming, cumbersome, and disorganized. The reader will feel as if he or she is plodding through the document. An unorganized report loses its influence, utility, and credibility.

5.4.5 Provide a Brief Description of Assessment Instruments

Prior to introducing test results it is important to provide a narrative summary of the instrument whose results are being presented. This description should include the following information:

(a) Description of the instrument and the construct being evaluated including the age range and scale (e.g., mean = 100; std. dev = 15) being used.
(b) Description of index and subtest scores.
(c) Chart to follow the above description.
(d) Narrative description of results.

Over the years my graduate students have consistently asked me for verbiage regarding a new instrument that they used during the evaluation process. The above offered framework may useful for this purpose.

5.4.6 Use Tables and Charts to Present Results

Most psychoeducational reports contain tables of test results either within the body of the report or as an addendum to the report. These charts are preceded by an introduction that describes the instrument. This is followed by a chart of test results, which in turn is followed by a brief description of the results. The use of a chart to present test results is good practice. On the other hand, reports that merely use a descriptive approach to the presentation of test results are less efficient and more cumbersome. This style of reporting test results is not recommended.

5.4.7 Put Selected Statements Within Quotations to Emphasize a Point

During the course of your interviews with the child, caregivers, or collateral contacts the interviewees will sometimes make statements that most efficiently and clearly describe the point they were trying to make. In such cases, it is a good practice to enclose those statements within quotation marks. For example, we could paraphrase a child who complains of sadness as follows:

> Jill notes that she is frequently sad and does not wish to participate in activities that used to interest her. She described suicidal ideation.

However, when we enclose direct remarks from Jill it emphasizes the struggles that she is facing:

> Jill explained that she "…no longer wants to play soccer, baseball or ride her bike." Jill stated that she does not understand why she does not want to participate: "I just lost interest and feel like crying all the time." Jill also described recent feelings of suicidality: "There are times when I wonder whether it would be better to be dead. I just feel so bad."

As noted above, the statements from the adolescent reveal an additional layer of perspective that does not come through without the direct quotations.

5.4.8 Improve Your Writing Style

By this stage in your education, you should have decent command of standard written English. If not, you have some work to do. I suggest reading thoroughly the APA Guide to Style and *The Elements of Style* by Strunk and White. You may also wish to review reports written by experienced psychologists and those offered in this book. You may have the best analytical skills the world has ever seen in a psychologist, but if your report is not clearly written than your analytical prowess is wasted.

5.5 Conclusion

The above report writing guidelines, combined with specific section-by-section report writing guidance, should assist the beginning graduate student in school and clinical-child psychology avoid many of the pitfalls of report writing that may be frequently encountered by the field.

References

Blau, T. H. (1991). *The psychological examination of the child*. New York, NY: Wiley.

Brenner, E. (2003). Consumer-focused psychological assessment. *Professional Psychology: Research and Practice, 34*, 240–247.

Brenner, E., & Holzberg, M. (2000). Psychological testing in child welfare: Creating a statewide psychology consultation program. *Consulting Psychology Journal: Practice and Research, 52*, 162–177.

Butcher, J., Perry, J., & Hahn, J. (2004). Computers in clinical assessment: Historical developments, present status, and future challenges. *Journal of Clinical Psychology, 60*, 331–345.

Groth-Marnat, G., & Horvath, L. S. (2006). The psychological report: A review of current controversies. *Journal of Clinical Psychology, 62*, 73–81.

Harvey, V. S. (1997). Improving readability of psychological reports. *Professional Psychology:Research and Practice, 28*, 271–274.

Harvey, V. S. (2006). Variables affecting the clarity of psychological reports. *Journal of Clinical Psychology, 62*, 5–18.

Kamphaus, R. W. (2001). Clinical assessment of child and adolescent intelligence (2nd ed.). New York, NY: Springer.

Lichtenberger, E. O. (2006). Computer utilization and clinical judgment in psychological assessment reports. *Journal of Clinical Psychology, 64*, 19–32. doi:10.1002/jclp.20197.

Matlin, M. W., & Gawron, V. J. (1979). Individual differences in pollyannaism. *Journal of Personality Assessment, 43*(4), 411–412. doi:10.1207/s15327752jpa4304_14.

Martin, R. P. & Dombrowski, S. C. (2008). Prenatal exposures: Psychological and behavioral consequences for children. Springer: New York.

Michaels, M. H. (2006). Ethical considerations in writing psychological assessment reports. *Journal of Clinical Psychology, 62*, 47–58.

Mussman, M. C. (1964). Teachers' evaluations of psychological reports. *Journal of School Psychology, 3*, 35–37.

Ownby, R. L. (1997). *Psychological reports: A guide to report writing in professional psychology* (3rd ed.). New York, NY: Wiley.

Rhee, S., Furlong, M. J., Turner, J. A., & Harari, I. (2001). Integrating strength-based perspectives in psychoeducational evaluations. *California School Psychologist, 6*, 5–17.

Salvagno, M., & Teglasi, H. (1987). Teacher perceptions of different types of information in psychological reports. *Journal of School Psychology, 25*, 415–424.

Shectman, F. (1979). Problems in communicating psychological understanding: Why won't they listen to me? *American Psychologist, 34*, 781–790.

Shively, J., & Smith, D. (1969). Understanding the psychological report. *Psychology in the Schools, 6*, 272–273.

Snyder, C. R., Ritschel, L. A., Rand, K. L., & Berg, C. J. (2006). Balancing psychological assessments: Including strengths and hope in client reports. *Journal of Clinical Psychology, 62*, 33–46. doi:10.1002/jclp.20198.

Tallent, N. (1993). *Psychological report writing* (4th ed.). Englewood Cliffs, NJ: Prentice Hall.

Tidwell, R., & Wetter, J. (1978). Parental evaluations of psychoeducational reports: A case study. *Psychology in the Schools, 15*, 209–215.

Watkins, M. W. (2014). *Writing psychological reports*. Unpublished manuscript.

Wedding, R. R. (1984). Parental interpretation of psychoeducational reports. *Psychology in the Schools, 21*, 477–481.

Weiner, J. (1985). Teachers' comprehension of psychological reports. *Psychology in the Schools, 22*, 60–64.

Weiner, J. (1987). Factors affecting educators' comprehension of psychological reports. *Psychology in the Schools, 24*, 116–126.

Weiner, J. & Kohler, S. (1986). Parents' comprehension of psychological reports. *Psychology in the Schools, 23*, 265–270.

Witt, J. C., Moe, G., Gutkin, T. B., & Andrews, L. (1984). The effect of saying the same thing in different ways: The problem of language and jargon in school-based consultation. *Journal of School Psychology, 22*, 361–367.

Part II
Section-by-Section
Report Writing Guidance

This section offers a section-by-section discussion of report components with a chapter devoted to each report section within Chaps. 6 through 10.

Chapter 6
Identifying Information and Reason for Referral

6.1 Introduction

This chapter offers a discussion of how to present the identifying information and the reason for referral sections of a report. Both sections are among the first you will encounter when reading a psychoeducational report. They present important contextual information that set the stage for the rest of the report.

6.2 Identifying Information

The identifying section of a report is the initial section of a report that provides demographic information about the child. It will include the full name of the child, the parent's names and address, caregiver contact information, the grade of the child, the child's date of birth, the date of report completion, and the date the report was sent to the caregivers. At the top of the report can be found the title. This is often "Psychoeducational Report" or "Psychological Report" with the word "Confidential" placed underneath the word "Psychoeducational Report." Placed beneath the words "Confidential" will be the identifying information.

The following example with furnish the reader with an idea of how this section is formatted. Your school district or university clinic may have a slightly different format for the title and identifying section, but much of what is presented below is fairly standard.

© Springer Science+Business Media New York 2015
S.C. Dombrowski, *Psychoeducational Assessment and Report Writing*,
DOI 10.1007/978-1-4939-1911-6_6

Example Identifying Section

Pyschoeducational Report	
Confidential	
Name: Jane Doe	Date of Birth: 1/20/2003
Grade: 5th	Age of Child: 10 years 4 months
Date of Report: May 10, 2016	Date Sent: May 11, 2016
Parents: John and Ruby Doe	Examiner's Name: Sean Parker, B.A.
Address: 124 Main Street	Supervisor's Name: Stefan C. Dombrowski, Ph.D.
Glastonbury, CT	
(203) 555-1212	
Local Education Agency:	Glastonbury Public Schools

Depending upon the school district, clinic, or psychologist, additional information may be included in the identifying section. This section of the report should be presented in an aesthetically appealing fashion with a visual balance between the right and left columns noted above. The title of the report should be centered.

6.3   Reason for Referral

The reason for referral is an important section and should contain referral questions that need to be addressed by the report (Brenner, 2003). The omission of referral questions within a report is considered by most texts and articles on report writing to be poor practice (Ownby, 1997; Tallent, 1993; Watkins, 2014; Weiner, 1985, 1987). The reason for referral helps to focus the report and assures that issues of concern are addressed by the psychologist. The reason for referral section is generally about a paragraph long and should be written concisely. It is inappropriate to incorporate too much information or information that makes this section into a mini-background section. Instead, the reason for referral section should discuss specific referral concerns. Most referrals for psychoeducational reports stem from concerns about a student's cognitive, academic, social, emotional, behavioral, communicative, or adaptive functioning. Often, but not always, the reason for referral will include a referral source. In the case of psychoeducational reports, the source is usually the parents/caregivers or the multidisciplinary team.

There are generally two approaches to writing the reason for referral section. One is to include a generic reason for referral and the other is to list specific referral questions *a priori* that need to be addressed. As mentioned the latter is the preferred approach by most texts and articles on report writing. However, when focusing a report through the provision of referral questions it will be important for the psychologist to be mindful to not overlook additional issues that will need to be addressed. For this reason, a combination of the specific and general referral question—a hybrid approach—may be useful.

6.3.1   Generic Referral

The generic referral question can sometimes be seen used for psychoeducational evaluations conducted within a school setting. This is utilized when the exclusive focus of the report is on classification eligibility. It is noted that the field has moved away from the test-and-place paradigm of yesteryear, but psychoeducational reports continue to serve the function of providing a child access to specially designed instruction. This is not best practice by any means and I do not advocate this practice that the report function in the service of gatekeeping. However, when the sole purpose of the report is to determine eligibility then the following format might be incorporated.

Example 1: Following concerns about his academic and behavioral progress at school, Jack was referred for a comprehensive evaluation to determine his present level of functioning and whether he might qualify for specially designed instruction. Recommendations to enhance Jack's functioning are also provided.

Example 2: Jack was referred for a comprehensive evaluation following concerns about his academic functioning and to determine whether he might qualify for special education support.

These two referral questions present a generic framework that might be employed for practitioners interested in a global referral question. There are both advantages and disadvantages to this approach.

Advantages: Permits the psychologist to retain a panoramic perspective and be a bit more unconstrained in targeting additional areas of concern following commencement of the evaluation. For instance, at the outset of the evaluation, perhaps there was the suspicion that the child solely had an issue with reading and attention. A specifically targeted referral may overlook the fact that the child also has issues with anxiety and possibly even depression.

Disadvantages: The psychologist may not sufficiently focus the evaluation on specific areas of need or may miss areas that should have been targeted. This could render the evaluation less useful to parents and teachers and be potentially off target.

6.3.2   Specific Referral

Listing of specific referrals questions is generally recommended as a best practice. It permits the psychologist to focus the report on areas of concern. The following are two examples of a reason for referral that is of a specific nature.

Example 1: Jack was referred following concerns about low progress in reading. Specifically, he struggles with automatically decoding words and comprehension of text. Jack also struggles with remaining seated for long periods of time and cannot focus on his classwork. This evaluation will determine whether Jack has a learning disability or whether his attentional difficulties have an impact on his educational progress.

Example 2: Jack is struggling with understanding social nuance which tends to hamper his capacity to get along with other children at school. Jack also struggles when his routines at school are changed. The school district wonders whether Jack has an autism spectrum diagnosis and will benefit from specially designed instruction.

Advantages: This approach focuses the report, providing evaluation goals for the psychologist. It also permits the psychologist to thoroughly evaluate the referral questions to be addressed and offer targeted feedback.

Disadvantages: The psychologist may overlook additional, uncovered issues by too narrowly focusing efforts solely on the referral question.

6.3.3   Hybrid Referral Question

A combination of the specific and general referral question may capture the advantages of both approaches. The following furnishes several examples of a hybrid type of reason for referral (i.e., combines the generic with the specific noted in the above discussion). I have found that this combined approach is useful. It not only serves to guide the reader and focus the report on salient concerns that led to the referral, but also permits the option to explore additional, uncovered issues not originally addressed within the referral.

6.3.4   Example Referrals for IDEA Categories

6.3.4.1   Referral for Suspected Learning Disabilities

Joquim struggles with sounding out words and understanding written text. His teachers have furnished him with additional intervention in this area but he still continues to struggle. Ms. Smith, Joquim's mother, noted that Joquim has had a tutor over the past year but still experiences difficulty with reading. Joquim was referred for a comprehensive evaluation to determine whether he qualifies for specially designed instruction. Recommendations to support Joquim's reading progress are also offered.

6.3.4.2   Referral for Suspected Emotional Disturbance

Matthew struggles with getting along with other children in the classroom. He misperceives other children's intent and views their words and actions toward him as hostile even though this is not the case. When this occurs, Matthew will argue with and often hit, kick or punch other children. Teacher reports indicate that Matthew disregards teacher redirection and has sometimes cussed out the teacher or thrown his books across the room when frustrated or upset. Matthew was referred for a comprehensive evaluation to determine whether he qualifies for special education support and what recommendations and accommodations might be appropriate to support his behavior in school.

6.3.4.3   Referral for Suspected Autism

Nick struggles with communicating and socializing at an age expected level. He rarely makes eye contact when being addressed by or speaking with others. He vocalizes sounds "eee aw eee aw" repetitively. Nick becomes distressed when his routines are changed and seems lost during times of transition. Nick was referred for a comprehensive evaluation to determine whether he qualifies for special education support and what recommendations and accommodations will be appropriate to support his learning and behavior in school.

6.3.4.4   Referral for Suspected Intellectual Disability

Tina faces considerable difficulty with all kindergarten tasks. She still cannot distinguish between numbers and letters and cannot identify colors. Tina can only recognize the letters in her name and the letters /a/, /b/, and /c/. Tina enjoys playing with other students and she is generally well liked. However, she sometimes cannot communicate her needs to them and so she will grab and hit when things do not go her way. Tina was referred for a comprehensive evaluation to determine whether she qualifies for special education support and what recommendations will be appropriate to support her learning and behavior in school.

6.3.4.5   Referral for Other Health Impaired

Aaron has an outside classification of Attention-Deficit/Hyperactivity Disorder (ADHD) from his pediatrician. In class, he struggles with staying seated, remaining on task, following directions, and calling out at inappropriate times. With redirection, structure and support, Aaron is able to persist and complete his classwork. Aaron is presently reading above grade level and is in one of the higher math groups. Ms. Jones, Aaron's mother, sought an evaluation to determine what supports are available to Aaron. Aaron is undergoing a comprehensive evaluation to determine whether he qualifies for special education support and what recommendations will be appropriate to support his learning and behavior in school.

6.3.4.6   Referral for Giftedness

Lukas reads several grades above level and has extremely high mathematics abilities. Lukas is interested in a wide variety of subjects and requires differentiated instruction because of his advanced academic skills. Lukas was referred for a comprehensive psychoeducational evaluation to determine whether he qualifies for the district's gifted program and what enrichment activities might be appropriate for him.

6.4   Conclusion

It is understood that the field of school psychology has moved away from its singular focus on being the gatekeeper of special education but an important purpose of the report is to determine eligibility for special education services. Because of this the reason for referral should include specific referral questions that need to be addressed along with a generic statement that indicates that the purpose of the report is to determine whether the child qualifies for special education support. The reason for referral should be sufficiently detailed to offer the reader a panoramic perspective—an executive summary statement of sorts—of what the comprehensive psychoeducational report will entail.

References

Brenner, E. (2003). Consumer-focused psychological assessment. *Professional Psychology: Research and Practice, 34*, 240–247.

Ownby, R. L. (1997). *Psychological reports: A guide to report writing in professional psychology* (3rd ed.). New York, NY: Wiley.

Tallent, N. (1993). *Psychological report writing* (4th ed.). Englewood Cliffs, NJ: Prentice Hall.

Watkins, M. W. (2014). *Writing psychological reports*. Unpublished manuscript.

Weiner, J. (1985). Teachers' comprehension of psychological reports. *Psychology in the Schools, 22*, 60–64.

Weiner, J. (1987). Factors affecting educators' comprehension of psychological reports. *Psychology in the Schools, 24*, 116–126.

Chapter 7
Assessment Methods and Background Information

7.1 Introduction

This chapter has two parts. The first part discusses the assessment methods section while the second part discusses the background section.

7.2 Assessment Methods

The assessment methods section is important and provides the reader with a detailed listing of the sources of data used to understand and evaluate the child. It also demonstrates that the clinician has engaged in due diligence and suggests whether the evaluation was indeed comprehensive. If this section is sparse then it might detract from the credibility of the report. The Methods of Assessment (or Assessment Methods) section serves as a type of table of contents except without the page numbering. The Assessment Methods section should be formatted in a particular way. Generally, it is a good idea to list the names of broad band cognitive ability, achievement and adaptive behavior followed by narrow band measures of the same. For instance, a cognitive ability test such as the Stanford–Binet should be listed first followed by the Woodcock–Johnson Tests of Cognitive Ability. In turn, this is followed by a narrow band measures such as the Peabody Picture Vocabulary Test, Fourth Edition and the Comprehensive Test of Phonological Awareness. Following the presentation of cognitive ability and academic achievement measures, broad band measures of behavior (e.g., BASC-2) followed by narrow band measures of behavior (e.g., Beck Depression Inventory) are presented.

© Springer Science+Business Media New York 2015
S.C. Dombrowski, *Psychoeducational Assessment and Report Writing*,
DOI 10.1007/978-1-4939-1911-6_7

The general framework presented below along with a specific example will be useful in elucidating the approach to this section.

- Cognitive Ability.
  - Narrow band measures.
- Academic Achievement including norm-referenced and curriculum-based measures.
  - Narrow Band Measures.
- Adaptive Behavior.
- Broad band behavior tests.
  - Narrow band behavior tests.
- Listing of Interviewees.
- Observations.
- Review of Records.

Assessment Methods

- *Wechsler Intelligence Scale for Children—Fifth Edition (WISC-V).*
- *Wechsler Individual Achievement Test—Third Edition (WIAT-III).*
- *Bender-Gestalt Second Edition (Bender).*
- *Behavior Assessment System for Children, Second Edition (BASC-2).*
  - Ms. Jonna Smith (Teacher Rating Scale).
  - Mr. Bill McFly (Teacher Rating Scale).
  - Ms. Jean Gonzalez (Parent Rating Scale).
- *BASC-2 Student Observation System.*
  - Joan Baez, Ph.D.
- *BASC-2 Structured Developmental History.*
  - Ms. Jean Gonzalez (Mother).
- *Vineland-II Adaptive Behavior Scales.*
  - Ms. Jean Gonzalez (Parent/Caregiver Rating Form).
- *Childhood Autism Rating Scale, Second Edition (CARS-2).*
  - John H. Smith, Ph.D.
- Student Interview.
  - Matthew Gonzalez.
- Teacher Interviews.
  - Jennifer Cramer (Resource Room Language Arts Teacher; 10/29/14).
  - Lauren Crane (Resource Room Math Teacher; 10/22/14).
  - William McMan (In-Class Support Special Education Teacher; 10/17/14).
- Speech-Language Pathologist Interview.
  - Mary Ann Lares (Speech-Language Pathologist; 10/18/14).
- Parent Interview.
  - Jean Gonzalez (Mother; 10/10/14 and 10/18/14).
- Classroom Observations (10/10/14, 10/12/14, and 10/22/14).
- Review of Educational and Psychological Records.
  - Psychoeducational Report (Dr. Barbara West; completed 9/9/14).

7.3 Background Information and Early Developmental History

Within the background and early developmental history section, you will summarize much of the information gathered via observations, questionnaire forms, interview results, and review of educational, psychological, and medical records. This section of the report has several components as noted below:

- Introduction.
- Prenatal, Perinatal, and Early Developmental History.
- Medical and Health.
- Cognitive, Academic, and Language Functioning.
- Social, Emotional, Behavioral, and Adaptive Functioning.
- Strengths.
- Conclusion.

7.3.1 Introduction

Within this component of the background section you will introduce the child by presenting the child's age, the child's grade, and the salient issues faced by the child. It should not be longer than a paragraph.

For example, the Background section might begin with an introductory statement as follows:

> Matthew Osbourne is a 7-year-old child in the first grade at the Hopewell Public School (HPS). Matthew faces difficulty with paying attention, organization, and remaining on task. Background information revealed difficulty with reading comprehension. Ms. Osbourne indicates that Matthew has been diagnosed with Attention-Deficit/Hyperactivity Disorder (ADHD) and Oppositional Defiant Disorder (ODD). Matthew is not presently taking any medication for the management of his symptoms, but Ms. Osbourne reports that he is scheduled for a psychotropic medication evaluation in mid-October. Matthew is reported to be an friendly child, but one who struggles with symptoms of inattention, distractibility, impulsivity, and loss of focus. His behavioral difficulties are having an impact on his educational functioning at school.

7.3.2 Prenatal, Perinatal, and Early Developmental History

This section of the background requires a discussion of pertinent factors that may impact a child's developmental functioning. Research is well established that disruptions to or complications during prenatal and perinatal development are associated with a host of adverse developmental outcomes (see Dombrowski & Martin, 2009; Dombrowski, Martin, & Huttunen, 2003; 2005; Dombrowski, Noonan, & Martin, 2007; Martin & Dombrowski, 2008; Martin, Dombrowski, Mullis, & Huttunen, 2006). Similarly, children who are delayed in their early developmental history often face later difficulties with their development. For these reasons, a discussion of prenatal, perinatal, and early developmental history is especially important.

> **Example Prenatal, Perinatal, and Early Developmental History Section**
>
> Ms. Jones reports that her pregnancy with Michael was complicated by premature rupture of membranes at approximately 33 weeks gestation. Ms. Jones indicated that she was prescribed Magnesium Sulfate to delay labor for several days and was given a second medication (steroids) that enhanced Matthew's lung development. Matthew was born at 33 weeks gestation weighing 4 pounds, 8 ounces. His Apgar scores were 7 at 1 min and 10 at 5 min. He had a 13-day stay in the neonatal intensive care unit (NICU) during which time he was placed under bilirubin lights for jaundice. Upon release from the NICU, Matthew was given a vaccine to prevent the respiratory synstitycal virus (RSV). Ms. Jones noted that Matthew's early developmental milestones were roughly on target. She explained that Matthew rolled over, sat up and crawled within age expected limits. Ms. Jones noted that Matthew walked at 13 months gestation. She explained that all other milestones were accomplished within normal limits with the exception of babbling. Ms. Jones explained that Matthew was not much of a babbler although he was a very social baby. Ms. Jones noted that Matthew experienced extreme colic until about 6 months of age. She described Matthew as a shy child who experienced distress during his first year of preschool. Ms. Jones expressed regret about putting Matthew in preschool at age 2 ½ and noted that she should have delayed his preschool entry a year. Otherwise, Ms. Jones described Matthew as a happy and healthy child.

7.3.3 Medical and Health

Psychologists view the world through a psychological lens and place their gaze upon these factors. However, there are numerous medical/health conditions that need to be ruled out as they could present as a symptom of one of the IDEA/DSM categories but have their origins in a health/medical condition. There are myriad medical and genetic conditions some of which are widely known (e.g., Down syndrome or fetal alcohol syndrome) and others less well known (e.g., Chiriari Malformation). Suffice to say that information from pediatric and other medical providers should be ascertained so that important medical or health conditions are investigated.

Example Medical and Health Section

Ms. Winkler noted that Isabella was born with Tetralogy of Fallot, a congenital heart defect. Inspection of records from Isabella's pediatrician also revealed a food allergy to tree nuts, asthma, and sickle cell anemia. Ms. Winkler indicated that Isabella carries an inhaler and noted that she had to expend considerable effort to document with Hometown Public Schools that it was a medically necessary medication since the school rarely permits students to carry inhalers. Isabella's hearing and vision are all intact. Isabella's physical health is otherwise intact and age appropriate. She has never experienced a major injury, accident or head trauma.

7.3.4 Cognitive, Academic, and Language Functioning

A large percentage of psychoeducational evaluations will have as its primary focus a child's cognitive, academic, and language functioning. The child's functioning in these areas, therefore, will need to be thoroughly discussed. Within this component of the background section, you will not discuss present norm-referenced measures. You will only discuss those from outside evaluations or from a prior report. You will, however, discuss a summary of the child's progress within the classroom as noted by parents, teachers, and grade reports.

Example Cognitive, Academic, and Language Functioning Section

Juan presently experiences significant difficulty with reading and writing in the third grade. He struggles with word decoding, spelling and reading comprehension. He also struggles with expressive language. English is Juan's second language and is not spoken in the home. At home, Juan speaks only Spanish. He has received intervention for children with ELL since his arrival at Newfield Public School in first grade but his teachers do not feel as if he is making appropriate progress in the third grade curriculum and wonder whether he might struggle with a learning disability. Additionally, Juan struggles with pronouncing words that begin with /r/ and /fr/. He is presently receiving speech-language support. His expressive language functioning was found to be in the below average range (see Speech-Language evaluation dated 2/23/14). Juan's cognitive ability had previously been evaluated in first grade after moving from Guatemala. His performance on the Unit (Std. Score = 110; 75th Percentile) was high average. His academic achievement abilities were not assessed at that time because he had just moved 6 months previously to the USA.

7.3.5 Social, Emotional, Behavioral, and Adaptive Functioning

Within this area of the background section, you will discuss the child's functioning in the social, emotional, behavioral, and adaptive domain from early in development through the present time period. You should not include a detailed developmental history within this section, but you may consider indicating the continuity of a difficulty or strength from earlier phases of development. For instance, if the child has struggled since preschool with social skills, and continues to struggle with such difficulties, then it is appropriate to discuss this information. Likewise, if the child has always had difficulty with overactivity, task persistence, and organization then it is appropriate to mention those characteristics.

Example of Social–Emotional and Behavioral Functioning

Jayden has always struggled in his interaction with peers. He is primarily nonverbal and will only occasionally use simple language to communicate his needs. Jayden rarely participates in group activities. Jayden's social and behavioral functioning at school has improved over the past year. He less frequently engages in behaviors that annoy other children and has learned to follow the basic classroom routines in his first grade room. Ms. Wong, Jayden's teacher, reports that he unpacks every morning, is able to transition to different activities and usually stays in his "spot" whether at a table or sitting on the rug. Most academic work is too difficult for Jayden, but he will pretend to do what everyone else is doing. He looks around and even looks at what others are doing and tries to copy them. Ms. Wong indicates that Jayden very much wants to feel part of our classroom and wants to be able to do it on his own (without an adult sitting with him). Jayden's interest in affiliating with and emulating of peers is a significant strength for Jayden and suggests continued need for access to age typical peers.

7.3.6 Strengths and Interests

It is good practice to conduct a strength-based assessment of children's skills. This is required by IDEA and also consistent with the positive psychology literature base. As part of this process, the child's hobbies and interests should be ascertained. Much of report writing emphasizes difficulties faced by children, which serves to make a case for the classification decision that will be made. However, it is difficult for caregivers to have negative aspects of their children discussed and emphasized. Imagine spending twenty or more minutes listening to a team of individuals emphasize where and how your child is struggling. This would be fairly disconcerting. A strengths-based assessment of the child's functioning along with the child's hobbies/interests is an important component of the psychoeducational report.

Example of Strengths and Interests Section

Mike is a child who is polite, helpful, and gets along well with others. He is good at drawing and enjoys most sports particularly baseball and soccer. Mike has several close friends with whom he plays Minecraft and builds model airplanes. Ms. Jones explains that Mike is family-oriented and helps her out with his younger sister. She explained that he is a compassionate child with many friends.

7.3.7 Conclusion

Within the conclusion to the background section, you will provide an overarching statement of the problem faced by the child that supports the case for the psycho-educational evaluation of the child. It is a generally brief statement that ties all aspects of the background and developmental history together and leaves the reader with the conclusion that an evaluation is necessary.

Example of Conclusion Section

Jayden has made progress in his behavioral and social functioning since last evaluation. Background information suggests continued difficulties in these areas and continued need for accommodation for social, behavioral, communication, and academic difficulties.

References

Dombrowski, S. C., & Martin, R. P. (2009). *Maternal fever during pregnancy: Association with infant, preschool and child temperament.* Saarbrucken: VDM Verlag.

Dombrowski, S. C., Martin, R. P., & Huttunen, M. O. (2003). Association between maternal fever and psychological/behavioral outcomes: An hypothesis. *Birth Defects Research A: Clinical and Molecular Teratology, 67,* 905–910.

Dombrowski, S. C., Martin, R. P., & Huttunen, M. O. (2005). Gestational smoking imperils the long term mental and physical health of offspring. *Birth Defects Research Part (A): Clinical and Molecular Teratology, 73,* 170–176.

Dombrowski, S. C., Noonan, K., & Martin, R. P. (2007). Birth weight and cognitive outcomes: Evidence for a gradient relationship in an urban poor African-American birth cohort. *School Psychology Quarterly, 22*(1), 26–43.

Martin, R. P., & Dombrowski, S. C. (2008). *Prenatal exposures: Psychological and educational consequences for children.* New York, NY: Springer Science.

Martin, R. P., Dombrowski, S. C., Mullis, C., & Huttunen, M. O. (2006). Maternal smoking during pregnancy: Association with temperament, behavioral, and academics. *Journal of Pediatric Psychology, 31*(5), 490–500.

Chapter 8
Assessment Results

8.1 Introduction

The assessment results section contains an organized presentation of all the norm-referenced (e.g., standardized test results) and informal (e.g., curriculum-based measures; observations; interview results) assessment results that have been ascertained during the assessment process. This section is structured with headings and subheadings to give an organized flow and for ease of reading. The end user of the report should be able to easily access sections of the report such as the full scale IQ test scores or ratings on behavior assessment instruments.

8.2 Organization of Assessment Results Section

The assessment results section has a generalized organizational format with four major headings:

1. Cognitive Ability and Academic Achievement.
2. Social, Emotional, Behavioral, and Adaptive Functioning.
3. Observations.
4. Interview Results.

The first two major sections will be organized such that broad band, norm-referenced measures are presented first followed by narrow band, norm-referenced measures. After all norm-referenced measures are presented within these first two sections then informal measures such as CBA/CBM, and any additional instruments are to be presented. Following this presentation, observations and interview results are presented in separate subsections.

© Springer Science+Business Media New York 2015
S.C. Dombrowski, *Psychoeducational Assessment and Report Writing*,
DOI 10.1007/978-1-4939-1911-6_8

The formatting of the assessment results section will look like the following:

Assessment Results

Cognitive Ability and Academic Achievement

- Full Scale IQ Measures
  - Narrow band cognitive ability measure (e.g., CTOPP-2; Memory, executive functioning, visual motor functioning)
- Broad Band Achievement Measures
  - Narrow band, full scale achievement measures (e.g., KeyMath; WRMT)

Social, Emotional, Behavioral, and Adaptive Functioning

- Broad band behavior rating scales
  - Narrow full band behavior rating scales (e.g., Beck Depression Inventory)
- Broad band adaptive behavior scales

Interview Results

- Student Interview
- Parent Interviews
- Teacher Interviews
- Other Interviews

Observations

- Classroom Observations
- Assessment Observations

8.3   Format for Presentation of Assessment Instruments

When presenting any assessment instrument, whether norm-referenced or informal, it is important to incorporate the instrument's title along with a narrative description of the instrument followed by a chart detailing the results. This section has three main characteristics:

1. Underlined, bolded or italicized title of the test which makes for easy reference to the instrument when a parent or professional wishes to locate that section in the report.
2. A description of the instrument that includes what the instrument measures, age range, and scaling (i.e., mean of 100 with standard deviation of 15 or mean of 50

with standard deviation of 10). The test manual may be referenced for the appropriate verbiage describing the instrument.

Following the general description include a chart that incorporates the names of the index and subtests in addition to their respective scores, the percentiles, the confidence interval and a descriptive classification.

Test of Cognitive Ability
The test of cognitive ability is an individually administered measure of intellectual functioning normed for individuals between the ages of 3 and 94 years. The test of cognitive ability contains several individual tests of problem solving and reasoning ability that are combined to form a Verbal Intelligence Index (VIQ) and a Nonverbal Intelligence Index (NIQ). The subtests that compose the VIQ assess verbal reasoning ability and vocabulary and is a reasonable approximation of crystallized intelligence. The NIQ comprises subtests that assess nonverbal reasoning and spatial ability and is a reasonable approximation of fluid intelligence and spatial ability. These two indexes of intellectual functioning are then combined to form a full scale IQ.

	Score	Percentile	95 % Conf. interval	Descriptive classification
Full scale IQ	100	50	96–104	Average
Verbal IQ	97	48	92–103	Average
Nonverbal IQ	103	53	98–108	Average

Jackie scored in the average range on the Test of Cognitive ability (FSIQ = 100; 50th percentile) with a similar average score on the verbal IQ (standard score = 97; 48th percentile) and nonverbal IQ (standard score = 103; 53rd percentile).

The inclusion of a chart is critically important and should not be omitted. Parents and especially other professionals can expediently make their own determination of a child's functioning from viewing the numbers presented within the charts. The chart formatting is fairly straightforward and offers information on the name of the tests, the standard scores, the confidence interval, and the descriptive classification.

The description of any norm-referenced instrument can be amended directly from the test publisher's manual. As noted in the report writing chapter, each test should have a title in bolded formatting to set it apart from the rest of the document and make it easier for the reader to locate the discussion of the instrument within the body of the report. This is not the section to integrate and synthesize information. This is the section where scores are just presented.

For example, when a child scores a 100 on the WISC-V Full Scale IQ and a 65 on the Working Memory Index then you are to report the following:

> Sarah scored in the average range on the WISC-V FSIQ (Std. Score = 100; 50th percentile) and in the below average range on the Working Memory Index (Std. Score=65; 2nd percentile).

Do not interpret by discussing the child's memory abilities and how the child's low memory abilities might contribute to difficulties with reading comprehension and acquisition of number facts. This would move into the realm of conceptualization which is reserved for a later section of the report.

As another example, consider a child who scored a 65 on the BASC-2 Internalizing Composite and a 73 on the Depression clinical scales. For the BASC-2 performance, you should only report that the student scored in the at-risk range on the Internalizing composite and in the clinically significant range on the Depression scale of the BASC-2. Do not, at this point in the report, launch into a discussion of how the child's findings on the BASC-2 are consistent with a clinically significant elevation of the Beck Depression Inventory, Second Edition and with teacher impressions that the child is sad relative to other fourth grade children. Instead, just state where the child scored (average, at-risk or clinically significant range). There will be time within the conceptualization and classification section to synthesize and integrate information to discuss the possibility of depression, to rule out need for additional evaluation in this area, and to offer recommendations for treatment (within the recommendation section).

There is another important point that must be made. Be wary of excluding numbers from your report and just reporting descriptive classification information. I understand the temptation to take this approach to spare feelings of the parent or because the practitioner may think the scores are invalid, but this practice degrades the value of the report and potentially harms the credibility of the psychologist. If you feel that the instrument's results are invalid then express that sentiment with supporting evidence. The clinical aptitude of psychologists who exclude numbers from the report without furnishing a valid clinical or psychometric reason for doing could be called to question.

Let's consider the following examples using the Reynolds Intellectual Assessment Scales (RIAS) and the Behavior Assessment System for Children, Second Edition (BASC-2).

Reynolds Intellectual Assessment Scale (RIAS)

Malayiah was administered the Reynolds Intellectual Assessment Scales (RIAS). The RIAS is an individually administered measure of intellectual functioning normed for individuals between the ages of 3 and 94 years. The RIAS contains several individual tests of intellectual problem solving and reasoning ability that are combined to form a Verbal Intelligence Index (VIX)

(continued)

(continued)

and a Nonverbal Intelligence Index (NIX). The subtests that compose the VIX assess verbal reasoning ability along with the ability to access and apply prior learning in solving language-related tasks. Although labeled the Verbal Intelligence Index, the VIX is also a reasonable approximation of crystallized intelligence. The NIX comprises subtests that assess nonverbal reasoning and spatial ability. Although labeled the Nonverbal Intelligence Index, the NIX also provides a reasonable approximation of fluid intelligence and spatial ability. These two indexes of intellectual functioning are then combined to form an overall Composite Intelligence Index (CIX). By combining the VIX and the NIX into the CIX, a strong, reliable assessment of general intelligence (g) is obtained. The CIX measures the two most important aspects of general intelligence according to recent theories and research findings: reasoning or fluid abilities and verbal or crystallized abilities.

The RIAS also contains subtests designed to assess verbal memory and nonverbal memory. Depending upon the age of the individual being evaluated, the verbal memory subtest consists of a series of sentences, age-appropriate stories, or both, read aloud to the examinee. The examinee is then asked to recall these sentences or stories as precisely as possible. The nonverbal memory subtest consists of the presentation of pictures of various objects or abstract designs for a period of 5 s. The examinee is then shown a page containing six similar objects or figures and must discern which object or figure has previously been shown. The scores from the verbal memory and nonverbal memory subtests are combined to form a Composite Memory Index (CMX), which provides a strong, reliable assessment of working memory and may also provide indications as to whether or not a more detailed assessment of memory functions may be required. In addition, the high reliability of the verbal and nonverbal memory subtests allows them to be compared directly to each other.

Each of these indexes is expressed as an age-corrected standard score that is scaled to a mean of 100 and a standard deviation of 15. These scores are normally distributed and can be converted to a variety of other metrics if desired.

Following are the results of Malayiah's performance on the RIAS.

	Composite IQ	Verbal IQ	Nonverbal IQ	Memory index
RIAS index	89	82	101	86
Percentile	23	12	53	18
Confidence interval (95 %)	84–95	76–90	95–107	80–93
Descriptive classification	Low average	Low average	Average	Low average

(continued)

(continued)

On testing with the RIAS, Malayiah earned a Composite Intelligence Index of 89. On the RIAS, this level of performance falls within the range of scores designated as low average and exceeded the performance of 23 % of individuals at Malayiah's age. Her Verbal IQ (Standard Score = 82; 12th percentile) was in the low average range and exceeded 12 % of individuals Malayiah's age. Malayiah's Nonverbal IQ (Standard Score = 101; 53rd percentile) was also in the average range, exceeding 53 % of individuals Malayiah's age. Malayiah earned a Composite Memory Index (CMX) of 86, which falls within the low average range of working memory skills and exceeds the performance of 18 out of 100 individuals Malayiah's age.

Behavior Assessment System for Children, Second Edition (BASC-2)

The Behavior Assessment System for Children, Second Edition (BASC-2) is an integrated system designed to facilitate the differential diagnosis and classification of a variety of emotional and behavioral conditions in children. It possesses validity scales and several clinical scales, which reflect different dimensions of a child's personality. Scores in the Clinically Significant range (T-Score > 70) suggest a high level of difficulty. Scores in the At-Risk range (T-Score 60–69) identify either a significant problem that may not be severe enough to require formal treatment or a potential of developing a problem that needs careful monitoring. On the Adaptive Scales, scores below 30 are considered clinically significant while scores between 31 to 40 are considered at-risk.

Ms. Smith

Clinical scales	T-Score	Percentile
Hyperactivity	85**	99
Aggression	72**	95
Conduct problems	85**	99
Anxiety	43	26
Depression	47	51
Somatization	46	46
Attention problems	73**	99
Learning problems	73**	99
Atypicality	43	19
Withdrawal	55	74
Adaptability	30**	3
Social skills	41	22
Leadership	47	43
Study skills	38	15
Functional communication	43	25

(continued)

(continued)

Clinical scales	T-Score	Percentile
Externalizing problems	83**	99
Internalizing problems	44	30
Behavioral symptoms index	66*	93
Adaptive skills	38	12
School problems	67*	94

  * = At-risk
  ** = Clinically Significant

The above results indicate clinically significant elevations on externalizing problems composite with an at-risk score on the behavioral symptoms index. The above results also indicate clinically significant elevations on the hyperactivity, aggression, conduct problems, attention problems, learning problems, and adaptability clinical scales. All other composite and clinical scales were in the average range.

As noted in the above examples each of these tests is interpreted in a hierarchical fashion starting with the global composites and then moving to index level followed by subtest level interpretation. At the present moment, interpretation at the subtest level within tests of cognitive ability is a practice that is hotly debated. Several researchers have cautioned the field about such practice (Dombrowski & Watkins, 2013; Dombrowski, 2013; Dombrowski, 2014a; 2014b; McDermott & Glutting, 1997; McDermott, Fantuzzo & Glutting, 1990; Watkins & Canivez, 2004). Still, others suggest it may be an acceptable practice when placed in the context of a well-grounded theory (e.g., Fiorello, Hale, Holdnack & Kavanagh, 2007; Keith & Reynolds, 2010). The debate is sure to continue.

8.4   Understanding Standard and Scaled Scores

Your basic measurement class should have furnished you with the background to understand the relationship among standard scores, scaled scores, and percentile ranks. These scores are all based on the normal curve. You should be able to quickly and efficiently approximate the standard score when given a percentile rank and when given a scaled score. If not, I would recommend spending time revisiting the normal curve and reviewing the chart below. Most standardized assessment instruments furnish standard scores with a mean of 100 and a standard deviation of 15. Some of these tests, primarily tests of intellectual abilities, also include scaled subtest scores which have a mean of 10 and a standard deviation of 3. Behavior rating scales such as the BASC-2 furnish standard scores (t-scores) with a mean of 50 and a standard deviation of 10. However, the norm referenced score is scaled it can be converted to a percentile rank for ease of interpretation.

The below chart serves as a guide for approximating the percentile rank of various scores. The test manual should be consulted for the specific relationship between the scale and the percentile rank as they can differ slightly from the below chart depending upon the age of the child and the norming process of the instrument.

Standard Score	Scaled Score	T-Score	Percentile
145	19	80	99.9
140	18		99.6
135	17		99
130	**16**	**70**	**97.5**
125	15		95
120	14		91
115	13	60	84
110	12		75
105	11		63
100	10	50	50
95	9		37
90	8		25
85	7	40	16
80	6		9
75	5		5
65	3		1
60	2		0.5
55	1	20	0.1

*Interquartile range = 90 to 110

Threshold for Intellectual Disability = 70

Threshold for Giftedness = **130**

You should know fluently several points on the normal curve including the mean, the interquartile range, and one, two and three standard deviations above the mean including corresponding percentile ranks. There is one important point to keep in mind and perhaps convey to caregivers. The percentile rank or the standard score is not akin to the percentage correct on a given test. Rather, the percentile rank provides a comparison of how well a child did relative to his or her age mates. Take for instance a standard score of 90. This equates to a percentile rank of 25 % and suggests that the child did better than 25 % of the normative group (or 25 out of 100 students of the same age taking the exam). This is quite different than a score of 90 % on an exam. Some caregivers may confuse the two scales so this will need to be explained to them.

In terms of classification, I find the below descriptive classification framework to be useful. With this framework the average range falls between a standard score of 90 and 110 (25th to 75th percentile) which reflects the interquartile range. A gifted/ superior score is 130 and above while a score in the significantly below average/ delayed range is <70.

Standard Score range	Descriptive classification
>130	Superior/gifted
121–129	Above average
111–120	High average
90–110	Average
80–89	Low average
70–79	Below average
<70	Significantly below average/delayed

You should use the descriptive classification that your supervisor, school district, or agency uses if it is different from the below classification approach. When a score falls close to one of the ranges, it makes sense to use both of the descriptive classifications. For instance, if a child attains a score of 89 on a test of cognitive ability then it may be appropriate to offer a descriptive classification of low average/ average.

8.4.1 Comment on Raw, Grade and Age Equivalent Scores

There is an important concept that must be clearly understood by graduate students in school and clinical child psychology. Raw scores have little clinical or psychometric relevance and only serve to crowd charts and confuse consumers of reports. Raw scores are superfluous, less clinically relevant and should not be reported or presented in charts. They are difficult to interpret and potentially misleading because they are not based upon equal scaling metrics. Let's first consider grade equivalent (GE) scores. GE scores give the impression that they are linked to the curriculum, but this is incorrect. Grade equivalent (and age equivalent) scores are norm-referenced, not criterion referenced, and reflect median level performance relative to the standardization population (Reynolds, 1981). Take a child who is in 5th grade and scores at a 12th grade equivalent level. This child is clearly advanced but the child is not on the same level as a 12th grader who is taking calculus. Conversely, consider a fifth grader who is reading at a first grade equivalent level. This individual is not reading at a guided level F—the approximate first quarter first grade guided reading level—but is much higher and at a level M. This is still low by fifth grade standards but certainly not at a first grade guided reading level. As another example, consider the aforementioned fifth grade child where the median GE is a fifth grade equivalency. An eighth grade level might be akin to one standard deviation above the mean (i.e., standard score of 115) while an 11th grade level could be a score of just four items higher (i.e., a standard score of 119)! What is the explanation for this specious scaling metric? Age and grade based scores are not based upon equal intervals and are therefore exceedingly problematic for interpretation. The presentation and use of grade or age equivalent scores could lead to erroneous interpretive practices and therefore should be avoided.

8.5   Conclusion

Assessment results should be presented in an organized, logical and aesthetically appealing fashion. Each instrument should be introduced in the report with a title followed by a description of the instrument. Following the title a chart should be included reporting standard scores, confidence intervals and percentile ranks. Grade and age equivalent scores should not be reported.

References

Dombrowski, S. C. (2013). Investigating the structure of the WJ-III at school age. *School Psychology Quarterly, 28*, 154–169.

Dombrowski, S. C. (2014a). Exploratory bifactor analysis of the WJ-III cognitive in adulthood via the Schmid–Leiman procedure. *Journal of Psychoeducational Assessment, 32*, 330–341. doi:10.1177/0734282913508243.

Dombrowski, S. C. (2014b). Investigating the structure of the WJ III cognitive in early school age through two exploratory bifactor analysis procedures. *Journal of Psychoeducational Assessment, 32*, 483–494. doi:10.1177/0734282914530838.

Dombrowski, S. C., & Watkins, M. W. (2013). Exploratory and higher order factor analysis of the WJ-III full test battery: A school-aged analysis. *Psychological Assessment, 25*, 442–455.

Fiorello, C. A., Hale, J. B., Holdnack, J. A., Kavanagh, J. A., Terrell, J., & Long, L. (2007). Interpreting intelligence test results for children with disabilities: Is global intelligence relevant? *Applied Neuropsychology, 14*, 2–12.

Keith, T. Z., & Reynolds, M. R. (2010). Cattel-Horn-Carroll theory and cognitive abilities: What we've learning from 20 years of research. *Psychology in the Schools, 47*, 635–650.

McDermott, P. A., Fantuzzo, J. W., & Glutting, J. J. (1990). Just say no to subtest analysis: A critique on Wechsler theory and practice. *Journal of Psychoeducational Assessment, 8*, 290–302.

McDermott, P. A., & Glutting, J. J. (1997). Informing stylistic learning behavior, disposition, and achievement through ability subtest patterns: Practical implications for test interpretation. Special Issue, *School Psychology Review, 26*,163–175.

Reynolds, C. R. (1981). The fallacy of "two years below grade level for age" as a diagnostic for reading disorders. *Journal of School Psychology, 19*(4), 350–358.

Watkins, M. W., & Canivez, G. L. (2004). Temporal stability of WISC-III subtest composite: Strengths and weaknesses. *Psychological Assessment, 16*, 133–138.

Chapter 9
Conceptualization and Classification

9.1 Introduction

This chapter presents the process of integrating data from multiple methods of assessment and sources of data to generate a data-driven portrait (i.e., conceptualization) of a child's functioning across multiple domains. The psychoeducational assessment process of integrating data and conceptualizing a child's functioning is similar to, but likely more data-driven, than the case formulation process within a therapeutic framework. When conceptualizing a child's functioning it is important to be mindful about straying too far from the data and into the realm of speculation or story creation. Following the presentation of how to conceptualize a child's functioning, you will be in the position to offer a classification decision that is supported by the data.

The conceptualization and classification section within a psychoeducational report is divided into four parts: (1) an introduction; (2) cognitive and academic functioning; (3) social, emotional, behavioral, and adaptive (if applicable) functioning; and (4) a conclusion. Within the conceptualization and classification section, you will discuss the integrated, summarized findings from each domain. After that, you will make a case for classification, ruling in or out various conditions. An example of each type of IDEA classification is discussed after the presentation of how to integrate information and write the conceptualization and classification section.

9.2 Integration of Information

Integration of data collected during the psychoeducational assessment process is a necessary prerequisite to writing the conceptualization and classification section of the psychoeducational report, but can be overwhelming to the graduate student or

© Springer Science+Business Media New York 2015
S.C. Dombrowski, *Psychoeducational Assessment and Report Writing*,
DOI 10.1007/978-1-4939-1911-6_9

neophyte psychologist. The capacity to properly integrate and then conceptualize requires a higher level of cognitive processing and sufficient experience with the process. Further confounding the integration process, several research sources indicate that the information collected during the comprehensive evaluation process is inconsistent and there is generally a lack of agreement among sources (e.g., Achenbach et al., 1987; Konold et al., 2004). Integration of information is one of the more difficult tasks that lay before the psychologist. It requires the psychologist to distill essential information from superfluous, to reconcile inconsistent sources of data, and to prioritize the most important findings that will be used to formulate a conceptualization within the report. This practice also draws upon understanding of the scientific literature so that conclusions drawn do not stray far from the research base. By necessity, this process is iterative. In other words, the psychologist may have engaged in what they thought was a comprehensive psychoeducational evaluation only to come to find that he or she needs to gather additional data to assist with the integration and conceptualization process. In fact, I tell my students that when you feel uneasy about conceptualizing a child's functioning and offering a classification decision then it generally means that you have not collected sufficient assessment information.

Of course, the perfectionistic, new psychologist must guard against the tendency to continuously seek additional data to support a potential classification decision. Unfortunately, the comprehensive psychoeducational assessment process may not always furnish a completely clear portrait of the child so the psychologist must make the most informed data-based decision possible. Psychologists may take a lesson from the legal system. The standard of evidence within the family court system is preponderance of the evidence. The criminal court system requires a higher standard of evidence (i.e., beyond a reasonable doubt). In certain cases, the information collected during the psychoeducational evaluation process allows the psychologist to draw a classification conclusion that is beyond a reasonable doubt, but in most cases the psychologist must use a preponderance of the evidence standard when determining a classification. The ambiguity of this decision-making process may cause a high degree of angst in the graduate student or psychologist who may seek (and wish for) for a straightforward classification decision.

9.2.1 Guidelines for the Integration of Results

The following guidelines will be helpful for the psychologist when integrating evaluation results in the service of conceptualizing a child's functioning and making a classification decision.

A. Review all sources of data and information collected during the evaluation.

B. Determine where there are major concerns (e.g., reported difficulties, low performance or at-risk/clinically significant findings) and strengths (e.g., reported strengths, high scores) on the following sources of data:

   i. Developmental history questionnaires, educational, medical, and behavioral records, interview results, and classroom observations.

   ii. Cognitive ability and academic achievement tests. When considering standardized assessment results, prioritize full scale composites over index scores which in turn are prioritized over subtest scores.
   iii. Social-Emotional, behavioral, and adaptive functioning instruments. Determine low scores on the adaptive behavior measures and at-risk to clinically significant findings on social, emotional, and behavioral measures. Determine where relative strengths might exist on the same measures.

C. Determine where sources of information/data (e.g., test results, interview results, observations, questionnaire results, background information) converge. When sources of information converge, then this lends greater support to the likelihood of a difficulty, deficit, or strength in that area.

D. Determine where sources of information diverge. When information/data sources diverge from another, then this may require follow-up with informants and possible additional evaluation.

E. Attempt to explain discrepancies/divergence but be very cautious about misattributing information. There can be numerous reasons for divergent findings including eye of the behavior issues (Martin, 1988), measurement error, situational factors and environmental factors. If you can find an explanation, then this can be valuable when formulating a conceptualization of the child's functioning and offering recommendations. If you cannot find a data-based explanation for the discrepant findings, then just state that the information sources do not all agree. Be wary of offering further explanation, unless you have definitive evidence, because you may just be speculating at that point.

F. Prioritize what information you will include in the report when conceptualizing the child's functioning. You have collected a significant amount of information, all of which will not necessarily be incorporated into the report.

G. Write the Conceptualization and Classification Section. You now have the task before you of writing succinctly the conceptualization and classification section of the report. It is difficult to synthesize complex psychoeducational data. The next section of this chapter provides a framework for writing the conceptualization and classification section of a psychoeducational report.

9.3   General Framework for the Conceptualization and Classification Section

Within this section you will follow a framework for writing the conceptualization and classification section that describes the child's progress in the cognitive, academic, social, emotional, behavioral, and adaptive domains. This is where you consider the integration process described in the previous section of this chapter. There are four main components to this section.

1. Opening statement.
2. Cognitive and Academic Functioning.

3. Social, Emotional, Behavioral, and Adaptive Functioning.
4. Concluding statement regarding eligibility.

The Cognitive and Academic functioning and the Social, Emotional, and Behavioral functioning sections have additional subsections. When writing the conceptualization section, you should have reviewed and integrated all relevant information collected during the comprehensive assessment process.

A general approach to writing the conceptualization and classification section is presented below. An example follows this general guidance.

1. Start with an opening statement that portrays how you arrived at your conceptualization and classification.

> **Example**
>
> Multiple methods of assessment and sources of data inform the conceptualization of Nikia's cognitive, academic, social-emotional, and behavioral functioning including whether he qualifies for special education support. Details in support of these findings are offered below.

2. Discuss your integration-based conceptualization of the child's cognitive and academic functioning.

   a. Start with a presentation of norm-referenced cognitive ability measures and then academic achievement measures.

> **Example**
>
> Nikia's overall cognitive ability is in the average range (WISC-V FSIQ=94; 34th percentile). According to cognitive assessment results, Nikia's working memory abilities fall in the below average range (WMS Standard score=92; 30th percentile). Nikia also struggled on a measure of phonological awareness generally scoring in the low average to below average range on this measure (CTOPP-2). Nikia's standardized academic achievement test results were similarly below average across the broad reading cluster (WJ IV Achievement Broad Reading Cluster=73; 4th percentile). His performance on measures of writing (WJ IV Achievement Broad Writing cluster=92, 28th percentile) and mathematics (WJ IV Achievement Broad Mathematics=95, 45th percentile) was average. It is possible that Nikia's difficulties with phonological awareness combined with working memory difficulties contribute to his decoding, fluency, and comprehension difficulties in reading.

b. Present information regarding functional academic performance including CBA/CBM data.

> **Example**
>
> Nikia's performance on Reading Curriculum-Based Measurement (R-CBM) is at 45 words per min below the expected range of 69–120 min expected of an average 2nd grade student. According to the AIMSweb Growth Table, Nikia is performing below an instructional level and in the below average range.

c. Discuss the child's progress in school as noted on his grade reports and via interviews with his teachers and parents.

> **Example**
>
> Teacher reports and academic grade reports suggest considerable difficulty with all aspects of reading including fluency, decoding and comprehension. Nikia has been receiving additional support through the reading specialist two times per week. Ms. Jones reports that Nikia participates in tutoring for one hour per week after school. Despite these efforts, Nikia continues to struggle with reading.

d. Discuss whether the sources of data and methods of assessment are consistent with one another.

   i. If so, state that methods of assessment and sources of data including norm-referenced achievement, grade reports, and teacher interview results converge to suggest that the student struggles with a particular academic area.

> **Example**
>
> Nikia has received additional, more intensive intervention via the reading specialist, but still continues to struggle. He also receives outside tutoring support. Background information, teacher reports, norm-referenced assessment, curriculum-based measurement, and school grade reports converge to suggest that Nikia faces considerable struggles with tasks that require him to read and understand written information.

   ii. If not, state where there might be areas of convergence and state where there are inconsistencies. This may occur, for instance, when the norm-referenced results are higher than school furnished data (i.e., grades or teacher interviews). This may also occur when classroom observations lack agreement with teacher interview results or behavior rating scales.

> **Example**
>
> John has received additional, more intensive intervention via the reading specialist because of struggles reading within the second grade curriculum. His mother reports that she provides him with outside tutoring support. Nikia's teachers indicate that his guided reading is at level H, below where he should be at this time of year (level K). Nikia's performance on the WIAT-III, however, indicate average reading performance (Reading Composite Std. Score = 93; 30th percentile).

e. Make the case for whether or not the child qualifies for special education services (or is eligible for a DSM classification if in Canada or if using a clinic-based approach).

> **Example**
>
> Multiple methods of assessment (e.g., norm-referenced and curriculum-based assessment) and sources of data including interview results, review of records, grade reports and classroom observations suggest that Nikia is eligible for special education support under a classification of learning disabilities.

3. Discuss your integration-based conceptualization of the child's social, emotional, behavioral, and adaptive functioning.

a. Present a discussion of the child's struggles in particular social, emotional, behavioral, and adaptive domains.

> **Example**
>
> (Nikia LD Example)
> Several methods of assessment including the BASC-2, classroom observations, review of grade reports, and teacher and parent interviews indicate that Nikia is a well-liked child who gets along with others. Ms. Davis explained that Nikia sometimes feels badly about himself and sometimes expresses that he is "dumb." The BASC-2 reported an at-risk elevation on the depression clinical scale. Both suggested problems with self-esteem and depression. All other areas of social-emotional and behavior functioning was within normal limits. Nikia enjoys drawing, singing, playing sports, and spending time with family. Ms. Davis reports that he is very helpful with his younger sister.

(continued)

(ED Example)

Mark struggles with struggles with inattentiveness, loss of focus, impulsivity, and distractibility. He also faces significant struggles with processing of social information. Mark frequently misperceives ambiguous and even benign interaction with other students as harmful or being directed negatively toward him. At these times, Mark will overreact, sometimes through physical aggression and other times through verbal threats. Mark has previously been sent to juvenile detention (September, 2015) for bringing in scissors and threatening another child. Mark has a preoccupying fascination with guns and weapons. He states that he wants to become a spy to gain access to the repertoire of guns available to spies so that he can defend himself against those who would bully him.

b. Present a discussion of the child's strengths in relevant social, emotional, behavioral, and adaptive domains.

Example

Nikia's strengths include his verbal expressiveness and creativity. Ms. Davis notes that Nikia can strike up a conversation with anyone and has many friends. Nikia has also been described as a caring child who can be helpful with his younger sister. Nikia loves animals and also assumes responsibility for caring for his dog.

c. When writing the conceptualization and classification section for emotional disturbance, delineate each line item of the special education code and address whether the child's symptoms meets that particular criterion. Consult your state's special education criteria for emotional disturbance.

Example

The following criteria from the Pennsylvania Special Education Code guided classification of emotional disturbance.

Emotional disturbance means a condition exhibiting one or more of the following characteristics over a long period of time and to a marked degree that adversely affects a child's educational performance:

A. *An inability to learn that cannot be explained by intellectual, sensory, or health factors.*

There are no intellectual, sensory or health factors that contribute to Mark's learning difficulties. This criterion is not applicable at this time.

B. *An inability to build or maintain satisfactory interpersonal relationships with peers and teachers.*

Mark struggles in his interaction with peers and teachers. He has used and continues to use physical threats and actual aggression when relating to other students. Mark has been suspended for physical aggression, verbal threats, and cussing out teachers (e.g., telling a teacher he "hates" them or to "fuck off"). Mark struggles with social-cognitive information processing distortions (i.e., understanding social nuance) where he misperceives ambiguous and even benign social interaction as being negatively directed, and even harmful, toward him. These characteristics and behaviors intrude upon his ability to build and maintain satisfactory interpersonal relationships with peers and teachers.

C. *Inappropriate types of behavior or feelings under normal circumstances.*

Mark displays several behaviors and feelings that are inappropriate under normal circumstances. His reaction to peers, teachers, and situations that frustrate him can be aggressive and volatile. He has cussed out teachers (e.g., telling them he "hates them" or to "fuck off"). Mark also tends to overreact to actual or perceived insults directed toward him by peers. At these times he will physically aggress, make verbal threats, or become disproportionately upset. Even when interaction with peers is appropriate, Mark frequently misperceives the interaction as negative and will become extremely upset and sometimes become either verbally or physically aggressive. Mark has been observed to flip a switch and go from being calm to extremely upset to a mildly frustrating circumstance. For instance, he has been observed to be fine one moment, but then extremely upset and angry the next moment when he struggled with opening his locker. Mark has a preoccupying fascination with guns and has stated an interest in learning how to use guns as a means to protect himself from other children who might aggrieve upon him.

D. *A general pervasive mood of unhappiness or depression.*

Multiple sources of evaluation data do not indicate that Mark is pervasively depressed or unhappy. He does sometimes become volatile when upset or denied his own way. This criterion is not applicable at this time.

> E. *A tendency to develop physical symptoms or fears associated with personal or school problems.*
>
> Multiple sources of evaluation data do not indicate that Mark develops physical symptoms or fears associated with personal or school problems. This criterion is not applicable at this time.
>
> *Emotional disturbance includes schizophrenia. The term does not apply to children who are socially maladjusted, unless it is determined that they have an emotional disturbance.*
>
> This is not applicable at this time.

4. Offer a concluding statement where you make a decision regarding classification.

> **Example**
>
> (For Learning Disabilities—Nikia Example)
> Multiple methods of assessment and sources of data suggest that Nikia faces considerable struggles with all aspects of reading. These difficulties impinge upon his educational progress at school and suggest that he is eligible for special education support under a classification of learning disabilities. Multiple methods or assessment and sources of data indicate that Nikia is a well-liked child with many friends. He struggles with low self-esteem but is a creative and friendly child who gets along well with others.
>
> (For Emotional Disturbance)
> Multiple methods of assessment and sources of data suggest that Mark faces considerable struggles in the social, emotional, and behavioral arena. These difficulties impinge upon his educational progress at school and suggest that he is eligible for special education support under a classification of emotional disturbance.

This above presented general framework may be followed for each of the IDEA categories and will be helpful in making a case for the classification decision and recommendations that will be offered.

9.4 Specific Conceptualization and Classification Examples

What follows are specific examples of the classification and conceptualization approach and write-up regarding LD, ED, Autism, and ID. Further guidance regarding best practices in classifying of individuals with suspected disabilities in each of these categories is offered in the next section of this book under separate chapters

(Chaps. 10–16). Please note all scenarios and iterations cannot be discussed within this text. Suffice to say that the general framework presented can be readily followed and will create an organized and easy to follow flow to your psychoeducational reports.

9.4.1   Learning Disabilities Conceptualization and Classification

Here is an example of a conceptualization and classification section in a child who struggles with dyslexia.

Conceptualization and Classification (Example)

Multiple data sources and methods of assessment inform the conceptualization of Jack's cognitive, academic, social-emotional, and behavioral functioning including whether he qualifies for special education support. Details in support of these findings are offered below.

Cognitive and Academic Functioning

Jack's overall cognitive ability is in the average range (WISC-V FSIQ=94; 34th percentile). According to cognitive assessment results, Jack's working memory abilities fall in the average range (WMS Standard score=92; 30th percentile). Jack struggled on a measure of phonological awareness generally scoring in the low average to below average range on this measure (CTOPP-2). He scored in the below average range on a measure of memory (WMS=74; 4th percentile). Jack's standardized academic achievement test results were similarly below average across the broad reading cluster (WJ IV Achievement Broad Reading Cluster=73; 4th percentile). His performance on measures of writing (WJ IV Achievement Broad Writing cluster=92, 28th percentile) and mathematics (WJ IV Achievement Broad Mathematics Cluster=95, 45th percentile) was average. Background information, teacher reports, and school records converge to suggest that Jack faces considerable struggles with task that require him to read written information. Jack has received additional, more intensive intervention via the reading specialist, but continues to struggle. He also receives outside tutoring support. Multiple sources of data and methods of evaluation converge to suggest that he will benefit from special education support under a classification of learning disabilities.

Social-Emotional and Behavioral Functioning

Jack is a well-liked child who gets along with peers and adults alike. He can be compassionate and caring. Jack has several close friends and a host of extracurricular activities including athletics, drawing, and piano. Jack is a quiet child who is anxious and self-conscious about his performance in school. This is supported by interview results and BASC-2 ratings in the at-risk range on anxiety. Jack is also beginning to struggle with self-esteem and feel badly about himself. Again, this is consistent with elevations of the BASC-2 and supported by parent interview results. Jack's difficulty with anxiety and self-esteem should continue to be monitored.

Summary

Based upon multiple methods and sources of evaluation including the dual academic deficit model of learning disabilities supported by clinical judgment, the IEP team concludes that Jack qualifies for special education services under a classification of learning disabilities. He will benefit from specially designed instruction for his difficulties with a reading disability.

9.4.2 Emotional Disturbance Conceptualization and Classification

When conceptualizing a child with suspected ED, it is critical to list and then address the classification criteria because the definition and diagnostic approach to ED is vague and elusive. There is not a linkage to specific DSM criteria and the definition of ED has not changed in over half a century since Bower (1982) first discussed the condition. What was then described as a landmark classification category can now be thought of as an anachronism.

Conceptualization and Classification (Example)

Multiple data sources and methods of assessment inform the conceptualization of Margaret's cognitive, academic, social-emotional, and behavioral functioning including whether she qualifies for special education support. Details in support of these findings are offered below.

Cognitive and Academic Functioning

Margaret's present performance on measures of cognitive ability was low average (Composite IQ=89, 23rd percentile; VIQ=82, 12th percentile; NIQ=101, 53rd percentile). Margaret's performance on the WJ-IV Achievement was below average across the mathematics cluster, low average on the writing cluster and average on the reading cluster. Margaret's standardized achievement test performance is consistent with prior evaluation results which suggested a classification of learning disabilities. Margaret's difficulties with distractibility and loss of focus during non-structured activities intensify her academic struggles. Margaret will benefit from specially designed instruction for her academic difficulties.

Social and Emotional Functioning

Margaret is a child who struggles with rule compliance, respect for authority, and use of coercion in her interaction with other children. She tends to use intimidation and verbal threats when she does not get her way. Margaret, however, can be an influential child with strong leadership potential but who sometimes uses those leadership abilities in negative ways. Still, Margaret can be supportive of and kind to others. When confronted about her behavior, Margaret has been observed to role her eyes, argue with teachers, and shut down. She displays low frustration tolerance and becomes upset when things do not go her way. Margaret also struggles with symptoms of inattention, distractibility, and impulsivity.

Margaret came to Smith Public School with a prior classification of emotional disturbance which she received in the second grade. In the prior evaluation dated October 16, 2013, a classification of emotional disturbance was deferred. It was determined that her emotional and behavioral functioning at that time was not sufficiently severe to meet the threshold for emotional disturbance. Events that have transpired since that evaluation now indicate, with a reasonable degree of clinical certainty, that Margaret meets criteria for a classification of emotional disturbance. Details in support of this decision are outlined below.

The following criteria from the Pennsylvania Special Education Code guided classification of emotional disturbance.

Emotional disturbance means a condition exhibiting one or more of the following characteristics over a long period of time and to a marked degree that adversely affects a child's educational performance:

A. *An inability to learn that cannot be explained by intellectual, sensory, or health factors.*

   There are no intellectual, sensory or health factors that contribute to Margaret's learning difficulties. This criterion is not applicable at this time.

B. *An inability to build or maintain satisfactory interpersonal relationships with peers and teachers.*

   Since October, 2013, Margaret has experienced an escalation in her difficulties with peers and teachers. She is oppositional with teachers and argues with or disregards their requests. She has flat out refused to return to class or continued to hang out in the bathroom despite being warned against such behavior. Background information revealed that although Margaret can be an influential, and sometimes a popular child with significant social influence, she struggles with getting along with those who do not share her perspective. When this occurs, she may intimidate, manipulate or bully those who disagree with her. During times of disagreement with other children, Margaret will become upset and lash out persistently. This style of interacting has even transcended the school environment where Margaret has engaged in cyberbullying. Margaret's escalated and intensified struggles with peers and teachers suggest that she now meets criterion B for a classification of emotional disturbance.

C. *Inappropriate types of behavior or feelings under normal circumstances.*

Margaret sometimes becomes upset when denied her own way or when redirected by teachers or other adults in the classroom. She also acts out, disregards, and argues with those in authority. Background information suggests that Margaret's response to teacher requests or disagreement with peers is inappropriately aggressive and intense. Margaret spent all of December, 2013 in the Horsham Clinic for behavioral and emotional difficulties. Although some of Margaret's behaviors are considered oppositional and socially maladjusted, many of her behaviors and feelings are inappropriate and sometimes even quite extreme. She responds aggressively to those with whom she does not agree. She also disregards common teacher requests to stay on task and follow classroom rules. Margaret's inappropriate behaviors and feelings under normal circumstances suggest that she now meets criterion C for a classification of emotional disturbance.

D. *A general pervasive mood of unhappiness or depression.*

Multiple sources of outside evaluation data indicate that Margaret suffers from a Mood Disorder, NOS. Mr. Ford notes that Margaret's affect is generally flat and she is rarely joyful with the exception of events such as her birthday. He also notes that Margaret has in the past been fairly "depressed" for an extended 2-week period. Margaret appears at times an hedonic and unhappy. Her difficulties in this area should continue to be monitored. Although Margaret experiences periods of anhedonia and unhappiness, evaluation results do not suggest that she is pervasively unhappy or depressed.

E. *A tendency to develop physical symptoms or fears associated with personal or school problems.*

Multiple sources of evaluation data do not indicate that Margaret develops physical symptoms or fears associated with personal or school problems. This criterion is not applicable at this time.

Emotional disturbance includes schizophrenia. The term does not apply to children who are socially maladjusted, unless it is determined that they have an emotional disturbance.

This is not applicable at this time.

Conclusion

Multiple methods of assessment and sources of data suggest that Margaret now meets criteria for a classification of Emotional Disturbance. She would also benefit from support for learning related difficulties.

9.4.3 Conceptualization and Classification of Autism

When conceptualizing and classifying a possible autism spectrum, it will be important to describe the core features of the syndrome and whether the child meets diagnostic criteria. According to IDEA, these features include verbal and nonverbal communication, social interaction, repetitive activities and stereotyped movements, unusual responses to sensory experience and difficulty with environmental change and changes in daily routines.

Conceptualization and Classification (Example)

Multiple data sources and methods of assessment inform the conceptualization of Mike's cognitive, academic, social-emotional, and behavioral functioning including whether she qualifies for special education support. Details in support of these findings are offered below.

Cognitive and Academic Functioning

Mike's present performance on a measure of cognitive ability was in the low average range (RIAS Composite Intelligence Index Standard Score = 85; 16th percentile). His performance on standardized measures of academic achievement suggest that he struggles with reading comprehension and applied mathematics problems. His progress on rote academic tasks including spelling and sight word recognition was in the average range. Within the classroom, Mike recognizes and identifies all of his letters and most of his sounds. He occasionally mixes up a few of the commonly confusing letters: b/d, g/q. He has basic concepts of print awareness including which way to open and read a book and where to find letters on the page. Ms. McCormack notes that Mike is starting to read small sight word books with 50–70 % accuracy. He writes down letters and his name and some sight words, but he struggles with carrying meaning along with his writing. In math, he identifies and writes his numbers and counts with one-to-one correspondence. Ms. McCormack notes that Mike cannot follow along with us when we break numbers into parts (e.g., saying "7 is 4 and how many more?") Mike struggles with expressive language and communication and receives speech-language support as a result.

Social, Emotional, and Behavioral Functioning

Multiple data sources and methods of assessment including interview results, classroom observations, and rating forms indicate that Mike struggles with communication, socialization, following classroom rules, and overactivity. When asked a direct question, Mike struggles with producing a clearly understood verbal response. Sometimes this occurs because his speech can be difficult to understand and even unintelligible. At other times Mike responds with a tangential statement that is unrelated to the question asked of him. Mike receives speech services for his communication difficulties. Mike struggles with relating to other children in an age expected manner. He seeks out other children with whom to play, but does so primarily in a way that tends to alienate him from them. Mike can also be physical with other children (e.g., hitting, punching, sliding into, or pushing them) sometimes intentionally and at other times accidentally. Additionally, Mike struggles with interpersonal boundaries and will encroach upon children's personal space or will get up in their face with his hands. Sometimes he engages in this behavior to play with them. At other times he engages in this behavior to get their attention or to get a response from them. This interactional style tends to alienate him from other children in the classroom. Although Mike seeks out social opportunities, he struggles with developing peer relationships at a developmentally appropriate level. Still, Mr. and Mrs. Jones note that Mike can be a compassionate and helpful child. Mike can be quite active in the classroom and frequently darts from one location to another. He loses focus easily and struggles with low task persistence for activities that he does not prefer. Mike is responsive to adult instruction when in a one-on-one situation than when in a group setting. At these times he is more easily redirected. Mike seems to enjoy playing in the sand tray including the sensation of feeling the sand on his hands. Over the past few days, Mike has been also observed to play with his hands while wearing a glove with the face of a cartoon bear (i.e., talk to his hands; interact with his hands). Mike has been wearing his gloves throughout the entire class day over the past several days. At other times, Mike will show his gloves to peers in the classroom. During one observation, most of these peers did not share Mike's excitement and interest in his gloves. Mike has been observed to elicit noises repeatedly (e.g, "ee-ah-ee-ah-you-your") and laugh while looking at his hands. Mike was asked about his gloves and he revealed that they can make ice cream or bring in fish. Mike struggles with following classroom and teacher rules. He will protest when requested to do something he does not prefer. These protests are much more intense than that of a typical kindergarten child. However, with considerable prompting, structure and support, Mike eventually complies. Still, his behaviors can be disruptive to other children around him and at times the entire class. Mike often can be observed with his back to the teacher and therefore the activity being discussed in class. At other times, he has been observed to stare blankly or play with an object such as a pebble or a string on the floor. This causes him to miss much of what is being discussed in the classroom. Mike's cluster of symptoms are impairing his social and behavioral functioning and also contributing to difficulties with his academic functioning. Mike will benefit from accommodations for symptoms consistent with a classification of autism.

Conclusion

Mike faces significant struggles with communication and socialization. Mike also displays atypical mannerisms including repetitive speech sounds and wearing gloves in school. At times, Mike disregards teacher requests and classroom rules, seeking to do what he prefers. Multiple methods of assessment and sources of data suggest that Mike meets criteria for a classification of autism.

9.4.4   Classification of Intellectual Disability

Cognitive and Academic Functioning (Example)

Keith's present performance on a measure of cognitive ability was in the delayed range (RIAS Composite IQ=48; 0.03 percentile; VIQ=49, 0.03 percentile; NIQ=62, 1st percentile). This is consistent with his prior performance (January, 2009) in the delayed range on a measure of cognitive ability (RIAS Composite IQ=50; 0.04 percentile; Verbal IQ=44; <0.01 percentile; Nonverbal IQ=74; 4th percentile). Keith's performance on the WJ-IV Achievement was also in the delayed range across all academic areas. Keith's extremely delayed cognitive ability and academic achievement performance suggests a need for intensive supports in a more restrictive environment. Keith's level of intellectual functioning is in the moderate intellectually disabled range.

Social, Emotional, and Adaptive Functioning

Keith experiences delays in two major adaptive behavior areas: communication and functional academics. His performance on an intelligence test revealed scores in the moderate intellectual disability range (RIAS Composite IQ=48; 0.03 percentile). The combination of moderate delays in cognitive ability and deficits in adaptive behavior (e.g., functional academics and communication) suggests, with a reasonable degree of clinical certainty, a classification of intellectual disability.

Keith also displays some areas of strength in his social-emotional and behavioral functioning. He has a capacity to emulate other children's behavior, which helps him to blend in with them. However, when Keith attempts to engage in reciprocal interaction, other children struggle to understand what he is saying. Although Keith can be charming and will often smile at or tease other children in an endearing way, he can be assertive, if not aggressive, in his interaction with them. For instance, in his attempt to be first in line, Keith will push others out of his way. This tends to alienate Keith from other children. Keith also struggles with reading and interpreting social cues. And, although he may successfully enter into a conversation or social interaction with other children in the classroom, he struggles to maintain that interaction. Keith will require more intensive social and communication intervention.

9.4.5   Conceptualization and Classification of OHI

Conceptualization and Classification (Example)

Tina's present performance on measures of cognitive ability was in the average range (Composite IQ=104; 61st percentile; VIQ=109, 73rd percentile; NIQ=98, 45th percentile). Tina's performance on the WJ-IV Achievement was low average in writing, reading and mathematics. Her attentional difficulties appear to impact her performance on rote, timed academic tasks.

Tina struggles with impulsivity, inattentiveness, disorganization, and following directions. She also struggles in her interaction with other children in the classroom. Tina tends to misperceive the intent of others and considers even benign interaction as hostile. On occasion, Tina will disregard teacher and classroom rules. She will benefit from teacher guidance and support for her social and behavioral difficulties.

Considering multiple data sources and methods of assessment, Tina will qualify for specially designed instruction under a classification of Other Health Impaired since her documented difficulties with Attention-Deficit/Hyperactivity Disorder are adversely impacting her progress in the classroom. The team concludes that specially designed instruction is called for in this case. The following recommendations might benefit her.

9.5 Conclusion

As noted throughout this section, the conceptualization and classification section requires psychologists to synthesize information, describe what animates (i.e., conceptualize) a child's functioning, and arrive at a classification decision. The approach presented in this chapter offers a framework for this purpose.

References

Achenbach, T. M., McConaughy, S. H., & Howell, C. (1987). Child/adolescent behavioral and emotional problems: Implications of cross-informant correlation for situational specificity. *Psychological Bulletin, 101*, 213–232.

Bower, E. M. (1982). Severe emotional disturbance: Public policy and research. *Psychology in the Schools, 19*, 55–60.

Konold, T. R., Walthall, J. C., & Pianta, R. C. (2004). The behavior of child ratings: Measurement structure of the child behavior checklist across time, informants, and child gender. *Behavioral Disorders, 29*, 372–383.

Martin, R. P. (1988). *Assessment of personality and behavior problems: Infancy through adolescence*. New York, NY: Guilford Press.

Chapter 10
Summary and Recommendations

10.1 Introduction

This chapter is comprised of three sections. The first incorporates a brief discussion of the summary section of a report. The second section describes how to write report recommendations. The report recommendation section itself is broken into two subsections that discuss recommendations for learning/academic based problems and behaviorally based problems. The third section addresses accommodations that will permit the child to access the academic curriculum.

10.2 Summary Section

The summary section of a report is vitally important. In many respects, it may be the section that is most carefully read. Some stakeholders in the schools as well as other professionals will skip immediately to the summary section to quickly understand the main findings. Other individuals may read the entire report but then refer to the summary section as a refresher after reading for the first time. If the report is ever contested in some way, then the summary section could come into focus as it will likely be the first section read by hearing officers and administrative law judges. For this reason, the summary section should be carefully prepared. Some psychologists may indicate that the summary section is redundant and adds to report length. However, a summary section, like a concluding section to any research article or term paper, is a natural way to conclude a psychoeducational report and transition into the recommendations section. When including a summary section it is critically important to make sure that any statement included within the summary has adequate support and does not contain new information.

© Springer Science+Business Media New York 2015
S.C. Dombrowski, *Psychoeducational Assessment and Report Writing*,
DOI 10.1007/978-1-4939-1911-6_10

10.2.1 Contents of the Summary Section

Within this section, you will restate key points from the reason for referral, your assessment and observation results, your conceptualization of the child, and your classification decision. Keep your summary concise. Do not include new information in the summary. This is the place where you reiterate your classification decision with a brief synthetical statement and then flow into the recommendations section. It is suggested that you avoid including a summary of the numbers from you test results within this section.

> *Example of a Summary Section*: Jaquil was referred for an evaluation because of difficulties with reading and writing and to determine whether he qualified for specially designed instruction. Multiple sources of data and methods of assessment including norm-referenced achievement testing in reading and writing, student grade reports, parental interviews, and teacher information all converge to indicate long standing and intense struggles with reading. Jaquil's achievement test results combined with classroom based academic difficulties suggests that he will qualify for special education support under a classification of learning disabilities.

As shown in the above example, the summary section offers a concluding statement or paragraph—a synopsis of the psychoeducational report—that then flows into the recommendations section. If the reader wishes to ascertain more detailed information then the reader can review that information within the report's body.

10.3 Recommendations Section

The universe of academic and behaviorally based issues is vast and it is not the intent of this chapter to offer a recommendation for every academic/learning or behaviorally based problem. Instead, a framework for the provision of useful recommendations to parents/caregivers, the multidisciplinary team, and other stakeholders is offered.

Recommendations may include academic and behaviorally based intervention or instructional strategies as well as accommodations. The recommendations that are offered should be empirically guided. If there is not an empirical basis, then there should be a sufficient theoretical rationale for the specific presentation of a recommendation. There are evidence-based resources for academic or behavioral problems. These resources typically use either a problem-solving (e.g., employ behavioral and/or cognitive behavioral principles) approach or a standard protocols approach (e.g., Words Their Way literacy, Bear et al., 2005; NASP PREPaRE Model, Brock et al., 2009). Recommendations may also include empirically based accommodations that permit the child to access the curriculum.

The recommendation section contains valuable information that provides intervention guidance to parents, teachers, and other key stakeholders for improving the social, emotional, behavioral, academic, cognitive, and language functioning of a child.

The multidisciplinary team considers the report's recommendations when determining IEP goals and objectives for the student including relevant accommodations.

To the degree possible, the psychoeducational report should set the stage for intervention planning whether or not the child is found eligible for special education services. (Children who do not qualify still benefit from intervention and accommodation recommendations). A caveat should be presented. It is important to understand your state's rules and regulations regarding the provision of recommendations within a psychoeducational report written by a school psychologist working for a public school. In New Jersey, for instance, the school psychologist does not incorporate recommendations and solely brings the written report to a meeting. From there the multidisciplinary team determines eligibility and appropriate intervention.

10.3.1   Why do Psychologist's Exclude Recommendations?

Some psychoeducational reports focus the recommendations singularly on whether a child is eligible for special education. It is argued (and in certain states codified into law) that the IEP team will determine specific, measurable objectives for the IEP so the inclusion of recommendations is unnecessary. This approach may miss an opportunity to offer guidance to multiple parties for intervention and educational planning. Cruickshank (1977) noted nearly four decades ago that diagnosis should be a springboard off of which intervention/treatment recommendations are offered.

10.3.2   State Practices

Certain states require that selected stakeholders prepare sections of the report independently. For instance, New Jersey has a model that utilizes numerous professionals when evaluating a child for eligibility. Let's consider an evaluation for learning disabilities eligibility. In New Jersey, the school psychologist conducts the cognitive assessment and then puts together a report that is brought to the multidisciplinary meeting. A professional called a Learning Disabilities Teacher Consultant (LDTC) conducts the achievement testing and then prepares a report for the IEP meeting. Sometimes school districts in New Jersey require that the school social worker conducts the adaptive behavior assessment. All professionals then bring their assessment data to a feedback/eligibility meeting and arrive at a decision for the child. If it is determined that the child is eligible for special education services then the team will create an IEP document that details educational planning for the child. No instructional or behavioral recommendations are offered within the reports of any practitioners involved. In other states recommendations may be frequently offered.

In Pennsylvania, for instance, the school psychologist will be responsible for completing a significant portion of the comprehensive psychoeducational evaluation and incorporates recommendations within the report.

10.3.2.1 Psychologist and School District Practice

Certain school districts and psychologists may choose to avoid offering recommendations within a report. Instead, the psychologist will write something akin to the following in the recommendation section:

> The IEP team will convene a meeting to determine whether Johnny is eligible for specially designed instruction and which interventions and accommodations are appropriate for Johnny.

The psychologist and the school district may take this approach to avoid incorporating an inappropriate recommendation that might cause present or future litigation. For instance, if a psychologist mistakenly recommends a private school placement for a child with autism spectrum or outside tutoring for a child with dyslexia then the school district may be held legally responsible for the provision of such services to the child. Because of these concerns, it is the policy of some school districts and psychologists to avoid incorporation of recommendations or solely incorporate recommendations that are vague or very general. Also, some school districts take this approach contending that special education eligibility and the provision of services should be based upon a multidisciplinary team decision-making process.

10.3.3 Importance of Recommendations

The recommendation section of the report provides guidance to teachers and care-givers on how to improve the academic or behavioral functioning of a child. For some psychologists, the main purpose of the recommendation section is to reinforce and restate the classification of a particular disability category. However, the recommendation section has greater relevance. In reports that list specific referral questions, the recommendation section should address those referral questions. The recommendation section may also offer strategies and interventions for improving children's outcomes as well as accommodations that permit the child to access the curriculum. Sometimes, traditional psychoeducational reports are criticized because they do not offer useful recommendations. This is a complaint that has been cited in the literature (Brenner, 2003; D'Amato & Dean, 1987; Tallent, 1992). However, to be considered high quality and useful a psychoeducational report should strive to offer specific recommendations that will assist with intervention and educational planning (Borghese & Cole, 1994).

10.4   General Recommendation Writing Guidelines

The following discussion offers general guidelines for writing recommendations followed by specific examples of recommendations. The recommendation section of a report is typically the last section and follows the summary/concluding section. The following is a suggested framework for writing recommendations:

1. Present an enumerated list with the general theme of the recommendation under-lined and subthemes offered in italics. The general recommendation title/theme is then followed by specific details about the recommendation. The recommen-dation moves from the general to the specific or from the broad to the narrow.

   Here are two examples of the framework that utilizes an enumerated list.

Example A:

1. *Social Skills Difficulties*: John struggles in his relationships with peers. He will benefit from the following recommendations.

   a. *Social Stories*: Specific details here.
   b. *Written Scripts*: Specific details here.
   c. *Social Video Monitoring*: Specific details here.

2. *Anger Control Difficulties*: John displays difficulties with temper outbursts and anger control. He will benefit from intervention for his difficulties in this area as follows:

   a. *Relaxation Training*: Specific details here.
   b. *Cognitive Reframing*: Specific details here.
   c. *Self-Monitoring of Triggers*: Specific details here.

Whenever possible, be specific with the recommendations so that the reader can understand the nature of the recommendation and then look to the empirical litera-ture for even more detailed information regarding how to implement the recommen-dation. Avoid vague and too general language. For instance, do not just indicate "teach social skills." Rather, offer one of the many appropriate evidence-based social skill interventions that are available (e.g., Gresham, 2010). The recommenda-tions offered should move from general to very specific and targeted.

Example A

Assume a child has a learning disability in reading that is related to phonological awareness difficulties. A recommendation such as "Jenny needs additional support for her reading difficulties" is not only vague but also less useful. Instead, it would be an improvement to incorporate something to the following effect:

> Jenny struggles with reading comprehension due to a lack of automatic word decoding skills. Jenny will benefit from additional intervention targeted at her phonological/phone-mic awareness and sight word knowledge.

Although this recommendation is better it could incorporate more specific details. The second example below deals with a child who struggles with reading comprehension. This recommendation moves from inadequate to best.

Example B

Inadequate:

Johnny struggles with reading and will require support for these difficulties.

Better:

Johnny struggles with the comprehension of written text and will benefit from pre-reading and organizational strategies that attempt to improve skills in this area.

Best:

1. *Reading Comprehension.* Johnny struggles with the comprehension of written text and will benefit from pre-reading and organizational strategies that attempt to improve this skill area. Following are a few suggestions that will likely benefit Johnny:

   a. Before reading preview the text by looking at the title and illustrations.
   b. Encourage the creation of a possible story from the illustrations.
   c. Make predictions about the story based on story features prior to reading the story.
   d. During reading, generate questions about the story that are directly related to the text and that require thinking beyond the text.
   e. After reading spend time reflecting upon the material and relating it to experiences and events the child has encountered.
   f. After reading have Johnny engage in the reading material using text summarizing.

2. Enhance recommendation readability and organization by numbering each recommendation and underlining each key recommendation point. After that indent and use italics with additional numbering/lettering. If each recommendation were just organized as a giant paragraph, then it becomes cumbersome to read.

Here is an example of a suggested format.

1) *Support for Difficulties with Reading Comprehension, Phonological Awareness, Sight Word Recognition, Word Decoding, and Reading Fluency*: Sam struggles with all aspects of reading including word decoding, phonological/phonemic awareness, reading fluency and reading comprehension. Sam requires specially designed instruction for his reading difficulties, as noted below.

   a. *Phonological Awareness and Sight Word Knowledge Skills.* Sam will benefit from continued intervention with basic phonemic awareness skills, such as emphasizing instruction on basic rimes (ack, ame, all, ake). Sam would be well served to increase his familiarity with reading fundamentals through a focus on words via alliteration lessons (e.g., tongue twisters), a personal dictionary of sight words (i.e., most frequently used words), and word family study (e.g., neat, beat, heat; noise, poise, choice).
   b. *Reading fluency.* Sam should practice oral reading fluency. Accordingly, Sam will benefit from repeated reading of the same passage until an appropriate grade level fluency rate is attained. The research literature suggests that

improvements in oral reading fluency via repeated passage reading generalizes to improvements in overall reading ability.

c. *Reading Comprehension.* Sam struggles with the comprehension of written text and will benefit from pre-reading and organizational strategies that attempt to improve this skill area. Following are a few suggestions that will likely benefit Sam:

   i. Before reading, preview the text by looking at the title and illustrations.
   ii. Encourage the creation of a possible story from the illustrations.
   iii. Make predictions about the story based on story features prior to reading the story.
   iv. During reading, generate questions about the story that are directly related to the text and that require thinking beyond the text.
   v. After reading, spend time reflecting upon the material and relating it to experiences and events the child has encountered.
   vi. After reading, have Sam engage in the reading material using text summarizing.

3. Offer supplementary resources in handouts that may be offered to the parents or caregivers at the feedback meeting.

4. Offer valuable website support group information in the recommendation section with a host of disabilities including learning disabilities, autism spectrum disorder, intellectual disability, and attention-deficit/hyperactivity disorder.

5. Offer accommodations that will assist the child in accessing the curriculum. The provision of accommodations will be discussed in the final section of this chapter. The accommodation section need not be a separate section and, in fact, accommodation recommendations are often commingled with intervention recommendations in the recommendation section of the report and indistinguishable from intervention recommendations.

10.5 Why Recommendations Are Not Implemented?

There are several reasons why recommendations are not implemented. Some specific reasons are presented below.

- Too general and lack specific, targeted information that renders them useful.
- Too complex and lengthy.
- Inappropriate for the setting, child's ability, or developmental stage.
- Too difficult to implement.
- Recipient lacks the resources, knowledge or skill set to implement.
- If recommendations do not become part of an IEP or Section 504 document then there is no legal responsibility to implement. (Of course, there is an ethical responsibility to implement).

If a recommendation is offered then ensure that it is able to be carried out by parents or teachers. Sometimes teachers lack the skill set, knowledge base, or time to implement the recommendation. Teachers are overburdened with multiple demands in a milieu with increasing class size and decreasing funding for aides and support staff. Teachers may have the desire to implement the interventions recommended in the report, but not have the time or resources. At other times, the recommendation may seem self-evident to the teacher or something the teacher feels he or she has already implemented (i.e., preferential seating; extended time, etc.).

10.6 Recommendation Examples

What follows are selected examples of recommendations for academic, behavioral, social, and emotional difficulties. As noted previously, it is not possible within this chapter to list the universe of recommendations for every behavioral or academic difficulty. Instead, the framework presented above should be referenced as you individualize your recommendations for the child. Some behavioral and social-emotional issues are best addressed through further evaluation (i.e., a functional behavioral assessment). More generally, a behavioral problem-solving model that uses applied behavioral analysis principles or a standards protocol approach for both academic and behavioral problems is well support in the literature (e.g., Shinn & Walker, 2010) and generally evidenced-based. Recommendations that are linked to these approaches are appropriate.

Presented below are selected examples of academic interventions followed by behaviorally based recommendations.

10.6.1 Sample Recommendations for Commonly Faced Academic Difficulties

10.6.1.1 Reading Difficulties

Students with reading difficulties manifest problems in several areas: (1) early literacy skills; (2) word decoding; (3) fluency (4) comprehension and (5) vocabulary. When considering where to intervene, there are six broad areas that may be the target for intervention (Byrnes, 2008): (1) print awareness (i.e., which direction to turn pages in a book, distinguishing letters from numbers; recognizing letters of the alphabet); (2) phonological awareness (i.e., the ability to discern and apply speech sounds to pronounce words); (3) sight word knowledge; (4) reading fluency (i.e., speed and ease of reading); (5) comprehension of written text; and (6) reading strategies (i.e., pre-reading skills; self-monitoring).

In accord with the above difficulties, the following is an example of a reading recommendation that is evidenced-based and might be incorporated into a psychoeducational report. This does not include all the possible intervention recommendations for reading difficulties (i.e., print awareness skills for a child in kindergarden) but it offers a useful exemplar.

1. *Support for Difficulties with Reading Comprehension, Phonological awareness, Sight Word Recognition, Word Decoding, and Reading Fluency*: Sam struggles with all aspects of reading including word decoding, phonological/phonemic awareness, reading fluency and reading comprehension. Sam requires specially designed instruction for his reading difficulties, as noted below.

   a) *Phonological Awareness and Sight Word Knowledge Skills*. Sam will benefit from continued intervention with basic phonemic awareness skills, such as emphasizing instruction on basic rimes (ack, ame, all, ake). Sam would be well served to increase his familiarity with reading fundamentals through a focus on words via alliteration lessons (e.g., tongue twisters), a personal dictionary of sight words (i.e., most frequently used words), and word family study (e.g., neat, beat, heat; noise, poise, choice).

   b) *Reading fluency*. Sam should practice oral reading fluency. Accordingly, Sam will benefit from repeated reading of the same passage until an appropriate grade level fluency rate is attained. The research literature suggests that improvements in oral reading fluency via repeated passage reading generalizes to improvements in overall reading ability.

   c) *Reading Comprehension*. Sam struggles with the comprehension of written text and will benefit from pre-reading and organizational strategies that attempt to improve this skill area. Following are a few suggestions that will likely benefit Sam:

      i. Before reading preview the text by looking at the title and illustrations.
      ii. Encourage the creation of a possible story from the illustrations.
      iii. Make predictions about the story based on story features prior to reading the story.
      iv. During reading, generate questions about the story that are directly related to the text and that require thinking beyond the text.
      v. After reading, spend time reflecting upon the material and relating it to experiences and events the child has encountered.
      vi. After reading have Sam engage in the reading material using text summarizing.

10.6.1.2   Writing Difficulties

Recommendations for written language may be broken down into four areas: (1) handwriting; (2) basic writing skills including punctuation and grammar; (3) spelling; and (4) written expression. One of these areas is often of greater concern than others. Some children, for instance, have relatively intact written expression skills, but difficulty with spelling. Spelling difficulties, like reading difficulties, have their origins in a language based difficulty. Other students struggle with handwriting to the extent that the recommendation might include a request for an occupational therapy evaluation.

Example

1. *Difficulties with Writing*: Nicki struggles with written expression including spelling. Accordingly she will benefit from the following recommendations.

   A. *Written Expression*: Nicki struggles with expressing her ideas in written form. The recommendations may be appropriate for her:

      i. Assist Nicki in generating ideas about a topic and then show her how to put the ideas in an outline.
      ii. Demonstrate for Nicki outlining principles. Have her practice what you just demonstrated so that she can distinguish between main ideas and supporting ideas.
      iii. Assist Nicki in creating a paragraph and then show her that that paragraphs require an introduction, a middle, and a conclusion. Require that Nicki generate her own paragraph and offer corrective feedback.
      iv. Require Nicki to proofread her written work and provide corrective feedback when appropriate.

   B. *Spelling*: Nicki struggles with spelling words in a phonetically plausible manner and the following recommendations may be appropriate for her:

      i. Have Nicki practice spelling words each day that require selected phonetic sounds. Introduce new words as Nicki has mastered the old words. The Cover, Copy, Compare, or Folding-in techniques are appropriate for this purpose and have strong research support learning new spelling words.
      ii. Ensure that Nicki hears correctly the sounds in the words that she misspells. Require Nicki to read the words aloud to determine whether she recognizes the letter units or phonemes in the words.
      iii. Require Nicki to use a phonetic approach to spelling any words she does not know how to spell.
      iv. Permit Nicki to practice spelling through a computer software program that provides immediate corrective feedback.

10.6.1.3 Mathematics Difficulties

Students who struggle with mathematics generally do so in two areas: mathematical calculation skills and mathematical problem solving/reasoning skills (Byrnes, 2008). Mathematics abilities tend to be hierarchical with failure to learn preceding skills contributing to difficulty with later concepts. Therefore, basic addition and subtraction skills are a necessary prerequisite to multiplication skills which in turn are necessary for division understanding. These skills are often mastered in the elementary school years. Additionally, in the elementary school years, children acquire a range of strategies for solving decontextualized addition and subtraction problems and word problems. Children with mathematics disabilities experience procedural and fact retrieval deficits. Byrnes (2008) notes that children with mathematics disabilities use less mature strategies (e.g., count-all versus min), make more frequent calculation errors, and perform strategies with less speed. Other mathematics deficiencies noted in the research include rapid number naming, comparing skills, and speed of processing of basic mathematics facts (Fuchs et al., 2005; Geary et al., 1999).

The following is an example recommendation for a child who struggles with math reasoning (i.e., word problems) and math calculation (e.g., basic addition and subtraction facts).

Example

1. *Mathematics including basic math facts and math reasoning*: James struggles with all aspects of mathematics including reasoning and mathematics calculation. He will benefit from intervention for difficulties in those areas as noted below.

    A. *Basic Mathematics Facts*: James struggles with acquisition of basic addition and subtraction facts. The following recommendations may be beneficial for him:

        i. Provide James with concrete examples to help learn and remember addition and subtraction concepts. For example, use coins, paper clips, or wooden blocks to form groupings to teach basic addition and subtraction facts.
        ii. Permit student to learn math facts using computer programs that make acquisition of this information fun since relatively immediate feedback is furnished.
        iii. Reinforce already acquired mathematics facts. Introduce new math facts one at a time.
        iv. Review daily the concepts the student just learned.
        v. Find opportunities for James to apply math facts to real-life situations (e.g., setting the table with the appropriate number of plates, utensils).
        vi. Practice math facts using the Cover, Copy, Compare or Folding-in technique. Both has strong research support for the acquisition of basic math facts.

    B. *Math Word Problems*: James struggles with mathematics word problems and will benefit from the following recommendations.

        i. Ask James to identify the primary question that is to be answered to solve the word problem. Make sure the student understands that extraneous information is sometimes included in a math word problem.
        ii. Teach James to look for hint words in word problems that indicate the mathematical operations.

    iii. Have James restate the math word problem in his own words.

    iv. Teach James to break down the math word problem into specific steps before attempting to solve it.

    v. Provide James a list of phrases or word that usually indicate an addition (e.g., sum, in all, total, altogether) and subtraction (e.g., difference, how many left, how many remain).

10.6.2 Sample Recommendations for Social, Emotional, and Behavioral Difficulties

Children in the schools are frequently referred for social, emotional, and behavioral difficulties. Difficulties run the gamut from self-esteem issues and depression to attentional issues and rule noncompliance. The universe of recommendations for social, emotional, and behavioral difficulties will not be addressed within this chapter. Instead, a selected sample of a few recommendations will be offered. There are numerous books and intervention manuals available in the literature that provide empirically guided interventions upon which the recommendations can be based. When writing a recommendation, it will be important to guide the reader including the multidisciplinary team toward empirically supported interventions for various skills deficit areas.

10.6.2.1 Recommendations for ADHD

One of the most common behavioral difficulties experienced by children involves difficulties with attention, hyperactivity, distractibility, and impulsivity. These children may even present with an outside classification of ADHD. Many children with ADHD, particularly those who experience hyperactivity and impulsivity, experience difficulties with rule noncompliance, assignment completion, and social skills. For children with symptoms of ADHD it is common to see a several-fold recommendation list. The first may include ecological considerations. The second may be a targeted behavioral intervention that can be implemented within the school and across settings (e.g., daily behavior report card; check in, check out (DuPaul & Stoner, 2003; Hawken & Horner, 2003; Simonsen et al., 2008). The third may involve parental education to help the parent understand how to effectively shape the child's behavior. Finally, the recommendation may be for the child to visit with a psychiatrist to determine whether medication management of symptoms might be worthwhile.

    Following is an example of recommendations for ADHD-like symptoms in the school. This is followed by a recommendation for a referral to a medical professional to assess need for psychotropic medication. A referral to a psychiatrist or physician for psychotropic medication is offered only after all additional intervention options have been exhausted.

1. *Strategies for difficulties with Attention, Distractibility, Hyperactivity, Impulsivity, and Loss of Focus:* Background reports indicate that Margaret experiences difficulty with attention and distractibility. As such, the following recommendations might be beneficial for her:

   A. *Check In, Check Out, and Behavior Report Card*: Margaret should have her behavioral expectations reviewed at the beginning of the school day. She should check in with an adult periodically throughout the day to determine whether her goals are being met. At the end of the day, Margaret should check out with that same adult and receive a behavior report card that acknowledges her behavioral performance and is sent home to her caregivers.

   B. *Provision of Directions by Teacher*: When Margaret's teachers interact with her, she should be encouraged to repeat and explain instructions to ensure understanding. The provision of directions to Margaret will be most effective when the teacher makes eye contact, avoids multiple commands, is clear and to the point, and permits repetition of directions when needed or asked for.

   C. *Positive Reinforcement and Praise for Successful Task Completion*: Margaret's teachers should provide positive reinforcement and immediate feedback for completion of desired behaviors or tasks. Initially, praise and reinforcement should be offered for successful effort on a task or behavior regardless of quality of performance.

   D. *Time on Task*: Communicate to Margaret how long she will need to engage in or pay attention on a particular task. Open ended expectations can be distressing to any child, let alone one with attentional difficulties.

   E. *Prepare Student Discreetly for Transitions*: Furnish Margaret with verbal prompts and visual cues that a new activity or task is about to start. This should be accomplished discreetly so as to avoid student embarrassment.

   F. *Recess Time*: Margaret should be permitted to participate in recess. Recess should not be a time to complete unfinished classwork or homework.

   G. *Extended Time, Teacher Check In's, Assignment Adjustment, and Frequent Breaks*: Margaret should be permitted additional time to complete academic tasks and projects. Margaret's teachers should also consider review of classwork as Margaret progresses on an assignment or project to assist Margaret in avoiding careless mistakes. She may benefit from chunking assignments or assignment reduction. More frequent breaks than what is typical may also reduce careless mistakes and help to maintain focus.

10.6.2.2   Referral to a Child Psychiatrist for a Psychotropic
                Medication Evaluation

Children are sometimes referred for an evaluation by a psychiatrist or physician for psychotropic medication evaluation or follow up monitoring. It is noted that the psychologist within a report should never recommend the use of psychotropic medications. This is beyond the scope of the psychologist's training and competence.

Referral to a Child Psychiatrist for a Psychotropic Medication Evaluation: James would benefit from a psychotropic medication evaluation for the host of behavioral difficulties he faces including impulsivity, hyperactivity, anger control, attention, mood, and possible low grade depression.

A psychiatrist friend once described the prescription of medication as "carefully reasoned speculation." I do not know whether this anecdotal story is actual best psychiatric practice, but it impressed upon me the need for continuous monitoring of a child's medication involving multiple stakeholders (e.g., child, parents, teachers) when monitoring a child's response to medication intervention.

Psychotropic Medication Compliance and Monitoring: Benaiah will benefit from continued compliance with his physician-determined medication plan. Since he recently changed medication from Ritalin to Concerta, it might be beneficial for Ms. Davis to consult with Benaiah's physician regarding a monitoring plan to determine the effectiveness of his medication.

10.6.2.3   Recommendations for Counseling

Frequently, children with social, emotional, and behavioral issues will receive recommendations for counseling. The following approach to the provision of counseling recommendations may be useful. Again, note the tiered approach with titles and subtitles.

1. *Counseling:* Chris will benefit from counseling for the following concerns:

   a. *Social-Cognitive Processing Deficits*: Chris tends to misperceive ambiguous and even benign situations as negative toward him. He will benefit from counseling for these difficulties.

   b. *Themes of Aggression*: Chris frequently discusses and appears to fantasize about aggressive themes including the use of guns. Some of this discussion may be based upon prior exposure to violence; others may be routed in an active fantasy life. Nonetheless, this theme, and Chris's possible exposure to trauma and violence, should be explored in counseling.

2. *Individual Counseling and Behavioral Support:* Benaiah will benefit from counseling and behavioral support for the following difficulties:

   a. Boundary awareness.
   b. Low frustration tolerance.

  c. Feelings of low self-esteem and possible low grade depression from his consistent lack of success at school.

  d. Oppositionality and rule noncompliance.

  e. Social skills difficulties including aggression toward other students.

  f. Being disrespectful to adults in the classroom.

10.6.2.4 Social Skills Intervention Recommendations

Social skills are a frequently targeted area for children within psychoeducational reports. Social skills interventions encompass a broad category for intervention recommendations. In fact, Gresham, Sugai, and Horner (2001) reports five different broad categories of social skills (e.g., peer relational skills, self-management skills, academic skills, compliance skills, assertion skills). When writing a recommendation for social skills difficulties it is critically important to guide the reader to where the child is experiencing difficulty. For instance, one child might need intervention targeted at his or her social-cognitive processing because that child tends to distort benign and even ambiguous social stimuli as being negatively directed toward him (e.g., Dodge & Coie, 1987). Other children might struggle with entering into and sustaining conversations and so the target of intervention is in this area. Still other children may fail to understand the perspective of others and encounter social difficulties as a result. The spectrum of social skills difficulties is broad so it is not possible to list all possible options within this chapter (Gresham, 2010). The following is an example of a child who struggles with entering into, sustaining and negotiating social interaction.

Social Skills Support: Luke will benefit from guidance in learning socially appropriate behavior. The following might be appropriate for Luke:

  a. How to join into conversations and play activities with other children.

  b. How to sustain conversations and play activities in a give-and-take fashion.

  c. Modeling of acceptable mannerisms and verbal behaviors when playing with other children.

  d. How to ask questions of other children to show interest in what they are doing.

  e. How to use verbal, rather than physical, means to resolve conflicts or gain attention from peers or adults.

10.6.2.5 Social Skills Recommendations for Children with Autism Spectrum

Children with autism spectrum encounter significant difficulties with social skills as this is a core deficit area. There is a wide body of intervention literature targeting children with autism spectrum disorders. Thus, writing recommendations that are linked to evidenced-based interventions is possible. Here is an example of two possible recommendations for social skills for children with autism spectrum.

Both recommendations have an empirical basis (e.g., Scattone, 2007) and have been researched within the autism literature as being tentatively successful. Scattone (2007) notes that social stories and written scripts (i.e., script fading), although having some empirical validation, will require additional empirical scrutiny. A social story is a short, individualized story designed to teach a child with autism a certain skill, event, concept, or social behavior (Gray, 1998, 2010). It is generally written in the first person to make it easier for a child to identify with the situation described in the story. A social story provides information about what is happening and why, who will participate, when an event or activity will take place, and the appropriate response expected from the child during a given social situation.

1. *Social Skills Difficulties including Social Pragmatics.* John struggles with initiating interaction with peers and can be quite disruptive to the class when enters into it. He does not realize his impact upon the classroom. The following may be beneficial to John.

   A. *Written Scripts*: John struggles with initiating play interaction with peers. The following use of script fading may be useful in assisting John with difficulties. Additional information regarding script fading is available from Krantz and McClannhan (1998).

      i. Develop the script around John's desire to play Pokeman with a peer.
      ii. The script may contain a single word for beginning readers or several full sentences for children with reading ability.
      iii. Manually assist the child in reading aloud one of the scripted statements by following the words with a pointer and using verbal prompts where necessary.
      iv. Physically guide the target child to face a peer, say the scripted statement, and place a check mark next to the scripted statement just made.
      v. Once the target child learns to use the scripts, the scripts may be faded over several steps. The following is an example:
         1. "John, do you want to play Pokémon today?"
         2. "John, do you want to play"
         3. "John, do you"
         4. "John, do"
         5. Child should have acquired target behavior.

   B. *Social Stories*: Create a social story to assist John with his struggles with entering into a classroom quietly. The follow general procedure should be used to create the story with additional information available from Gray (2010).

      i. Specify the behavior that is to be developed or changed in John.
      ii. Work on one behavior at a time with John.
      iii. Create a story and write it in the first person.
      iv. Use drawings and/or photographs of the activity.

     v. When appropriate, have John participate in the development of the social story.
    vi. Present a detailed description of the situation that presents John with difficulty.
   vii. Describe the desired behavior.
  viii. Conclude with a description of the desired, acceptable behavior.

10.6.2.6   Crisis Recommendations

Recommendations in anticipation of a crisis or following a crisis become critically important to ensure the safety of the student and others who might come into contact with the student. They are sometimes incorporated into the recommendations section of a report.

Crisis Management Plan: The Smith School has a crisis management plan in place because Jack has in the past physically aggressed toward other students or objects in the classroom. He also has jeopardized his own safety by leaving the building. Jack is transferring out-of-district and his next setting should formalize a crisis management plan for these infrequent situations. The following is an example of a plan that might be established:

a. Be aware of cues that Jack is upset.
b. Try to calm student. Separate Jack from peers if possible.
c. If problem gets worse, notify school principal.
d. The school psychologist will come to talk with Jack and escort him to her office.
e. Jack will take a 10-min time-out in the school psychologist's.
f. Jack will be verbally praised for calming himself and for taking time-out appropriately.
g. The school psychologist will remind Jack of expectations and the card system upon returning to class.
h. The school psychologist (or other adult) will escort Jack back to class.

Threats to Others: Last year, Chris reported that he threatened to kill another student and was sent to juvenile detention for part of the day until midnight. Even if Chris was being dramatic in his threat and never intended to follow through, he needs to understand that the school and community take such threats seriously and there will be significant consequences from making a threat to the physical safety of another individual. Accordingly, any future threats to others should continue to be monitored by the school and appropriate protective action taken (i.e., contact law enforcement; contact Ms. Smith; contact the intended victim) following a credible threat to another individual.

Suicidal Ideation: John has made suicidal overtures and been hospitalized for such behavior. Should John express suicidal ideation or make explicit gestures, then this should be taken seriously and appropriate protective action taken. This should include contacting John's legal guardian to ensure that he is taken to a crisis center or hospital.

10.6.2.7 Parental Recommendations

Recommendations for parents and caregivers may be appropriate when coordination of care between the school and home is necessary. Presented below are two examples of recommendations that could be furnished within a report.

Parental Monitoring of Preoccupation with Guns: Though not an issue for special education, Ms. Jones is strongly advised to monitor and regulate Chris's preoccupation with guns given his tendency to misperceive social situations and considering his impulsive style. Background information revealed that Chris displays an interest in learning how to use guns as a means to protect himself from those who would aggrieve upon him. Chris's access to environments where guns might be available to him should be clearly circumscribed. Resources and possible training materials (i.e., classes) to promote safety may be available through local law enforcement and Chris should undertake such training.

Suicidal Ideation and Overtures: Although Jenna has repeatedly stated that she would not hurt herself, her suicidal ideation and gesturing should be taken seriously by Ms. Smith and appropriate protective action taken when Jenna makes such threats. Appropriate protective action means to take Jenna to a crisis center or hospital. If Jenna refuses to go, then law enforcement should be contacted.

10.7 Accommodations

Accommodations are frequently offered in a psychoeducational report within the recommendations section. Sometimes accommodation recommendations are difficult to distinguish from intervention recommendations within a report. Accommodations serve the purpose of providing access to the curriculum. They level the playing field for a child with a disability. Accommodations are distinguished from recommendations in that they do not discuss direct instruction or intervention services. Instead, accommodations are intended to alter the environment, alter the assignment, alter the test or adapt sensory experiences (e.g., noise filtering headphones; FM audio system). The accommodations furnished in the recommendations section of your report should be based upon the psychoeducational assessment and linked to the individualized needs of the child.

Some of the more widely recognized accommodations are for individuals with physical and communication disabilities. This might include the need for Braille for a child with a visual impairment or extended time to travel between classes for a child who requires a walker for mobility. Accommodations may also be available to children with learning and behavioral needs. These may include books on tape for a child with dyslexia or extended time for a child with ADHD who qualifies under OHI or who has a Section 504 plan.

The following are just a few examples of accommodations which might be applicable given various difficulties faced by a child. They are certainly not exhaustive but will furnish the reader with a brief sampling.

10.7.1   Environmental Accommodations

- Provide student with preferential seating near the teacher.
- Provide student with preferential seating in an area free from distractions and away from the door.
- To reduce distractions, use headphones in the classroom while other children are using computer equipment.
- Provide student with a quiet location in the room during reading assignments.
- Use an FM audio system in the classroom to assist student in hearing teacher remarks.

10.7.2   Testing Accommodations

- Provide the student with extended time (time-and-a-half) during math tests.
- Permit student to furnish responses orally rather than in writing.
- Read tests out loud to student.
- Permit student to take a break half-way through testing.
- Permit student to type rather than write short answer questions.
- Provide student with a calculator to double-check math calculation for which the work has been presented.
- Read test questions to student when requested.

10.7.3   Homework/Classwork Modifications

- Permit student to use books on tape.
- Allow student to complete every other homework question.
- Permit student to start an assignment and then approach the teacher for corrective feedback.
- Ensure that student has written down homework assignment in daily schedule in each before leaving school.
- Reduce amount of homework for student so she can complete assignments in same time as others.
- Permit student to work with a peer during in class writing assignments.

The accommodations offered above are a small subset of the available accommodations to children. The accommodations that are offered within a report should be linked to the individualized needs of the child being evaluated. Accommodations may be included as a separate subsection although they are frequently incorporated and interspersed with intervention recommendations throughout the recommendation section.

10.8   Website Suggestions

Selected websites provide a guide regarding assessment, intervention and accommodation practices. A few selected websites that may be of use to parents and psychologists are listed below.

ADHD
Children and Adults with Attention Deficit/Hyperactivity Disorder (CHADD): http://www.chadd.org/.

Autism
http://www.autism-society.org/.

Learning Disabilities
Learning Disabilities Association of America http://ldaamerica.org/.
National Center for Learning Disabilities (LDA): www.ncld.org.

Intellectual Disability
The ARC: http://www.thearc.org/.

Additional Useful Websites
National Association of School Psychologists (NASP): www.nasponline.org.
Council for Exceptional Children (CEC): www.cec.sped.org.
National Dissemination Center for Children with Disabilities: http://nichcy.org/.
American Foundation for the Blind: http://www.afb.org/.
American Academy of Pediatrics: www.aap.org.
National Center on Intensive Intervention: http://www.intensiveintervention.org/.
Best Evidence Encyclopedia: http://www.bestevidence.org/.
National Registry of Evidence-based Programs and Practices: http://www.nrepp.samhsa.gov/Index.aspx.
Promising Practices Network: http://www.promisingpractices.net/.

This is certainly not an exhaustive list and I have likely overlooked additional, valuable Internet resources, but it represents a starting point for immediately accessible sources of assessment and intervention information.

10.9   Conclusion

The summary section of a report is critically important. It provides a brief overview of the report including the classification decision. It may be the first section read within the report. Recommendations within a psychoeducational report guide parents and teachers on needed interventions and accommodations. Within this book, it is not possible to offer recommendations for the universe of academic and behaviorally based problems. Instead, this chapter offered a model for how to prepare report recommendations. When writing recommendations it is necessary to keep in mind the evidenced-based literature. Applied behavioral analysis principles via a problem-solving model undergird successful interventions for behaviorally based problems and academic learning difficulties. Also, a standards protocol approach for academic and behaviorally based problems has also been found to have linkages with the empirical literature. The interventions recommended should be empirically based or linked to the theoretical literature. The accommodations offered within the recommendation section should have an empirical linkage and, at a minimum, provide the child with access to the academic curriculum. The summary and recommendation section of a report is critically important.

References

Bear, D. R., Invernizzi, M., Templeton, S., & Johnston, F. (2005). *Words their way: Word study phonics, vocabulary, and spelling instruction* (3rd ed.). Upper Saddle River, NJ: Merrill Publishing.

Borghese, N., & Cole, E. (1994). Psychoeducational recommendations: Perceptions of school psychologists and classroom teachers. *Canadian Journal of School Psychology, 10*, 70–87.

Brenner, E. (2003). Consumer-focused psychological assessment. *Professional Psychology: Research and Practice, 34*, 240–247.

Brock, S. E., Nickerson, A. B., Reeves, M. A., Jimerson, S. R., Lieberman, R., & Feinberg, T. (2009). *School crisis prevention and intervention: The PREPaRE training model.* Bethesda, MD: National Association of School Psychologists.

Byrnes, J. P. (2008). *Cognitive development and learning in instructional contexts* (3rd ed.). New York, NY: Allyn & Bacon.

Cruickshank, W. M. (1977). Least-restrictive placement: Administrative wishful thinking. *Journal of Learning Disabilities, 10*, 193–194.

D'Amato, R. C., & Dean, R. S. (1987). Psychological reports, individual education programs, and daily lesson plans: Are they related? *Professional School Psychology, 2*, 93–101.

Dodge, K. A., & Coie, J. D. (1987). Social information processing factors in reactive and proactive aggression in children's peer groups. *Journal of Personality and Social Psychology, 53*, 1146–1158.

DuPaul, G. J., & Stoner, G. (2003). *ADHD in the schools: Assessment and intervention strategies* (2nd ed.). New York, NY: Guilford.

Fuchs, L. S., Compton, D. L., Fuchs, D., Paulsen, L., Bryant, J. D., & Hamlet, C. L. (2005). The prevention, identification, and cognitive determinants of math difficulty. *Journal of Educational Psychology, 97*, 493–513.

Geary, D. C., Hoard, M. K., & Hamson, C. O. (1999). Numerical and arithmetical deficits in learning disabled children: Relation to dyscalculia and dyslexia. *Aphasiology, 15*, 645–647.

Gray, C. (1998). Social stories and comic strip conversations with students with Asperger syndrome and high-functioning autism. In E. Schopler (Ed.), *Asperger Syndrome or High Functioning Autism?* (pp. 167–194). New York, NY: Plenum Press.

Gray, C. (2010). *The New Social Story™ book.* Arlington, TX: Future Horizons.

Gresham, F. M. (2010). Evidence-based social skills interventions: Empirical foundations for instructional approaches. In M. R. Shinn & H. M. Walker (Eds.), *Interventions for achievement and behavior problems in a three-tier model including RTI* (pp. 337–362). National Association of School Psychologists: Bethesda, MD.

Gresham, F. M., Sugai, G., & Horner, R. H. (2001). Interpreting outcomes of social skills training for students with high-incidence disabilities. *Exceptional Children, 67*(3), 331–344.

Hawken, L. S., & Horner, R. H. (2003). Evaluation of a targeted intervention within a schoolwide system of behavior support. *Journal of Behavioral Education, 12*, 225–240.

Krantz, P. J., & McClannahan, L. E. (1998). Social interaction skills for children with autism: A script-fading procedure for beginning readers. *Journal of Applied Behavior Analysis, 31*, 191–202.

Scattone, D. (2007). Social skills interventions for children with autism. *Psychology in the Schools, 44*, 717–726.

Shinn, M. R., & Walker, H. M. (2010). *Interventions for achievement and behavior problems in a three-tier model including RTI.* Bethesda, MD: National Association of School Psychologists.

Simonsen, B., Fairbanks, S., Briesch, A., Myers, D., & Sugai, G. (2008). Evidence based practices in classroom management: Considerations for research to practice. *Education and Treatment of Children, 31*, 351–380.

Tallent, N. (1992). *The practice of psychological assessment.* Upper Saddle River, NJ: Prentice Hall.

Part III
Guidance Regarding Assessment and Classification of IDEA Categories Including Sample Reports

The forthcoming section will provide generalized guidance regarding the identification and classification of the major categories for which psychologists in the schools are responsible. This includes LD, ED, Autism, Intellectual disability, OHI and section 504. Sample reports are offered for each of these IDEA diagnostic categories and for the section 504 classification. Guidance is also furnished for the process of assessment and identification of hearing impairment/deafness, visual impairment/blindness, traumatic brain injury, orthopedic impairment and culturally and linguistically diverse learners.

Chapter 11
Learning Disabilities

11.1 Overview

The assessment of learning disabilities will be among the most common of your evaluations. Research shows that it comprises approximately 51 % of all special education classifications with 7.66 % of the school-aged population receiving a classification (Boyle et al., 2011). Two major classification systems address the needs of children and adolescents with learning disabilities (LD): the system based on special education law (e.g., Individuals with Disabilities Act (IDEA) and the system used by the clinical community (Diagnostic and Statistical Manual (DSM). The definition and classification approach from the two diagnostic systems lack specificity but has distanced itself from the discrepancy approach.

11.2 Historical Considerations

Researchers spanning nearly 100 years have investigated children's difficulties with learning to read, write, and perform mathematical operations (Hinshelwood, 1917; Kirk, 1981; Orton, 1925). To the consternation of some in the educational community, early definitions of learning disabilities (LD) were medically oriented (e.g., brain injured, perceptually impaired, dyslexic, and neurologically impaired). In an effort to move away from a medically oriented conceptualization, Samual Kirk, a professor of special education, introduced the term learning disability:

> A learning disability refers to a retardation, disorder, or delayed development in one or more of the processes of speech, language, reading, writing, arithmetic, or other school subjects resulting from a psychological handicap caused by a possible cerebral dysfunction and/or emotional or behavioral disturbances. It is not the result of mental retardation, sensory deprivation, or cultural and instructional factors (Kirk, 1962, p. 263).

© Springer Science+Business Media New York 2015
S.C. Dombrowski, *Psychoeducational Assessment and Report Writing*,
DOI 10.1007/978-1-4939-1911-6_11

Kirk's definition had a significant influence on subsequent generations of LD definitions within psychiatric (e.g., DSM) and educational (e.g., IDEA) taxonomies. Kirk's definition did not contain specific mention of a discrepancy between intellectual ability and achievement (Kirk & Bateman, 1962) but it was still considered too medically oriented (Mercer, Forgnone, & Wolking, 1976). In an effort to move away from a medically oriented LD definition that was less educationally relevant and to provide the field with a method to assess the construct, the field adopted the discrepancy model as a primary defining characteristic. Barbara Bateman (1965), one of Kirk's students, was the first to provide an LD definition that included a reference to a discrepancy between ability and achievement. This definition was thought to be more parsimonious and have greater educational relevance. Rutter and Yule (1975) and Yule (1973) wrote the first articles that provided what was then considered an empirical basis for the IQ–achievement discrepancy. Their research (i.e., the Isle of Wight study) influenced the field's conceptualization of LD and fostered incorporation of the discrepancy diagnostic heuristic into subsequent generations of DSM and IDEA LD classification taxonomy. However, numerous studies across the next 40 years challenged Rutter and Yule's conclusion that an IQ–achievement discrepancy model can be reliably and validly used for LD diagnosis and educational classification (Aaron, 1997; Dombrowski, Kamphaus, & Reynolds, 2004; Dombrowski, Ambrose, & Clinton, 2007; Dombrowski, Kamphaus et al., 2006).

Instead, most researchers have argued that the discrepancy model has made the LD definition just as educationally irrelevant as prior medically oriented definitions (Aaron, 1997; Dombrowski et al., 2004; Dombrowski & Gischlar, 2014; Lyon, 1995; Siegel, 1999). After more than four decades of use and when considering the accumulated research evidence against the discrepancy model, the research community and most practicing psychologists in the fields of school and clinical child psychology have finally cast aside the discrepancy approach as a means of classification.

11.3 Definition and Identification of Learning Disabilities

There are three learning disabilities definitions and identification procedures that will be presented including IDEA, DSM, and NJCLD. Keep in mind that you will need to adhere to your respective state's eligibility criteria when making a classification decision. State criteria are generally aligned with IDEA criteria.

IDEA Definition and Identification Procedures

(10) Specific learning disability. (i) General. Specific learning disability means a disorder in one or more of the basic psychological processes involved in understanding or in using language, spoken or written, that may manifest itself in the imperfect ability to listen, think, speak, read, write, spell, or to do mathematical calculations, including conditions such as perceptual disabilities, brain injury, minimal brain dysfunction, dyslexia, and developmental aphasia.

(ii) Disorders not included. Specific learning disability does not include learning problems that are primarily the result of visual, hearing, or motor disabilities, of mental retardation, of emotional disturbance, or of environmental, cultural, or economic disadvantage.

The multidisciplinary team may determine that a child has a specific learning disability if the child does not achieve adequately for the child's age or meet State-approved grade-level standards in one or more of the following areas, when provided with learning experiences and instruction appropriate for the child's age or state-approved grade–level standards:

- Oral expression.
- Listening comprehension.
- Written expression.
- Basic reading skills.
- Reading fluency skills.
- Reading comprehension.
- Mathematics calculation.
- Mathematics problem solving.

The child does not make sufficient progress to meet age or state-approved grade-level standards in one or more of the areas identified above when using a process based on the child's response to scientific, research-based intervention; or the child exhibits a pattern of strengths and weaknesses in performance, achievement, or both, relative to age, state-approved grade-level standards, or intellectual development.

Under IDEA a child cannot be classified as having a learning disability if it is determined that the child's struggles are the result of the following:

- A visual, hearing, or motor disability;
- Mental retardation;
- Emotional disturbance;
- Cultural factors;
- Environmental or economic disadvantage;
- Limited English proficiency;
- Lack of appropriate instruction.

(continued)

(continued)

> IDEA permits several approaches to identification of learning disabilities:
>
> 1. Response to scientific, research-based interventions (presumably intended to mean Response to Intervention);
> 2. A pattern of strengths and weaknesses in performance, achievement, or both, relative to age, State-approved grade-level standards, or intellectual development; or
> 3. Alternative research-based procedures.
>
> Additionally, IDEA specifically references the discrepancy, but only by indicating that a state "must not require the use of a severe discrepancy between intellectual ability and achievement for determining whether a child has a specific learning disability." Some states continue to permit use of the discrepancy approach in its varied iterations.
> [34 CFR 300.307] [20 U.S.C. 1221e-3; 1401(30); 1414(b)(6)]

Note that some of the LD categories specified in the IDEA definition cross over into the realm of speech-language (i.e., oral expression). Because of this the services of a speech-language therapist may need to be involved in assessment and eligibility determination for SLD.

> **DSM-5**
>
> Specific Learning disorder is defined in the DSM-5 (American Psychiatric Association, 2013) as follows (p66):
>
> (A) Difficulties learning and using academic skills, as indicated by the presence of at least one of the following symptoms that have persisted for at least 6 months, despite the provision of interventions that target those difficulties.
>
> 1. Inaccurate or slow and effortful word reading (e.g., reads single words aloud incorrectly or slowly and hesitantly, frequently guesses words, has difficulty sounding out words).
> 2. Difficulty understanding the meaning of what is read (e.g., may read text accurately but not understand the sequence, relationships, inferences, or deeper meanings of what is read).
> 3. Difficulties with spelling (e.g., may add, omit, or substitute vowels or consonants).
> 4. Difficulties with written expression (e.g., makes multiple grammatical or punctuation errors within sentences; employs poor paragraph organization; written expression of ideas lacks clarity).

(continued)

(continued)

5. Difficulties in mastering number sense, number facts, or calculation (e.g., has poor understanding of numbers, their magnitude, and relationships; counts on fingers to add single-digit numbers instead of recalling the math fact as peers do; gets lost in the midst of arithmetic computation and may switch procedures).
6. Difficulties with mathematical reasoning (e.g., has severe difficulty applying mathematical concepts, facts, or procedures to solve quantitative problems).

(B) The affected academic skills are substantially and quantifiably below those expected for the individual's chronological age, and cause significant interference with academic or occupational performance, or with activities of daily living, as confirmed by individually administered standardized achievement measures and comprehensive clinical assessment. For individuals age 17 years and older, a documented history of impairing learning difficulties may be substituted for the standardized assessment.

(C) The learning difficulties begin during school-age years but may not become fully manifested capacities (e.g., as in timed tests, reading or writing lengthy complex reports for a tight deadline, excessively heavy academic loads).

(D) The learning difficulties are not better accounted for by intellectual disabilities, uncorrected visual or auditory acuity, other mental or neurological disorders, psychosocial adversity, lack of proficiency in the language of academic instruction, or inadequate educational instruction.

Omitted from the DSM definition but included within IDEA is the notion of difficulties with listening comprehension and oral language. Included within the DSM definition are the customary rule outs (e.g., intellectual disability; environmental, socioeconomic, and cultural factors; lack of adequate instruction; hearing, vision or other disabling conditions).

The DSM-5 generally suggests that a learning disability is predicated upon the following areas of academic achievement.

1. Word Decoding and fluency.
2. Reading comprehension.
3. Spelling.
4. Written expression.
5. Mathematical calculation and operations.
6. Mathematical reasoning.

The National Joint Committee on Learning Disabilities (NJCLD) comprises 11 organizations that conduct research in LD and academic achievement. The NJCLD approach to classification is presented next and presents a solid framework for LD identification.

NJCLD Definition

Learning disabilities is a general term that refers to a heterogeneous group of disorders manifested by significant difficulties in the acquisition and use of listening, speaking, reading, writing, reasoning, or mathematical abilities. These disorders are intrinsic to the individual, presumed to be due to central nervous system dysfunction, and may occur across the life span. Problems in self-regulatory behaviors, social perception, and social interaction may exist with learning disabilities but do not by themselves constitute a learning disability. Although learning disabilities may occur concomitantly with other handicapping conditions (for example, sensory impairment, mental retardation, serious emotional disturbance), or with extrinsic influences (such as cultural differences, insufficient or inappropriate instruction), they are not the result of those conditions or influences.

Instruments and Procedures for Comprehensive Assessment and Evaluation

To obtain a comprehensive set of quantitative and qualitative data, accurate and useful information about an individual student's status and needs must be derived from a variety of assessment instruments and procedures including RTI data, if available. A comprehensive assessment and evaluation should

1. Use a valid and the most current version of any standardized assessment.
2. Use multiple measures, including both standardized and nonstandardized assessments, and other data sources, such as

   - Case history and interviews with parents, educators, related professionals, and the student (if appropriate);
   - Evaluations and information provided by parents;
   - Direct observations that yield informal (e.g., anecdotal reports) or data-based information (e.g., frequency recordings) in multiple settings and on more than one occasion;
   - Standardized tests that are reliable and valid, as well as culturally, linguistically, developmentally, and age appropriate;
   - Curriculum-based assessments, task and error pattern analysis (e.g., miscue analysis), portfolios, diagnostic teaching, and other nonstandardized approaches;
   - Continuous progress monitoring repeated during instruction and over time.

(continued)

(continued)

3. Consider all components of the definition of specific learning disabilities in IDEA 2004 and/or its regulations, including

   - Exclusionary factors;
   - Inclusionary factors;
   - The eight areas of specific learning disabilities (i.e., oral expression, listening comprehension, written expression, basic reading skill, reading comprehension, reading fluency, mathematics calculation, mathematics problem solving);
   - The intra-individual differences in a student, as demonstrated by "a pattern of strengths and weaknesses in performance, achievement, or both relative to age, State-approved grade level standards or intellectual development" 34 CFR 300.309(a)(2)(ii).

4. Examine functioning and/or ability levels across domains of motor, sensory, cognitive, communication, and behavior, including specific areas of cognitive and integrative difficulties in perception; memory; attention; sequencing; motor planning and coordination; and thinking, reasoning, and organization.

5. Adhere to the accepted and recommended procedures for administration, scoring, and reporting of standardized measures. Express results that maximize comparability across measures (i.e., standard scores).
   Age or grade equivalents are not appropriate to report.

6. Provide confidence interval and standard error of measure, if available.

7. Integrate the standardized and informal data collected.

8. Balance and discuss the information gathered from both standardized and nonstandardized data, which describes the student's current level of academic performance and functional skills, and informs decisions about identification, eligibility, services, and instructional planning.

Source: Reproduced with permission. National Joint Committee on Learning Disabilities. (2010, June). *Comprehensive Assessment and Evaluation of Students With Learning Disabilities.* Retrieved on March 31, 2014 from www.ldonline.org/njcld.

NASP also produced a position statement regarding the identification of students with suspected learning disabilities. This position paper offers similar guidance to that of the NCJLD (e.g., comprehensive evaluation; rule out exclusionary features; does not mention use discrepancy; consider cultural and linguistic factors) but is slightly less specific.

148

11 Learning Disabilities

**NASP Position Regarding the Comprehensive Evaluation
of Children with Suspected Specific Learning Disabilities**

The National Association of School Psychologists (NASP) adopted a position statement on July 16, 2011 regarding the comprehensive evaluation of children with suspected learning disabilities. NASP indicates that the purpose of the evaluation for SLD is to gather relevant functional, developmental and academic information to determine eligibility and make recommendations regarding educational place and instructional interventions. The procedures recommended by NASP are presented below as adapted and reorganized.

1. Review data including prior evaluations, current classroom-based assessments, local or state assessments, classroom observations, and input from parents
2. Use a variety of assessments and other evaluation methods that must not be discriminatory on a racial or cultural basis and must be administered in the language that will yield accurate (i.e., reliable and valid) information.
3. Must consider whether the determining factor is the lack of appropriate instruction in reading or math, limited English proficiency, or cultural and linguistic differences.
4. Use assessment techniques that are culturally sensitive and adequately address the issues related to English language learners.
5. Identification and eligibility determinations should not be based on any single method or measure.
6. A comprehensive evaluation may include historical trends of performance and current measures of academic skills (norm-referenced, criterion-referenced, and/or curriculum-based), cognitive abilities and processes, and social–emotional competencies and oral language proficiency as appropriate; classroom observations; and indirect sources of data (e.g., teacher and parent reports).
7. When conducting the evaluation, look toward the evaluation's utility for subsequent intervention.

Source: Adapted from National Association of School Psychologists. (2011). *Identification of Students With Specific Learning Disabilities (Position Statement)*. Bethesda, MD: Author.

All major diagnostic taxonomies (i.e., IDEA and DSM) and agencies (e.g., NJCLD and NASP) recommend that LD be identified using a comprehensive evaluation based upon multiple methods of assessment and sources of data. NJCLD and DSM do not make reference to the IQ-Achievement discrepancy. IDEA permits use of the IQ-Achievement discrepancy. All three groups rule out visual, hearing and motor impairments along with intellectual disability and emotional issues. Additional rule outs include cultural factors, environmental factors, economic disadvantage and limited English proficiency.

11.4 General Guidance Regarding the Psychoeducational Assessment of Learning Disabilities

For psychologists working within a private practice or clinic the DSM is typically referenced for guidance regarding diagnosis. If the psychoeducational evaluation is conducted by an outside psychologist and is to be furnished to the school then the outside psychologist may wish to reference both IDEA and DSM when making a classification. This will increase the relevance of the outside evaluation and make a better case for an education classification when it is considered by the multidisciplinary team.

Outside clinicians are further cautioned about the need to observe the child within the school-based setting and acquire information from teachers including interview results and rating forms. These two features of assessment may be overlooked by the private practitioner, but will limit the relevance of the completed report.

Psychologists working in the schools should follow state guidelines when determining eligibility but may wish to consider the NJLCD's and NASP's position regarding identification of LD where flexibility of classification is offered. Whether the evaluation is conducted by a school psychologist or a psychologist in a private practice, the above two approaches offer appropriate guidance regarding assessment and identification. Of course, state guidelines, predicated upon IDEA, must be referred to when making a classification decision in the school.

11.5 Comment on Use of IQ Tests

Some argue that IQ is an unnecessary part of the comprehensive evaluation process. I am in disagreement with this perspective. IQ is one of the most extensively researched constructs in the field of psychology (Ceci & Williams, 1997; Dombrowski & Gischlar, 2014; Dombrowski et al., 2007; Kaufman & Litchenberger, 2006). It can be used to rule out ID and provides a sense of a child's academic trajectory. The literature is convincing in indicating that IQ is related to academic achievement. It may offer promise for some children and potentially set realistic expectations for others. It is a valuable metric and provides valuable information.

11.6 Conclusion

The assessment of LD in children is one of the most prevalent evaluations undertaken by child psychologists. Nearly 8 % of children in the schools are classified with an SLD. Assessment guidance is offered via agencies (e.g., NJCLD and NASP) and diagnostic systems (e.g., DSM and IDEA). Most systems and organizations are united in their expectation for a comprehensive evaluation for the identification of LD. Even though the DSM-5 may provide a more empirically grounded definition and diagnostic approach, IDEA and state regulations supersede the diagnostic criteria offered by DSM when making classification decisions in US public schools.

Appendix: LD Report Example

Psychological Report
Confidential

Name: Nick Jones   Date of Report: March 22, 2016
Date of Birth: 4/10/2008   Chronological Age: 7 years 11 months
Grade: 2nd   School: Goodwin Public Schools

Name of Examiner: Stefan C. Dombrowski, Ph.D.

Parent Name and Address: Cynthia Jones
                              1234 State Street
                              Philadelphia, PA 19138

Phone: 215-555-1234

Reason for Referral:
Nick struggles with all basic academic skills (e.g., reading, writing and mathematics) in the second grade curriculum. Specifically, Nick struggles with word decoding and comprehension of written text. He also struggles with expressing ideas in writing and with both math reasoning and mathematics calculation skills. Nick was referred for a comprehensive evaluation to determine his present level of functioning and whether he might qualify for specially designed instruction.

Assessment Methods and Sources of Data
Reynolds Intellectual Assessment Scale (RIAS)
Woodcock–Johnson Tests of Achievement, Fourth Edition (WJ-IV)
Bender Visual Motor Gestalt, Second Edition (Bender-2)
Comprehensive Test of Phonological Processing-Second Edition (CTOPP-2)
Wechsler Memory Scale-Fourth Edition (WMS-IV)
Behavior Assessment System for Children, Second Edition (BASC-2)

- Ms. Jenny McMahon (Second Grade Teacher)
Teacher Interview
- Ms. Jenny McMahon (Second Grade Teacher)
- Ms. Mia Riley (Reading Specialist)
Parent Interview
- Ms. Cynthia Jones (Mother)
Student Interview
- Nick Jones
Classroom Observations (2/10/16; 2/10/16)
Review of Academic Grade Reports
Review of School Records

Background Information and Developmental History
Nick is a 7-year-old second grade elementary school student who lives with his parents in Philadelphia, PA. He has received intensive intervention for his academic difficulties in the classroom but has failed to respond adequately to such intervention.

Prenatal, Perinatal, and Early Developmental History: Ms. Jones noted that Nick was born early at 32 weeks gestation weighing 4 lb 8 oz. She explained that Nick spent 11 days in the NICU and received bilirubin lights for jaundice. Ms. Jones was 35 years old at the birth of Nick. Ms. Jones indicated that Nick was evaluated for early intervention services but was not found eligible. Nick was slightly delayed in walking (14 months) but he sat up and rolled over at age expected limits. Ms. Jones indicated that Nick suffered from colic for the first 6 months of life and would scream most of the day over that time period. She explained that he began sleeping through the night at 8 months. Ms. Jones explained that Nick never really babbled as baby and just seemed to skip to talking. He spoke his first sentences at an age expected time period. Ms. Jones indicated that Nick was shy as a baby and protested vigorously when she left for work. All other early developmental milestones were attained within normal limits.

Medical: Nick's hearing is intact. He suffered from chronic otitis media and received hearing aids at age four as a result. Ms. Jones explained that Nick would continually be sick in daycare the first few years. She mentioned that he has fairly robust health but presently suffers from asthma. She notes that Nick contracted the RSV virus at 3 months of age and required hospitalization for a week. Nick wears glasses and has needed such since age 3. He has never suffered any head injury, and other infection.

Cognitive, Academic, and Language Functioning: Ms. Jones reports that Nick is a bright child but just struggles to understand basic academic skills. She noted that Nick can become frustrated as a result. Ms. Jones explained that she spends a great deal of time with Nick on his homework but that it just does not sink in. Ms. Jones wonders whether Nick has dyslexia. Ms. Jones explained that Nick really struggles with sounding out words and with spelling. She mentioned that he also struggles with mathematics and seems to confuse the signs. Ms. Jones noted that Nick receives support from the reading specialist but needs even more intense support. She explained that mathematics and writing are difficult for Nick as well.

Social-Emotional and Behavioral Functioning: Ms. Jones describes Nick as a quiet but well-liked child. He has many friends and gets along well with others. Ms. Jones indicated that Nick has never had a behavior problem at school. She commented on her concerns about his self-esteem, noting that Nick is beginning to feel badly about himself because of his difficulties at school.

Strengths: Nick is a compassionate and well-liked child with solid social skills. He participates in soccer and basketball. Nick is respectful of adults in the classroom. He is a gifted artist and loves drawing. Nick also plays piano.

Summary: Nick struggles with reading, writing, and mathematics, despite more intensive intervention in those areas. He is well behaved and gets along well with peers and adults alike. Nick is a competent artist and pianist.

Cognitive and Academic Functioning

Reynolds Intellectual Assessment Scale (RIAS)

Nick was administered the Reynolds Intellectual Assessment Scales (RIAS). The RIAS is an individually administered measure of intellectual functioning normed for individuals between the ages of 3 and 94 years. The RIAS contains several individual tests of intellectual problem solving and reasoning ability that are combined to form a Verbal Intelligence Index (VIX) and a Nonverbal Intelligence Index (NIX). The subtests that compose the VIX assess verbal reasoning ability along with the ability to access and apply prior learning in solving language-related tasks. Although labeled the Verbal Intelligence Index, the VIX is also a reasonable approximation of crystallized intelligence. The NIX comprises subtests that assess nonverbal reasoning and spatial ability. Although labeled the Nonverbal Intelligence Index, the NIX also provides a reasonable approximation of fluid intelligence and spatial ability. These two indexes of intellectual functioning are then combined to form an overall Composite Intelligence Index (CIX). By combining the VIX and the NIX into the CIX, a strong, reliable assessment of general intelligence *(g)* is obtained. The CIX measures the two most important aspects of general intelligence according to recent theories and research findings: reasoning or fluid abilities and verbal or crystallized abilities.

The RIAS also contains subtests designed to assess verbal memory and nonverbal memory. Depending upon the age of the individual being evaluated, the verbal memory subtest consists of a series of sentences, age-appropriate stories, or both, read aloud to the examinee. The examinee is then asked to recall these sentences or stories as precisely as possible. The nonverbal memory subtest consists of the presentation of pictures of various objects or abstract designs for a period of 5 s. The examinee is then shown a page containing six similar objects or figures and must discern which object or figure has previously been shown. The scores from the verbal memory and nonverbal memory subtests are combined to form a Composite Memory Index (CMX), which provides a strong, reliable assessment of working memory and may also provide indications as to whether or not a more detailed assessment of memory functions may be required. In addition, the high reliability of the verbal and nonverbal memory subtests allows them to be compared directly to each other.

Each of these indexes is expressed as an age-corrected standard score that is scaled to a mean of 100 and a standard deviation of 15. These scores are normally distributed and can be converted to a variety of other metrics if desired.

Following are the results of Nick's performance on the RIAS.

	Composite IQ	Verbal IQ	Nonverbal IQ	Memory index
RIAS index	94	95	96	92
Percentile	34	37	39	30
Confidence interval (95 %)	87–100	89–102	90–102	86–99

On testing with the RIAS, Nick earned a Composite Intelligence Index of 94. On the RIAS, this level of performance falls within the range of scores designated as average and exceeded the performance of 34 % of individuals at Nick's age. His Verbal IQ (Standard Score=95; 37th percentile) was in the average range and exceeded 37 % of individuals Nick's age. Nick's Nonverbal IQ (Standard Score=96; 39th percentiile) was in the average range, exceeding 39 % of individuals Nick's age. Nick earned a Composite Memory Index (CMX) of 92, which falls within the average range of working memory skills and exceeds the performance of 30 out of 100 individuals Nick's age.

Woodcock–Johnson Tests of Achievement-IV (WJ-IV)
The WJ-IV is an achievement test used to measure basic reading, writing, oral language, and mathematics skills. The Reading subtest includes letter and word identification, vocabulary, and comprehension skills. The Writing subtest includes spelling, writing fluency, and simple sentence writing. The Mathematics subtest includes calculation, practical problems, and knowledge of mathematical concepts and vocabulary.

Nick obtained the following scores in each of the areas of measurement:

	Standard score	Percentile	Descriptive classification
Broad reading	71	3	Below average
Letter-word ID	77	6	Below average
Sentence reading fluency	71	3	Below average
Passage comprehension	68	2	Below average
Broad writing	66	1	Below average
Sentence writing fluency	71	3	Below average
Writing samples	82	11	Low average
Spelling	67	1	Below average
Broad mathematics	76	5	Below average
Math facts fluency	71	3	Below average
Applied problems	78	8	Below average
Calculation	86	18	Low average

Standardized achievement test results revealed below average performance across all academic areas.

Bender Visual-Motor Gestalt Test, Second Edition (Bender-II)

The Bender-II measures visual-motor integration skills, or the ability to see and copy figures accurately. A quantitative and qualitative analysis of Nick's drawings suggests that his visual-motor integration abilities (e.g., fine motor skills for paper and pencil tasks) are high average (Copy Standard Score = 114; 82nd percentiile).

Comprehensive Test of Phonological Processing-Second Edition (CTOPP-2)

The CTOPP-2 is a standardized test of phonological processing that yield three composite scores: (1) Phonological Awareness; (2) Phonological Memory; and (3) Rapid Naming. The Phonological Awareness composite measures a student's ability to access the phonological structure of oral language. The Phonological Memory composite measures the ability to code information phonologically for temporary storage in working or short-term memory. The Rapid Naming Composite measures a student's ability to retrieve phonological information from memory and the ability to complete a sequence of operations quickly and repeatedly. Nick's performance across the three index composite areas was as follows:

	Scaled Score	Percentile	Description
Phonological awareness	71	3	Below average
Phonological memory	66	1	Below average
Rapid naming	77	6	Below average

Nick's profile on the CTOPP-2 revealed a child who falls within the below range. The current test administration appears to provide an accurate estimate of Nick's present phonological processing.

Wechsler Memory Scale-Fourth Edition (WMS-IV)

The WMS-IV is an individual memory test that yields five index scores: (1) Auditory Memory; (2) Visual Memory; (3) Visual Working Memory; (4) Immediate Memory; and (5) Delayed Memory. The Auditory Memory Index measures a student's ability to listen to oral information, repeat it immediately, and then repeat it again after a 20–30 min delay. The Visual Memory Index is a measure of visual details and spatial location. The Visual Working Memory Index is a measure of a student's ability to temporarily hold and manipulate spatial locations and visual details. The Immediate Memory Index measures recall of verbal and visual information immediately after a stimulus is presented. The Delayed Memory Index measures a student's ability to recall visual and verbal information after a 20–30 min delay.

Nick obtained the following scores in each of the areas of measurement:

	Standard score	Percentile	Confidence Interval (95 %)	Descriptive classification
Auditory memory	98	45	92–104	Average
Visual memory	95	37	90–101	Average
Visual working memory	103	58	96–110	Average
Immediate memory	105	63	99–111	Average
Delayed memory	88	31	82–95	Low average

Standardized memory test results revealed that Nick scored in the average range for all Indexes, with the exception of Delayed Memory which was in the Low Average range (88; 31st percentile).

Social-Emotional and Behavioral Functioning

Behavior Assessment System for Children, Second Edition (BASC-2)

The Behavior Assessment System for Children, Second Edition (BASC-2) is an integrated system designed to facilitate the differential diagnosis and classification of a variety of emotional and behavioral conditions in children. It possesses validity scales and several clinical scales, which reflect different dimensions of a child's personality. *T*-scores between 40 and 60 are considered average. Scores greater than 70 (*T* > 70) are in the Clinically Significant range and suggest a high level of difficulty. Scores in the At-Risk range (*T*-Score 60–69) identify either a significant problem that may not be severe enough to require formal treatment or a potential of developing a problem that needs careful monitoring. On the Adaptive Scales, scores below 30 are considered clinically significant while scores between 31 and 40 are considered at-risk.

	Ms. McMahon	
Clinical scales	*T*-score	Percentile
Hyperactivity	50	50
Aggression	45	35
Anxiety	62*	86
Depression	63*	89
Somatization	67*	93
Atypicality	48	47
Withdrawal	56	77
Attention problems	49	48
Adaptability	49	49
Social skills	57	65
Functional communication	45	35
Externalizing problems	48	47
Internalizing problems	64*	91
Behavioral symptoms index	51	53
Adaptive skills	53	62

*At-risk rating

BASC-2 ratings suggested an at-risk elevation on the internalizing behaviors composite with an average rating on the behavioral symptoms index and externalizing composite. BASC-2 rating suggested an at-risk elevation on the anxiety, depression and somatization clinical scales.

Interview Results

Student Interview (March 18, 2016): Nick was interviewed to ascertain impressions of his progress at school. Nick indicated that he likes school "because of the teachers." Nick explained that he struggles with reading and writing. He said that his progress in mathematics is "okay." When asked about his behavioral and social progress at school, Nick noted that his behavior at school is good and he generally does not get into trouble. He explained that he is a generally happy child. Nick discussed his fears. He noted that he is afraid of the dark. He also said that he is "not that smart." Nick stated that he has a number of friends at school. Nick stated that his strengths include sports, math, and drawing. He indicated that his hobbies include playing sports and playing video games.

Parent Interview (March 15, 2016): Ms. Cynthia Jones, Nick's mother, was interviewed to ascertain her impressions of Nick's cognitive, academic, social, and behavioral progress. Ms. Jones noted that Nick is "okay with mathematics." Ms. Jones explained that Nick struggles with mathematics when there are words problems. She explained that math today is different when she grew up in that it includes a lot of reading. Ms. Jones indicated, however, that Nick's main struggles are with reading, writing, and his memory. She also noted that his confidence level is down because of his academic struggles. Ms. Jones commented that socially, Nick is a very a very shy child and needs to speak up a bit more. Ms. Jones explained that Nick has always been a pleasant student to have in the classroom. This year, Ms. Jones explained that Nick seems to be a bit more defiant in class, noting that he has had two letters sent home which is different from prior years. Nick's strengths include being a pleasant and kind child and video games. She explained that he also plays piano. Ms. Jones also indicated that Nick can be very motivated about a task that interests him. Ms. Jones expressed concerns about the possibility that Nick will be retained. Ms. Jones stated that she is concerned that Nick will become resentful if he is retained. On the other hand, Ms. Jones explained that she does not want him to lose out on important academic information.

Teacher Interview (March 23, 2016): Ms. Jennifer McMahon, Nick's second grade teacher, was interviewed regarding Nick's academic, behavioral, emotional, social, and adaptive functioning. Ms. McMahon explained that Nick struggles with reading and she is really concerned about this. Ms. McMahon indicated that any language-based topic is difficult for Nick. Ms. McMahon explained that Nick regressed in reading this past summer and had forgotten his pre-reading/pre-literacy skills. Ms. McMahon indicated that phonological skills are a problem for Nick. She also mentioned that Nick has low sight word knowledge and places at the pre-primer level. Ms. McMahon explained that Nick's writing is also low. Ms. McMahon stated that Nick does okay in mathematics, but word problems (number stories) are hard for him. Ms. McMahon explained that Nick's strengths include his behavior, his pleasant demeanor, and his cheerful attitude about school despite his struggles. She also noted that Nick is imaginative and draws well.

Teacher Interview (April 5, 2016): Ms. Mia Riley, reading specialist, was asked to furnish her impressions of Nick's progress in school. Ms. Riley indicated that Nick is eager to learn and willing to try whatever is put in front of him. However, Ms. Riley explained that Nick struggles with phonological awareness and with sight word decoding. Ms. Riley comments that this impacts his comprehension of written text. Additionally, Ms. Riley stated that Nick struggles with spelling and writing at a grade expected level. She noted that he has good handwriting but really struggles with conveying information on paper. Ms. Riley explained that she has been working on fostering Nick's basic understanding of phonemic awareness skills.

Observations

Classroom Observation (March 25, 2016): Nick was observed for thirty minutes during math instruction led by Ms. McMahon's student-teacher. For the first ten minutes of the class, Nick was observed to be engaging in the whole group instruction. He was occasionally active at his seat where he would fidget with items and shift around. About ten minutes into the whole group instruction, Nick started working on math problems in his workbook though he also directed his gaze toward the student-teacher. Nick also was noted to occasionally doodle on a piece of paper during the instructional activity. After the math instruction, the class transitioned to the carpet area. Nick appropriately followed classroom rules, packed up his desk and went to the carpet. He sat attentively listening to the teacher read at story about being a good sport on a team. Two students near Nick were talking, but Nick continued to listen to the teacher read to the class. Impressions of the observation were that Nick was attentive to class instructions and engaged in the activity of the class.

Observation during Assessment: Throughout the assessment process, Nick was engaged and task persistent. He seemed to enjoy the one-on-one attention he received. At one point, Nick asked to use the restroom but returned and quickly resumed engagement in the testing activities. Nick was responsive to the evaluator's questions of him. His affect and mood were positive. He maintained a high energy level. The results appear to be a valid representation of his abilities.

Conceptualization and Classification

Multiple data sources and methods of assessment inform the conceptualization of Nick's cognitive, academic, social-emotional, and behavioral functioning including whether he qualifies for special education support. Details in support of these findings are offered below.

Cognitive and Academic Functioning: Nick's overall cognitive ability is in the average range (Standard score = 94; 34th percentiile). According to cognitive assessment results, Nick's working memory abilities fall in the average range (Standard score = 92; 30th percentiile). Nick struggled on a measure of phonological awareness generally scoring in the low average to below average range on this measure (CTOPP-2). His standardized academic achievement test results were similarly below average across the reading, writing and mathematics clusters. Nick faces considerable struggles with the academic curriculum. He has received additional, more intensive intervention via the reading specialist. Nick receives outside tutoring support.

Social-Emotional and Behavioral Functioning: Nick is a well-liked child who gets along with peers and adults alike. He can be compassionate and caring. Nick has several close friends and a host of extracurricular activities including athletics, drawing, and piano. Nick is a quiet child who is anxious and self-conscious about his performance in school. This is supported by interview results and BASC-2 ratings in the at-risk range on anxiety. Nick is also beginning to struggle with self-esteem and feel badly about himself. Again, this is consistent with elevations of the BASC-2 and supported by parent interview results. Nick's difficulty with anxiety and self-esteem should continue to be monitored.

Summary: Based upon multiple methods and sources of evaluation including the dual academic deficit model of learning disabilities supported by clinical judgment, the IEP team concludes that Nick qualifies for special education services under a diagnosis of learning disabilities.

Summary and Recommendations

Nick's overall cognitive ability falls within the average range. Nick's performance on measures of academic achievement (WJ-III Achievement) was in the average to low average range. Based on teacher interview results, review of academic records, standardized test performance, student observations, parent interview results, and current classroom performance, Nick qualifies for special education services under a diagnosis of learning disabilities.

Considering Nick's performance on measures of achievement and cognitive ability, combined with actual classroom performance, academic grade reports, parent interviews, behavior observations, and teacher interviews, Nick continues to be eligible for special education support. The team concludes that specially designed instruction is called for at this time. The following recommendations might benefit Nick.

1. *Support for Difficulties with Reading Comprehension, Phonological Awareness, Sight Word Recognition, Word Decoding, and Reading Fluency*: Nick struggles with all aspects of reading including word decoding, phonological/phonemic awareness, reading fluency and reading comprehension. Nick requires specially designed instruction for his reading difficulties as noted below.

   (a) *Phonological Awareness and Sight Word Knowledge Skills.* Nick will benefit from continued intervention with basic phonemic awareness skills, such as emphasizing instruction on basic rimes (ack, ame, all, ake). Nick would be well served to increase his familiarity with reading fundamentals through a focus on words via alliteration lessons (e.g., tongue twisters), a personal dictionary of sight words (i.e., most frequently used words), and word family study (e.g., neat, beat, heat; noise, poise, choice).

   (b) *Reading fluency.* Nick should practice oral reading fluency. Accordingly, Nick will benefit from repeated reading of the passage until an appropriate grade level fluency rate is attained. The research literature suggests that improvements in oral reading fluency via repeated passage reading generalizes to improvements in overall reading ability.

(c) *Reading Comprehension.* Nick struggles with the comprehension of written text and will benefit from pre-reading and organizational strategies that attempt to improve this skill area. Following are a few suggestions that will likely benefit Nick:

  (i) Before reading, preview the text by looking at the title and illustrations.
  (ii) Encourage the creation of a possible story from the illustrations.
  (iii) Make predictions about the story based on story features prior to reading the story.
  (iv) During reading, generate questions about the story that are directly related to the text and that require thinking beyond the text.
  (v) After reading, spend time reflecting upon the material and relating it to experiences and events the child has encountered.
  (vi) After reading, have Nick engage in the reading material using text summarizing.

2. *Difficulties with Writing*: Nick struggles with written expression including spelling. Accordingly she will benefit from the following recommendations.

  (A) *Written Expression*: Nick struggles with expressing her ideas in written form. The recommendations may be appropriate for her:

    (i) Assist Nick in generating ideas about a topic and then show him how to put the ideas in an outline.
    (ii) Demonstrate for Nick outlining principles. Have him practice what you just demonstrated so that he can distinguish between main ideas and supporting ideas.
    (iii) Assist Nick in creating a paragraph and then show him that that paragraphs require an introduction, a middle, and a conclusion. Require that Nick generate his own paragraph and offer corrective feedback.
    (iv) Require Nick to proofread his written work and provide corrective feedback when appropriate.

  (B) *Spelling*: Nick struggles with spelling words in a phonetically plausible manner and the following recommendations may be appropriate for him:

    (i) Have Nick practice spelling words each day that require selected phonetic sounds. Introduce new words as Nick has mastered the old words. The Cover, Copy, Compare or Folding-in techniques are appropriate for this purpose and have strong research support learning new spelling words.
    (ii) Ensure that Nick hears correctly the sounds in the words that she misspells. Require Nick to read the words aloud to determine whether he recognizes the letter units or phonemes in the words.

    (iii) Require Nick to use a phonetic approach to spelling any words he does not know how to spell.

    (iv) Permit Nick to practice spelling through a computer software program that provides immediate corrective feedback.

(C) *Math Word Problems*: Nick struggles with mathematics word problems and will benefit from the following recommendations.

    (a) Ask Nick to identify the primary question that is to be answered to solve the word problem. Make sure the student understands that extraneous information is sometimes included in a math word problem.

    (b) Teach Nick to look for hint words in word problems that indicate the mathematical operations.

    (c) Have Nick restate the math word problem in his own words.

    (d) Teach Nick to break down the math word problem into specific steps before attempting to solve it.

    (e) Provide Nick a list of phrases or word that usually indicate an addition (e.g., sum, in all, total, altogether) and subtraction (e.g., difference, how many left, how many remain).

3. *Self-Esteem*: Background information suggests that Nick's academic difficulties have contributed to reduced self-confidence and a tendency to give up more readily when faced with tasks he perceives as difficult. Nick should be offered additional support, encouragement, and praise for effort made toward completing tasks.

Stefan C. Dombrowski, Ph.D.
Licensed Psychologist
Certified School Psychologist

LD Report Example 2 with Concurrent ADHD Diagnosis

Psychological Report
Confidential

Name: Matthew Osbourne   Date of Report: October 30, 2013
Date of Birth: 11/1/2006   Chronological Age: 7
Grade: 1   School: Hopewell Public School
Name of Examiner: Stefan Dombrowski

Parent and Address: Sharon Osbourne

Phone: (609) 555-1234

Reason for Referral:
Background information and teacher reports reveal that Matthew struggles with reading and writing. Specifically, Matthew experiences difficulty with oral reading fluency and comprehension of written information. He also struggles with quickly and efficiently producing written work. Additionally, Matthew's faces difficulties with attention, hyperactivity and distractibility. Matthew was referred for a comprehensive evaluation to determine his present level of functioning and whether or not he might qualify for specially designed instruction.

Assessment Methods and Sources of Data

Reynolds Intellectual Assessment Scale (RIAS)
Woodcock–Johnson Tests of Achievement, Fourth Edition (WJ-IV)
Bender Visual Motor Gestalt, Second Edition (Bender-2)
Behavior Assessment System for Children—Second Edition (BASC-2)

– Ms. Mindy Kaling (First Grade Teacher)
– Ms. Sharon Osbourne (Mother)
Teacher Interview
– Ms. Mindy Kaling (First Grade Teacher)
Parent Interview
– Ms. Sharon Osbourne
Student Interview
– Matthew Osbourne
Classroom Observations (10/2/2013)
Review of Academic Grade Reports
Review of School Records

Background Information and Developmental History

Matthew Osbourne is a 7-year-old child in the first grade at the Hopewell Public School (HPS). Matthew faces difficulty with paying attention, organization, and remaining on task. Background information revealed difficulty with reading comprehension. Ms. Osbourne indicates that Matthew has been diagnosed with Attention-Deficit/Hyperactivity Disorder (ADHD) and Oppositional Defiant Disorder (ODD). Matthew is not presently taking any medication for the management of his symptoms, but Ms. Osbourne reports that he is scheduled for a psychotropic medication evaluation in mid-October.

Prenatal, Perinatal, and Early Developmental History: Ms. Osbourne noted that she had gestational diabetes. Matthew was born with Erb's Palsy at 37 weeks weighing 9 lb. He had a 2 week stay in the Neonatal Intensive Care (NICU). Matthew's early developmental milestones were generally attained within normal limits with the exception of walking. Matthew was slightly delayed and did not walk until 14 months of age.

Medical: Ms. Osbourne indicated that Matthew is not currently taking any medications but suffers from migraines. Matthew will be evaluated by a child psychiatrist mid-October for possible psychotropic medication. Matthew's hearing and vision are intact. Ms. Osbourne reported no incidence of head injury or major infection.

Cognitive, Academic, and Language Functioning: Background information and teacher reports indicate that Matthew struggles with reading and writing. Ms. Kaling commented that Matthew's reading is below level, noting that he rarely stays focused on the lesson or during independent reading time. Ms. Kaling also mentioned that Matthew's writing is similarly below level again noting that he rarely stays focused on the lesson or during independent writing time. Teacher reports confirmed difficulties with these academic areas. Background reports indicated that Matthew's mathematics progress is at grade level. She indicated that he has a good understanding of the current unit (e.g., addition, although he sometimes misses parts of problems because he does not (or cannot) read all of the instructions).

Social-Emotional and Behavioral Functioning: Ms. Kaling indicated that Matthew is a friendly child. Every once in a while he gets upset and stomps/throws pencils/ slams his book. He usually calms down but he can sulk for a long time. She noted that he needs to pay attention to whole class instruction, stay focused on independent work, keep his body under control by not bothering those around him, and listen to and follow teachers' instructions. Ms. Kaling indicated that Matthew has been sent to the ReSet room numerous times and this sometimes seems to help his behavior.

Strengths: Matthew's strengths include helping out around the classroom when asked by a teacher. He has also been described as a child with good artistic ability, a good sense of humor and one who enjoys life.

Summary: Matthew struggles with symptoms of inattentiveness, hyperactivity, and impulsivity. He also struggles with comprehension of written text. Matthew enjoys helping in the classroom and wants to do well at school. He struggles with both academics and behavior at school.

Interview Results

Parent Interview (October 6, 2013): Ms. Sharon Osbourne was contacted to ascertain impressions of Matthew's academic, behavioral, and social-emotional functioning at school. Ms. Osbourne commented first regarding Matthew's behavioral issues. She noted that he has been diagnosed with ADHD and ODD. Commenting next on Matthew's academic progress, Ms. Osbourne noted that Matthew struggles with reading and his handwriting can be sloppy. Ms. Osbourne indicated that his mathematics is okay. She indicated that her concerns are "more behavioral than academic." Ms. Osbourne commented that at school Matthew was suspended last year in kindergarten. She noted that his records indicated that Matthew hit the teacher, although Matthew has a different account of what happened. Ms. Osbourne explained that she has tried to get the suspension removed from his record, but the teacher is no longer working at the school so the school would not remove the suspension. Ms. Osbourne indicated that Matthew has a few additional instances of not listening, not controlling his body, being put in time out from recess, and where he had to be picked him up early from school. Ms. Osbourne explained that he was sent home once thus far this year. She noted that Matthew has some good days. Commenting next on his social progress, Ms. Osbourne indicated that socially Matthew is okay as long as other kids do not do anything to trigger his anger. Ms. Osbourne discussed Matthew's areas of strength and need. She noted that he can focus for long periods if he is interested in a topic. Ms. Osbourne also indicted that Matthew likes to draw and play outside. She noted that Math is one of his strengths. She also mentioned that Matthew is very athletic and loves to play all types of sports.

Student Interview (October 10, 2013): Matthew was interviewed to ascertain impressions of his progress at HCS. Matthew stated that he likes HCS especially discovery, art and recess. When asked about his academic progress, Matthew explained that mathematics is sometimes difficult for him, but reading and writing are good. Matthew next discussed his behavior at school. He explained that he sometimes gets into trouble for "doing something bad." When asked to elaborate, Matthew indicted that he once went to CARES for making noises with his throat. Matthew indicated that he has several friends. He stated that he enjoys going outside and playing.

Teacher Interview (June 3, 2013): Ms. Mindy Kaling, Matthew's first grade teacher, was interviewed regarding Matthew's academic, behavioral, emotional, and social functioning. Ms. Kaling provided the following information. She stated that Matthew's reading and writing are both below grade level. Ms. Kaling explained that Matthew can demonstrate some level of competence if a teacher is able to sit with him and coach him.

Observations

Classroom Observation (October 2, 2013): Matthew was observed for 15 min in Ms. Kaling's classroom. The observation occurred during a reading activity where students were being instructed on how to make connections between books with a partner. During this whole group instruction, Matthew was observed to sit attentively and listen to Ms. Kaling. When the activity shifted and students were asked to partner with another student to share their connections, Matthew again complied with this request. Impressions of the observation were that Matthew was on task and compliant with teacher requests.

Observation during Assessment: Matthew was very compliant during the beginning of assessment, though he struggled in both cognitive and achievement tests. Matthew grew frustrated during the passage comprehension subtest of the WJ-III and was furnished with encouragement for his efforts on this subtest. Matthew responded well to encouragement and was engaged in the subtest. Test results are considered a valid representation of Matthew's abilities.

Cognitive and Academic Functioning

Reynolds Intellectual Assessment Scale (RIAS)

Matthew was administered the Reynolds Intellectual Assessment Scales (RIAS). The RIAS is an individually administered measure of intellectual functioning normed for individuals between the ages of 3 and 94 years. The RIAS contains several individual tests of intellectual problem solving and reasoning ability that are combined to form a Verbal Intelligence Index (VIX) and a Nonverbal Intelligence Index (NIX). The subtests that compose the VIX assess verbal reasoning ability along with the ability to access and apply prior learning in solving language-related tasks. Although labeled the Verbal Intelligence Index, the VIX is also a reasonable approximation of crystallized intelligence. The NIX comprises subtests that assess nonverbal reasoning and spatial ability. Although labeled the Nonverbal Intelligence Index, the NIX also provides a reasonable approximation of fluid intelligence and spatial ability. These two indexes of intellectual functioning are then combined to form an overall Composite Intelligence Index (CIX). By combining the VIX and the NIX into the CIX, a strong, reliable assessment of general intelligence (g) is obtained. The CIX measures the two most important aspects of general intelligence according to recent theories and research findings: reasoning or fluid abilities and verbal or crystallized abilities.

The RIAS also contains subtests designed to assess verbal memory and nonverbal memory. Depending upon the age of the individual being evaluated, the verbal memory subtest consists of a series of sentences, age-appropriate stories, or both, read aloud to the examinee. The examinee is then asked to recall these sentences or stories as precisely as possible. The nonverbal memory subtest consists of the presentation of pictures of various objects or abstract designs for a period of 5 s. The examinee is then shown a page containing six similar objects or figures and must discern which object or figure has previously been shown. The scores from the verbal memory and nonverbal memory subtests are combined to form a Composite Memory Index (CMX), which provides a strong, reliable assessment of working memory and may also provide indications as to whether or not a more detailed assessment of memory functions may be required. In addition, the high reliability of the verbal and nonverbal memory subtests allows them to be compared directly to each other.

Each of these indexes is expressed as an age-corrected standard score that is scaled to a mean of 100 and a standard deviation of 15. These scores are normally distributed and can be converted to a variety of other metrics if desired.

Following are the results of Matthew's performance on the RIAS.

	Composite IQ	Verbal IQ	Nonverbal IQ	Memory index
RIAS index	84	79	93	97
Percentile	14	8	32	42
Confidence interval (95 %)	79–90	73–87	87–100	91–103

On testing with the RIAS, Matthew earned a Composite Intelligence Index of 84. On the RIAS, this level of performance falls within the range of scores designated as low average and exceeded the performance of 14 % of individuals at Matthew's age. His Verbal IQ (Standard Score = 79; 8th percentile) was in the below average range and exceeded 8 % of individuals Matthew's age. Matthew's Nonverbal IQ (Standard Score = 93; 32nd percentile) was in the average range, exceeding 32 % of individuals Matthew's age. Matthew earned a Composite Memory Index (CMX) of 97, which falls within the average range of working memory skills and exceeds the performance of 42 out of 100 individuals Matthew's age.

Woodcock–Johnson Tests of Achievement-IV (WJ-IV)

The WJ-IV is an achievement test used to measure basic reading, writing, oral language, and mathematics skills. The Reading subtest includes letter and word identification, vocabulary, and comprehension skills. The Writing subtest includes spelling, writing fluency, and simple sentence writing. The Mathematics subtest includes calculation, practical problems, and knowledge of mathematical concepts and vocabulary.

Matthew obtained the following scores in each of the areas of measurement:

	Standard score	Percentile	Descriptive classification
Broad Reading	79	8	Below average
Letter-word ID	89	23	Low average
Passage comprehension	79	8	Below average
Sentence reading fluency	77	7	Below average
Broad writing	87	20	Low average
Sentence writing fluency	79	8	Below average
Writing samples	92	29	Average
Spelling	92	30	Average
Broad mathematics	93	32	Average
Math facts fluency	95	38	Average
Applied problems	99	48	Average
Calculation	90	25	Average

Standardized achievement test results revealed below average performance across broad reading cluster, low average broad writing performance and average performance on the mathematics cluster.

Bender Visual-Motor Gestalt Test, Second Edition (Bender-II)

The Bender-II measures visual-motor integration skills, or the ability to see and copy figures accurately. A quantitative and qualitative analysis of Matthew's drawings suggests that his visual-motor integration abilities (e.g., fine motor skills for paper and pencil tasks) are low average (Copy Standard Score=81; 10th percentiile).

Comprehensive Test of Phonological Processing-Second Edition (CTOPP-2)

The CTOPP-2 is a standardized test of phonological processing that yield three composite scores: (1) Phonological Awareness; (2) Phonological Memory; and (3) Rapid Naming. The Phonological Awareness composite measures a student's ability to access the phonological structure of oral language. The Phonological Memory composite measures the ability to code information phonologically for temporary storage in working or short-term memory. The Rapid Naming Composite measures a student's ability to retrieve phonological information from memory and the ability to complete a sequence of operations quickly and repeatedly. Matthew's performance across the three index composite areas was as follows:

	Scaled Score	Percentile	Description
Phonological awareness	121	92	Above average
Phonological memory	100	50	Average
Rapid naming	118	88	High average

Matthew's profile on the CTOPP-2 revealed a child who falls within the average range. The current test administration appears to provide an accurate estimate of Sofia's present phonological processing.

Social-Emotional and Behavioral Functioning

Behavior Assessment System for Children, Second Edition (BASC-2)
The Behavior Assessment System for Children, Second Edition (BASC-2) is an integrated system designed to facilitate the differential diagnosis and classification of a variety of emotional and behavioral conditions in children. It possesses validity scales and several clinical scales, which reflect different dimensions of a child's personality. Scores in the Clinically Significant range (*T*-Score >70) suggest a high level of difficulty. Scores in the At-Risk range (*T*-Score 65–69) identify either a significant problem that may not be severe enough to require formal treatment or a potential of developing a problem that needs careful monitoring. On the Adaptive Scales, scores below 30 are considered clinically significant while scores between 31 and 35 are considered at-risk.

	Ms. Kaling		Ms. Osbourne	
Clinical scales	*T*-Score	Percentile	*T*-Score	Percentile
Hyperactivity	85**	99	72**	95
Aggression	72**	95	66*	92
Conduct problems	85**	99	71**	93
Anxiety	43	26	54	67
Depression	47	51	59	85
Somatization	46	46	45	44
Attention problems	73**	99	75**	96
Learning problems	73**	99	73**	99
Atypicality	43	19	45	23
Withdrawal	55	74	53	70
Adaptability	30**	3	32*	5
Social skills	40	20	40	22
Leadership	47	43	45	40
Study skills	38*	15	–	–
Functional communication	43	25	44	28
Activities of daily living	–	–	41	26
Externalizing problems	83**	99	74**	96
Internalizing problems	44	30	45	32
Behavioral symptoms index	66*	93	64*	90
Adaptive skills	38*	12	40	14
School problems	67*	94	–	–

*At-risk rating
**Clinically significant rating

The above results indicate clinically significant elevations on externalizing problems composite with an at-risk score on the adaptive skills composite and behavioral symptoms index. The above results also indicate clinically significant elevations on the hyperactivity, aggression, conduct problems, attention problems, learning problems, and adaptability (at-risk for parent rating) clinical scales.

Conceptualization and Classification

Multiple data sources and methods of assessment inform the conceptualization of Matthew's cognitive, academic, social-emotional, and behavioral functioning including whether he qualifies for special education support. Details in support of these findings are offered below.

Cognitive and Academic Functioning: Matthew's present performance on measures of cognitive ability was low average (Composite IQ = 84, 14th percentile; VIQ = 79, 8th percentile; NIQ = 93, 32nd percentile). Matthew's performance on the WJ-IV Achievement was below average in reading, low average in writing and average in mathematics. This performance is consistent with teacher reports where Matthew was noted to struggle with reading, perform higher in writing with structure and support, and be at grade level in mathematics.

Social and Emotional Functioning: Matthew is described as a child who struggles with attention, loss of focus, distractibility, and hyperactivity. This is consistent with BASC-2 results where he scored in the clinically significant range on the inattention and hyper-activity clinical scales. Background information and standardized behavior rating scales revealed that Matthew sometimes disregards classroom rules and teacher requests and needs structure and support for these difficulties. Although Matthew will sulk when redirected, he is generally able to gather himself and return to the task required of him. Matthew can be a helpful child when a teacher requests his assistance.

Summary: Based upon multiple methods and sources of evaluation including the dual academic deficit model of learning disabilities supported by clinical judgment, the IEP team concludes that Matthew qualifies for special education services under a diagnosis of learning disabilities. Matthew will also benefit from support for his attention-related difficulties.

Summary and Recommendations

Matthew's overall cognitive ability falls within the low average range. Matthew's performance on measures of academic achievement (WJ-III) was in the below aver-age to average range. Based on teacher interview results, review of academic records, standardized test performance, student observations, parent interview results, and current classroom performance, Matthew qualifies for special education services under a diagnosis of learning disabilities. The team concludes that specially designed instruction is called for at this time. The following recommendations might benefit Matthew.

1. *Strategies for difficulties with Attention, Distractibility, and Loss of Focus*:
   Background reports indicate that Matthew experiences difficulty with attention
   and distractibility. As such, the following recommendations might be beneficial
   for him:

   (A) *Seating*. Matthew should continue to sit in a location where there are mini
       mal distractions.

   (B) *Provision of Directions by Teacher:* When Matthew's teachers interact with
       him, he should be encouraged to repeat and explain instructions to ensure
       understanding. The provision of directions to Matthew will be most effec-
       tive when the teacher makes eye contact, avoids multiple commands, is
       clear and to the point, and permits repetition of directions when needed or
       asked for.

   (C) *Positive Reinforcement and Praise for Successful Task Completion:*
       Matthew's teachers should provide positive reinforcement and immediate
       feedback for completion of desired behaviors or tasks. Initially, praise and
       reinforcement should be offered for successful effort on a task or behavior
       regardless of quality of performance.

   (D) *Time on Task*: Communicate to Matthew how long he will need to engage in
       or pay attention on a particular task. Open ended expectations can be dis-
       tressing to any child, let alone one with attentional difficulties.

   (E) *Prepare Student Discreetly for Transitions*: Furnish Matthew with verbal
       prompts and visual cues that a new activity or task is about to start. This
       should be accomplished discreetly so as to avoid student embarrassment.

   (F) *Recess Time*: Matthew should be permitted to participate in recess. Recess
       should not be a time to complete unfinished classwork or homework.

   (G) *Extended Time, Teacher Check In's, and Frequent Breaks*: Matthew should
       be permitted additional time to complete academic tasks and projects.
       Matthew's teachers should also consider review of classwork as Matthew
       progresses on an assignment or project to assist Matthew in avoiding
       careless mistakes. More frequent breaks than what is typical may also
       reduce careless mistakes and help to maintain focus.

2. *Support for Difficulties with Reading Comprehension, Phonological Awareness,
   Sight Word Recognition, Word Decoding, and Reading Fluency*: Matthew struggles with all aspects of reading including word decoding, phonological/phone-
   mic awareness, reading fluency and reading comprehension. Matthew requires
   specially designed instruction for his reading difficulties, as noted below.

   (A) *Phonological Awareness and Sight Word Knowledge Skills*. Mattthew will
       benefit from continued intervention with basic phonemic awareness skills,
       such as emphasizing instruction on basic rimes (ack, ame, all, ake). Mattthew
       would be well served to increase his familiarity with reading fundamentals
       through a focus on words via alliteration lessons (e.g., tongue twisters), a

personal dictionary of sight words (i.e., most frequently used words), and word family study (e.g., neat, beat, heat; noise, poise, choice).

(B) *Reading fluency.* Mattthew should practice oral reading fluency. Accordingly, Mattthew will benefit from repeated reading of the passage until an appropriate grade level fluency rate is attained. The research literature suggests that improvements in oral reading fluency via repeated passage reading generalizes to improvements in overall reading ability.

(C) *Reading Comprehension.* Matthew struggles with the comprehension of written text and will benefit from pre-reading and organizational strategies that attempt to improve this skill area. Following are a few suggestions that will likely benefit Mattthew:

    (i) Before reading, preview the text by looking at the title and illustrations.

    (ii) Encourage the creation of a possible story from the illustrations.

    (iii) Make predictions about the story based on story features prior to reading the story.

    (iv) During reading, generate questions about the story that are directly related to the text and that require thinking beyond the text.

    (v) After reading, spend time reflecting upon the material and relating it to experiences and events the child has encountered.

    (vi) After reading, have Matthew engage in the reading material using text summarizing.

3. *Support for Writing*: Matthew struggles with written expression, which requires sustained attention and organization, but performs better with support and structure. Matthew will require additional assistance in this area.

(A) *Written Expression*: Mattthew struggles with expressing her ideas in written form. The recommendations may be appropriate for him:

    (i) Assist Matthew in generating ideas about a topic and then show him how to put the ideas in an outline.

    (ii) Demonstrate for Matthew outlining principles. Have him practice what you just demonstrated so that he can distinguish between main ideas and supporting ideas.

    (iii) Assist Matthew in creating a paragraph and then show him that that paragraphs require an introduction, a middle, and a conclusion. Require that Mattthew generate him own paragraph and offer corrective feedback.

    (iv) Require Matthew to proofread him written work and provide corrective feedback when appropriate.

(B) *Spelling*: Matthew struggles with spelling words in a phonetically plausible manner and the following recommendations may be appropriate for him:

    (i) Have Matthew practice spelling words each day that require selected phonetic sounds. Introduce new words as Matthew has mastered the old words. The Cover, Copy, Compare or Folding-in techniques are appropriate for this purpose and have strong research support learning new spelling words.

(ii) Ensure that Matthew hears correctly the sounds in the words that he misspells. Require Matthew to read the words aloud to determine whether he recognizes the letter units or phonemes in the words.

(iii) Require Matthew to use a phonetic approach to spelling any words he does not know how to spell.

(iv) Permit Matthew to practice spelling through a computer software program that provides immediate corrective feedback.

Stefan C. Dombrowski, Ph.D.
Licensed Psychologist (PA and NJ)
Certified School Psychologist (PA and NJ)

References

Aaron, P. G. (1997). The impending demise of the discrepancy formula. *Review of Educational Research, 67*, 461–502.

Bateman, B. (1965). Learning disabilities: An overview. *Journal of School Psychology, 3*(3), 1–12.

Boyle, C. A., Boulet, S., Schieve, L. A., Cohen, R. A., Blumberg, S. J., Yeargin-Allsopp, S. V., & Kogan, M. D. (2011). Trends in the prevalence of developmental disabilities in US Children, 1997–2008. Pediatrics. Retrieved May 22, 2014 from http://pediatrics.aappublications.org/content/early/2011/05/19/peds.2010-2989

Ceci, S. J., & Williams, W. M. (1997). Schooling, intelligence, and income. *American Psychologist, 52*, 1051–1058.

Dombrowski, S. C., Ambrose, D. A., & Clinton, A. (2007). Dogmatic insularity in learning disabilities diagnosis and the critical need for a philosophical analysis. *International Journal of Special Education, 22*(1), 3–10.

Dombrowski, S. C., & Gischlar, K. L. (2014). Ethical and empirical considerations in the Identification of learning disabilities. *Journal of Applied School Psychology, 30*, 68–82.

Dombrowski, S. C., Kamphaus, R. W., et al. (2006). The Solomon Effect in learning disabilities diagnosis: Have we not yet learned from history? *School Psychology Quarterly, 21*(3), 359–373.

Dombrowski, S. C., Kamphaus, R. W., & Reynolds, C. R. (2004). After the demise of the discrepancy: Proposed approach to learning disabilities classification. *Professional Psychology: Research and Practice, 35*(4), 364–372.

Hinshelwood, J. (1917). *Congenital word blindness*. London: HK Lewis.

Individuals with Disabilities Education Improvement Act of 2004 (IDEA), Pub. L. No. 108–446, 118 Stat. 2647 (2004). [Amending 20 U.S.C. §§ 1400 et seq.].

Kaufman, A. S., & Litchenberger, E. O. (2006). *Assessing adolescent and adult intelligence* (3rd ed.). Hoboken, NJ: Wiley.

Kirk, S. A. (1962). *Educating exceptional children*. Boston: Houghton Mifflin.

Kirk, S. A. (1981). Learning disabilities: A historical note. *Academic Therapy, 17*(1), 5–11.

Kirk, S. A., & Bateman, B. (1962). Diagnosis and remediation of learning disabilities. *Exceptional Children, 29*(2), 73–78.

Lyon, G. R. (1995). Toward a definition of dyslexia. *Annals of Dyslexia, 45*, 3–27.

Mercer, C. D., Forgnone, C., & Wolking, W. D. (1976). Definitions of learning disabilities used in the United States. *Journal of Learning Disabilities, 9*, 376–386.

National Association of School Psychologists. (2011). *Identification of students with specific learning disabilities (position statement).* Bethesda, MD: Author.

National Joint Committee on Learning Disabilities. (2010, June). Comprehensive assessment and evaluation of students with learning disabilities. Retrieved March 31, 2014 from www.ldonline.org/njcld

Orton, S. (1925). Word blindness in school children. *Archives of Neurology and Psychiatry, 14*, 581–613.

Rutter, M., & Yule, W. (1975). The concept of specific reading retardation. *Journal of Child Psychology and Psychiatry, 16*, 181–197.

Siegel, L. S. (1999). Issues in the definition and diagnosis of learning disabilities: A perspective on Guckenberger v. Boston University. *Journal of Learning Disabilities, 32*(4), 304–319.

Yule, W. (1973). Differential prognosis of reading backwardness and specific reading retardation. *British Journal of Educational Psychology, 43*, 244–248.

Chapter 12
Autism

12.1 Overview

The prevalence of autism within the general population is estimated at approximately 0.47 % (Boyle et al., 2011). Certain states, such as New Jersey, report a considerably higher prevalence at 2.22 % (Baio, 2014). Within the DSM, the definition of autism spectrum disorder has recently been revised and eliminated Asperger's and Rhett's Disorder from the fifth edition. Individuals previously classified with Asperger's will now likely receive the classification of high functioning autism. The authors of the DSM reported that the change reflected a more empirically sound approach despite the disapproval of some in the lay and practitioner community.

12.2 Definition of Autism Within IDEA

(i) Autism means a developmental disability significantly affecting verbal and nonverbal communication and social interaction, generally evident before age three, that adversely affects a child's educational performance. Other characteristics often associated with autism are engagement in repetitive activities and stereotyped movements, resistance to environmental change or change in daily routines, and unusual responses to sensory experiences.

(ii) Autism does not apply if a child's educational performance is adversely affected primarily because the child has an emotional disturbance, as defined in paragraph (c)(4) of this section.

(iii) A child who manifests the characteristics of autism after age three could be identified as having autism if the criteria in paragraph (c)(1)(i) of this section are satisfied.

© Springer Science+Business Media New York 2015   175
S.C. Dombrowski, *Psychoeducational Assessment and Report Writing*,
DOI 10.1007/978-1-4939-1911-6_12

The IDEA definition of autism does not furnish detailed guidance regarding classification. It still lacks a specific description of the characteristics of ASD. Because of this, some psychologists look to the DSM-5's definition and diagnostic approach to assist with the classification of autism with the understanding IDEA/state procedures drive classification decisions in the public schools. Be cautious about the temptation to be overly reliant on the DSM. The classification decision should still be predicated upon the IDEA definition when working in a public school district (Zirkell, 2011).

12.3   Definition of Autism Within DSM-5

The DSM-5 definition and diagnostic approach may be referenced as a resource to assist with the classification of ASD under IDEA. It may help to clarify decision-making as it furnishes additional details and examples of ASD. When making a private practice, clinic-based or agency diagnosis the DSM-5 is the resource that is customarily referenced.

Autism Spectrum Disorder 299.00

A. Deficits in social communication and social interaction across multiple contexts as manifested by the following (May be other examples):

1. Deficits in social-emotional reciprocity, ranging, for example from abnormal social approach and failure of normal back-and-forth conversation; to reduced sharing of interests, emotions, or affect; to failure to initiate or respond to social interactions.
2. Deficits in nonverbal communication used for social interaction (e.g., poorly integrated verbal and nonverbal communication; abnormalities in eye contact and body language; deficits in understanding and use of gestures; a total lack of facial expressions and nonverbal communication).
3. Deficits in developing, maintaining, and understanding relationships (e.g., difficulties adjusting behavior to suit various social contexts; difficulties in sharing imaginative play or in making friends; absence of interest in peers).

B. Restricted, repetitive patterns of behavior, interests, or activities as manifested by at least two of the following:

1. Stereotyped or repetitive motor movements, use of objects, or speech (e.g., simple motor stereotypies, lining up toys or flipping objects, echolalia, idiosyncratic phrases).
2. Insistence on sameness, inflexible adherence to routines, or ritualized patterns of verbal or nonverbal behavior (e.g., extreme distress at small change, difficulties with transitions, rigid thinking patterns, greeting rituals, need to take same route or eat same food every day).

3. Highly restricted, fixated interests that are abnormal in intensity or focus (e.g., strong attachment to or preoccupation with unusual objects, excessively circumscribed or perseverative interests).
4. Hyper- or hyporeactivity to sensory input or unusual interest in sensory aspects of the environment (e.g., apparent indifference to pain/temperature, adverse response to specific sounds or textures, excessive smelling or touching of objects, visual fascination with lights or movement).

C. Symptoms must be present in the early developmental period and cause clinically significant impairment in social, occupational, or other areas of functioning.

Source: Diagnostic and Statistical Manual of Mental Disorders, Fifth Edition, American Psychiatric Association (2013).

One of the considerations for a classification of ASD is whether the child is higher or lower functioning. This is often demarcated by the child's level of cognitive ability and adaptive behavior. Children with higher functioning autism spectrum disorders generally have IQ's above the ID range (i.e., IQ > 70) with a similar level of adaptive functioning (>70). Children with moderate to severe ASD often will have a co-occurring or comorbid classification of ID as IQ's and adaptive behavior results are generally lower than 70.

12.4   Identification of Autism

The definition of autism within IDEA guides classification within US public schools. There may be instances where a child receives a classification of autism within the schools but who may not have received a diagnosis from an outside clinic or medical professional. This typically occurs in instances of higher functioning ASD where the child's language, cognitive, and academic achievement are generally intact. The converse could also be true. A child may have an outside classification of autism from his pediatrician or from an outside agency, but not receive a classification in the schools. This situation is likely rare and largely theoretical though it is possible. A child may receive a DSM-5 diagnosis but not experience an adverse impact on educational performance. In this circumstance, the child may not be found eligible for a classification under IDEA since IDEA and state regulations drive classification in the schools. (The child could be found eligible for a Section 504 plan. See Chap. 15).

Presented in the following table is each of the classification characteristics found in the IDEA definition followed by example signs and symptoms of autism that might be indicative of an ASD. These examples are not contained in the federal guidelines and are not exhaustive, but may assist the psychologist in arriving at a school-based classification decision.

IDEA 2004 Classification Criteria for Autism

Communication (verbal and nonverbal)	Social interaction	Repetitive activities and stereotyped movements
• Displays echolalia (i.e., saying words and phrases repeatedly) • Provides tangential answers to direct questions • Experiences delayed speech and language skills • Does not respond to gestures such as waving good bye • Reverses pronouns (e.g., says "you" instead of "I") • Gives unrelated answers to questions • Uses few or no gestures (e.g., does not wave hello or goodbye) • Talks in a flat, robot-like, pedantic or sing-song voice • Does not understand jokes, sarcasm, or teasing • Does not use or fully understand gestures, tone of voice or body language • Facial expressions and gestures may be incongruent with what is said	• Does not acknowledge or respond to their names by 10–12 months • Does not share objects that the child finds interesting (e.g., show a toy; point out a train passing by) by 14 months • Does not engage in symbolic play (i.e., pretend to feed a baby; pretend to shave) by 18–24 months • Does not play games like peek-a-boo or patty cake • Prefers to play alone • Avoids eye contact • Only interacts to achieve a desired goal • Has flat or inappropriate facial expressions • Does not understand personal space boundaries • Is not comforted by others during distress • Has trouble understanding other people's feelings or talking about own feelings • May seek friendships but not know how to get or maintain them • Difficulty taking turns and sharing	• Flaps hands, makes rocking movements, or spins in circles • Has obsessive interests in toys, cartoon characters, video games, or television shows • Has perseverative and even obsessive interests • Lines up toys or other objects • Likes parts of objects (e.g., wheels)
Unusual response(s) to sensory experience	**Environmental change and change in daily routines**	
• Has unusual sensory reactions to sounds, smells, tastes, sights, and textures (e.g., does not like tags on shirts; will not eat vegetables; cannot tolerate bright lights) • Restricted food interests • Displays underreaction or overreaction to pain • Become distressed by loud noises • Have unusual sleeping habits (e.g., need for only 5 h of sleep per night) • Avoids, resists or is sensitive to physical contact such as cuddling or being touched	• Plays with toys the same way every time • Becomes upset by changes in routines (e.g., dropping off or picking up from school) • Gets upset by minor changes • Has to follow certain routines	

Because IDEA only offers a generalized definition of autism, it might be helpful to refer to the above chart when making a classification of autism within a U.S. public school setting.

12.5   General Guidance Regarding Psychoeducational Assessment of ASD

When possible, the child with suspected ASD should be assessed across multiple domains of functioning including cognitive, adaptive, achievement, speech-language, gross and fine motor, sensory and medical. The speech pathologist, occupational therapist, and physical therapist are often critically important professionals who participate in the evaluation and treatment planning of children with ASD. The speech-language pathologist will conduct an evaluation of the child's expressive, receptive and pragmatic communication abilities. The occupational therapist and physical therapist will evaluate fine and gross motor coordination skills.

A comprehensive evaluation should include a problem-solving approach that uses multiple methods of assessment and multiple sources of data. These assessment sources include a detailed developmental history, review of medical and early school records, interviews (caregivers, parents, teachers, and other personnel), observations, standardized cognitive, academic, adaptive, social-emotional, motor, speech/language, and behavioral functioning.

Children with ASD present with numerous behavioral issues that may require both broad and narrow band measures of behavior. These behaviors may range from self-stimulation and pica to noncompliance, aggression and self-injury. Norm-referenced (e.g., BASC; CARS-2) instruments are often used to better understand a child's functioning across multiple domains. The assessment of adaptive behavior is also critically important when the presence of ASD is suspected. Measures such as the Vineland-II and ABAS-II are two of the more commonly used measures for this purpose. Performance on cognitive ability and adaptive behavior is often used to demarcate the line between high functioning and moderate/low functioning ASD. In addition to the traditional psychoeducational assessment, a functional behavioral assessment may be necessary for intervention planning when ASD is suspected. There are numerous resources for this purpose (e.g., O'Neil, Albin, Storey, & Horner, 2014; Watson & Steege, 2003).

An exploration of the child's early developmental and medical history becomes extremely important when assessing for ASD since selected signs and symptoms are generally present within the first 2 years of life and there are various medical and genetic conditions that are associated with ASD including seizures (Filipek, 2005), tuberous sclerosis (Harris, 2010) and Fragile X syndrome (Harris, 2010). Often, the child's pediatrician will have identified the child as having an ASD and the child will have received early intervention services. If a child enters the school system without a classification of autism, and a multidisciplinary team suspects an ASD, then the school psychologist may be charged with overseeing the evaluation. In certain states such as New Jersey the school system requires a neurologist or a developmental pediatrician to furnish a classification to the school before the child will be classified with an ASD so state regulations must be considered. There are additional considerations regarding the psychoeducational assessment of children with ASD.

12.5.1 Consider Comorbidity and Rule Out Selected Disorders

ASD does not exist in isolation. Individuals with ASD often experience co-occurring or comorbid disorders including anxiety disorders, intellectual disability, and Tourette's/tics. Anxiety disorders are one of the most frequently observed comorbid conditions. Children with ASD may experience obsessive compulsive disorder, separation anxiety, panic disorder, and agoraphobia (Saulnier & Ventola, 2012). This comes as little surprise as individuals with ASD experience distress in social situations, when routines are changed, or when placed in new environments. Children with ASD may respond functionally, but inappropriately to such changes. For example, a child may respond aggressively when placed in a novel environment with new children. Children with ASD also sometimes experience tic disorders or Tourette's disorder. Tic disorders involve the presence of either motor or vocal tics while Tourette's disorder contains both motor and vocal tics. An additional consideration when evaluating children with ASD is to determine whether the child has an ID exclusively or in combination with ASD. This is sometimes difficult to differentiate and the psychologist must consider social and language features when ruling out one or the other conditions. Sometimes children with ASD are thought to have a variant of ADHD (Gadow, DeVincent, & Pomeroy, 2006; Matson & Nebel-Schwalm, 2007). Be cautious about misconstruing fixation with inattention and poor response to social cues with impulsivity. Certainly, some children with ASD have higher activity levels and react impulsively but it will be important to distinguish between inappropriate response to social/environmental stimuli and organically based inattention/impulsivity when ruling in or out ADHD (Saulnier & Ventola, 2012). Previously, the DSM-IV did not allow comorbid autism and ADHD diagnosis. The DSM-5 removed this prohibition and now permits a concurrent autism and ADHD classification. A final consideration when evaluating for suspected ASD is a communication or language disorder. This is where the expertise of the speech-language pathologist is needed. The language impairment may be consistent with ASD's communication impairment, but the child will not experience the relational and social skills deficits common in children with ASD.

12.5.2 Cognitive Ability

The assessment of intellectual ability in children with ASD may provide useful information. Expressive language and communication deficits may preclude the administration of the verbal portion of an IQ test, resulting in a purely nonverbal evaluation of the child's cognitive ability. At other times, the child's cognitive ability may not be able to be evaluated using standardized tests of cognitive ability. Commonly used IQ tests should be incorporated into a comprehensive evaluation of a child with ASD. At times, these children may only be assessed using the verbal portion of the IQ test or may require the use of a nonverbal IQ test (e.g., UNIT or TONI-3). When attempting to evaluate a child with ASD the process may need to be spaced out or attempted when it is perceived that the child will be able to participate in the process.

12.5.3   Academic Achievement

Certain children with higher functioning autism will require that their progress in academic achievement is assessed. This should involve the assessment of a child's reading, writing, mathematics, oral comprehension and listening comprehension abilities. Some children with higher functioning ASD may display hyperlexia (Grigorenko, Klin, & Volkmar, 2003) wherein their word decoding abilities are much higher than reading comprehension and cognitive ability. They also tend to be precocious, and almost obsessive, readers (Saulnier & Ventola, 2012). Generally, children with higher functioning ASD will perform better on rote academic activities but struggle when faced with the requirement to synthesize information and comprehend more abstract content.

12.5.4   Communication and Language

An impairment in the ability to communicate and use language is a core feature of ASD. Particularly in younger children the question of a speech-language impairment versus an ASD arises. Speech-Language impairments are defined by deficits in expressive and receptive language abilities. However, children with speech-language impairments will not experience the delays in social communication that are common in children with ASD. Children with speech-language deficits struggle with communicating and using language but their understanding of relationships and the social world around them is intact. A speech-language evaluation will assist when seeking to understand communication and language abilities and when desiring a differentiation between the two conditions.

12.5.5   Adaptive Functioning

The assessment of adaptive behavior is a critical aspect when evaluating a child with ASD. It is important to understand what a child can do independently in their daily lives. For instance, does a child reciprocate in conversation when spoken to.

Does the child acknowledge and appreciate compliments? There are several measures of adaptive behavior including the Vineland Adaptive Behavior Scales II (Sparrow, Cicchetti, & Balla, 2005) and the Adaptive Behavior Assessment System, Second Edition; Harrison & Oakland, 2003). The Vineland is one of the more widely used and researched measure of adaptive behavior. The Vineland-II has a teacher rating form and a parent or caregiver semi-structured interview to assess the areas of socialization, communication, and daily living skills. With a child with suspected ASD, including higher functioning children with solid cognitive capacity, research suggests that adaptive functioning may be a more important predicator of independent living and life success than IQ (Howlin, Goode, Hutton, & Rutter, 2004).

12.5.6 Fine and Gross Motor Skills

Children with ASD often struggle with gross motor skills. For instance, they may be clumsy or demonstrate an awkward gait or posture. These children may also find it difficult to write or draw. Therefore, an occupational and physical therapy evaluation is a critical component of the comprehensive evaluation.

12.6 Conclusion

A thorough evaluation is necessary for accurate diagnosis and appropriate treatment planning. ASD is a disorder with heterogeneous presentation with no two individuals alike. There are common core features of ASD that include deficits in socialization and communication and often difficulties with stereotyped movements. Multiple stakeholders should be involved in the multidisciplinary evaluation including the school psychologist, the speech-language pathologist, and the occupational and physical therapists.

Appendix: Sample Report 1: High Functioning Autism Example

Psychological Report
Confidential

Name: Noah Puckerman   Date of Report: January 10, 2014
Date of Birth: 5/22/2008   Chronological Age: 5 years 6 months
Grade: Kindergarten   School: McKinley Public School

Parent Name and Address: Mrs. Puckerman
                         Lima, OH 12345

Phone: (609) 555-1234

Name of Examiner: Stefan C. Dombrowski, Ph.D.

Reason for Referral:
Noah understands selected basic academic skills but struggles with comprehension and processing of abstract information. Noah also struggles with communicating and relating to other children. He was referred for a comprehensive evaluation to determine his present level of functioning and whether he might qualify for specially designed instruction.

Assessment Methods and Sources of Data
Stanford–Binet Intelligence Scales—Fifth Edition (SB5)
Woodcock–Johnson Tests of Achievement, Fourth Edition (WJ-IV)
Bender Visual Motor Gestalt, Second Edition (Bender II)
Behavior Assessment System for Children, Second Edition (BASC-2)

– Mr. Shuester
– Mrs. Pukerman
Gilliam Autism Rating Scale—Second Edition (GARS-2)
– Mr. Shuester
– Mrs. Puckerman
Childhood Autism Rating Scale, Second Edition (CARS 2)
– Stefan C. Dombrowski, Ph.D.

Teacher Interview
- Mr. Will Shuester (Kindergarten Teacher)
- Mrs. Emma Pillsbury (Teacher's Assistant)
Parent Interview
  Mr. Jacob Puckerman
- Mrs. Natasha Puckerman
Student Interview
- Noah Puckerman
Classroom Observations (11/20/13; 1/8/14)
Review of Academic Grade Reports
Review of School Records

Background Information and Developmental History
Noah Puckerman is a 5-year-old kindergarten student at the McKinley Public School (MPS). He struggles with the academic, behavioral, and social aspects of the kindergarten curriculum and was referred for an evaluation as a result.

Prenatal, Perinatal, and Early Developmental History: Mrs. Puckerman noted that her pregnancy with Noah was normal. Noah was born at term and without complication. She explained that all early developmental milestones were within normal limits with the exception of communication. Mrs. Puckerman stated that Noah would point instead of say what he wanted and did not start talking in sentences until about age three. Mrs. Puckerman explained that Noah would also mispronounce words. Instead of saying \milk\, he would say \mook\. Noah received early intervention services.

Medical: Mrs. Puckerman noted no medical concerns with Noah. Noah's vision and hearing are intact. He has never experienced a head injury or a major infection.

Cognitive, Academic, and Language Functioning: Noah receives speech-language support for difficulties with expressive language and communication. Noah did not start talking until approximately 3 years of age. His communication difficulties persist. His speech is difficult to understand and sometimes unintelligible. He also tends to respond in a tangential way to questions asked of him. Although Noah has an understanding of rote kindergarten academic information (e.g., sight word knowledge spelling; number sense), Noah faces difficulty with aspects of the academic curriculum in kindergarten that require higher level processing (e.g., retelling basic aspects of a story he just read; basic emergent writing skills; basic addition and subtraction).

Social-Emotional and Behavioral Functioning: Mr. and Mrs. Puckerman describe Noah as an affectionate child who is impatient and who struggles with attention, communication, and processing of information. Mrs. Puckerman expressed that Noah gets along with other children and that she does not have any concerns about his social progress. She commented that Noah sometimes does not realize when somebody wants to stop playing. Mr. and Mrs. Puckerman explain that Noah has difficulty with focusing. Background information and evaluation results revealed that Noah struggles with social, behavioral, and communication functioning.

Strengths: Noah has been described as an affectionate and compassionate child. He takes pride and responsibility in his classroom job of being the door holder. He knows he is the first one in line, and does not forget. Math has been described as an area of strength for Noah.

Summary: Noah experiences difficulties with communication, socialization, and processing of information particularly more abstract information. Further details in support of this classification and the need for specially designed instruction are offered in the body of this report.

Interview Results

Parent Interview (December 11, 2013): Mrs. Natasha Puckerman, Noah's mother, was interviewed regarding her perspective on Noah's academic, behavioral, social, emotional, and adaptive progress. Mrs. Puckerman commented that Noah does not seem to process information the way other children his age process information. For instance, when Mrs. Puckerman helps Noah with homework and with letters, he struggles to struggles to comprehend what he was just taught. Mrs. Puckerman wondered whether his struggles are related to a lack of focus. She will tell him to look on the paper and he will look somewhere else. When he doesn't want to focus on something she noted that it is very difficult for him. When he takes his time he does it correctly. Mrs. Puckerman also mentioned that Noah struggles with waiting for what he wants and will get upset if he does not get it. She noted that he will persistently ask for something until he gets it. Mrs. Puckerman explained that Noah's main difficulty is that it takes him additional time to calm himself and get focused. She explained that she sees this at home and his teachers also report this difficulty.

Mrs. Puckerman commented on Noah's social progress. She noted that he gets along with other children and that she does not have any concerns about his social progress. Mrs. Puckerman commented that Noah sometimes does not realize when somebody wants to stop playing. Mrs. Puckerman described Noah as an affectionate child who enjoys giving hugs. She noted that he is affectionate toward her and asks how her baby is doing. Mrs. Puckerman explained that Noah jumps into groups situations and participates. She explained that he is able to imitate others. Mrs. Puckerman commented that when Noah misses directions or instructions, he will imitate others and follow along. Mrs. Puckerman reiterated that Noah does not have issues socially. She noted that his issues are related to a lack of focus and difficulty with communicating. Mrs. Puckerman explained that Noah gets frustrated really quickly when things don't go his way. She noted that he does not have issues with transitions or novelty. Mrs. Puckerman explained that Noah has always had difficulty with communicating. She explained that he did not speak in sentences until about age three. Noah received early intervention services. Mrs. Puckerman explained that Noah will use the phrase "all the time" in many sentences. Mrs. Puckerman indicated that Noah makes a clicking noise with his mouth when he is engaged in an activity and will hum as he eats. Otherwise, Mrs. Puckerman indicated that Noah does not engage in echoing of words. She noted that he generally uses his pronouns properly, but will occasionally say \him\ instead of \he\. He also will occasionally confuse pronoun usage (e.g., "I'm not her sister anymore' for 'She's not my sister anymore").

Mrs. Puckerman indicated that her pregnancy with Noah was normal. She also noted that all early developmental milestones were within normal limits with the exception of communication. Mrs. Puckerman explained that Noah would point instead of say what he wanted and did not start talking in sentences until about age three. Mrs. Puckerman explained that Noah would also mispronounce words. Instead of saying \milk\, he would say\mook\. Mrs. Puckerman commented on Noah's strengths. She indicated that his strengths include his inquisitiveness. She explained that he is very interested in where babies come from. He is also curious about Christmas time. Mrs. Puckerman explained that Noah has an outgoing personality. Mrs. Puckerman expressed that Noah needs to focus better. She also explained that he struggles with writing including handwriting and he does not show too much interest in reading. Mrs. Puckerman explained that Noah's mathematics progress is pretty good, but he sometimes skips numbers. Mrs. Puckerman was asked whether an outside classification such as ADHD or autism was ever mentioned. She noted that she "does not see autism. I see it as a big issue with focus and communication." Mrs. Puckerman indicated that she works for the Center for Autism in Philadelphia.

Parent Interview (January 6, 2014): Mr. Jacob Puckerman, Noah's father, was interviewed regarding his perspective on Noah's academic, behavioral, social, emotional, and adaptive progress. Mr. Puckerman indicated that his biggest concern is attention span. He noted that Noah has difficulty keeping focus, loses interest easily, and struggles with sitting with the rest of the class. Mr. Puckerman explained that listening is a constant struggle for Noah. He noted that Noah struggles with following directions. Mr. Puckerman also explained that speech is an area of concern, but indicated that Noah has been making a lot of progress lately especially a home. Mr. Puckerman next commented that Noah does find socially. He noted that he has not been able to observe him much at school, but explained that outside of school he interacts a lot with his younger sister and they seem to get along. Mr. Puckerman indicated that when Noah is around cousins and friends, he seems to play for hours without issues. Mr. Puckerman explained that he has not heard any reports about Noah having any problems in the social arena. Mr. Puckerman indicated that Noah is into rhythm and music so he will make sounds with his mouth when he is actively engaged (e.g., clicking, humming sounds rhythmically). Mr. Puckerman next discussed Noah's early childhood. He stated that speech and communication was the biggest concern. Mr. Puckerman indicated that Noah was allowed to gesture and not use words for such a long time. Or he would communicate with one word (e.g., milk) and Mrs. Puckerman and I would just infer what he wanted. Mr. Puckerman explained that Noah continues to struggle with communicating, but it is related to the clarity of his speech. Mr. Puckerman indicated that Noah received services around age 3 from Elwyn because it was difficult to understand what he was saying. Mr. Puckerman commented on Noah's strengths which include being aware of his environment, his memory, and his caring and compassionate way. Mr. Puckerman indicated that Noah can also be empathetic noting that when someone is hurt, he will say, "are you okay?" He explained that Noah is very helpful and is always offering to help out. He noted that Noah's hobbies include toys, cars, and playing video games.

Teacher Interview (November 30, 2013): Mr. Will Shuester, Noah' kindergarten teacher, was interviewed regarding Noah's academic, behavioral, emotional, and social functioning. Mr. Shuester provided the following information. Noah recognizes and identifies all of his letters and most of his sounds. He occasionally mixes up a few of the commonly confusing ones: b/d, g/q, etc. He has basic concepts of print awareness (e.g., which way to open and read a book; where to find letters on the page). He is starting to read small sight word books with approximately 50–70 % accuracy. In writing, Noah writes down letters and his name and some sight words, but he does not necessarily carry meaning along with his writing. He does not say what he wants to say, write it down, and then read it back. In math, he identifies and writes his numbers and counts with one to one correspondence. Mr. Shuester indicates that Noah cannot follow along with us when we break numbers into parts like saying "7 is 4 and how many more?"

Behaviorally, Mr. Shuester explained that Noah has a difficult time recognizing what the group is doing and following along with them. In any transition, he often lingers around the classroom, looking for things, talking about something else he wants to do, or seeking people out to play with. Mr. Shuester explained that she has been working with him to look at her and say "I'm listening" when she says his name because he often doesn't look when his name is called. He noted that he does not see Noah's behavior as oppositional or defiant, just unfocused and a little unaware of what is exactly being expected from him. He explained that when the class is working together on the carpet Noah is usually actively talking to others, poking them with little things he finds on the rug, or if he is self-contained he is making constant noises and usually moving his face or hands in a repetitive motion. During independent work, he sometimes follows along, but for a much smaller portion of the task than the rest of the students. If most of the class writes for 20–30 min, he can usually write for about 5-10 and once he is done. Mr. Shuester explained that she has not found a way to prompt him to extend his work further. During clean up or other transitions where there is a lot of moving around, he starts waving his head back and forth or running in circles or making noises with more intensity.

Socially and emotionally, he seeks out students who are also playful and easily distracted. He will typically focus on one thing for a few weeks. Right now, whenever he has an opportunity he will say "feet" to other people to get them to laugh. He doesn't understand when other people are helping him. For example, if we are cleaning up and someone puts away his crayons so that their table gets cleaned on time, he will cry and say "They're mean. They took my crayons." Sometimes, when he needs to transition he will cry and say "but I don't want to." He was sick a few weeks ago and since then he says "But I don't feel good" after nearly every direction he is given. Sometimes he does not understand the need to put things away and move on and will take it as a punishment. If he is really engaged in something and we all clean up from it, occasionally he will cry and wail as though all of his privileges were taken away. In terms of communication, he often answers questions with a number a response that he thinks will get him what he wants, instead of expressing what's really going on (like the "I don't feel good" comment). He does a pretty good job with his own name and gender pronouns. Sometimes he mixes up negative prefixes like "Can you untie my shoes please?"

He does a good job taking care of his belongings and keeping track of where they are. He does a nice job in his illustrations, making them clear and remembering what is what. When he is able to follow directions in math, his work is accurate. In terms of areas of need, he needs to be able to meet his physical needs for movement and noise, in a way that helps him focus on what the class is doing instead of distracting from it.

Teacher Assistant Interview (December 11, 2013): Ms. Emma Pillsbury, Noah's teaching assistant, was interviewed regarding Noah's academic, behavioral, emotional, and social functioning. Ms. Pillsbury noted that she taught Noah last summer in the Springboard program so she has been able to observe his behavior since that time period. Ms. Pillsbury provided the following information. Academically, Noah knows the letters and sounds, can count to 100 and knows the numerals. He can retell parts of a story. He does not complete worksheets or writing assignments. He has poor writing and coloring skills. His classroom behavior keeps him from attending to the lessons. Noah really struggles academically.

Behaviorally, Noah is unable to focus for more than 30–45 s. He is loud and exhibits anger when sent to his seat or take a break in the form of feet stomping, yelling, telling us he hates school, he won't be here tomorrow or to shout that so and so got him in trouble. He calls children names and hits them or throws things at them, like pencils, small pieces of paper, or a block. He used to keep calling out the word "feet" to make people laugh but has since changed his word choice to "dookie." Noah is not always aware of what the other students are doing. When asked what the students are doing he is not always sure. If asked to do what the other students are doing he doesn't always know what he should do. When he is sent back to his seat or to take a break he doesn't understand why, even if he is told something like "you were calling out again, so you'll have to go back to your seat." He likes to blame others and say that they got him in trouble. During recess he engages in inappropriate play, such as throwing sand at people, knocking people to the ground, name calling and hitting things or people with sticks. Most of the time when given a direction that he doesn't want to do, like put your crayons away, he will generally comply with the request with a count down from 3. He usually follows the direction by the time I get to 0. Noah requires help with focus, treating peers with kindness, and self-control of his body and language.

Student Interview (December 4, 2013): Noah was interviewed to ascertain a sense of his progress at MPS. When asked, "How do you like going to school at MPS?" Noah responded "there was not school yesterday" even though there was school. He was next asked whether he likes going to kindergarten to which he replied, "I like going to kindergarten." He was then asked his favorite thing to do in kindergarten. Noah indicated that he enjoys playing activities like dinosaurs, cars, and snacks. At one point during the interview, Noah expressed that he must hurry up because he is "late for morning meeting." Noah was asked who his friends are at school. He replied "I don't know." He was then asked to name several classmates and he was able to name a few. Noah indicated that he does not get into trouble at school. He explained that his hobbies including playing with cars and his Buzz Lightyear doll. Noah also explained that he enjoys playing Angry Birds on his father's iPad. He explained that he likes recess at school and plans to play soccer. Noah explained that "soccer is for children while football is for grown-ups." At times Noah was difficult to understand and required numerous attempts clarify questions for him to directly respond.

Observations

Observation (November 20, 2013): Noah was observed for 50 min during kindergarten class. The class was transitioning from quiet time following lunch to an activity at the carpet. Mr. Shuester instructed the class to go and sit at the carpet. Noah ignored the first request. He was offered individual instruction to head to the carpet. Noah replied, "I don't feel like it." After about 1 min, he joined the class at the carpet. While sitting at the carpet, Noah picked up a string and started playing with it. The teacher asked the class to show three fingers. Noah was not focusing on this request and instead continued playing with the string. He also attempted to talk to another student seated near him. At that point, Noah was instructed to turn and face the chart that the teacher was using to present a topic. Noah complied but was observed to be rock back and forth and be active as he was seated. He also found a rock on the floor and started playing with that object. Noah was also observed to make sucking noises with his teeth. Ms. Pillsbury was instructing the class how to draw a picture of a leaf. Underneath the picture of the leaf students were to write a letter. Mr. Shuester asked the class what part of a letter goes on the line. Noah replied out loud, "a tiger." After about 10 min into the presentation Noah started focusing on the teacher guided instruction. There was one additional time when another child lifted up the carpet where Noah was sitting and Noah screamed at the child to stop.

Observation (January 8, 2014): Noah was observed during lunch, transition back to class, and then during class time. The observation occurred over a span of 2 h. During lunch, Noah was observed to be wearing gloves, one blue with a facial design of a cartoon bear, and the other, solid red. During lunch, Noah seemed quite interested in playing with the blue glove with the design. He would hold it up in front of his face and look at it. He also played with a drink bottle that had a toy figure as part of the cap. At one point, Noah approached the psychologist and pointed out the hat on the figure. At other times, Noah would attempt to interact with other students at his lunch table. His interaction was observed to be physical where he would poke and touch the other student. One student imitated Noah's nonverbal interactional style and engaged by poking and prodding Noah in return. Next, Noah transitioned to his classroom. When his table was called to line up, Noah was observed to cut in front of other students and head to the front of the line. Noah entered the classroom and stood by the examiner and started at him. This occurred for a period of about 2 min after which point the examiner reminded Noah to return to his seat. Noah stated that he was going to play in the sand tray table. Mr. Shuester acknowledged that it was Noah's turn to play with the sand tray. Noah took off his gloves, placed them in his cubby, and began playing in the sand table. While he was running his hands through the sand, Noah was observed to make a humming and clicking noise. At one point, Noah mentioned to the examiner that he recognizes a character on a lunch box (e.g., Mater from the movie, *Cars*). For the next 10 min, Noah was observed to continue to make loud vocalizations, talk to himself, and generally play loudly with the sand tray. The class was engaged in quiet time, but Noah seemed unaware of the need to be quiet. Instead, he would make vocalizations and talk to himself. His also seemed unaware of the requirement to keep noise to a low level since it was quiet time. When Mr. Shuester indicated that the class was finished with quiet time, Noah remarked out loud, "I'm done now." He then proceeded to his cubby and put his gloves back on. After that, Noah joined the rest of the class at his desk. Mr. Shuester instructed the class to float over quietly to the carpet. Noah remained at his desk, stared at his gloves raised up in front of his face, and made vocalization sounds (e.g., \ee\, \ah\; \ee\, \ah\, \you\, \your\) over and over. Noah was given a warning to head to the carpet. He expressed frustration over such request and protested on his way to the carpet. As he entered the carpet area, he slides into another student who protested. He also punched a second student who was seated in front of him. Noah was told to sit down, and he screamed out, "I don't want to sit." Noah complied with this request for approximately 1 min at which point he got up from the carpet and began to play with a shelf near the carpet. Noah was instructed to return to the carpet and he complied. However, he sat too close to another student in the class, and that student expressed annoyance and moved away from Noah. Noah then picked up the carpet underneath another student, prompting that student to scream out in frustration. That student was sent to take a break away from the carpet area. Mr. Shuester asked the class to sit "like a student" (e.g., pretzel style). Noah was able to comply with this request. While Mr. Shuester instructed the class, Noah screamed out, "rocket ship." It is unknown what prompted this vocalization, but Noah seemed to be engaged in solitary imaginative play. Noah was requested to face the teacher as he spent approximately 50 % of the time with his back to her. He complied for several minutes, but was observed to roll around on the floor. At one point, Noah was observed to sit with his back to the teacher and stare for approximately 90 s. Noah got up and attempted to wander the classroom. He was instructed again to sit at the carpet. Noah responded by saying, "I don't want to sit on the carpet." Noah complied after prompting for about 20 s. He then resumed playing with his hands (gloves on them). At one other point, Noah attempted to engage with another student. He did so by making fairly unintelligible vocalizations and through the use of taunting gestures with his hands. The other student become upset and moved away from Noah. Noah then began playing with a pebble on the carpet.

Since Noah seemed preoccupied with the gloves and playing with them, the examiner took Noah out to the hallway to discuss the gloves. Noah commented that he makes ice cream with the blue glove. He communicated that there are buttons on this glove. He demonstrated how this occurs. Noah also indicated that he uses this glove to "bring his fish." Noah also indicated that his red glove on his other hand is a razor. He demonstrated how it works as a razor by moving his red gloved hand across his blue gloved hand. Noah and the examiner returned to the classroom. The class was engaged in a writing activity where the class was asked to sound out and write several words (e.g., bug). Noah seemed uncertain what to do, so he looked at other students and was then able to complete this task. Impressions of the observation were that Noah experienced considerable difficulty following classroom rules and remaining focused. He was quite active and struggled with communicating and interacting in an age appropriate manner with other students, at times poking and prodding them in an effort to get their attention or a reaction from them. Impressions of the observation were that Noah requires considerable prompting, structure and support.

Observation during Assessment: Noah was active and inattentive and required significant redirection and support during the testing session. He made eye contact and smiled. However, his responses to direct questions were often tangential. Occasionally Noah would stare off into space and require redirection. Noah also observed a particular doll (e.g., a superhero) in the room. He perseverated on playing with this doll to the extent that it had to be removed from the room. Although Noah required structure, support and occasional redirection, his testing session is considered a valid and accurate representation of his abilities.

Cognitive and Academic Functioning

Stanford-Binet Intelligence Scales-Fifth Edition (SB5)
Noah was administered the Stanford–Binet Intelligence Scales—Fifth Edition
(SB5). The SB5 is an individually administered measure of intellectual functioning
normed for individuals between the ages of 2 and 85+ years. The SB5 contains five
factor indexes for each the VIQ and NVIQ: Fluid Reasoning, Knowledge,
Quantitative Reasoning, Visual Spatial, and Working Memory. Fluid reasoning represents an individual's ability to solve verbal and nonverbal problems and reason
inductively and deductively. Knowledge represents the accumulated fund of general
information acquired at home, school, work, or in life. Quantitative reasoning
reflects facility with numbers and numerical problem solving, whether with word
problems or figural relationships. Quantitative reasoning emphasizes problem solving more than mathematical knowledge. Visual-spatial processing reflects the ability to see patterns, relationships, spatial orientation, and the connection among
diverse pieces of a visual display. Working memory is a measure of short-term
memory processing of information whether verbal or visual, emphasizing the brief
manipulation of diverse information.

The SB5 provides three intelligence score composites and five factor indices
with a mean of 100 and a Standard deviation of 15. Scores between 90 and 110 are
considered average.

	Standard	95 % Conf.	Descriptive	
	Score	Percentile	Interval	Classification
IQ scores				
Full scale IQ (FSIQ)	85	16	81–89	Low average
Nonverbal IQ (NVIQ)	86	15	82–90	Low average
Verbal IQ (VIQ)	82	13	78–86	Low average
Factor index scores				
Fluid reasoning (FR)	81	12	77–85	Low average
Knowledge (KN)	80	11	75–85	Low average
Quantitative reasoning (QR)	78	9	74–82	Below average
Visual spatial (VS)	88	22	84–92	Low average
Working memory (WM)	89	24	85–93	Low average

The above table may be referenced to obtain Noah's performance in each of
these areas while the following is a description of each of the factor index scores.
Fluid reasoning represents an individual's ability to solve verbal and nonverbal
problems and reason inductively and deductively. Knowledge represents the accumulated fund of general information acquired at home, school, work, or in life.
Quantitative reasoning reflects facility with numbers and numerical problem solving,
whether with word problems or figural relationships. Quantitative reasoning emphasizes problem solving more than mathematical knowledge. Visual-spatial processing
reflects the ability to see patterns, relationships, spatial orientation, and the connection

among diverse pieces of a visual display. Working memory is a measure of short-term memory processing of information whether verbal or visual, emphasizing the brief manipulation of diverse information.

The SB5 includes ten subtest scores with a mean of 10 and a Standard deviation of 3. Scores between 8 and 12 are considered average. Noah's individual subtest scores were as follows:

Nonverbal tests		Verbal tests	
Fluid reasoning	7	Fluid reasoning	16
Knowledge	7	Knowledge	6
Quant. Reasoning	6	Quant. Reasoning	7
Visual spatial	8	Visual spatial	8
Working memory	8	Working memory	7

On testing with the SB5, Noah earned a Full Scale IQ of 85. On the SB5, this level of performance falls within the range of scores designated as low average and exceeded the performance of 16 % of individuals at Noah's age. His Verbal IQ (Standard Score = 82; 12th percentile) was in the low average range and exceeded 12 % of individuals Noah's age. Noah's Nonverbal IQ (Standard Score=86; 13th percentile) was in the low average range, exceeding 13 % of individuals Noah's age.

Woodcock-Johnson Tests of Achievement-IV (WJ-IV)

The WJ-IV is an achievement test used to measure basic reading, writing, oral language, and mathematics skills. The Reading subtest includes letter and word identification, vocabulary, and comprehension skills. The Writing subtest includes spelling, writing fluency, and simple sentence writing. The Mathematics subtest includes calculation, practical problems, and knowledge of mathematical concepts and vocabulary.

Brandon obtained the following scores in each of the areas of measurement:

	Standard	Descriptive	
	Score	Percentile	Classification
Brief reading	94	35	Average
Letter-word ID	101	53	Average
Passage comprehension	77	6	Below average
Brief writing	96	39	Average
Writing samples	96	39	Average
Spelling	98	44	Average
Brief mathematics	79	8	Below average
Applied problems	78	7	Below average

Standardized achievement test results revealed below average passage comprehension and applied mathematics problems skills with average writing and letter word identification skills.

Bender Visual-Motor Gestalt Test, Second Edition (Bender-II)

The Bender-II measures visual-motor integration skills, or the ability to see and copy figures accurately. A quantitative and qualitative analysis of Noah's drawings suggests that his visual-motor integration abilities (e.g., fine motor skills for paper and pencil tasks) are below average (Copy Standard Score = 75; 5th percentile).

Social, Emotional, and Behavioral Assessment

Behavior Assessment System for Children, Second Edition (BASC-2)

The Behavior Assessment System for Children, Second Edition (BASC-2) is an integrated system designed to facilitate the differential diagnosis and classification of a variety of emotional and behavioral conditions in children. It possesses validity scales and several clinical scales, which reflect different dimensions of a child's personality. T-scores between 40 and 60 are considered average. Scores greater than 70 ($T > 70$) are in the Clinically Significant range and suggest a high level of difficulty. Scores in the At-Risk range (T-Score 60–69) identify either a significant problem that may not be severe enough to require formal treatment or a potential of developing a problem that needs careful monitoring. On the Adaptive Scales, scores below 30 are considered clinically significant while scores between 31 and 35 are considered at-risk.

	Mr. Shuester		Mr. Puckerman	
Clinical scales	T-score	Percentile	T-score	Percentile
Hyperactivity	73**	96	58	80
Aggression	60*	86	55	75
Anxiety	55	76	50	54
Depression	63*	89	51	55
Somatization	67*	93	54	72
Atypicality	73**	95	54	70
Withdrawal	56	77	53	70
Attention problems	66*	93	55	75
Adaptability	37*	11	41	33
Social skills	45	34	50	52
Functional communication	45	35	45	35
Activities of daily living	–	–	45	35
Externalizing problems	67*	94	53	55
Internalizing problems	64*	91	52	57
Behavioral symptoms index	70**	96	56	62
Adaptive skills	41	18	45	42

*At-risk rating
**Clinically significant rating

The ratings of Noah on the BASC-2 by Mr. Schuester and Mrs. Puckerman produced different results. Mrs. Puckerman rated Noah in the average range across all composites and clinical scales. Mr. Schuester's ratings on the BASC-2 ratings suggested a clinically significant elevation on the behavioral symptoms index composite with an at-risk rating on the internalizing and externalizing behaviors composites. Mr. Schuester's BASC-2 rating also suggested a clinically significant elevation on the hyperactivity and atypicality clinical scales with an at-risk rating on the aggression, depression, adaptability, somatization, and attention problems clinical scales.

Gilliam Autism Rating Scale-Second Edition (GARS-2)

The GARS-2 is a screening instrument used for the assessment of individual's ages 3–22 who have severe behavioral problems that may be indicative of autism. The GARS-2 is composed of three subscales that are based on the definition of autism: stereotyped behaviors, communication, and social interaction. The Social Interaction subscale comprises items that describe social interactive behaviors, expression of communicative intent, and cognitive and emotional behaviors. The stereotyped behavior subscale comprises items that describe restricted and stereotyped behaviors that are characteristic of Asperger's. The social interaction subscale contains items that evaluate the individual's ability to relate appropriately to people, events and objects. An Autism Index of 85 or higher indicates a very likely presence of autism. An index score of 70 to 84 indicates a possible classification of autism while a score below 70 indicates an unlikely presence of autism

	Teacher	Father
	Std. Score	Std. Score
Stereotyped behaviors	7	4
Communication	11	6
Social interaction	10	4
Autism index	96	61

Ratings of Noah by his teacher on the GARS-2 suggest a very likely probability of Autism. Mr. Scheuster's ratings suggest a low probability of autism.

Childhood Autism Rating Scale, Second Edition (CARS 2)

The CARS 2 is a behavior rating scale developed to identify children across the autism spectrum. Children are rated on fifteen characteristics including relationship to others; body use; emotional response; adaptation to change; taste, smell and touch response; fear or nervousness; visual response; object use; imitation; verbal and nonverbal communication; intellectual ability; activity level and listening response. Children (ages 2–12) with scores on the CARS below 30 generally do not receive a classification of an autism spectrum disorder. Children with scores between 30 and 36.5 are considered to have mild to moderate autism while scores above 37 reflect severe autism. Noah's rating on the CARS 2 was 30, suggesting mild to moderate symptoms of an Autism Spectrum Disorder.

Conceptualization and Classification

Multiple data sources and methods of assessment inform the conceptualization of Noah's cognitive, academic, social-emotional, and behavioral functioning including whether he qualifies for special education support. Details in support of these findings are offered below.

Cognitive and Academic Functioning: Noah's present performance on a measure of cognitive ability was in the low average range (SB5 FSIQ = 85; 16th percentile). His performance on standardized measures of academic achievement suggest that he struggles with reading comprehension and applied mathematics problems. His progress on rote academic tasks including spelling and sight word recognition was in the average range. Within the classroom, Noah recognizes and identifies all of his letters and most of his sounds. He occasionally mixes up a few of the commonly confusing letters: b/d, g/q. He has basic concepts of print awareness including which way to open and read a book and where to find letters on the page. Mr. Shuester notes that Noah is starting to read small sight word books with 50–70 % accuracy. He writes down letters and his name and some sight words, but he struggles with carrying meaning along with his writing. In math, he identifies and writes his numbers and counts with one-to-one correspondence. Mr. Shuester notes that Noah cannot follow along with us when we break numbers into parts (e.g., saying "7 is 4 and how many more?") Noah struggles with expressive language and communication and receives speech-language support as a result.

Social, Emotional, and Behavioral Functioning: Multiple data sources and methods of assessment including interview results, classroom observations, and rating forms indicate that Noah struggles with communication, socialization, following classroom rules, and overactivity. When asked a direct question, Noah experiences difficulty with producing a clearly understood verbal response. Sometimes this occurs because his speech can be difficult to understand and even unintelligible. At other times Noah responds with a tangential statement that is unrelated to the question asked of him. Noah receives speech services for his communication difficulties. Noah struggles with relating to other children in an age expected manner. He seeks out other children with whom to play, but does so primarily in a way that tends to alienate him from them. Noah can also be physical with other children (e.g., hitting, punching, sliding into, or pushing them) sometimes intentionally and at other times accidentally. Additionally, Noah struggles with interpersonal boundaries and will encroach upon children's personal space or will get up in their face with his hands. Sometimes he engages in this behavior to play with them. At other times he engages in this behavior to get their attention or to get a response from them. This interactional style tends to alienate him from other children in the classroom. Although Noah seeks out social opportunities, he struggles with developing peer relationships at a developmentally appropriate level. Mr. and Mrs. Puckerman note that Noah can be a compassionate and helpful child. Noah can be quite active in the classroom and frequently darts from one location to another. He loses focus easily and struggles with low task persistence for activities that he does not prefer. Noah is more responsive to adult instruction when in a one-on-one situation than when in a group setting. At these times he is more readily redirected. Noah seems to enjoy playing in the sand tray including the sensation of feeling the sand on his hands. Over the past few days, Noah has been also observed to play with his hands while wearing a glove with the face of a cartoon bear (i.e., talk to his hands; interact with his hands). Noah has been wearing his gloves throughout the entire class day over the past several days. At other times, Noah will show his gloves to peers in the classroom. During one observation, most of these peers did not share Noah's excitement and interest in his gloves. Noah has been observed to elicit noises repeatedly (e.g., "ee-ah-ee-ah-you-your") and laugh while looking at his hands. Noah was asked about his gloves and he revealed that they can make ice cream or bring in fish. Noah struggles with following classroom and teacher rules. He will protest when requested to do something he does not prefer. These protests are much more intense than that of a typical kindergarten child. However, with considerable prompting, structure and support, Noah eventually complies. Still, his behaviors can be disruptive to other children around him and at times the entire class. Noah often can be observed with his back to the teacher and therefore the activity being discussed in class. At other times, he has been observed to stare blankly or play with an object such as a pebble or a string on the floor. This causes him to miss much of what is being discussed in the classroom.

Summary: Noah's cluster of symptoms are impairing his social and behavioral functioning and also contributing to difficulties with his academic functioning. Noah will benefit from accommodations for symptoms consistent with a classification of autism.

Summary and Recommendations

Considering multiple data sources and methods of assessment, Noah will benefit from accommodations for the host of academic, behavioral, social, emotional, and communication deficits that are associated with a classification of an autism spectrum disorder. Selected recommendations are offered below.

1. *Accommodations for Academic Tasks*: Noah will benefit from accommodations for academic skills including reading, writing and mathematics.

2. *Occupational Therapy Evaluation*: Noah struggles with fine motor skills for paper and pencil tasks and will benefit from an occupational therapy evaluation.

3. *Speech-Language Therapy*: Noah struggles with verbal communication. At times his speech can be difficult to understand. At other times his speech is unintelligible. Noah's communication style can also be tangential when he is asked a direct question and then responds with an unrelated comment. His communication difficulties interfere not only with his academic progress, but also with his social progress. He will benefit from continued speech-language support as indicated in the speech pathologist's report.

4. *Social Skills Training including Stories and Social Pragmatics Interventions*: Noah may benefit from exposure to social stories, role plays and behavioral modeling as a way to improve social skills and increase more appropriate engagement with peers during interaction with them.

5. *Behavioral Support*: Noah may benefit from support for the following behaviors associated with his classification:

   (a) Low frustration tolerance when required to engage in an activity he does not prefer.
   (b) Difficulty with following directions from teachers.
   (c) Peer interaction including how to engage in a more appropriate manner than grabbing, poking, or hitting other children.
   (d) Difficulty with transition from one activity to another.
   (e) High activity level and low task persistence.

Stefan C. Dombrowski, Ph.D.
Licensed Psychologist (PA and NJ)
Certified School Psychologist (PA and NJ)

Sample Report 2: Low to Mid Functioning Autism

Psychological Report
Confidential

Name: Eric Berry   Date of Report: December 14, 2016
Date of Birth: 6/5/20011   Chronological Age: 5
Grade: Kindergarten   School: Washington Public School
Name of Examiner: Stefan Dombrowski

Parent Name and Address: Shelby Berry

Phone: (609) 555-1234

Reason for Referral:

Eric faces significant struggles with communicating and socializing in an appropriate manner. He is generally a nonverbal child and rarely produces verbal responses to questions asked of him. Eric has an outside classification of Autism from his pediatrician. He was referred for a comprehensive evaluation to determine his present level of functioning and whether he might qualify for specially designed instruction. Recommendations and accommodations appropriate for Eric will also be offered.

Assessment Methods and Sources of Data
Universal Nonverbal Intelligence Test (UNIT)
Peabody Picture Vocabulary Test, Fourth Edition (PPVT-4)
Behavior Assessment System for Children, Second Edition (BASC-2)

– Ms. Mary Corcoran
Gilliam Autism Rating Scale—Second Edition (GARS-2)
– Ms. Mary Corcoran
Vineland Adaptive Behavior Scale, Second Edition (Vineland-II)
– Ms. Mary Corcoran
Childhood Autism Rating Scale, Second Edition (CARS 2)
– Stefan C. Dombrowski, Ph.D.
Teacher Interview
– Ms. Mary Corcoran (Kindergarten Teacher)
– Ms. Britney Pierce (Teacher's Aide)
Parent Interview
– Ms. Shelby Berry
Classroom Observations
Review of Academic Grade Reports
Review of School Records

Background Information and Developmental History
Prenatal, Perinatal, and Early Developmental History: Eric was born prematurely at 34 weeks gestation weighing 4 pounds 4 ounces. His mother's pregnancy was complicated by gestational diabetes and problems with weight gain (only 15 pounds during pregnancy). Ms. Berry was 39 years old at the time of Eric's birth. Delivery was uncomplicated although Eric was admitted to the Neonatal Intensive Care Unit (NICU) at Albert Einstein Medical Center for 1 week due to poor oral intake and insufficient weight gain. Eric walked at 15 months and said his first words at less than a year. Background information revealed that Eric may have lost other sounds by the time he was nearly 3 years old. Eric has always been a picky eater avoiding meat or vegetables. He used to choke and gag on food, but background results revealed that he no longer does so. Eric drools a lot and often protrudes his tongue out of his mouth. Eric attended a daycare where he received speech therapy two times per week. Eric is still primarily nonverbal.

Medical: Eric experiences asthma and a peanut allergy. He also suffers from seasonal allergies primarily during the fall. Eric has never experienced a head injury. His hearing and vision are intact. No further medical history is available.

Cognitive, Academic, and Language Functioning: Prior evaluation results from April 2010 revealed that Eric's receptive and expressive language was at about a 12 month level. Recent speech language results revealed higher receptive language abilities (PPVT-4 Std. Score = 94; average range). His expressive language abilities were lower (Expressive One Word Vocabulary Picture Vocabulary Test Std. Score = 78; below average). Background information revealed considerable difficulties with all aspects of the kindergarten curriculum.

Social-Emotional and Behavioral Functioning: Eric has always struggled in his interaction with peers. He is primarily nonverbal and will only occasionally use simple language to communicate his needs. Eric rarely participates in group activities. He sometimes attempts to engage other children in the classroom, but does so in an inappropriate fashion that alienates him from them. For instance, Eric has been observed to hit, poke or bump into other students to get their attention. Eric also struggles with the reciprocal aspects of communication, does not participate in group activities, and can throw extreme temper tantrums when denied his own way. Additionally, Eric struggles with overactivity and needs structure, support, and prompting for periods of transition. At the beginning of the academic year, Eric had intensive behavioral difficulties. He struggled with his adjustment to Washington Public School but with behavioral support has now adjusted to the new environment and routines of the classroom.

Strengths: Eric is described as a sweet child who enjoys making other people laugh. He has demonstrated a degree of resiliency in his capacity to adjust to an entirely new school environment.

Summary: Prior evaluation results indicated likelihood of an autism spectrum disorder (see Consultation Report from ABC Healthcare Network; April, 2, 2010). This consultation report also recommended early intervention services including speech-language therapy. Eric continues to struggle with difficulties with socialization, communication, and understanding the perspective of others.

Interview Results
Parent Interview (October 22, 2016): Ms. Shelby Berry, Eric's mother, was interviewed regarding her impressions of Eric's functional in the cognitive, academic, social, emotional, adaptive, and behavioral arena. Ms. Berry explained that Eric has an outside classification of autism and received early intervention services. Ms. Berry commented that Eric rarely participates in conversations with other children and adults. She mentioned that he says only a few words. Ms. Berry noted that Eric said his first words by 12 months of age, but lost most language abilities by age three. Ms. Berry commented that Eric seeks to interact (nonverbally) with other children, but struggles in his interaction with them. She noted that he is unaware of his body and frequently runs into other children and objects. She noted that he is clumsy. Ms. Berry explained that when things do not go his way or when Eric is introduced to a

new environment, then he has a tendency to throw temper tantrums. She mentioned that this occurred when he first arrived at Washington Public School, but that Eric has since adjusted to the school and its routines. Ms. Berry commented that her pregnancy with Eric was complicated by gestational diabetes. She indicated that Eric was born prematurely at 34 weeks gestation. Eric required a stay in the NICU. Ms. Berry explained that Eric's hearing and vision are intact. She noted that he has never experienced a head injury or major infection.

Teacher Interview (October 26, 2016): Ms. Mary Corcoran, Eric' kindergarten teacher, was interviewed regarding Eric's academic, behavioral, emotional, and social functioning. Ms. Corcoran first discussed Eric's behavioral progress. She noted that Eric has struggled with transitioning to a new school and the associated people in his life at school. Ms. Corcoran explained that Eric would enter a new classroom and would require about 30 min to finally settle down. She explained that Eric is a wanderer and would walk around the classroom and be disruptive. Ms. Corcoran explained that one time he wrote all over the white board with regular markers and ripped down the calendar. Ms. Corcoran explained that she gave him something to chew was has helped him. She explained that Eric has sensory issues. He likes to play in the sand table. He also likes sensory stimulation and does well when writing with shaving cream. Ms. Corcoran explained that it is difficult for Eric to stay in one place. He has extreme difficulty sitting in a chair or on the carpet. Ms. Corcoran indicated that Eric can be aggressive toward other students. She indicated that he sometimes hits other children for no reason. Ms. Corcoran noted that his behavior has improved since the beginning of the school year, but that he still struggles. Ms. Corcoran indicated that Eric has been sent to the CARES office on a number of occasions. Ms. Corcoran stated that Eric loves physical education. She noted that Eric faces social struggles. For instance, she explained that he drools a lot and seems to get a kick out of getting other children's reaction. Ms. Corcoran noted that Eric faces difficulty with making friends. Academically, Ms. Corcoran indicated that Eric writes on a 2–3-year-old level. She explained that he can only consistently make the /J/ in his name. Ms. Corcoran explained that on some days, Eric can count to ten and name the alphabet. Ms. Corcoran indicated that Eric can recognize some colors although he cannot draw shapes.

Teacher Interview (November 13, 2016): Ms. Mary Corcoran, kindergarten teacher, was interviewed again to better understand the perceived functions of Eric's behavior. Ms. Corcoran noted that Eric struggles with following classroom rules and when required to conform, he can act out by throwing a tantrum. She noted that this also occurs when he does not get his way. Ms. Corcoran indicated that Eric prefers to do what he chooses and will become upset when asked to change his routine. She reiterated that Eric has a hard time following classroom rules and procedures. Ms. Corcoran further indicated that Eric struggles with sitting in one place. She noted that he attempts to avoid academic work and tries to play with something so he wanders and then starts getting into things. On one occasion, Ms. Corcoran reiterated that Eric used regular markers on the white board. Ms. Corcoran explained that Eric seeks to escape from academic tasks. She also explained that Eric he wishes to do what he wants and will protest when denied his own way. Additionally, Ms. Corcoran explained that Eric finds certain activities such as sitting in one place distressing because it may be hard for him. On these occasions, Ms. Corcoran noted that Eric will get up and wander. Finally, Ms. Corcoran explained that Eric's behavioral difficulties intensify later in the day when he becomes tired.

Teacher's Aide Interview (November 13, 2016): Ms. Britney Pierce, teacher's aide, was interviewed for her impressions of the functions of Eric's behavior at school. Ms. Pierce explained that Eric struggles during transitions, later in the day, and when required to engage in a task that he does not prefer. She also noted that sitting on the carpet without some kind of support (i.e., someone to lean against) can be difficult for him. Ms. Pierce explained that Eric sometimes will display tantrums when denied his own way. She also noted that this has improved since the start of the school year. Ms. Pierce noted that transitions are difficult for Eric and he requires advanced prompting and cues to successfully make transitions from one activity to another. She explained that Eric also seeks attention from other students in the classroom, but can seek this attention in an inappropriate way. For instance, he has been observed to hit or poke other students rather than use his words. Ms. Pierce also noted that Eric enjoys the attention of selected adults in the classroom. Ms. Pierce further explained that Eric enjoys playing in the sand table, with his "chewy," and his coat. Apparently, he obtains sensory stimulation from these objects or activities. Ms. Pierce further noted that Eric attempts to escape from selected activities or settings including mathematics where he is required to sit on the carpet. When denied his own way, Eric has been observed to tantrum, although this has improved since the beginning of the school year. Ms. Pierce noted that during the first few weeks of school, Eric was completely nonverbal and would just grunt. At present, Ms. Pierce indicated that Eric uses a few words to express his needs. She commented that he is responsive to intervention.

Observations

Observation 1 (November 13, 2016): Eric was observed for 20 min during lunch. He was accompanied by a student teacher who assisted him in retrieving his lunch and finding his seat. Eric was observed to carry his lunch tray from the lunch line to his table. The student teacher assisted Eric in locating his seat. For the next 10 min Eric was observed to eat his meal and occasionally interact nonverbally with the student teacher. On one occasion, the student teacher opened a drink container for Eric.

Observation 2 (November 13, 2016): Eric was observed during his evaluation session with the occupational therapist and the psychologist. During the evaluation with the occupational therapist, Eric was initially reluctant to engage with the therapist, but warmed up and interacted with her in a nonverbal manner. He would attempt to comply with requests from the therapist, but was generally nonverbal. He was noted, however, to smile when she would joke and play with him. During this session, Eric seemed engaged and interested in the tasks, but rarely spoke to her.

Observation 3 (November 28, 2016; 11:15–11:30 AM): Eric was observed during the occupational therapist evaluation. He was noted to comply with requests to put beads on a small string, zip up his jacket, and put on gloves. He faced considerable difficulty responding to verbal requests such as what is the color of this toy and how many toys are there in this pile. Eric appeared engaged in the activity though he rarely looked to the examiner for reinforcement. On several occasions, Eric was asked to demonstrated excitement over completing a task by raising his arms and saying "yeah," but Eric never imitated these gestures. During the course of the physical therapist evaluation, Eric's attention sometimes drifted. He would then start moving toward an object of interest until redirected.

Observation 4 (November 28, 2016; 12:15–12:45 PM): Eric was observed in Ms. Corcoran's kindergarten classroom during whole group mathematics and language instruction. The class was initially requested to count to 100 along with the teacher. During a good portion of this observation, Eric was noted to stare in the direction of the teacher or a classmate who just responded to a teacher's request. He did raise his hand when Ms. Corcoran asked a question of the class, but when called upon he did not respond. For the remainder of the observation Eric never appeared to be following along. The class activity next switched to a verbal analogy game. Several minutes after the start of this game, Eric laid down on the floor. After 5 min, he sat back up with his jacket draped over his left shoulder. The class activity ended and students were instructed to line up by the door when they heard the first letter of their names. Eric waited until he heard his letter, which was offered after everyone else's name was called.

Observation 5 (November 28, 2016; 12:45–1:05 PM): Eric was observed as he entered library for instruction by Ms. Parker. As he walked to the library, Eric followed the directions to walk in line. Open arriving at the library, Eric proceeded to disregard teacher's rules to proceed in order to a table. Instead, he cut ahead of every class mates and sat down at a table in the library. Throughout instruction by Ms. Parker, who was discussing the arrival of the Scholastic Book Fair, Eric sat appropriately in his seat. However, he did not participate in the whole class discussion nor did he seem interested in engaging in the activity.

Observation during Assessment: During the assessment session with the psychologist, Eric struggled with and was reluctant to participate in verbal activities. As a result, an evaluation of his verbal cognitive ability via a standardized measure is not available at this time. However, Eric readily engaged in nonverbal portions of a cognitive ability test. Eric seemed to enjoy the one-on-one attention he received during the assessment process. Following verbal instructions to draw a picture of himself, Eric attempted to draw a picture. He also attempted to draw a picture of a rainbow. At one point, Eric even attempted to initiate conversation with the psychologist. Eric asked a question of the psychologist which was not understood by the psychologist. When Eric did not receive an answer, he said "asked you a question." Eric was very active and required considerable redirection, structure and support throughout the evaluation session.

Observation during Assessment: Eric was a bit slow to warm up during the assessments. He complied with all requests during assessment but faced considerable difficulties with the language portions and began to grow frustrated. He required a 5 min bathroom break and when he returned complied throughout the rest of the assessment.

Cognitive and Academic Functioning

Universal Nonverbal Intelligence Test (UNIT)
The UNIT is an individually administered nonverbal test of intelligence that is given with only pantomime instructions. All items are nonverbal and require no speech. It is made up of four subtests that provide four Quotient Scores and a Full Scale IQ score.

The following are the results of Nick's performance on the UNIT. The UNIT quotients provide scores with a mean of 100 and a standard deviation of 15. Scores between 85 and 115 are considered average.

	Full scale IQ	Memory	Reasoning	Symbolic	Nonsymbolic
UNIT quotient	79	82	79	87	81
Percentile	8	11	8	19	10
Confidence interval (95 %)	76–82	76–87	76–82	80–94	74–87

The UNIT subtests provide scores with a mean of 10 and a standard deviation of 3. Scores between 7 and 13 are considered average.

UNIT subtests	Scaled score
Symbolic memory	5
Cube design	6
Spatial memory	4
Analogic reasoning	5

Eric's overall performance on the UNIT (FSIQ=79; 8th percentile) was in the below average range suggesting that he performed better than 8 out of 100 children his age.

Peabody Picture Vocabulary Test, Fourth Edition
The Peabody Picture Vocabulary Test, Fourth Edition, Form B is a norm-referenced instrument that measures the receptive vocabulary of persons age ranging from 2 years and 6 months to 19 and above. The PPVT-4 scale measures the understanding of the spoken word in standard American English, assessing only receptive vocabulary.

Assessment results	Standard score	95 % CI	Percentile rank
PPVT-4	82	78–87	11

Eric obtained a Standard Score of 82 (11th percentile) placing him in the low average range.

Social-Emotional and Behavioral Functioning

Behavior Assessment System for Children, Second Edition (BASC-2)

The Behavior Assessment System for Children, Second Edition (BASC-2) is an integrated system designed to facilitate the differential diagnosis and classification of a variety of emotional and behavioral conditions in children. It possesses validity scales and several clinical scales, which reflect different dimensions of a child's personality. T-scores between 40 and 60 are considered average. Scores greater than 70 ($T>70$) are in the Clinically Significant range and suggest a high level of difficulty. Scores in the At-Risk range (T-Score 60–69) identify either a significant problem that may not be severe enough to require formal treatment or a potential of developing a problem that needs careful monitoring. On the Adaptive Scales, scores below 30 are considered clinically significant while scores between 31 and 39 are considered at-risk.

Ms. Corcoran

Clinical scales	T-score	Percentile
Hyperactivity	83**	99
Aggression	84**	99
Anxiety	42	21
Depression	56	78
Somatization	40	14
Atypicality	65*	91
Withdrawal	70**	95
Attention problems	66*	93
Adaptability	30**	1
Social skills	32*	3
Functional communication	36*	6
Externalizing problems	85**	99
Internalizing problems	45	35
Behavioral symptoms index	77**	98
Adaptive skills	30**	2

*At-risk
**Clinically significant

BASC-2 ratings suggested a clinically significant elevation on the externalizing problems, adaptive skills and behavior symptoms index composites. BASC-2 rating suggested a clinically significant elevation on the hyperactivity, aggression, withdrawal, and adaptability scales with a rating in the at-risk range on the atypicality, attention problems, functional communication, and social skills scales.

Vineland II Adaptive Behavior Scales

The Vineland measures a student's performance of the daily activities necessary for taking care of oneself, socializing, and getting along with others. Ms. Lord completed the teacher rating form that assesses Doug's functioning in the areas of Communication (receptive, expressive, and written), Daily Living Skills (personal, academic, school community), and Socialization (Interpersonal relationships, Play and leisure time, coping skills).

Domain	Ms. Corcoran		
	Std. Score	Percentile	95 % CI
Communication	60	<1	±7
Daily living skills	68	1	±8
Socialization	67	1	±5
Motor skills	66	1	±10
Adaptive behavior composite	61	1	±4

Results indicate that Eric is performing in the significantly below average range on the Vineland-II across all adaptive skills composites.

Gilliam Autism Rating Scale-Second Edition (GARS-2)

The GARS-2 is a screening instrument used for the assessment of individuals ages 3–22 who have severe behavioral problems that may be indicative of autism. The GARS-2 is composed of three subscales that are based on the definition of autism: stereotyped behaviors, communication, and social interaction. The Social Interaction subscale comprises items that describe social interactive behaviors, expression of communicative intent, and cognitive and emotional behaviors. The stereotyped behavior subscale comprises items that describe restricted and stereotyped behaviors that are characteristic of Asperger's. The social interaction subscale contains items that evaluate the individual's ability to relate appropriately to people, events and objects. An Autism Index of 85 or higher indicates a very likely presence of autism. An index score of 70–84 indicates a possible classification of autism while a score below 70 indicates an unlikely presence of autism.

Ms. Corcoran

	Std. Score
Stereotyped behaviors	8
Communication	9
Social interaction	10
Autism index	94

Ratings of Eric on the GARS-2 suggest a very likely probability of Autism.

Childhood Autism Rating Scale, Second Edition (CARS 2)

The CARS 2 is a behavior rating scale developed to identify children across the autism spectrum. Children are rated on fifteen characteristics including relationship to others; body use; emotional response; adaptation to change; taste, smell and touch response; fear or nervousness; visual response; object use; imitation; verbal and non-verbal communication; intellectual ability; activity level and listening response. Children (ages 2–12) with scores on the CARS below 30 generally do not receive a classification of an autism spectrum disorder. Children with scores between 30 and 36.5 are considered to have mild to moderate autism while scores above 37 reflect severe autism. Eric's rating on the CARS 2 was 33, suggesting that he experiences mild to moderate symptoms of an Autism Spectrum Disorder.

Conceptualization and Classification

Multiple data sources and methods of assessment inform the conceptualization of Eric's cognitive, academic, social-emotional, and behavioral functioning including whether he qualifies for special education support. Details in support of these findings are offered below.

Cognitive and Academic Functioning: Eric's present cognitive ability performance could only be partially ascertained. Eric scored in the below average range on the UNIT, a measure of nonverbal ability (Standard Score = 79; 8th percentile). Eric faces considerable struggles with verbal expression and it is likely that his significant difficulties with these abilities contributed to his inability to produce a verbal response. Generally, Eric presents as a nonverbal youngster, so his struggles with the verbal portions of tests of cognitive ability are consistent with these overall diffi-culties. An evaluation by the speech-language pathologist revealed that Eric's receptive vocabulary understanding is higher than his expressive abilities. Eric's per-formance on the Peabody Picture Vocabulary Test, Fourth Edition (PPVT-4) was in the low average range (Std. Score = 84; 11th percentile). This test suggests that Eric has superior receptive than expressive verbal understanding.

Social, Emotional, and Behavioral Functioning: Multiple data sources including interview results, classroom observations, and rating forms indicate that Eric struggles with communicating and interacting in a socially appropriate fashion. For instance, when asked a direct question, Eric is generally unable to produce a verbal response. He also finds most academic (e.g., alphabet principle) and behavioral (e.g., sitting in class) requirements difficult. There has been improvement since Eric arrived at the beginning of the year. He is better able to wait his turn, sit in a whole group setting, and avoid temper tantrums when denied his own way or denied access to a preferred activity. Still, Eric struggles with developing peer relationships at a developmentally appropriate level and displays a lack of social and emotional reciprocity.

Summary: Eric's cluster of behavioral, communication, and social-emotional difficulties are impairing his social and behavioral functioning and also contributing to difficulties with his academic functioning. Eric will benefit from accommodations for symptoms consistent with a classification of autism.

Summary and Recommendations

Eric faces significant struggles with the academic curriculum. He also faces challenges with expressing himself orally and with the fine motor aspects of writing. Eric was not able to be evaluated on a standardized measure of academic achievement due to significant deficits in verbal understanding and expression. This is consistent with his with classroom based performance where he struggles with producing a response to written or orally furnished questions. Eric will require specially designed instruction to make gains in the academic curriculum.

Considering multiple data sources and methods of assessment, Eric will benefit from accommodations for the host of academic, behavioral, social, emotional, and communication deficits that are associated with a classification of an autism spectrum disorder. Selected recommendations are offered below while additional recommendations are presented in the functional behavioral assessment that accompanies this report.

1. *Accommodations for Academic Tasks*: Eric struggles with most academic tasks in the kindergarten curriculum and will benefit from intervention for very basic academic skills including letter, number, shape and color recognition. He will also benefit from guidance regarding how to write his numbers and letters, a task he finds difficult.

2. *Speech-Language Therapy*: Eric is a nonverbal child who generally speaks softly and produces only a few words. This interferes not only with his academic progress, but also with his social progress. He will benefit from speech-language support as indicated in the speech pathologists report.

3. *Social Skills Training including Stories and Social Pragmatics Interventions*: Eric may benefit from exposure to social stories, role plays and behavioral modeling as a way to improve social skills and increase more appropriate responses to peers during interaction with them.

4. *Behavioral Support*: Eric may benefit from support for the following behaviors associated with his classification:

   (a) Transition to new activities or environments.
   (b) Low frustration tolerance when required to engage in an activity he does not prefer.
   (c) Difficulty with following multistep directions.
   (d) Peer interaction including how to engage in a more appropriate manner than grabbing or poking other children.

5. *Support for Caregivers*: The following website provides useful information regarding children with an autism spectrum disorder classification: http://www. autism-society.org . Ms. Stokeham may wish to reach out to resources in the community for families with a child on the autistic spectrum.

6. *Functional Behavioral Assessment*: Additional recommendations are offered in the accompanying functional behavioral assessment report.

Stefan C. Dombrowski, Ph.D.
Licensed Psychologist (PA and NJ)
Certified School Psychologist (PA and NJ)

Sample Report 3: Lower Functioning Autism

Name: Mike Smith   Date of Report: November 7, 2016
Date of Birth: 1/24/2010   Chronological Age: 6
Grade: K   School: San Juan Unified School District (SJUD)
Name of Examiner: Stefan Dombrowski

Parent and Address: Maria Smith

Phone: (609) 555-1234

Reason for Referral

Mike is a nonverbal child with an outside classification of autism. He makes only a few sounds that are reminiscent of words. Mike experiences considerable difficulty with all aspects of the kindergarten curriculum including cognitive, academic, behavioral, social-emotional and adaptive. Mike was referred for a comprehensive evaluation to determine his present level of functioning and whether he might qualify for specially designed instruction. Appropriate recommendations and accommodations are offered.

Assessment Methods and Sources of Data
Behavior Assessment System for Children, Second Edition (BASC-2)

- Mrs. Tina Norbury
Vineland Adaptive Behavior Scale, Second Edition (Vineland-II)
- Mrs. Tina Norbury
Childhood Autism Rating Scale, Second Edition (CARS 2)
- Stefan C. Dombrowski, Ph.D.
Teacher Interview
- Mrs. Tina Norbury (Kindergarten Teacher)
- Mrs. Evelyn Crabtree (Therapeutic Support Staff)
- Mrs. Sue Sylvester (Learning Support Teacher)
Parent Interview
- Mrs. Maria Smith and Mr. Matthew Smith
Classroom Observations
Review of Academic Grade Reports
Review of School Records

Background Information and Developmental History
Mike Smith is a 6-year-old kindergarten student at the San Juan Unified School District (SJUD). He struggles with all aspects of the kindergarten curriculum and was referred for an evaluation as a result.

Prenatal, Perinatal, and Early Developmental History: Mike was born prematurely at 32 weeks gestation. He was the product of a multiple birth and his twin brother is in kindergarten. Mike spent 30 days in the Neonatal Intensive Care Unit (NICU) following his birth. Mrs. Smith notes that Mike was delayed by about 6 months in most early developmental milestones including walking, saying his first words, rolling over, and sitting up. Mike received early intervention speech, occupational therapy and physical therapy through Elwyn. He has an outside diagnosis of Autism. Mike is still primarily nonverbal and continues to walk on his toes.

Medical: Mike's hearing and vision are intact. He experienced a fall down the top of the stairs at 3 years of age and experienced a concussion. Mike also contracted influenza at age 4 and required a 2-week hospitalization. Mike has an outside classification of Autism. Mr. and Mrs. Smith reported additional medical concerns at this time.

Cognitive, Academic, and Language Functioning: A test of cognitive ability including a nonverbal test of cognitive ability was not able to be administered to Mike at the present time. Mike did not appear interested in the evaluation. Because of Mike's interest in using a pointer within the classroom, he was asked to point to specific letters and numbers on a large board. Mike was not able to comply with this task.

Mike occasionally uses his Picture Exchange Communication Systems (PECS) to communicate his needs. Mike has no additional standardized cognitive or academic achievement results. Classroom information indicates extreme difficulties with communication and with understanding basic academic skills.

Social-Emotional, Behavioral, and Adaptive Functioning: Mike has always struggled in his interaction with peers. He is primarily nonverbal and will only occasionally use simple language to communicate his needs. For instance Mike has been observed to vocalize approximately three words at school (e.g., \muh\ for \more\; \wah\ for \ walk\ and \bye-bye\). Mrs. Smith and Mr. Smith indicated that Mike can vocalize about ten words. Mike rarely participates in group activities. Instead, he plays alone or plays in parallel with other children. If a peer has something that interests Mike, then he will just walk over and attempt to grab the object. Mike likes the feeling of selected items over his head such as leaves, mulch, and blocks. He walks on his toes. Mike pumps his arms/fists when excited. He wears a pull-up because of a lack of independent toileting skills. Mike is better with urination than defecation. He is assisted at least twice daily with trips to the bathroom at school. Mike has recently been darting out of the classroom.

Strengths: When asked about Mike's strengths, Mrs. Norbury described Mike as a kind and sweet child. Mrs. Sylvester indicated that Mike can be sweet, kind, and affectionate and has a very agreeable disposition. Mrs. Crabtree explained that Mike does respond to redirection from her. She noted that he can be charming through his use of smiling and seems to enjoy one-on-one attention.

Summary: Mr. Smith and Mrs. Smith report that Mike has an outside classification of autism. The present evaluation indicates that Mike faces considerable struggles with communication, socialization, academic, and adaptive skills.

Interview Results

Parent Interview (November 6, 2016): Mrs. Smith and Mr. Smith were interviewed together regarding Mike's functioning. Mrs. Smith noted that Mike is a twin and was born prematurely 8 weeks early; he had a stay in the NICU for 30 days. Mrs. Smith explained that Mike was approximately 6 months behind his twin brother in all early developmental milestones. She noted that this prompted her to seek consultation and ultimately receive early interventions support (e.g., OT, PT, Speech). Mrs. Smith explained that Elwyn provided the Picture Exchange Communication System (PECS) for Mike. Mr. Smith and Mrs. Smith explained that Mike has an outside diagnosis of autism. Mrs. Smith explained that Mike can approximately vocalize 10 words. Mr. Smith explained that Mike can independently spell several words using his finger including cat, dog and stop. Mrs. Smith and Mr. Smith explained that Mike is a generally happy child. They noted that whether he engages in a particular task depends upon his mood. Mr. Smith explained that if Mike wants the computer or iPad then that is what he wants and it is hard to break him away from that activity. Mrs. Smith explained that Mike tends to play by himself. She noted that he will not share with others. Mrs. Smith explained that Mike. Mr. Smith and Mrs. Smith noted that Mike's needs include being independent. They noted that he is capable of doing many things, but needs a one-on-one assistant. Mr. Smith and Mrs. Smith explained that Mike's strengths include being a quick learner (i.e., he adjusted well considering being placed in a totally different environment). Mr. Smith indicated that Mike has adjusted to a new routine at HCS. Mrs. Smith stated that once Mike he learns a routine, he will comply. Both parents noted that Mike needs assistance in the bathroom particularly with defecating. Mrs. Smith explained that Mike will notify when he needs to use the bathroom through his PECS system or will take folks by the arm. Mrs. Smith and Mr. Philips explained that Mike needs "sameness" in routines and assistance with transitions. Mrs. Smith and Mr. Smith spent a considerable amount of time discussing possible options for services. Mrs. Smith and Mr. Smith commented that if the recommendation is to change Mike's placement, then they would need some time to discuss and consult with other experts. They discussed the pragmatic aspects of having to get three different children to three different places and were concerned about Mike's adjustment to another placement considering that his transition to HCS has gone pretty well.

Teacher Interview (October 11, 2016): Mrs. Mary Norbury, Mike's kindergarten teacher, was interviewed regarding Mike's academic, behavioral, emotional, adaptive, and social functioning. Mrs. Norbury indicated that Mike is primarily nonverbal. She noted that he does not show what he can do or know. Mrs. Norbury explained that Mike has a picture book describing different activities, but he does not always use it. She noted that he cannot demonstrate his knowledge through words or using the picture book to show his knowledge. During whole group instruction, Mrs. Norbury indicated that it seems like Mike is sometimes listening. She mentioned that he uses noise and utterances to communicate, but it is hard to decipher. Mrs. Norbury explained that Mike tends to wander the classroom but is getting better at sitting. She explained that Mike constantly needs a board book in hand and often turns through the pages. Commenting on Mike's social progress, Mrs. Norbury explained that Mike will play alongside other children but will not have much interaction with them. She noted that he does not initiate with other children. Mrs. Norbury explained that Mike does not communicate his need to use the bathroom. She explained that he wears pull-ups because of this. Mrs. Norbury noted that Mike needs constant monitoring.

Teacher Interview (November 13, 2016): Mrs. Sue Sylvester, Mike's learning support teacher, was interviewed regarding Mike's academic, behavioral, emotional, adaptive, and social functioning. Mrs. Sylvester first discussed Mike's communication abilities. She noted that Mike has very little verbal communication. Mrs. Sylvester expressed that Mike's communication is mostly through vocalizations. She indicated that Mike is starting to sign the word \more\ but it takes prompting.

Mrs. Sylvester indicated that Mike will make a vocalization that approximates \more\ but it is often with the preceding \m\ sound. Mrs. Sylvester indicated that Mike knows his letters and numbers. She indicated that he can write the letters of the alphabet but cannot do so on a line. Mrs. Sylvester indicated that Mike can also click on a computer numbers in proper order. Mrs. Sylvester noted that Mike can spell words such as \Super Why\ (one of the PBS shows), \sit\ and \comp\ for \computer\. Mrs. Sylvester explained that Mike understands the connection between \comp\ and \computer\ but does not write \sit\ when he wants to sit. Beyond that, Mrs. Sylvester expressed that Mike has limited communication abilities. She noted that he still does not communicate his need to go to the bathroom and does not recognize when he has just gone to the bathroom. For instance, Mrs. Sylvester discussed how Mike urinated in the classroom and his pants were wet and there was a pool of urine around him. She explained that Mike did not seem to notice. Commenting next on Mike's social abilities, Mrs. Sylvester explained that Mike seems unaware of other children in the classroom. She noted that Mike will interact with her only when she has directed the interaction; otherwise, he will wander off and do something else. Mrs. Sylvester explained that she is working on being less impulsive with clicking on the computer. She indicated that Mike now understands that he may have to wait for an application to load and less frequently clicks. Still, Mrs. Sylvester explained that the use of the computer is highly reinforcing for Mike. Mrs. Sylvester indicated that Mike has recently taken to getting up and wandering out of the classroom. She expressed concerns about Mike's safety because of this behavior. Mrs. Sylvester expressed that Mike needs more functional skills that focus on feeding, bathroom skills, use of utensils, and basic communication skills.

Therapeutic Support Staff Interview (TSS; October 23, 2016): Mrs. Evelyn Crabtree, Mike's TSS worker, was interviewed for her impressions of Mike's behavior at school. Mrs. Crabtree explained that Mike faces significant communication struggles. She noted that she has only heard him say three words and these words are not very clear (e.g., "muh" for /more/; "waaa" for /walk/; and "bye-bye"). Mrs. Crabtree explained that he will not be verbal every day. Mrs. Crabtree explained that Mike is getting better at using his picture book. She noted that 2 weeks ago he started using it and learning. Mrs. Crabtree explained that Mike has the capacity to communicate with his picture book, but must feel like using it to do so. Mrs. Crabtree explained that last week, for the first time, Mike used the picture book to explain that he has to go to the bathroom, but we do not know when he has to go until after he goes to the bathroom. As a result, Mrs. Crabtree indicated that Mike is taken to the bathroom two times per day. Mrs. Crabtree explained that Mike has limited interactions with other children in the classroom. She noted that he will either play alongside the other children and will only interact with them when he wants something, at which point he will just grab the toy or book. Mrs. Crabtree explained that Mike puts everything in his mouth. She also noted that he likes to put items over his head and hair. She explained that this includes mulch, leaves, and blocks. Mrs. Crabtree noted that Mike has no sense of routines or boundaries within the classroom. She noted that he walks on his toes and will arm/fist pump when excited. Mrs. Crabtree further explained that everything has to be done on Mike's left side. For instance, if his right shoe is untied, then she must take off and tie his left shoe first before tying the right shoe. Mrs. Crabtree explained that Mike sometimes breaks down and cries. She mentioned that she is uncertain why, but suspects he is frustrated.

Observations

Observation 1 (October 23, 2016): Mike was observed for 20 min while seated at his desk, during center time, and then during transition to recess. The rest of the class was working on a literacy activity. Mike was observed to be playing with a hard cover book along with a wooden, yellow truck. Mike attempted to get out of his seat on three occasions during seat work, but was redirected by Mrs. Crabtree. Mike complied with this request, but he was never engaged in any of the work the rest of the class was working on. Denoting a transition to center time, the student teacher asked students to put their heads upon their desks. Mike required prompting from Mrs. Crabtree, but complied with this request. Students were then asked to move to the carpet to begin center time. Mike needed considerable prompting to comply with this request. He moved to the carpet area while the student teacher provided a lesson on reading, but he had his back to the teacher. He needed prompting to face where the teacher was seated. Mike did not appear interested in this lesson. Instead, he was focused on his hard cover book along with his yellow, wooden, small truck. He was noted to make vocalizations during the center time and was observed to get up and wander the classroom on four occasions. Mike was then redirected by Mrs. Crabtree to return to the carpet.

Observation 2 (October 23, 2016): Mike was observed for 30 min during transition to recess and then during one-on-one time with the TSS worker and the psychologist. As the class transitioned from carpet time to recess, Mike did not seem aware of the transition and continued to play with his book and small, yellow truck. To ensure that Mike was in familiar surroundings, this psychologist attempt to conduct an evaluation of Mike's nonverbal cognitive ability. Mike was not interested in participating. Instead, Mike was interested in a pointer that his teacher uses to count numbers on the counting board. Mike used the pointer and uttered a sound as he pointed to each number. Since Mike seemed interested in using the pointer and the counting board, the psychologist asked Mike to point to specific numbers on the board. Mike was unable to complete this task. Mike was also asked to use the pointer to identify letters of the alphabet requested of him. Again, he was unable to complete this task. As the psychologist spoke with the TSS worker, Mike wandered the room. He would attempt to go through various items, but when redirected to stop, he complied. Mike became visibly upset when his right shoe became untied. Mrs. Crabtree started to tie the right shoe, but Mike made a sound and wanted her to untie his left shoe first and then move to the right shoe. Toward the end of the observation and evaluation, Mike started to utter crying like sounds and place his hands on his head. Mike then left with Mrs. Crabtree to finish the remainder of recess.

Observation 3 (October 30, 2016): Mike was observed for 20 min when the student teacher was demonstrating how to write \qu\ words. After approximately five attempts to get Mike to trace the letters, Mike attempted to trace the letters on the worksheet using his finger. He required considerable prompting and support to engage. Following completion of this activity, Mike used the picture system to roughly communicate that he wanted to leave the classroom with the speech-language pathologist. (Mike selected "outside" and then took the speech-language pathologist by the arm). The activity then switched to a whole group reading lesson. The entire class was prompted to go to the carpet. Mike continued turning the pages of a book and failed to regard the prompt. His TSS worker then prompted Mike to move to the carpet. Mike was able to comply, but sat with his back facing the rest of the class and the teacher. He had to be prompted again to turn and face the teacher.

Observation during Assessment: Mike was accompanied to the testing session by his TSS worker. Mike was unable to complete a nonverbal test of cognitive ability. Mike could not produce a verbal response to any questions asked of him. He attempted to emulate his teacher's use of a pointer to count or name letters of the alphabet. However, when Mike was asked to point to specific letters and numbers, he was unable to do so. Mike rarely used his PECS systems. It appeared to be cumbersome, cluttered and difficult to use. After approximately 20 min, Mike attempted to leave the testing session by taking the TSS working by the hand. The testing session ended at that time.

Cognitive and Academic Functioning

Due to Mike's significant struggles with communication and related symptoms of an autism spectrum classification, he was not able to participate in a conventional or a nonverbal test of cognitive ability.

Social-Emotional and Behavioral Functioning

Behavior Assessment System for Children, Second Edition (BASC-2)

The Behavior Assessment System for Children, Second Edition (BASC-2) is an integrated system designed to facilitate the differential diagnosis and classification of a variety of emotional and behavioral conditions in children. It possesses validity scales and several clinical scales, which reflect different dimensions of a child's personality. T-scores between 40 and 60 are considered average. Scores greater than 70 ($T > 70$) are in the Clinically Significant range and suggest a high level of difficulty. Scores in the At-Risk range (T-Score 60–69) identify either a significant problem that may not be severe enough to require formal treatment or a potential of developing a problem that needs careful monitoring. On the Adaptive Scales, scores below 30 are considered clinically significant while scores between 31 and 35 are considered at-risk.

Mrs. Norbury

Clinical scales	T-score	Percentile
Hyperactivity	53	70
Aggression	55	78
Conduct problems	56	78
Anxiety	39*	9
Depression	59	84
Somatization	42	19
Attention problems	67*	95
Learning problems	70**	94
Atypicality	79**	97
Withdrawal	69*	95
Adaptability	30*	1
Social skills	30*	1
Leadership	31*	1
Study skills	29**	1
Functional communication	21**	1
Externalizing problems	55	75
Internalizing problems	46	38
School problems	70**	97
Behavioral symptoms index	67*	94
Adaptive skills	25**	1

*At-risk
**Clinically significant

BASC-2 ratings suggested a clinically significant elevation on the school problems and adaptive skills composites with an at-risk rating on the behavioral symptoms index. BASC-2 rating suggested a clinically significant elevation on the learning problems, atypicality, study skills, and functional communication clinical skills with an at-risk rating on the attention problems, adaptability, anxiety, social skills, leadership skills, and withdrawal clinical scales.

Vineland II Adaptive Behavior Scales
The Vineland measures a student's performance of the daily activities necessary for taking care of oneself, socializing, and getting along with others. Mrs. Norbury completed the teacher rating form that assesses Mike's functioning in the areas of Communication (receptive, expressive, and written), Daily Living Skills (personal, academic, school community), and Socialization (Interpersonal relationships, Play and leisure time, coping skills).

Following are the results on the Vineland-II:

Domain	Mrs. Norbury		
	Std. Score	Percentile	95 % CI
Communication	38	<1	±7
Daily living skills	44	<1	±7
Socialization	55	<1	±5
Motor skills	43	<1	±11
Adaptive behavior composite	38	<1	±4

Results indicate that Mike is performing in the significantly below average range on the Vineland-II across all adaptive skills composites.

Childhood Autism Rating Scale, Second Edition (CARS 2)
The CARS 2 is a behavior rating scale developed to identify children across the autism spectrum. Children are rated on fifteen characteristics including the following: relationship to others; body use; emotional response; adaptation to change; taste, smell and touch response; fear or nervousness; visual response; object use; imitation; verbal and nonverbal communication; intellectual ability; activity level and listening response. Children (ages 2–12) with scores on the CARS below 30 generally do not receive a classification of an autism spectrum disorder. Children with scores between 30 and 36.5 are considered to have mild to moderate autism while scores above 37 reflect severe autism. Mike's rating on the CARS 2 was 40 (T-score=52; 58 percentile), suggesting that he experiences severe symptoms of an Autism Spectrum Disorder.

Conceptualization and Classification
Multiple data sources including interview results, classroom observations, and rating forms indicate that Mike struggles with symptoms of an autism spectrum disorder. Details in support of these findings are offered below.

Cognitive and Academic Functioning: Mike faces considerable difficulty relating to people in a typical manner. He only minimally imitates sounds, words or movements from others. He is able to approximately communicate the sounds of only a few words including /muh/ (for more) and /wah/ (for walk). Mike is primarily nonverbal in his communication, but still struggles to use the picture communication system he brings to school.

Social, Emotional, Behavioral, and Adaptive Functioning: Mike experiences considerable social, emotional, behavioral, and adaptive difficulties. He walks on his toes. When needing to put on articles of clothing or have his shoes tied (or retied), Mike needs to have that occur on the left side first. He insists that if it is only his right shoe that is untied, then the left be first untied and then retied before the right.

Mike enjoys the physical sensation of items (e.g., leaves, blocks, hands) touching his head. Mike generally does not reciprocate communication and plays alone. Background information indicates that his play with other children is entirely parallel when he happens to engage near them. If Mike wants an item from another child, he will simply walk over and grab the item. Mike wears a pull-up and requires assistance when going to the bathroom. When excited he will do a fist/arm pump motion. With prompting and considerable one-on-one support, Mike is able to follow selected classroom rules such as sitting at the carpet, putting his head on his desk, and heading to recess. However, if left without such support, Mike would remain unable to follow along.

Summary: Mike symptoms are significantly impairing his functioning in all domains at school. He will benefit from accommodations for symptoms consistent with a classification of autism.

Summary and Recommendations
Considering multiple data sources and methods of assessment, Mike will benefit from accommodations for the host of academic, behavioral, social, emotional, adaptive, and communication deficits that are associated with a classification of an autism spectrum disorder.

1. *More Intensive Intervention*: Mike's functional academic, behavioral, communication, socialization, and adaptive needs are not being met in the present setting. He will require more intensive programming and functional intervention for the host of struggles he faces. Additionally, it is recommended that Mike be evaluated for a new PECS system as his present one appears to be disorganized and difficult to use.

2. *Support for Caregivers*: The following website provides useful information regarding children with an autism spectrum disorder classification: http://www. autism-society.org. Mr. Smith and Mrs. Smith may wish to reach out to resources in the community for families with a child on the autistic spectrum.

Stefan C. Dombrowski, Ph.D.
Licensed Psychologist (PA and NJ)
Certified School Psychologist (PA and NJ)

References

Baio, J. (2014). Prevalence of autism spectrum disorder among children aged 8 years – autism and developmental disabilities monitoring network, 11 sites, United States, 2010. *Morbidity and Mortality Weekly Report (MMWR), 63*, 1–21.

Boyle, C. A., Boulet, S., Schieve, L. A., Cohen, R. A., Blumberg, S. J., Yeargin-Allsopp, S. V., & Kogan, M. D. (2011). Trends in the prevalence of developmental disabilities in US Children, 1997–2008. Pediatrics. Retrieved May 22, 2014 from http://pediatrics.aappublications.org/content/early/2011/05/19/peds.2010-2989

Filipek, P. A. (2005). Medical aspects of autism. In F. R. Volkmar, R. Paul, A. Klin, & D. Cohen (Eds.), *Handbook of autism and pervasive developmental disorders* (pp. 534–581). Hoboken, NJ: Wiley.

Gadow, K. D., DeVincent, C. J., & Pomeroy, J. (2006). ADHD symptom subtypes in children with pervasive developmental disorder. *Journal of Autism and Developmental Disorders, 36*, 271–283.

Grigorenko, E. L., Klin, A., & Volkmar, F. (2003). Annotation: hyperlexia: disability or superability? *Journal of Child Psychology and Psychiatry, 44*, 1079–1091.

Harris, J. C. (2010). Autism spectrum diagnoses in neurogenetic syndromes. In E. Hollander, A. Kolevzon, & J. T. Coyle (Eds.), *Textbook of autism spectrum disorders* (pp. 223–237). Washington, DC: American Psychiatric Publishing.

Harrison, P. L., & Oakland, T. (2003). *Adaptive behavior assessment system* (2nd ed.). San Antonio, TX: The Psychological Corporation.

Howlin, P., Goode, S., Hutton, J., & Rutter, M. (2004). Adult outcome for children with autism. *Journal of Child Psychology and Psychiatry, 45*, 212–229.

Matson, J. L., & Nebel-Schwalm, M. S. (2007). Comorbid psychopathology with autism spectrum disorder in children: An overview. *Research in Developmental Disabilities, 28*, 341–35.

O'Neil, R. E., Albin, R. W., Storey, K., & Horner, R. H. (2014). *Functional assessment and program development for problem behavior: A practical handbook.* Clifton Park, NY: Cengage Learning.

Saulnier, C. A., & Ventola, P. E. (2012). *Essentials of autism spectrum disorders evaluation and assessment.* Hoboken, NJ: Wiley.

Sparrow, S. S., Cicchetti, V. D., & Balla, A. D. (2005). *Vineland adaptive behavior scales* (2nd ed.). Circle Pines, MN: American Guidance Service.

Watson, S. T., & Steege, M. W. (2003). *Conducting school-based functional behavioral assessments: A practitioner's guide. The Guilford practical intervention in the schools series.* New York, USA: Guilford Press.

Zirkell, P. S. (2011). The role of DSM in IDEA case law. Communique, 39. Retrieved April 2, 2014 from www.nasponline.org.

Chapter 13
Emotional Disturbance

13.1 Overview

Bower (1960) originally conceived of the term emotionally disturbed. His definition, with slight modification, was subsequently incorporated into the federal definition in 1975 with the passage of the Education for All Handicapped Children (PL 42-175). The definition and diagnostic criteria for the category emotionally disturbed (ED) has persisted through the present rendition of IDEA. Neither the definition of ED nor the confusing and controversial diagnostic approach has changed since that time. There still remains little consensus as to what constitutes ED (Forness & Kavale, 2000; Kauffman & Landrum, 2012) and there is no universally accepted definition (Friedman, Kutash, & Duchnowski, 1996), rendering the term just as confusing and controversial as when it was first codified into the federal regulations. Complicating matters further, IDEA and DSM-5 do not offer interchangeable terminology. In other words, the special education classification of ED is not interchangeable with any DSM-5 diagnosis except schizophrenia. However, the prevalence of schizophrenia in childhood (Dombrowski, Gischlar, & Mrazik, 2011) is so rare that its alignment across taxonomies is nearly meaningless.

Della Toffalo and Pedersen (2005) note that the majority of youth classified with ED meet diagnostic criteria for a mental disorder. There are additional concerns that have been raised regarding ED. Males, African-Americans and children from lower SES backgrounds have been disproportionately classified as ED (Osher, Sims, & Woodruff, 2002). Moreover, there are no widely accepted, standardized measures that reliably and validly assess the five criteria from the federal definition for ED (Floyd & Bose, 2003). Instead, idiosyncratic assessment procedures using informal observations and ambiguous diagnostic criteria may form the basis for an ED classification within the schools (Handwerk & Marshall, 1988). One of the more confounding issues with the diagnostic criteria was the inclusion of the social maladjustment rule-out. Skiba and Grizzle (1992) note that this was added to the initial definition because of concerns over opening the floodgates to juveniles under

© Springer Science+Business Media New York 2015   221
S.C. Dombrowski, *Psychoeducational Assessment and Report Writing*,
DOI 10.1007/978-1-4939-1911-6_13

the supervision of the court system following contact with the law. Researchers, advocacy groups, professional organizations, and legal experts have attempted to distinguish between social maladjustment and emotional disturbance with little success (Kelly, 1988; Slenkovitch, 1992a, 1992b). Some consider social maladjustment as synonymous with disruptive disorders (e.g., ODD, CD). Others (e.g., NASP; APA) have suggested that children with externalizing behavior disorders should be eligible for special education services in the schools under a classification of ED. The debate is sure to continue until a well-operationalized definition is devised that is clinically and psychoeducationally relevant.

13.2   Definition

The federal definition of ED is as follows:

Emotional disturbance means a condition exhibiting one or more of the following characteristics over a long period of time and to a marked degree that adversely affects a child's educational performance:

(A) An inability to learn that cannot be explained by intellectual, sensory, or health factors.
(B) An inability to build or maintain satisfactory interpersonal relationships with peers and teachers.
(C) Inappropriate types of behavior or feelings under normal circumstances.
(D) A general pervasive mood of unhappiness or depression.
(E) A tendency to develop physical symptoms or fears associated with personal or school problems.

Emotional disturbance includes schizophrenia. The term does not apply to children who are socially maladjusted, unless it is determined that they have an emotional disturbance under paragraph (c)(4)(i) of this section (Federal Register, 2006, p. 46756).

13.3   Identification

As mentioned, the identification of ED is plagued by several issues. The foremost is an ambiguous definition that lacks clear operationalization. The definition has not changed materially since it was incorporated into federal legislation nearly 40 years ago. Suffice to say, the definition is a clinical and psychoeducational anachronism that requires significant updating.

Criterion A above is something that is readily understood as a rule out and makes clinical and educational sense. However, criteria B through D are sufficiently vague to permit idiosyncratic interpretation and diagnostic application. What does it mean to be unable to build or maintain satisfactory relationships? What does it mean to have inappropriate behavior or feelings under normal circumstances? If a child tends to develop somatic complaints associated with school, and therefore experiences an adverse educational impact, but is generally well-behaved and well-regarded by peers and teachers alike, would it be appropriate to label the child as "emotionally disturbed?" This becomes an especially salient concern in consideration of research that suggests the label itself is associated with commission of criminal offense. Wagner (1989) notes that within 3 years of leaving school more than 50 % of ED students have had at least one arrest. The term schizophrenia is listed as a specific criterion, but the incidence of schizophrenia in childhood (Dombrowski et al., 2011) is so low that it renders this inclusion criterion less applicable. As for criterion D above, it could be associated with depression as noted within the DSM, but the term "pervasively unhappy" is a singular symptom of depression rendering it illusive as a diagnostic characteristic. So, the field is left with a vague definition and must use clinical judgment, perhaps idiosyncratically, to arrive at a classification.

13.4   General Guidance Regarding Psychoeducational Assessment of ED

A comprehensive evaluation using multiple methods of assessment and multiple data sources becomes especially important in the classification of ED. As mentioned the stakes are high given the prospect of misdiagnosis particularly when evaluating African-Americans, males, and children from lower SES backgrounds. When conducting an evaluation for suspected ED, it is extremely important to consider cultural context. Additionally, if narrow band ED measures are used then it is best to use them qualitatively as an informal assessment due to their technical limitations. To support a classification of ED, I recommend listing each ED criteria and then specifically delineating whether the criteria was met. One of the more difficult decisions will be to differentiate between emotional disturbance and social maladjustment. Neither scholars nor practitioners have been able to successfully make this determination so it will take considerable reflection. What is clear, however, is that children with emotional and behavioral disorders are not receiving needed services given the low prevalence of the condition (less than 1 % despite estimates of mental disorders in school age children at over five times that amount) (Costello, Mustillo, Erkanli, Keeler, & Angold, 2003).

There are no widely accepted standardized measures of ED (Floyd & Bose, 2003). Those assessment instruments that are available have been criticized for having poor technical properties (Floyd & Bose, 2003). A wide variety of assessment tools have been created for the purpose of classifying students with suspected ED. These include the Scale for Assessing Emotional Disturbance (SAED; Epstein & Cullinan, 1998), the Differential Test of Conduct and Emotional Problems (DT/CEP; Kelly, 1990), and the Emotional and Behavior Problem Scale (EBPS; Wright, 1989). Yet, these tools have been severely criticized for technical limitations. It was argued by

Floyd and Bose (2003) that if they are used at all then these scales should be used as one component of a comprehensive multi-source, multi-method evaluation. For all the reasons cited above, the field often relies upon idiosyncratic descriptions, informal observations, clinical myth, and arbitrary assessment procedures (Becker, 2011; Handwerk & Marshall, 1998) when arriving at an ED classification.

The following example using the Pennsylvania Special Education Code is illustrative of the approach to classification of ED that I have found useful and appropriate.

Emotional Disturbance Example
The following criteria from the Pennsylvania Special Education Code guided classification of emotional disturbance.

Emotional disturbance means a condition exhibiting one or more of the following characteristics over a long period of time and to a marked degree that adversely affects a child's educational performance:

(A) *An inability to learn that cannot be explained by intellectual, sensory, or health factors.*

There are no intellectual, sensory or health factors that contribute to Crystian's learning difficulties. This criterion is not applicable at this time.

(B) *An inability to build or maintain satisfactory interpersonal relationships with peers and teachers.*

Crystian struggles in his interaction with peers and teachers. He has used, and continues to use, physical threats and actual aggression when engaging with other students. Crystian has been suspended for physical aggression, verbal threats, and cussing out teachers (e.g., telling a teacher he "hates" them or to "fuck off"). Crystian struggles with social-cognitive information processing distortions (i.e., understanding social nuance) where he misperceives ambiguous and even benign social interaction as being negatively directed toward him. These characteristics and behaviors intrude upon his ability to build and maintain satisfactory interpersonal relationships with peers and teachers. This criterion is applicable.

(C) *Inappropriate types of behavior or feelings under normal circumstances.*

Crystian's displays several behaviors and feelings that are inappropriate under normal circumstances. His reaction to peers, teachers, and situations that frustrate him can be aggressive and volatile. He has cussed out teachers (e.g., telling them he "hates them" or to "fuck off"). Crystian also tends to overreact to actual or perceived insults directed toward him by peers. At these times he will physically aggress, make verbal threats, or become disproportionately upset. Even when interaction with peers is appropriate, Crystian frequently misperceives the interaction as negative

(continued)

(continued)

and will become extremely upset and sometimes become either verbally or physically aggressive. Crystian has been observed to flip a switch and go from being calm to extremely upset to a mildly frustrating circumstance. For instance, he has been observed to be fine one moment, but then extremely upset and angry the next moment when he struggled with opening his locker. Crystian has a preoccupying fascination with guns and has stated an interest in learning how to use guns as a means to protect himself from other children who might aggrieve upon him. This criterion is applicable.

(D) *A general pervasive mood of unhappiness or depression.*

Multiple sources of evaluation data do not indicate that Crystian is pervasively depressed or unhappy. He does sometimes become volatile when upset or denied his own way. This criterion is not applicable at this time.

(E) *A tendency to develop physical symptoms or fears associated with personal or school problems.*

Multiple sources of evaluation data do not indicate that Crystian develops physical symptoms or fears associated with personal or school problems. This criterion is not applicable at this time.

Emotional disturbance includes schizophrenia. The term does not apply to children who are socially maladjusted, unless it is determined that they have an emotional disturbance.

This is not applicable at this time.

Conclusion: Based upon review of the above criteria, Crystian will be found eligible for special education support under a classification of learning disabilities.

13.5   Conclusion

Bower first introduced the term emotional disturbance and it was his conceptualization that was incorporated into the Education for All Handicapped Children Act of 1975. Congress inserted the socially maladjusted rule out and these seemingly opposing perspectives—emotionally disturbed vs. socially maladjusted—have served to hamper the definition and diagnostic approach ever since. The federal definition remains as problematic today as it was when it was codified into law 40 years ago. One of the most confounding aspects of ED is the exclusionary clause. Students who are socially maladjusted are generally not considered ED unless they are also emotional disturbed. A lack of consensual definition of ED impacts ED identification. One of the fundamental requirements of classification is a clear operational definition of a construct. ED suffers from a lack of clarity. Given the ambiguity, poor operational definition and controversy surrounding the definition, it is no surprise that there are significant challenges related to identification of ED.

Appendix: Sample Report 1—Emotional Disturbance

Psychological Report
Confidential

Name: Kyle Peterson   Date of Report: March 22, 2016
Date of Birth: 4/10/2004   Chronological Age: 12 years 11 months
Grade: 6th   School: JFK School

Parent Name and Address: Kim Peterson
                                                  1234 State Street
                                                  Philadelphia, PA 19138

 Phone: 215-555-1234

Name of Examiner: Stefan C. Dombrowski, Ph.D.

Reason for Referral
Kyle faces considerable social, emotional and behavioral issues at school. He is frequently off-task and generally disregards classroom rules. Kyle also tends to misperceive the intent of other children as hostile. As a result, he sometime engages in conflict with them. Kyle's mother wonders whether Kyle might be gifted. Kyle was referred for a comprehensive evaluation to determine his present level of functioning and whether he might qualify for specially designed instruction.

Assessment Methods and Sources of Data
Stanford–Binet Fifth Edition (SB5)
Wechsler Individual Achievement Test, Third Edition (WIAT-III)
Bender Visual Motor Gestalt, Second Edition (Bender-2)
Behavior Assessment System for Children—Second Edition (BASC-2)
– Teacher Version (Tina Chang, Sixth Grade Math/Science Teacher)

- Teacher Version (Colin Smith, Sixth Grade Language Arts/Social Science Teacher)
  ADHD Rating Scale IV
- School Version (Ms. Collen Lord, Sixth Grade Teacher)
- Home Version (Ms. Kim Peterson, Mother)

Teacher Interview
- Ms. Tina Chang (Sixth Grade Math/ScienceTeacher)
- Mr. Colin Waters (Sixth Grade Language Arts and Social Science Teacher)
- Ms. Rebecca Beans (Middle School Director)

School Counselor Interview
- Ms. Erin Crowley
  Parent Interview
- Ms. Kim Peterson

Student Interview
- Kyle Peterson

Classroom Observations
Review of Academic Grade Reports
Review of School Records

Background Information and Developmental History

Kyle Peterson is a 12-year-old child in the sixth grade at the JFK School (JFK). He transferred to JFK last year from John B. Lord Elementary School. Prior to attending Lord Elementary, Kyle attended Lee Elementary and Allen Locke Elementary. Since arriving at JFK, Kyle has experienced a host of social, emotional, and behavioral difficulties. Ms. Peterson, Kyle's mother, wonders whether Kyle is gifted.

Prenatal, Perinatal, and Early Developmental History: Ms. Peterson noted that Kyle was born early at 40 weeks gestation weighing 7 lb 8 oz. She explained that her pregnancy with him was without complication other than feelings of extreme stress. Ms. Peterson reported considerable family turmoil throughout her pregnancy with Kyle. She was 28 years old at the birth of Kyle. Ms. Jones commented that Kyle's early developmental milestones were attained within or in advance of developmental expectation. Ms. Peterson reports that Kyle was a precocious talker who was also inquisitive and asking questions. She described him as a loving and active child who enjoyed learning. Kyle participated in a Head Start preschool. Ms. Peterson indicted that there were no behavioral concerns early in his life.

Medical: Kyle's hearing and vision are intact. He had never suffered any head injury nor any other injury or infection. Ms. Peterson reports that Kyle has robust health and rarely gets sick. He has no other medical conditions.

Cognitive, Academic, and Language Functioning: Ms. Jones reports that Kyle is a bright child who is verbally expressive. Ms. Peterson wonders whether Kyle is gifted. Kyle has no prior history of special education support. Background information revealed that Kyle's difficulties with inattention and distractibility adversely impact his academic performance. Kyle's tendency toward oppositionality also impacts his functioning. He has been observed to disregard teacher requests to focus on an assignment in class and instead read a book. Kyle's teachers feel that he has academic potential but his difficulties with disorganization, inattention and oppositionality interfere with his ability to learn.

Social-Emotional and Behavioral Functioning: Kyle struggles with a host of emotional and behavioral issues. He faces difficulty with paying attention, disorganization, and loss of focus. He displays a general pattern of disregard of classroom rules and teacher requests. Kyle also tends to misperceive social situations, which creates difficulties for him with other children. Teacher reports indicate that Kyle has academic potential but his tendency to be off-task and inattentive creates academic problems. Background information and interview results revealed that Kyle sometimes is preoccupied with gun use as a means to protect himself. Kyle reports that he was placed in juvenile detention for part of a day following a threat to another student last September. Since Kyle's arrival at JFK, his emotional and behavioral difficulties have continued, if not escalated. He has been suspended for threatening other students, physically aggressing toward students, and for cussing off teachers.

Strengths: Kyle's strengths include his outgoing nature, his creativity, and his verbal expressiveness.

Summary: Kyle faces a host of emotional and behavioral issues at school that interfere with his learning. He is considered a verbally expressive child who is creative.

Interview Results
Parent Interview (October 3, 2016): Ms. Kim Peterson was interviewed regarding her perspective on Kyle's academic, behavioral, and social-emotional progress. Ms. Peterson first commented on Kyle's academic progress. She explained that he is doing "okay" academically, but struggles with mathematics. She noted that his reading and writing are fine and that he has never received prior learning support. Ms. Peterson explained that Kyle just needs a little tutoring in mathematics. Ms. Peterson next commented on Kyle's behavioral and social-emotional progress. She explained that Kyle indicates that other children tease him and make fun of his name. She noted that this bothers Kyle and makes him upset. As a result, he may react to their teasing and in turn get into trouble. Ms. Peterson explained that Kyle needs to learn how to properly react to teasing and bullying. Ms. Peterson noted that Kyle also struggles with the absence of his father in his life. Ms. Peterson commented that Kyle attended less desirable schools from kindergarten until fifth grade

and the negativity and poor attitudes of some of the children created a poor environment for learning within those schools. Ms. Peterson discussed Kyle's strengths. She noted that he is a creative child who is always talking about different animals. She explained that Kyle has social strengths and is able to strike up a conversation with anyone. Ms. Peterson noted that Kyle's areas of need include mathematics and not reacting to teasing. Ms. Peterson mentioned that all of Kyle's developmental milestones and early development were attained within normal limits.

Parent Interview (*October 18, 2016*): Ms. Kim Peterson was interviewed a second time specifically to discuss Kyle's preoccupation with guns and to discuss the prior incident where he was placed in juvenile detention following a threat to another student. Ms. Peterson noted that she was aware of Kyle's fascination with guns and "finds it disgusting." She also noted that it is something she discourages. Ms. Peterson explained that Kyle has had a long standing interest in guns. Ms. Peterson indicated that she always threw away toys that had gun themes because of his interest in them. Ms. Peterson wonders whether Kyle gets his fascination with guns from his father's side. During the course of this interview, this examiner emphasized to Ms. Peterson the need to keep Kyle away from any environments that provide access to guns.

Moving next to a discussion of Kyle's juvenile detention center placement, Ms. Peterson indicated that Kyle brought scissors to school to work on a project. On that day, she explained that he threatened another student, so the school put "two and two together" and called in the authorities. Ms. Peterson noted that Kyle was treated horribly and she has lodged a complaint against the school for how Kyle was treated.

Student Interview (*September 25, 2016*): Kyle was interviewed to ascertain impressions of his progress at WCS. He stated that he likes WCS because it is fun and the teachers make learning fun. Kyle was asked about his prior schooling. He noted that he attended Allen Locke Elementary, Lee Elementary, and John B. Lord Elementary prior to coming to WCS. When asked why he switched to WCS, Kyle noted that he wanted to see what the school would be like. He noted that if he liked it, then he would stay. Kyle explained that he has been bullied previously at his elementary schools, but has not experienced that since arriving at WCS. He explained one incident last September when he threatened to kill someone who was bullying him so he was sent to Juvenile detention center until about midnight. Kyle further explained that he becomes sad when other children tease and bully him. He explained that he one day hopes to become a spy so that he can learn how to better defend himself from others who might pick on him. He noted that he would also like access to the repertoire of guns available to spies. Kyle denied have any additional worries or concerns. Kyle was next asked about his academic progress. He noted that he does well in school but sometimes needs help with work, particularly mathematics. Kyle indicated that his hobbies include video games, basketball and going outside. He noted that he is good at reading, basketball and doing his school work. Kyle indicated that he needs help with mathematics.

Teacher Interview (September 30, 2016): Ms. Tina Chang, Kyle's sixth grade teacher, was interviewed regarding Kyle's academic, behavioral, emotional, and social functioning. Ms. Chang provided the following information.

Academic
Kyle has a lot of academic potential. When he knows what to do, he works quickly and efficiently, and is able to finish work well. His academic habits are impacted by disorganization; he often leaves his notebooks or textbooks out of the class.

Behavior
Kyle's behavior seems to be under his control at times, and not at others. He is occasionally explosive or dismissive when redirected (e.g., says he wasn't doing something, says that the teacher is not correct, will complain). He is often off-task in class, will read when he is supposed to be doing other work, or will distract other students. Since being moved to the front of the room, his behavior has improved somewhat. With a substitute present, he did almost no work for 90 min.

Social-Emotional Functioning
Kyle is easily frustrated and distracts other students frequently. He will raise his voice; his emotions become extremely elevated when he is upset. He often feels that students are doing inappropriate things to him when these things are not actually happening. Kyle takes very little responsibility for materials and coming to class prepared. His social-emotional presence appears to be immature for his age, but his awareness of other students seems to be more developed (i.e., the way he responds or interacts is younger than a sixth grader but his thinking is much higher). Kyle is friends with two students in the class who are often isolated or alienated by other kids.

Areas of Strength
Kyle is able to complete math work quickly and when focused. He is able to show higher level thinking or notice big ideas. Kyle will participate when constantly engaged or cold called.

Teacher Interview (October 2, 2016): Mr. Colin Waters, Kyle's sixth grade language arts and social science teacher, was interviewed regarding Kyle's academic, behavioral, emotional, and social functioning. Ms. Waters commented first regarding Kyle's academic progress. He explained that Kyle does not write very well. He noted that Kyle likes to read, but only certain kinds of books. Still, Mr. Waters explained that Kyle has trouble finishing books and does not want to participate in class. Mr. Waters noted that Kyle struggles with paying attention in class. For instance, he noted that Kyle is often focusing on one task (e.g., reading at his desk) when he is supposed to be involved with another activity. Mr. Waters indicated that Kyle requires considerable prompting for follow rules and remain on task, but becomes defensive when redirected. Mr. Waters explained that Kyle has a difficult time perceiving accurately social interaction. He noted that Kyle will think someone is saying something or acting badly toward him when they are not. Mr. Waters explained that Kyle is sometimes dishonest. He discussed one incident where Kyle entered another classroom late and told the teacher that Mr. Waters gave him approval to be late, when Mr. Waters never said that. Mr. Waters next described Kyle's areas of strength. He noted that Kyle can be quite expressive even though the topic being discussed is off-topic. Mr. Waters expressed that Kyle has social and behavioral needs (e.g., regard for authority figures and rules at school; how to navigate social conversations with peers; how to participate properly in class including group work).

Teacher Interview (November 13, 2016): Ms. Rebecca Beans, Middle School Director, was interviewed regarding Kyle's progress at school. Ms. Beans discussed the history of Kyle's behavior at WCS. She noted that since September Kyle has been written up or suspended for selected incidents including the following: Threatening to harm another student; physically aggressing toward a student and displaying explosive behavior; speaking improperly to teachers (e.g., telling a teacher to "fuck off"; telling a teacher "I hate you"); and general disregard of school rules (e.g., leaving the classroom without permission on numerous occasions; chewing gum; being out of uniform). Ms. Beans expressed concerns about Kyle's processing of social information and reaction to frustration. She explained that she will see Kyle in the hall and things are fine, but only to see him a short while later extremely upset because he could not open his locker. At these times, Ms. Beans explained that Kyle will overreact, become extremely upset, and take quite some time to calm down. Ms. Beans indicated that Kyle will flip a switch fairly quickly and become reactive. Ms. Beans explained that Kyle misperceives other students' actions and intentions toward him, and will overreact by using physical aggression or verbal threats. Ms. Beans discussed a situation conveyed to her by another teacher. She mentioned that Kyle was walking by a group of younger children and expressed that he "just wanted to punch them in the face." Ms. Beans discussed that Kyle struggles without considerable structure, prompting and support in the classroom. She noted that he frequently disregards the classroom activity and instead will pull out a comic book and start reading it. Ms. Beans also discussed confusion when Kyle first arrived at school. She explained that his legal name is completely different from the one he uses. Ms. Beans explained that Kyle has a compassionate and caring side as noted by his interest in holding and petting the school's bunny rabbits. Ms. Beans further indicated that Kyle seems intensely interested in the rabbits and is constantly asking to hold and pet them. She stated that she uses access to the rabbits as a way to reward Kyle for appropriate behavior.

Observations
Classroom Observation (September 25, 2016): Kyle was observed for 20 min in Mr. Waters's classroom. Kyle entered the classroom and retrieved a piece of paper on which to write because he could not locate his notebook. The class was involved in a lesson on architecture. The class then transitioned to another activity. Because the

class took some additional time to transition to this activity, Mr. Waters requested the class to place their heads upon their desks for 2 min. Kyle complied with this request. Afterwards, the class was requested to write eight characteristics of civilization. Instead of beginning work on the activity, Kyle was observed for the next 7 min to silently talk with a neighboring student in a way that did not disrupt the class, but kept him off-task. Impressions of the observation were that Kyle was generally off task but not disruptive to the class.

Observation during Assessment: Kyle was initially engaged in the assessment process and seemed to enjoy the individualized attention he was receiving. As the session progress, Kyle became irritable and would verbally externalize his frustration. This became particularly poignant during the introduction to the writing fluency subtest when Kyle stated, "why do I have to do this shit, anyway?" as he slammed his hand onto the desk in frustration. The examiner assured Kyle that he was working hard and would soon be finished. Kyle was able to gather himself and resume the assessment process but would frequently make loud sighs or gasp in frustration. Despite The results appear to be a valid representation of his abilities.

Cognitive and Academic Functioning

Stanford–Binet Intelligence Scales—Fifth Edition (SB5)
Kyle was administered the Stanford–Binet Intelligence Scales—Fifth Edition (SB5). The SB5 is an individually administered measure of intellectual functioning normed for individuals between the ages of 2 and 85+ years. The SB5 contains five factor indexes for each the VIQ and NVIQ: Fluid Reasoning, Knowledge, Quantitative Reasoning, Visual Spatial, and Working Memory. Fluid reasoning represents an individual's ability to solve verbal and nonverbal problems and reason inductively and deductively. Knowledge represents the accumulated fund of general information acquired at home, school, work, or in life. Quantitative reasoning reflects facility with numbers and numerical problem solving, whether with word problems or figural relationships. Quantitative reasoning emphasizes problem solving more than mathematical knowledge. Visual-spatial processing reflects the ability to see patterns, relationships, spatial orientation, and the connection among diverse pieces of a visual display. Working memory is a measure of short-term memory processing of information whether verbal or visual, emphasizing the brief manipulation of diverse information.

The SB5 provides three intelligence score composites and five factor indices with a mean of 100 and a Standard deviation of 15. Scores between 90 and 110 are considered average.

	Standard score	Percentile	95 % Conf. interval	Descriptive classification
IQ scores				
Nonverbal IQ (NVIQ)	88	23	84–92	Low average
Full Scale IQ (FSIQ)	86	15	82–90	Low average
Verbal IQ (VIQ)	90	25	86–94	Average
Factor index scores				
Fluid reasoning (FR)	81	12	77–85	Low average
Knowledge (KN)	90	25	85–95	Average
Quantitative reasoning (QR)	88	23	82–92	Low average
Visual spatial (VS)	88	22	84–92	Low average
Working memory (WM)	89	24	85–93	Low average

The above table may be referenced to obtain Kyle's performance in each of these areas while the following is a description of each of the factor index scores. Fluid reasoning represents an individual's ability to solve verbal and nonverbal problems and reason inductively and deductively. Knowledge represents the accumulated fund of general information acquired at home, school, work, or in life. Quantitative reasoning reflects facility with numbers and numerical problem solving, whether with word problems or figural relationships. Quantitative reasoning emphasizes problem solving more than mathematical knowledge. Visual-spatial processing reflects the ability to see patterns, relationships, spatial orientation, and the connection among diverse pieces of a visual display. Working memory is a measure of short-term memory processing of information whether verbal or visual, emphasizing the brief manipulation of diverse information.

The SB5 includes ten subtest scores with a mean of 10 and a Standard deviation of 3. Scores between 8 and 12 are considered average. Kyle's individual subtest scores were as follows:

Nonverbal tests		Verbal tests	
Fluid reasoning	7	Fluid reasoning	6
Knowledge	9	Knowledge	8
Quant. reasoning	6	Quant. reasoning	7
Visual spatial	8	Visual spatial	8
Working memory	7	Working memory	7

On testing with the SB5, Kyle earned a Full Scale IQ of 88. On the SB5, this level of performance falls within the range of scores designated as low average and exceeded the performance of 23 % of individuals at Kyle's age. His Verbal IQ (Standard Score = 90; 25th percentile) was in the average range and exceeded 25 % of individuals Kyle's age. Kyle's Nonverbal IQ (Standard Score = 86; 15th percentile) was in the low average range, exceeding 15 % of individuals Kyle's age.

Wechsler Individual Achievement Test, Third Edition (WIAT-III)

The WIAT-III is an individual achievement test that yields eight composite scores: (1) Oral Language; (2) Total Reading; (3) Basic Reading; (4) Reading Comprehension and Fluency; (5) Written Expression; (6) Mathematics; (7) Math Fluency; and (8) Total Achievement. All of the subtests on the WIAT-III, except for the Math Fluency subtests, contribute to the Total Achievement Composite. The WIAT-III is used to measure reading, writing, mathematics, and listening comprehension skills. The Oral Language Composite includes measures of both listening comprehension and oral expression. The Total Reading Composite includes measures of basic reading, reading fluency, and reading comprehension. The Basic Reading Composite includes letter and word identification, the ability to assess and apply phonetic decoding skills using both real words and nonsense words. The Reading Comprehension and Fluency Composite includes a measure of student's ability to understand what was just read and measures of speed, accuracy and prosody of oral reading. The Written Expression Composite includes measures of alphabet writing fluency, spelling, sentence composition, and essay composition. The Mathematics Composite includes measures of math problem solving and numerical operations. The Math Fluency Composite, which does not contribute to the Total Achievement Score, includes items that measure simple addition, subtraction, and multiplication speediness.

Kyle obtained the following scores in each of the areas of measurement:

	Standard score	Percentile	Confidence interval (95 %)	Descriptive classification
Oral language	103	58	95–111	Average
Listening comprehension	99	47	88–100	Average
Oral expression	107	68	97–117	Average
Total reading	103	58	98–108	Average
Basic reading	105	63	101–109	Average
Word reading	106	66	110–112	Average
Pseudoword decoding	107	68	101–113	Average
Reading comprehension and fluency	95	45	88–98	Average
Reading comprehension	86	15	78–91	Low Average
Oral reading fluency	98	45	91–105	Average
Written expression	103	58	96–110	Average
Sentence composition	94	34	82–106	Average
Essay composition	112	79	102–122	High Average
Spelling	102	55	96–108	Average
Mathematics	83	13	77–89	Below Average
Math problem solving	94	34	85–103	Average
Numerical operations	74	4	68–80	Below Average
Math fluency	80	9	73–87	Low Average
Math fluency (addition)	85	16	74–96	Low Average
Math fluency (subtraction)	84	14	74–94	Low Average
Fluency (multiplication)	76	5	66–86	Below Average
Total achievement	99	47	95–103	Average

Standardized achievement test results revealed a total achievement Std. Score of 99 (47th percentile), an average score. Kyle scored in the average range for all areas, with the exception of Mathematics and Math Fluency. In both Mathematics and Math Fluency, Kyle scored in the Below Average range (Std. Score = 83; 13th percentile, and Std. Score = 80; 9th percentile, respectively).

Bender Visual-Motor Gestalt Test, Second Edition (Bender-II)

The Bender-II measures visual-motor integration skills, or the ability to see and copy figures accurately. A quantitative and qualitative analysis of Kyle's drawings suggests that her visual-motor integration abilities (e.g., fine motor skills for paper and pencil tasks) are high average (Copy Standard Score = 115; 84th percentile).

Social, Emotional, and Behavioral Functioning

Behavior Assessment System for Children, Second Edition (BASC-2)

The Behavior Assessment System for Children, Second Edition (BASC-2) is an integrated system designed to facilitate the differential diagnosis and classification of a variety of emotional and behavioral conditions in children. It possesses validity scales and several clinical scales, which reflect different dimensions of a child's personality. Scores in the Clinically Significant range (T-Score > 70) suggest a high level of difficulty. Scores in the At-Risk range (T-Score 60–69) identify either a significant problem that may not be severe enough to require formal treatment or a potential of developing a problem that needs careful monitoring. On the Adaptive Scales, scores below 30 are considered clinically significant while scores between 31 and 35 are considered at-risk.

Clinical scales	Ms. Chang T-Score	Mr. Waters T-Score
Hyperactivity	69*	62
Aggression	74**	63
Conduct problems	84**	65*
Anxiety	63	56
Depression	75**	62
Somatization	47	47
Attention problems	78**	68*
Atypicality	89**	72**
Withdrawal	63	55
Adaptability	29**	35*
Social Skills	40	28**
Leadership	36*	34*
Study Skills	31*	31*
Functional communication	40	38*
Externalizing problems	77**	64
Internalizing problems	64	56

(continued)

(continued)

Clinical scales	Ms. Chang T-Score	Mr. Waters T-Score
Behavioral symptoms index	80**	67*
Adaptive skills	33*	31*
School problems	68*	62

*At-risk
**Clinically significant

The above results indicate clinically significant elevations on the externalizing composite index and the behavioral symptoms index. The above results indicate a score in the at-risk range on the adaptive skills and school problems indices. The following clinical scales were in the clinically significant range on at least one of the ratings above: aggression, conduct problems, depression, attention problems, social skills, atypicality, and adaptability. Kyle scored in the at-risk range on the hyperactivity and study skills scales.

ADHD Rating Scale IV

The ADHD Rating Scale IV is a rating scale consisting of ADHD symptoms based on the DSM V diagnostic criteria. In general, scores between the 85th and 93rd percentile are considered above average or "at-risk" for symptom cluster compared to the normative sample. Scores above the 93rd percentile are generally considered clinically significant. Kyle received the following scores:

Scale	Teacher percentile	Parent percentile
Hyperactivity/impulsivity	95th (clinically significant)	50–75th (average)
Inattention	94th (clinically significant)	50–75th (average)
Combined	97th (clinically significant)	50–75th (average)

Conceptualization and Classification

Multiple data sources and methods of assessment inform the conceptualization of Kyle's cognitive, academic, social-emotional, and behavioral functioning including whether he qualifies for special education support. Details in support of these findings are offered below.

Cognitive and Academic Functioning: Kyle's present performance on measures of cognitive ability was low average/average (FSIQ=88, 24th percentile; VIQ=90, 19th percentile; NIQ=86, 15th percentile). Kyle's performance on the WIAT-III Achievement was average across the reading and writing cluster, but below average in mathematics. More specifically, Kyle struggled with most basic math concepts. Kyle will benefit from specially designed instruction for his difficulties with mathematics.

Ms. Peterson also wondered whether Kyle is gifted. Within the public school setting in Pennsylvania, a child who scores 130 (97.5 percentile) or above on a measure of cognitive ability is considered gifted. Kyle scored in the low average range (Stanford–Binet 5 FSIQ = 88; 24th percentile) and would not be considered eligible for gifted programming.

Social and Emotional Functioning: Kyle is a sixth grade student who struggles with inattentiveness, loss of focus, impulsivity, and distractibility. He also faces significant struggles with processing of social information. Kyle frequently misperceives ambiguous and even benign interaction with other students as harmful or being directed negatively toward him. At these times, Kyle will overreact, sometimes through physical aggression, and other times through verbal threats. Kyle has previously been sent to juvenile detention (September, 2014) for bringing in scissors and threatening another child. Kyle has a preoccupying fascination with guns and weapons. He states that he wants to become a spy to gain access to the repertoire of guns available to spies so that he can defend himself against those who would bully him. Kyle's strengths include his verbal expressiveness and creativity. Ms. Peterson notes that Kyle can strike up a conversation with anyone.

The following criteria from the Pennsylvania Special Education Code guided classification of emotional disturbance.

Emotional disturbance means a condition exhibiting one or more of the following characteristics over a long period of time and to a marked degree that adversely affects a child's educational performance:

(A) *An inability to learn that cannot be explained by intellectual, sensory, or health factors.*

There are no intellectual, sensory or health factors that contribute to Kyle's learning difficulties. This criterion is not applicable at this time.

(B) *An inability to build or maintain satisfactory interpersonal relationships with peers and teachers.*

Kyle struggles in his interaction with peers and teachers. He has used and continues to use physical threats and actual aggression when relating to other students. Kyle has been suspended for physical aggression, verbal threats, and cussing out teachers (e.g., telling a teacher he "hates" them or to "fuck off"). Kyle struggles with social-cognitive information processing distortions (i.e., understanding social nuance) where he misperceives ambiguous and even benign social interaction as being negatively directed, and even harmful, toward him. These characteristics and behaviors intrude upon his ability to build and maintain satisfactory interpersonal relationships with peers and teachers.

(C) *Inappropriate types of behavior or feelings under normal circumstances.*

Kyle's displays several behaviors and feelings that are inappropriate under normal circumstances. His reaction to peers, teachers, and situations that frustrate him can be aggressive and volatile. He has cussed out teachers (e.g., telling them he "hates them" or to "fuck off"). Kyle also tends to overreact to actual or perceived insults directed toward him by peers. At these times he will physically aggress, make verbal threats, or become disproportionately upset. Even when interaction with peers is appropriate, Kyle frequently misperceives the interaction as negative and will become extremely upset and sometimes become either verbally or physically aggressive. Kyle has been observed to flip a switch and go from being calm to extremely upset to a mildly frustrating circumstance. For instance, he has been observed to be fine one moment, but then extremely upset and angry the next moment when he struggled with opening his locker. Kyle has a preoccupying fascination with guns and has stated an interest in learning how to use guns as a means to protect himself from other children who might aggrieve upon him.

(D) *A general pervasive mood of unhappiness or depression.*

Multiple sources of evaluation data do not indicate that Kyle is pervasively depressed or unhappy. He does sometimes become volatile when upset or denied his own way. This criterion is not applicable at this time.

(E) *A tendency to develop physical symptoms or fears associated with personal or school problems.*

Multiple sources of evaluation data do not indicate that Kyle develops physical symptoms or fears associated with personal or school problems. This criterion is not applicable at this time.

Emotional disturbance includes schizophrenia. The term does not apply to children who are socially maladjusted, unless it is determined that they have an emotional disturbance.

This is not applicable at this time.

Summary: Kyle will benefit from special education support under a classification of Emotional Disturbance.

Summary and Recommendations

Considering Kyle's performance on measures of achievement and cognitive ability, combined with actual classroom performance, academic grade reports, parent interviews, behavior observations, and teacher interviews, Kyle is eligible for special education support. The team concludes that specially designed instruction is called for at this time. The following recommendations might benefit Kyle.

1. Strategies for difficulties with Attention, Distractibility, Hyperactivity, Impulsivity, and Loss of Focus: Background reports indicate that Kyle experiences difficulty with attention and distractibility. As such, the following recommendations might be beneficial for her:

    (A) *Seating:* Kyle should continue to sit in a location where there are minimal distractions.

(B) *Provision of Directions by Teacher:* When Kyle's teachers interact with her, she should be encouraged to repeat and explain instructions to ensure understanding. The provision of directions to Kyle will be most effective when the teacher makes eye contact, avoids multiple commands, is clear and to the point, and permits repetition of directions when needed or asked for.

(C) *Positive Reinforcement and Praise for Successful Task Completion:* Kyle's teachers should provide positive reinforcement and immediate feedback for completion of desired behaviors or tasks. Initially, praise and reinforcement should be offered for successful effort on a task or behavior regardless of quality of performance.

(D) *Time on Task*: Communicate to Kyle how long she will need to engage in or pay attention on a particular task. Open ended expectations can be distressing to any child, let alone one with attentional difficulties.

(E) *Prepare Student Discreetly for Transitions*: Furnish Kyle with verbal prompts and visual cues that a new activity or task is about to start. This should be accomplished discreetly so as to avoid student embarrassment.

(F) *Recess Time*: Kyle should be permitted to participate in recess. Recess should not be a time to complete unfinished classwork or homework.

(G) *Extended Time, Teacher Check In's, and Frequent Breaks*: Kyle should be permitted additional time to complete academic tasks and projects. Kyle's teachers should also consider review of classwork as Kyle progresses on an assignment or project to assist Kyle in avoiding careless mistakes. More frequent breaks than what is typical may also reduce careless mistakes and help to maintain focus.

(H) *Check In, Check Out, and Behavior Report Card:* Kyle should have his behavioral expectations reviewed at the beginning of the school day. He should check in with an adult periodically throughout the day to determine whether his goals are being met. At the end of the day, Kyle should check out with that same adult and receive a behavior report card that acknowledges his behavioral performance and is sent home to his caregivers.

2. *Support for Mathematics*: Kyle struggles with mathematics, particularly basic math facts, and will benefit from specially designed instruction for mathematics skills.

3. *Social Skills*: Kyle tends to misperceive ambiguous and even benign social interaction as antagonistic toward him. For instance, he becomes easily upset and overreacts when he feels he is being teased. Kyle would be well served by instruction and guidance regarding appropriate perception of, and response to, social interaction.

4. *Counseling*: Kyle will benefit from counseling for the following concerns:

(i) *Social-Cognitive Processing Deficits*: Kyle tends to misperceive ambiguous and even benign situations as negative toward him. He will benefit from counseling for these difficulties.

(ii) *Themes of Aggression*: Kyle frequently discusses and appears to fantasize about aggressive themes including the use of guns. Some of this discussion may be based upon prior exposure to violence; others may be routed in an active fantasy life. Nonetheless, this theme, and Kyle's possible exposure to trauma and violence, should be explored in counseling.

5. *Parental Monitoring of Preoccupation with Guns*: Though not an issue for special education, Ms. Peterson is strongly advised to monitor and regulate Kyle's pre-occupation with guns given his tendency to misperceive social situations and considering his impulsive style. Background information revealed that Kyle displays an interest in learning how to use guns as a means to protect himself from those who would aggrieve upon him. Kyle's access to environments where guns might be available to him should be clearly circumscribed. Resources and possible training materials (i.e., classes) to promote safety may be available through local law enforcement.

6. *Threats to Others*: Last year, Kyle reported that he threatened to kill another student and was sent to juvenile detention for part of the day until midnight. Even if Kyle was being dramatic in his threat and never intended to follow through, he needs to understand that the school and community take such threats seriously and there will be significant consequences from making a threat to the physical safety of another individual. Accordingly, any future threats to others should continue to be monitored by the school and appropriate protective action taken (i.e., contact law enforcement; contact Ms. Peterson; contact the intended victim) following a credible threat to another individual.

Stefan C. Dombrowski, Ph.D.
Licensed Psychologist (PA and NJ)
Certified School Psychologist (PA and NJ)

Sample Report 2—Emotional Disturbance

Psychological Report
Confidential

Name: Christopher Smith   Date of Report: May 9, 2014
Date of Birth: 6/28/06   Chronological Age: 7
Grade: 2   School: McCrel Public School
Name of Examiner: Stefan C. Dombrowski

Parent name and address: Sharell Smith
                          1234 Sidney Ln
                          Philadelphia, PA, 19183

Reason for Referral

Chris was referred for a comprehensive evaluation following concerns about his emotional and behavioral progress in the classroom. This evaluation was conducted to determine Chris's present level of functioning and whether he is eligible for specially designed instruction.

Assessment Methods and Sources of Data

Reynolds Intellectual Assessment Scales (RIAS)
Wechsler Individual Achievement Test—Third Edition (WIAT-III)
Bender Visual Motor Gestalt, Second Edition (Bender-2)
Behavior Assessment System for Children—Second Edition (BASC-2)

– Ms. Collen Moon
Teacher Interview
– Ms. Collen Moon (Second Grade)
TSS Worker Interview
– Mr. Nick Man
Parent Interview
– Ms. Sharell Smith (Mother)
Student Interview
– Chris Smith
Classroom Observations
Review of School Records

Background Information and Developmental History
Chris is a second grade student at McCrel Public School. He currently faces deficits in social-emotional, behavioral, cognitive, and academic Functioning.

Prenatal, Perinatal, and Early Developmental History: Ms. Smith noted that she suffered from the flu during her pregnancy with Chris. She is concerned that the effects from her fever and elevated temperature may have had an adverse effect on Chris's development. Ms. Smith commented that Chris had some delays in language acquisition compared to that of his siblings. He met all other developmental milestones within normal limits.

Medical: Chris has prior diagnoses of Posttraumatic Stress Disorder (PTSD), Oppositional Defiant Disorder (ODD), and Attention-Deficit/Hyperactivity Disorder (ADHD). He takes celexa, clonidine and adderal for the management of his emotional and behavioral symptoms.

Cognitive, Academic, and Language Functioning: Because of Chris's emotional and behavioral difficulties, he is experiencing difficulty in the classroom curriculum. He rarely is on-task and often is found to be noncompliant with classroom rules. Chris's is in jeopardy of falling behind because of his emotional and behavioral difficulties.

Social-Emotional and Behavioral Functioning: At the beginning of last year, Chris was hospitalized for approximately 6 weeks for suicidal ideation. Ms. Smith, Chris's mother, did not provide much of the details, but only indicated that his hospitalization was related to behavioral issues. As a result of Chris's considerable emotional, social, and behavioral difficulties, he has been furnished with a TSS worker. Since January 2009, Chris has been working with Mr. Nick Man. Prior to Mr. Man, Chris had two TSS workers, one of whom quit because of concerns about her safety. Background information revealed that the former TSS work was concerned about Chris's physical aggressiveness. Chris has had a history of behavioral problems since kindergarten. Both Chris's kindergarten and first grade teachers expressed concerns about his behavioral, social, and emotional progress in their respective grade reports.

Strengths: Chris's strengths are described as mathematics, being helpful and personable.

Summary: Chris Smith is a 7-year-old, second grade student who experiences considerable emotional, social, and behavioral difficulties at school including aggression and

Interview Results
Parent Interview: Ms. Sharell Smith, Chris's mother, was interviewed on May 7, 2014 to ascertain her impressions of Chris's academic, social, emotional, and behavioral functioning. Ms. Smith indicated that Chris is struggling with reading and paying attention to his teachers. She noted that he cannot focus which causes him to

miss out on classwork. Ms. Smith was asked how Chris obtained a TSS worker. Ms. Smith explained that he got it "through Warren E. Smith." Ms. Smith was asked about Chris's hospitalization at the beginning of last academic year. She explained that Chris was hospitalized "for behavior," including acting out and doing things he should not be doing. When asked whether Chris ever attempted to hurt himself or others, Ms. Smith explained that Chris claimed that he wanted to hurt himself, but never followed through on it. Ms. Smith stated that Chris takes adderall, celexa, and clonidine for the management of his behavioral issues.

Student Interview (April 23, 2014): Chris was interviewed to ascertain impressions of his progress at WCS. Chris had considerable difficulty during the interview and subsequent assessment process. He required constant structure and support. The process had to be broken out across two different days because of Chris's struggles with remaining on task. When asked whether he enjoys WCS Chris stated, "yes." When asked to elaborate, Chris ignored the examiner's question, but proceeded to pick out a toy from the room. Chris was asked about a bloodshot eye. He stated that his mother "poked him in the eye" by accident when she was trying to calm him down. Chris was also asked about his emotional status. He stated that he is sometimes sad and sometimes happy. Chris was asked about why he was hospitalized. He stated that it occurred a long time ago. He noted that he was "sad and wanted to kill" himself. Chris stated that he forgot why he was sad. Chris stated that he is good at mathematics and enjoys playing outside, baseball, and basketball.

Teacher Interview (April 23, 2014): Ms. Collen Moon, Chris's teacher, was interviewed regarding Chris's academic, behavioral, emotional, social, and adaptive functioning. Ms. Moon commented first about Chris's behavior, noting that it is of greatest concern. She explained that he has extreme difficulty with impulsivity and oppositionality. Ms. Moon also noted that Chris struggle with inattentiveness and hyperactivity. Ms. Moon explained that Chris has a diagnosis of ADHD, ODD, and PTSD. She explained that Chris sometimes struggles with peer interactions, noting that some children become annoyed by him. Ms. Moon explained that at the beginning of January, Chris's behaviors escalated to the point where he was observed to fight with adults in the classroom and storm out of the classroom when denied his own way. Ms. Moon explained that as a result of Chris's behavioral and emotional difficulties, he has been furnished with a TSS worker. She explained that when his behavioral and emotional difficulties do not interfere with his academic progress, Chris performs at an approximate grade expected level. Ms. Moon commented that Chris's strengths include mathematics and noted that he can be a helpful child.

TSS Worker Interview (April 23, 2014): Nick Man, Chris's TSS worker, was interviewed for his impressions of Chris's academic, behavioral, emotional, and social functioning. Mr. Man indicated that he started working with Chris in January. Mr. Man noted that Chris has a diagnosis of ADHD and PTSD. Mr. Man commented that Chris's father physically abused him which resulted in a diagnosis of PTSD. Mr. Man explained that Chris is extremely impulsive and very controlling. He indicated that Chris is constantly moving, constantly talking, and does not have control over his behavior. Mr. Man discussed Chris's social progress. He noted that Chris is liked, but he can be disrespectful and nasty. For instance, Chris sometimes laughs at other people's misfortunes which tends to annoy them. Mr. Man noted that Chris has problems with limits. He stated that Chris is also oppositional and when upset or angered can take as long as 30 min to deescalate. Mr. Man noted that Chris has even attempted to hit him on several occasions. Mr. Man indicated that Chris requires anger management training and techniques for dealing with frustration. He also stated that Chris is desperate for attention. Mr. Man indicated that Chris's strengths include mathematics, being helpful, and being personable.

Observations

Classroom Observation (April 23, 2014): Chris was observed for 20 min in Mr. Moon's class. The class was involved in a whole group circle time instruction. Within the first minute of the observation, Chris's behavior required redirection. He was told to put down a marker attached to a string that he was swinging. Chris was also observed to be standing up, swinging his arms, spinning around and making noises. On another occasion, Chris was observed to spin in circles, hitting the air with his book. On his way to return a book to the shelf, Chris dropped his spelling/sight words and spent the next 5 min on the floor attempting to put them back on the circle ring. He became frustrated, and began to talk aloud and make noises. He continued to become frustrated, throwing the cards on the ground because he could not line up the whole punched circles and place the cards on the ring. The TSS came over and assisted Chris, demonstrating how to place the cards on the ring. Chris missed the entire instruction about how to approach the in-class math assignment. Chris then picked out a book for after math work, returned to his desk, and dropped the book to the floor making a loud noise. As Chris returned to his seat, he pretended to swing at another student. After that, Chris threw his book into the air, attempted to catch it. He then screamed out, "I don't have a pencil." Ms. Collen asked Chris to go to the hallway to spend 3 min calming down. Chris went out into the hallway, and proceeded to pick up the cushions trying to hit each one. He was also observed to do flips across the couch. Dean Paul passed by, and redirected Chris to sit down. Chris then returned to the classroom, but was told that his time was not up. He returned to the hallway, and was active. Ms. Tench sat on the couch, talking with Chris and attempting to redirect his behavior. Impressions from this observation were that Chris is extremely hyperactive and had difficulty controlling both his impulses and behavior.

Observation during Assessment (April 26, 2014): Chris was extremely distractible and active throughout the assessment process. He would frequently attempt to play with test items, get up out of his seat, and verge off into unrelated conversational topics. He required significant structure, support and redirection given his impulsive and active style. With the provision of redirection, structure and support, Chris was able to get back on task and complete the assessment process. The current test results are considered a valid representation of his abilities.

Cognitive and Academic Functioning

Reynolds Intellectual Assessment Scale (RIAS)

Chris was administered the Reynolds Intellectual Assessment Scales (RIAS). The RIAS is an individually administered measure of intellectual functioning normed for individuals between the ages of 3 and 94 years. The RIAS contains several individual tests of intellectual problem solving and reasoning ability that are combined to form a Verbal Intelligence Index (VIX) and a Nonverbal Intelligence Index (NIX). The subtests that compose the VIX assess verbal reasoning ability along with the ability to access and apply prior learning in solving language-related tasks. Although labeled the Verbal Intelligence Index, the VIX is also a reasonable approximation of crystallized intelligence. The NIX comprises subtests that assess nonverbal reasoning and spatial ability. Although labeled the Nonverbal Intelligence Index, the NIX also provides a reasonable approximation of fluid intelligence and spatial ability. These two indexes of intellectual functioning are then combined to form an overall Composite Intelligence Index (CIX). By combining the VIX and the NIX into the CIX, a strong, reliable assessment of general intelligence (g) is obtained. The CIX measures the two most important aspects of general intelligence according to recent theories and research findings: reasoning or fluid abilities and verbal or crystallized abilities.

The RIAS also contains subtests designed to assess verbal memory and nonverbal memory. Depending upon the age of the individual being evaluated, the verbal memory subtest consists of a series of sentences, age-appropriate stories, or both, read aloud to the examinee. The examinee is then asked to recall these sentences or stories as precisely as possible. The nonverbal memory subtest consists of the presentation of pictures of various objects or abstract designs for a period of 5 s. The examinee is then shown a page containing six similar objects or figures and must discern which object or figure has previously been shown. The scores from the verbal memory and nonverbal memory subtests are combined to form a Composite Memory Index (CMX), which provides a strong, reliable assessment of working memory and may also provide indications as to whether or not a more detailed assessment of memory functions may be required. In addition, the high reliability of the verbal and nonverbal memory subtests allows them to be compared directly to each other.

Each of these indexes is expressed as an age-corrected standard score that is scaled to a mean of 100 and a standard deviation of 15. These scores are normally distributed and can be converted to a variety of other metrics if desired.

Following are the results of Chris's performance on the RIAS.

	Composite IQ	Verbal IQ	Nonverbal IQ	Memory index
RIAS index	95	101	91	91
Percentile	39th	52nd	27th	27th
Confidence interval (95 %)	90–100	95–107	85–98	85–98

On testing with the RIAS, Chris attained a Composite Intelligence Index of 95. On the RIAS, this level of performance falls within the range of scores designated as average and exceeds the performance of 39 % of individuals at Chris's age. Chris attained a Verbal Intelligence Index of 101 (52nd percentile), which exceeds 52 % of individuals Chris's age. His Nonverbal IQ was 91 (27th percentile). Chris attained a Composite Memory Index (CMX) of 91, which falls within the average range of working memory skills and exceeds the performance of 27 out of 100 individuals Chris's age.

Wechsler Individual Achievement Test, Third Edition (WIAT-III)

The WIAT-III is an individual achievement test that yields eight composite scores: (1) Oral Language; (2) Total Reading; (3) Basic Reading; (4) Reading Comprehension and Fluency; (5) Written Expression; (6) Mathematics; (7) Math Fluency; and (8) Total Achievement. All of the subtests on the WIAT-III, except for the Math Fluency subtests, contribute to the Total Achievement Composite. The WIAT-III is used to measure reading, writing, mathematics, and listening comprehension skills. The Oral Language Composite includes measures of both listening comprehension and oral expression. The Total Reading Composite includes measures of basic reading, reading fluency, and reading comprehension. The Basic Reading Composite includes letter and word identification, the ability to assess and apply phonetic decoding skills using both real words and nonsense words. The Reading Comprehension and Fluency Composite includes a measure of student's ability to understand what was just read and measures of speed, accuracy and prosody of oral reading. The Written Expression Composite includes measures of alphabet writing fluency, spelling, sentence composition, and essay composition. The Mathematics Composite includes measures of math problem solving and numerical operations. The Math Fluency Composite, which does not contribute to the Total Achievement Score, includes items that measure simple addition, subtraction, and multiplication speediness.

Chris obtained the following scores in each of the areas of measurement:

	Standard score	Percentile	Confidence interval (95 %)	Descriptive classification
Oral language	100	50	95–105	Average
Listening comprehension	99	47	88–100	Average
Oral expression	103	56	97–107	Average
Total reading	103	58	98–108	Average
Basic reading	105	63	101–109	Average
Word reading	106	66	110–112	Average
Pseudoword decoding	107	68	101–113	Average
Reading comprehension and fluency	95	45	88–98	Average
Reading comprehension	86	15	78–91	Low Average
Oral reading fluency	98	45	91–105	Average
Written expression	103	58	96–110	Average
Sentence composition	94	34	82–106	Average

(continued)

(continued)

	Standard score	Percentile	Confidence interval (95 %)	Descriptive classification
Essay composition	112	79	102–122	High Average
Spelling	102	55	96–108	Average
Mathematics	103	57	97–108	Average
Math problem solving	114	84	85–103	High Average
Numerical operations	94	44	90–99	Average
Math fluency	93	43	89–97	Average
Math fluency (addition)	95	44	90–100	Average
Math fluency (subtraction)	94	43	89–99	Average
Fluency (multiplication)	96	45	91–101	Average
Total Achievement	99	47	95–103	Average

Standardized achievement test results revealed average performance across all academic areas.

Bender Visual-Motor Gestalt Test, Second Edition (Bender-II)
The Bender-II measures visual-motor integration skills, or the ability to see and copy figures accurately. A quantitative and qualitative analysis of Chris's drawings suggests that his visual-motor integration abilities (e.g., fine motor skills for paper and pencil tasks) are high average (Copy Standard Score = 114, 83rd percentile).

Social-Emotional and Behavioral Functioning

Behavior Assessment System for Children, Second Edition (BASC-2)
The Behavior Assessment System for Children, Second Edition (BASC-2) is an integrated system designed to facilitate the differential diagnosis and classification of a variety of emotional and behavioral conditions in children. It possesses validity scales and several clinical scales, which reflect different dimensions of a child's personality. Scores in the Clinically Significant range (*T*-Score > 70) suggest a high level of difficulty. Scores in the At-Risk range (*T*-Score 60–69) identify either a significant problem that may not be severe enough to require formal treatment or a potential of developing a problem that needs careful monitoring. On the Adaptive Scales, scores below 30 are considered clinically significant while scores between 31 and 40 are considered at-risk.

Ratings by Ms. Moon

Clinical scales	T-Score	Percentile
Hyperactivity	86**	99
Aggression	86**	99
Conduct problems	88**	99
Anxiety	50	51
Depression	56	78
Somatization	46	40
Attention problems	69*	96
Learning problems	68*	95
Atypicality	85**	99
Withdrawal	72**	99
Adaptability	26**	1
Social skills	32*	3
Leadership	36*	8
Study skills	32*	3
Functional communication	37*	9
Externalizing problems	90**	99
Internalizing problems	51	51
School problems	70**	97
Behavioral symptoms index	82**	99
Adaptive skills	30**	2

*At-risk
**Clinically significant

The above results indicate clinically significant rating on the externalizing, school problems, and adaptive skills composites. Chris scored in the clinically significant range on the behavioral symptoms index. Chris scored in the clinically significant range on the hyperactivity, aggression, conduct problems, atypicality, and withdrawal clinical scales. He scored in the at-risk range on the study skills, attention problems, leadership, functional communication, learning problems, and social skills scales.

Conceptualization and Classification

Multiple data sources and methods of assessment inform the conceptualization of Chris's cognitive, academic, social-emotional, and behavioral functioning including whether he qualifies for special education support. Details in support of these findings are offered below.

Cognitive and Academic Functioning: Chris's performance on measures of cognitive ability was in the average range (RIAS Composite IQ=95; 39th percentile). His performance on the memory scales of the RIAS was average (Std. Score=91; 27th percentile). Chris's performance on the WIAT-III across all academic areas was average. This is consistent with teacher reports of grade typical performance in the academic curriculum. However, there are times when Chris's emotional and behavioral difficulties are sufficiently florid that they interfere with his academic functioning in the classroom. During those times, Chris struggles to focus on his classwork and instead misses instruction.

Social-Emotional and Behavioral Functioning: Background information indicates possible physical abuse and a diagnosis of PTSD. Thus, some of Chris's behavioral difficulties may be a function of trauma. Additionally, Chris was hospitalized at the beginning of last academic year. Although hospitalization documentation is presently unavailable, background information and interview result indicate that Chris was hospitalized for suicidal ideation and other behavioral difficulties. Because of Chris's emotional difficulties, he struggles with age appropriate social skills and sometimes displays behavioral outbursts that are difficult to manage. Chris takes a combination of medications that attempt to help with the management of his emotional and behavioral symptoms. Chris is a child who experiences considerable emotional and behavioral difficulties at school. These emotional difficulties are having an adverse impact on Chris's educational performance. Chris requires intensive intervention to preserve his functioning in the classroom. A classification of emotional disturbance is warranted.

The following criteria from Pennsylvania's Special Education Code guided classification of emotional disturbance.

Emotional disturbance means a condition exhibiting one or more of the following characteristics over a long period of time and to a marked degree that adversely affects a child's educational performance:

(A) *An inability to learn that cannot be explained by intellectual, sensory, or health factors.*

There are no intellectual, sensory or health factors that contribute to Chris's learning difficulties. Instead, Chris's emotional difficulties are hampering his academic performance in the classroom.

(B) *An inability to build or maintain satisfactory interpersonal relationships with peers and teachers.*

Although Chris has demonstrated some capacity to relate to others in the classroom, Chris's emotional difficulties contribute to considerable interpersonal problems both with peers and adults in the classroom. When denied his own way, Chris has physically aggressed toward adults in the classroom. Two prior TSS workers have quit as a result of Chris's aggression. Chris's present TSS worker has been the recipient of physical aggression. At other times, Chris will be verbally or physically disruptive, calling out or leaving the classroom. Further, Chris experiences considerable difficulty entering into and sustaining peer relationships. Background information indicates that he sometimes annoys other children, which alienates him from them. He also can be impulsive and hostile during interpersonal interaction, further alienating him from peers.

(C) *Inappropriate types of behavior or feelings under normal circumstances.*

When denied his own way, Chris can become physically aggressive and oppositional. This emotional response does not appear volitional. In other words, Chris does not appear to have control over some of his behavioral and emotional outbursts. He also incorrectly misperceives even benign social situations as antagonistic, and can produce an emotional or behavioral response inconsistent with the circumstance.

(D) *A general pervasive mood of unhappiness or depression.*

Chris has is the past expressed suicidal ideation for which he was hospitalized for nearly 6 weeks. This would suggest a linkage to depressive tendencies, although at present any depressive symptomatology appears to manifest through externalizing behaviors.

(E) *A tendency to develop physical symptoms or fears associated with personal or school problems.*

This is not applicable at this time.

Emotional disturbance includes schizophrenia. The term does not apply to children who are socially maladjusted, unless it is determined that they have an emotional disturbance.

This is not applicable at this time.

Summary: Chris will benefit from special education support under a classification of Emotional Disturbance.

Summary and Recommendations

Multiple sources of data and approaches to evaluation suggest that Chris struggles with emotional and behavior difficulties. Considering Chris's performance on standardized behavior rating scales along with classroom observations, actual classroom performance, school records, parent interviews, and teacher interviews, Chris qualifies for special education services under a classification of emotional disturbance. The team concludes that specially designed instruction is called for in this case.

The following recommendations might benefit Chris:

1. *Psychotropic Medication Compliance and Monitoring*: Chris has in the past suddenly stopped taking his medications. Any decision made regarding medications should be done with the consultation of Chris's physician. Sudden cessation of medications such as clonidine can produce adverse side effects. In addition, any alteration in Chris's medication should be communicated to MPS so that his teachers, TSS worker, and other related school personnel can monitor for any behavioral changes and then communicate that to his mother.

2. *Monitoring for Suicidal Ideation*: Background information indicates that Chris was hospitalized for suicidality. Any future expression of intent to harm himself should be taken seriously and appropriate protective action by school personnel and others should be undertaken.

3. *Strategies for difficulties with Attention, Distractibility, and Loss of Focus*: Background reports indicate that Chris experiences difficulty with attention, impulsivity, and distractibility. As such, the following recommendations might be beneficial for him:

    (A) *Check In, Check Out, and Behavior Report Card:* Chris should have his behavioral expectations reviewed at the beginning of the school day. He should check in with an adult periodically throughout the day to determine whether his goals are being met. At the end of the day, Chris should check out with that same adult and receive a behavior report card that acknowledges his behavioral performance and is sent home to his caregivers.

    (B) *Provision of Directions by Teacher:* When Chris's teachers interact with him, he should be encouraged to repeat and explain instructions to ensure understanding. The provision of directions to Chris will be most effective when the teacher makes eye contact, avoids multiple commands, is clear and to the point, and permits repetition of directions when needed or asked for.

    (C) *Positive Reinforcement and Praise for Successful Task Completion:* Chris's teachers should provide positive reinforcement and immediate feedback for completion of desired behaviors or tasks. Initially, praise and reinforcement should be offered for successful effort on a task or behavior regardless of quality of performance.

    (D) *Time on Task*: Communicate to Chris how long he will need to engage in or pay attention on a particular task. Open ended expectations can be distressing to any child, let alone one with attentional difficulties.

    (E) *Prepare Student Discreetly for Transitions*: Furnish Chris with verbal prompts and visual cues that a new activity or task is about to start. This should be accomplished discreetly so as to avoid student embarrassment.

    (F) *Recess Time*: Chris should be permitted to participate in recess. Recess should not be a time to complete unfinished classwork or homework.

    (G) *Extended Time, Teacher Check In's, Assignment Adjustment, and Frequent Breaks*: Chris should be permitted additional time to complete academic tasks and projects. Chris's teachers should also consider review of classwork as Chris progresses on an assignment or project to assist Chris in avoiding careless mistakes. He may benefit from chunking assignments or assignment reduction. More frequent breaks than what is typical may also reduce careless mistakes and help to maintain focus.

4. *Individual Counseling*: Chris would benefit from counseling for behavioral and emotional issues. Background reports indicate that Chris was the victim of physical abuse and as a result has a subsequent PTSD diagnosis. Many of Chris's behaviors may be trauma-related. A qualified child counselor with experience with trauma may be an appropriate individual with whom Chris could engage in a therapeutic relationship.

Stefan C. Dombrowski, Ph.D.
Licensed Psychologist
Certified School Psychologist

References

Becker, S. P. (2011). Eligibility, assessment and educational placement issues for students classified with emotional disturbance: Federal and state-level analyses. *School Mental Health, 3*, 24–34.

Bower, E. H. (1960). *Early identification of emotionally handicapped children in schools.* Springfield, IL: Thomas.

Bower, E. M. (1982). Defining emotional disturbance: public policy and research. *Psychology in the Schools, 19*, 55–60.

Costello, E. J., Mustillo, S., Erkanli, A., Keeler, G., & Angold, A. (2003). Prevalence and development of psychiatric disorders in childhood and adolescence. *Archives of General Psychiatry, 60*, 837–844.

Della Toffalo, D. A., & Pedersen, J. A. (2005). The effect of a psychiatric diagnosis on school psychologists' special education eligibility decisions regarding emotional disturbance. *Journal of Emotional and Behavioral Disorders, 13*, 53–60.

Dombrowski, S. C., Gischlar, K., & Mrazik, M. (2011). *Assessing and treating low incidence/high severity psychological disorders and childhood.* New York, NY: Springer Science.

Epstein, M. H., & Cullinan, D. (1998). *Scale for assessing emotional disturbance.* Austin, TX: Pro-Ed.

Floyd, R. B., & Bose, J. B. (2003). Behavior rating scales for the assessment of emotional disturbance: A critical review of measurement characteristics. *Journal of Psychoeducational Assessment, 21*, 43–78.

Forness, S. R., & Kavale, K. A. (2000). Emotional behavioral disorders: Background and current status of the E/BD terminology and definition. *Behavioral Disorders, 25*, 264–269.

Friedman, R. M., Kutash, K., & Duchnowski, A. J. (1996). The population of concern: Defining the issues. In B. A. Stroul (Ed.), *Children's mental health: Creating systems of care in a changing society* (pp. 69–96). Baltimore, MD: Paul H. Brookes.

Handwerk, M. A., & Marshall, R. M. (1998). Behavioral and emotional problems of children with LD, SED, or both conditions. *Journal of Learning Disabilities, 31*, 327–339.

Kauffman, J., & Landrum, T. (2012). *Characteristics of emotional and behavioral disorders of children and youth* (10th ed.). Upper Saddle River, NJ: Pearson.

Kelly, E. J. (1988). Use of a self-concept test in differentiating between conduct disordered and emotionally disturbed students. *Psychological Reports, 62*, 363–367.

Kelly, E. J. (1990). *The differential test of conduct and emotional problems.* Aurora: Slosson.

Osher, D., Sims, A. E., & Woodruff, D. (2002). Schools make a difference: The overrepresentation of African-American youth in special education and the juvenile justice system. In D. J. Losen & G. Orfield (Eds.), *Racial inequality in special education.* Cambridge, MA: Harvard Education Press.

Skiba, R., & Grizzle, K. (1992). Qualifications vs. logic and data: Excluding conduct disorders from the SED definition. *School Psychology Review, 21*, 23.

Slenkovitch, J. (1992a). Can the language "social maladjustment" in the SED definition be ignored? *School Psychology Review, 21*, 21–22.

Slenkovitch, J. (1992b). Can the language "social maladjustment" in the SED definition be ignored? The final words. *School Psychology Review, 21*, 43–44.

U.S. Department of Education, Federal Register (2006) p. 46756, 300.8(c)(4)(i)).

Wagner, M. (1989). *The transition experiences of youth with disabilities: A report from the National Longitudinal Transition Study*. Menlo Park, CA: SRI International.

Wright, F. (1989). *Emotional and behavior problem scale*. Columbia, MO: Hawthorne Educational Services.

Chapter 14
Intellectual Disabilities

14.1 Overview

Intellectual disability, formerly mental retardation, is defined fairly consistently across most psychiatric (e.g., DSM, ICD), special education (e.g., IDEA) and organization-based (e.g., AAIDD) systems of classification. The definition generally shares three common core features: (1) deficits in intellectual functioning such as reasoning, problem solving, judgment, and abstract thinking; (2) deficits in adaptive behavior (conceptual, social, and practical) such as communication, daily living skills, and self-care; and (3) occurrence during the developmental period (i.e., before age 18). Each of the major taxonomies (e.g., IDEA, DSM, ICD) also have at the core of their definition and classification approach the requirement for a "dual deficit" in IQ and adaptive behavior. Psychologists working in the schools, where the preponderance of ID classification are offered, must work within the constraints of their respective state codes. State codes are generally aligned with the definition found within IDEA.

14.2 Definition

IDEA
On Tuesday, October 5, 2010, President Obama signed into law S. 2781 ("Rosa's Law") which replaced the term "mental retardation" in Federal statues including IDEA with the term "intellectual disability." Rosa's law was named after a child with Down syndrome from the state of Maryland. The family of Rosa and Senator Barbara Mikulski worked together to ensure that the word "mental retardation" was expunged from the federal code and replaced with the term intellectual disability.

© Springer Science+Business Media New York 2015
S.C. Dombrowski, *Psychoeducational Assessment and Report Writing*,
DOI 10.1007/978-1-4939-1911-6_14

According to the Federal Regulations under IDEA the definition of ID is as follows:

"Intellectual disability (ID) means significantly subaverage general intellectual functioning, existing concurrently with deficits in adaptive behavior and manifested during the developmental period, that adversely affects a child's educational performance." [34 CFR §300.8(c)(6)]

Source: CFR, Title 34, Chapter III, Part 300, §300.8 (Child with a disability), (c)(6)

State special education definitions are aligned with the federal definition but each state has autonomy to define the term and its approach to eligibility. Bergeron, Floyd, and Shands (2008) examined state level guidelines for identification of mental retardation and found considerable variation in definition including the terms cognitive impairment, cognitive disability, cognitive delay and severely limited intellectual capacity. Bergeron et al. (2008) indicated a general consensus surrounding the IQ cut score at approximately two standard deviations below the mean with some states (about 40 %) accounting for measurement error by specifying an IQ range (e.g., 70–75) or permitting consideration of confidence intervals.

AAIDD

The American Association on Intellectual and Developmental Disabilities (AAID), considered the authoritative source on intellectual disability, offers as similar definition (Schalock et al. 2010):

Intellectual disability is characterized by significant limitations both in intellectual functioning and in adaptive behavior as expressed in conceptual, social, and practical adaptive skills. This disability originates before age 18 (p1).

The AAIDD criterion specifies an IQ score that is approximately two standard deviations below the mean and considers the instrument's standard error of measurement and strengths and limitations. Importantly, the AAIDD indicates that a valid assessment of ID requires the consideration of cultural and linguistic diversity along with individual differences in communication, sensory, motor and behavioral factors. The significant limitation in adaptive behavior, noted in the above definition, is characterized by performance of approximately two standard deviations below the mean on either (A) an overall score on a standardized measure of conceptual, social, and practical skills; or (B) one of the following adaptive skills areas: conceptual, social or practical.

DSM 5 Definition

The newly revised DSM offers a definition of ID.

> Intellectual Disability (Intellectual Developmental Disorder 319) is a disorder with onset during the developmental period that includes both intellectual and adaptive functioning deficits in conceptual, social, and practical domains. The following three criteria must be met:
>
> (A) Deficits in intellectual function, such as reasoning, problem solving, planning, abstract thinking, judgment, academic learning, and learning from experience, confirmed by both clinical assessment and individualized, standardized intelligence testing.
> (B) Deficits in adaptive functioning that result in failure to meet developmental and sociocultural standards for personal independence and social responsibility. Without ongoing support, the adaptive deficits limit functioning in one or more activities of daily life, such as communication, social participation, and independent living, across multiple environments, such as home, school, work, and community.
> (C) Onset of intellectual and adaptive deficits during the developmental period.
>
> *Source*: Adapted from the Diagnostic and Statistical Manual of Mental Disorders, Fifth Edition (Copyright 2013). American Psychiatric Association.

14.2.1 Etiology

The causes of ID are myriad. Some genetic causes include Down syndrome, fragile X syndrome, and phenylketonuria (PKU). Prenatal and perinatal factors also play a role including fetal alcohol effects, prenatal infection by rubella, anoxia at birth, extreme prematurity, and other complications during pregnancy (see Martin & Dombrowski, 2008). Additional environmental exposures during the developmental period may also cause ID including exposure to infectious diseases such as whopping cough, measles, and meningitis or exposure to toxicants such as lead or poison.

14.2.2 Characteristics of Intellectual Disabilities

It is noted that head trauma or injury that results in a profile similar to ID is not in itself ID, but rather should be considered a Traumatic Brain Injury (TBI; see Chap. 16). It is similarly noteworthy that physical appearance is a misleading qualifier for the classification of ID. The prototypical child with ID does not have the characteristics of Down Syndrome. In fact, approximately 70 % of individuals with ID are in the mild ID range, whereas individuals with Down Syndrome have more moderate delays (Schalock et al. 2010). Some characteristics of ID include delays or difficulty, relative to other children the same age, in the following areas:

- Gross motor skills including sitting up, crawling, and walking.
- Communication skills including learning to talk or speak.
- Memory difficulties.
- Social pragmatic skills including difficulty with understanding social rules and seeing the consequences of actions.
- Executive functioning including problem-solving, cause-and-effect relationships, and prediction.

14.3   Identification of ID

Multiple methods of assessment and sources of data should be referenced when classifying ID. This may include a review of medical, educational, and early developmental history; interviews of caregivers; observations in the school setting; functional assessments; and norm-referenced measures of IQ, academic achievement (where possible), behavior and adaptive behavior.

14.4   General Guidance Regarding Psychoeducational Assessment

14.4.1   Dual Deficit in IQ and Adaptive Behavior

At the core of any approach to the evaluation of ID is what is known as a dual deficit approach. This requires the assessment of both intellectual functioning and adaptive behavior on psychometrically sound, nationally normed measures. These instruments should have a mean of 100 and a standard deviation of 15. When a child scores two standard deviations below the mean (approximately a 70 or lower), and when considering the standard error of measure (SEM) on both these instruments, then the child is considered to have an ID. The dual deficit approach should be supplemented, as necessary, by informal and functional measures of adaptive behavior.

14.4.2   Tests of Intelligence

Tests of cognitive ability such as the Wechsler scales and the Stanford–Binet have been the commonly accepted instruments suggested by diagnostic taxonomies and organizational guidelines such as the AAIDD. The AAIDD recommends against a screening instrument or a short form of an IQ test. Although the Wechsler Scales and the Stanford–Binet are frequently used IQ tests there are additional IQ instruments that may also be viable alternatives. When making a classification decision, the standard error of measurement should be considered in cases that are slightly above the 70 cut score. Please keep in mind that clinical judgment should always supplant rigid cut score application where permitted by state regulations. This is particularly the case with IQ tests which are prone to measurement error, the Flynn Effect, regression effects, and test differences (i.e., a test with numerous manipulatives may be inappropriate for a child with significant fine motor deficits). (Flynn, 1984, 1987; Kranzler & Floyd, 2013).

The application of a rigid cut score is frowned upon by clinicians with specific expertise in ID (e.g., AAIDD), by diagnostic systems (e.g., DSM-5), by ethical codes (e.g., APA, NASP) and test standards (APA, AERA, and NCME, 1999). The identification of ID should be complemented by multiple methods and sources of information including in depth background and developmental history, medical history, interviews of multiple caregivers including parents and teachers, standardized test scores, understanding of cultural differences, and sound clinical judgment. The foundation for the classification decision is the requirement to document a dual deficit in IQ and adaptive behavior. But the clinician should consider sensory/motor issues and cultural, social, ethnic and language differences. In some cases, a nonverbal test of cognitive ability may be appropriate (e.g., TONI or UNIT).

Other considerations include the use of a recently normed test (i.e., within the last 10 years) to avoid issues with the Flynn Effect. The IQ test should also have high reliability (internal consistency $\geq .95$; test–retest $\geq .90$). Kranzler and Floyd (2013) discuss two additional issues that must be considered when selecting an IQ test. They discuss the importance of paying attention to inadequate subtest floors and to subtest requirements that might interfere with accurate measurement of psychometric g. Inadequate floors occur when a child obtains a raw score of one (1) on an instrument and the standard score is within (i.e., higher than a 70) two standard deviations of the mean. This may be a problem for selected subtests from most of the IQ tests noted above, but it is not a problem when attempting to derive a full scale IQ score (i.e., psychometric g). Kranzler and Floyd (2013), Braden and Elliot (2003), and Phillips (1994) caution about selecting an instrument with too many manipulatives due to the common co-occurrence of sensory and motor disabilities in children and adolescents with ID. As an example, a child suspected of having ID but who has cerebral palsy and concomitant fine motor skills difficulties might benefit from administration of an IQ test that avoids manipulatives such as blocks or copying symbols quickly under timed conditions (Kranzler & Floyd, 2013).

14.4.3   Adaptive Behavior

Adaptive behavior is assessed using psychometrically sound adaptive behavior scales as well as clinical judgment. Several adaptive behavior assessment instruments are available to the field although two of the more commonly used instruments include the Vineland-II and the ADAS-II. Psychologists may wish to consider the following instruments for the purpose of adaptive behavior assessment:

- Adaptive Behavior Scale-School, Second Edition
- Adaptive Behavior Evaluations Scale-Revised, Second Edition
- Scales of Independent Behavior-Revised
- Adaptive Behavior Assessment System, Second Edition
- Vineland Adaptive Behavior Scales, Second Edition

When identifying adaptive behavior via a norm-referenced measure, psychologists should attempt to ascertain ratings and information from several knowledgeable respondents including parents and teachers. One of the confounding issues in the evaluation of children with ID may be found when interviewing parents. Parents sometimes mistake the occasional demonstration of a behavior with typically occurring behavior. Professionals need to focus on typically performing (i.e., actually demonstrating consistently) the behavior rather than on the parent's belief or statement that the child can do the behavior.

Along with norm-referenced measures of adaptive behavior, the clinician may wish to informally investigate adaptive behavior via interviews, accumulation of background and developmental history, and inspection of medical, educational, and psychological records in the following areas:

- Conceptual abilities (e.g., communication, language, problem solving, judgment, reading and writing, understanding of money, and concepts of time).
- Social abilities (e.g., interpersonal skills, social problem solving, understanding of nuance and idioms, social responsibility, rule compliance and naïveté).
- Practical abilities (e.g., personal care, hygiene, toileting, getting dressed, feeding oneself, understanding of travel directions, and health care safety).

The DSM-5 offers a comprehensive chart detailing specific adaptive abilities according to levels of severity (Mild, Moderate, Severe and Profound), across several stages of development, and among the three adaptive behavior domain areas (conceptual, social, and practical). When considering a classification of ID under special education regulations, the clinician may reference the DSM-5 to assist with decision-making but keep in mind that it is the IDEA/state criteria that drives classification in the schools.

Severity level	Conceptual domain	Social domain	Practical domain
Mild	For preschool children, there may be no obvious conceptual differences. For school-age children and adults, there are difficulties in learning academic skills involving reading, writing, arithmetic, time, or money, with support needed in one or more areas to meet age-related expectations. In adults, abstract thinking, executive functioning (i.e., planning, strategizing, priority setting, and cognitive flexibility), and short-term memory, as well as functional use of academic skills (e.g., reading, money management), are impaired. There is a somewhat concrete approach to problems and solutions compared with age-mates.	Compared with typically developing age-mates, the individual is immature in social interactions. For example, there may be difficulty in accurately perceiving peers' social cues. Communication, conversation, and language are more concrete or immature than expected for age. There may be difficulties regulating emotion and behavior in age-appropriate fashion; these difficulties are noticed by peers in social situations. There is limited understanding of risk in social situations; social judgment is immature for age, and the person is at risk of being manipulated by others (gullibility).	The individual may function age-appropriately in personal care. Individuals need some support with complex daily tasks in comparison to peers. In adulthood, supports typically involve grocery shopping, transportation, home and child-care organizing, nutritious food preparation, and banking and money management. Recreational skills resemble those of age-mates, although judgment related to wellbeing and organization around recreation requires support. In adulthood, competitive employment is often seen in jobs that do not emphasize conceptual skills. Individuals generally need support to make health care decisions and legal decisions, and learn to perform a skilled vocation competently. Support is typically needed to raise a family.
Moderate	All through development, the individual's conceptual skills lag markedly behind those of peers. For preschoolers, language and pre-academic skills develop slowly. For school-age children, progress in reading, writing, mathematics, and understanding of time and money occurs slowly across the school years and is markedly limited compared with that of peers. For adults, academic skill development is typically at an elementary level, and support is required for all use of academic skills in work and personal life. Ongoing assistance on a daily basis is needed to complete conceptual tasks of day-to-day life, and others may take over these responsibilities fully for the individual.	The individual shows marked differences from peers in social and communicative behavior across development. Spoken language is typically a primary tool for social communication but is much less complex than that of peers. Capacity for relationships is evident in ties to family and friends, and the individual may have successful friendships across life and sometimes romantic relationships in adulthood. However, individuals may not perceive or interpret social cues accurately. Social judgment and decision-making abilities are limited, and caretakers must assist the person with life decisions. Friendships with typically developing peers are often affected by communication or social limitations. Significant social and communicative support is needed in work settings for success.	The individual can care for personal needs involving eating, dressing, elimination, and hygiene as an adult, although an extended period of teaching and time is needed for the individual to become independent in these areas, and reminders may be needed. Similarly, participation in all household tasks can be achieved by adulthood, although an extended period of teaching is needed, and ongoing supports will typically occur for adult-level performance. Independent employment in jobs that require limited conceptual and communication skills can be achieved, but considerable support from coworkers, supervisors, and others is needed to manage social expectations, job complexities, and ancillary responsibilities such as scheduling, transportation, health benefits, and money management. A variety of recreational skills can be developed. These typically require additional supports and learning opportunities over an extended period of time. Maladaptive behavior is present in a significant minority and causes social problems.

(continued)

(continued)

Severity level	Conceptual domain	Social domain	Practical domain
Severe	Attainment of conceptual skills is limited. The individual generally has little understanding of written language or of concepts involving numbers, quantity, time, and money. Caretakers provide extensive supports for problem solving throughout life.	Spoken language is quite limited in terms of vocabulary and grammar. Speech may be single words or phrases and may be supplemented through augmentative means. Speech and communication are focused on the here and now within everyday events. Language is used for social communication more than for explication. Individuals understand simple speech and gestural communication. Relationships with family members and familiar others are a source of pleasure and help.	The individual requires support for all activities of daily living, including meals, dressing, bathing, and elimination. The individual requires supervision at all times. The individual cannot make responsible decisions regarding well-being of self or others. In adulthood, participation in tasks at home, recreation, and work requires ongoing support and assistance. Skill acquisition in all domains involves long-term teaching and ongoing support. Maladaptive behavior, including self-injury, is present in a significant minority.
Profound	Conceptual skills generally involve the physical world rather than symbolic processes. The individual may use objects in goal-directed fashion for self-care, work, and recreation. Certain visuospatial skills, such as matching and sorting based on physical characteristics, may be acquired. However, co-occurring motor and sensory impairments may prevent functional use of objects.	The individual has very limited understanding of symbolic communication in speech or gesture. He or she may understand some simple instructions or gestures. The individual expresses his or her own desires and emotions largely through nonverbal, nonsymbolic communication. The individual enjoys relationships with well-known family members, caretakers, and familiar others, and initiates and responds to social interactions through gestural and emotional cues. Co-occurring sensory and physical impairments may prevent many social activities.	The individual is dependent on others for all aspects of daily physical care, health, and safety, although he or she may be able to participate in some of these activities as well. Individuals without severe physical impairments may assist with some daily work tasks at home, like carrying dishes to the table. Simple actions with objects may be the basis of participation in some vocational activities with high levels of ongoing support. Recreational activities may involve, for example, enjoyment in listening to music, watching movies, going out for walks, or participating in water activities, all with the support of others. Co-occurring physical and sensory impairments are frequent barriers to participation (beyond watching) in home, recreational, and vocational activities. Maladaptive behavior is present in a significant minority.

Source: American Psychiatric Association. (2013). DSM-5. Pages 34–36.

14.5   Conclusion

The classification of ID in the schools is accomplished via a comprehensive psycho-educational evaluation but predicated upon a dual deficit in cognitive ability and adaptive behavior. Each state has its own definition, label and identification procedures, but these features are fairly consistent with the federal guidelines with a few minor exceptions.

Appendix: Sample Report

Intellectual Disability

Psychological Report
Confidential

Name: Keith Smith   Date of Report: May 15, 2016
Date of Birth: 5/22/2007   Chronological Age: 8 years 11 months
Grade: 2   School: Smith Public School
Name of Examiner: Stefan C. Dombrowski, Ph.D.

Parent Name and Address: Cher Haley
                             1234 Briar Cliff Lane
                             Philadelphia, PA, 19138

Phone: 609-585-1234

Reason for Referral

Keith faces continued difficulties with all aspects of the academic curriculum including reading, writing and mathematics. He is primarily non-verbal in his communication was referred for a comprehensive reevaluation to gain insight into his academic, behavioral, adaptive, and social progress in the classroom. The multidisciplinary team wonders whether Keith will be found eligible for a classification of intellectual disability and what recommendations might benefit Keith.

Assessment Methods and Sources of Data
Stanford–Binet Intelligence Scales—Fifth Edition (SB5)
Woodcock–Johnson Tests of Achievement, Fourth Edition (WJ-IV)
Bender Visual Motor Gestalt, Second Edition (Bender-2)

Behavior Assessment System for Children, Second Edition (*BASC-2*)
– Ms. Jennifer Lincoln (Second Grade Teacher)
Vineland Adaptive Behavior Scales, Second Edition (*Vineland-II*)
– Ms. Jennifer Lincoln (Second Grade Teacher)
– Ms. Jessie Miller (Special Education Teacher)
Teacher Interview
– Ms. Jennifer Lincoln (Second Grade Teacher)
– Ms. Jessie Miller (Special Education Teacher)
Parent Interview
– Cher Haley (Mother)
Student Interview
– Keith Smith
Classroom Observations
Review of Academic Grade Reports
Review of School Records

Background Information and Developmental History
Keith Smith is an 8 year, 11 month-old child in the second grade at the Smith Public
School (SPS). Keith experiences moderate delays in cognitive ability, functional
academics, and functional communication. These delays are sufficiently severe that
Keith will qualify for a classification of intellectual disability (formerly mental retardation). This classification reflects a revision to the diagnosis from January 2014
where a classification of mental retardation was deferred in favor of a classification
of learning disabilities and speech language delay. In 2014, Keith experienced cognitive delays and functional communication deficits, but his academic skills were in the
below/low average range. He also just entered kindergarten and other indicators at
that time (e.g., standardized achievement test scores; parental input; socialization
skills) suggested that the classification of intellectual disability be deferred. At the
present time, Keith's moderate delays in cognitive ability, functional academics, and
functional communication are sufficiently severe that a classification of intellectual
disability is now clinically indicated.

Prenatal, Perinatal, and Early Developmental History: Ms. Haley noted that Keith
was born prematurely at 32 weeks weighing 5 lb. He spent 1 week in the NICU but
experienced little to no medical concerns. Ms. Haley also reported suffering from
the flu during her first trimester with Keith. Keith experienced delays in walking and
talking. He did not say his first word until 13 months of age and walked at 15 months.
Ms. Haley reports that all other developmental milestones were attained within
normal limits.

Medical: Ms. Haley that Keith is in good health and has no medical concerns. She
indicated that his hearing and vision are intact. Keith has never experienced a head
injury or major infection.

Cognitive, Academic, and Language Functioning: Keith faces significant struggles with his academic progress. He can only recognize a few letters of the alphabet and struggles with counting up through 100. Keith's language ability is low. He struggles with verbal expression. Keith's prior performance on a measure of cognitive ability was in the delayed range (RIAS Composite IQ=50; 0.04 percentile; Verbal IQ=44; <0.01 percentile; Nonverbal IQ=74; 4th percentile). Keith's performance on the WJ-III Achievement was also in the delayed range across all academic areas. His language ability is low for his age and he struggles with verbal expression. Ms. Haley noted that Kevin's math ability is improving.

Social-Emotional and Behavioral Functioning: Both Ms. Haley and Ms. Lincoln noted that Keith struggles socially. He frequently misinterprets social cues and gets teased in class. He also struggles with following classroom rules because he sometimes is unaware of his lack of compliance. Keith demonstrates a strength in his ability to emulate other students' behavior and adapt to situations. He struggles with expressing himself at an age expected manner and is often difficult to understand when he speaks.

Strengths: Ms. Haley indicated that Keith's strengths include his helpfulness, his sociability, and his concern for others. Kevin is able to emulate other children in school.

Summary: Keith continues to experience significant deficits in the academic and communication arena. He struggles with all academic subjects and faces considerable difficulties with expressing himself orally and in writing.

Cognitive and Academic Functioning

Stanford–Binet Intelligence Scales—Fifth Edition (SB5)

Keith was administered the Stanford–Binet Intelligence Scales—Fifth Edition (SB5). The SB5 is an individually administered measure of intellectual functioning normed for individuals between the ages of 2 and 85+ years. The SB contains several individual tests of intellectual problem solving and reasoning ability that are combined to form a Verbal Intelligence Quotient (VIQ) and a Nonverbal Intelligence Quotient (NVIQ). These two indexes of intellectual functioning are then combined to form an overall Full Scale Intelligence Quotient (FSIQ). By combining the VIQ and the NVIQ into the FSIQ, a strong, reliable assessment of general intelligence (g) is obtained. The FSIQ measures the two most important aspects of general intelligence according to recent theories and research findings: reasoning or fluid abilities and verbal or crystallized abilities.

The SB5 contains five factor indexes for each the VIQ and NVIQ: Fluid Reasoning, Knowledge, Quantitative Reasoning, Visual Spatial, and Working Memory. Fluid reasoning represents an individual's ability to solve verbal and nonverbal problems and reason inductively and deductively. Knowledge represents the accumulated fund of general information acquired at home, school, work, or in life. Quantitative reasoning reflects facility with numbers and numerical problem solving, whether with word problems or figural relationships. Quantitative reasoning emphasizes problem solving more than mathematical knowledge. Visual-spatial processing reflects the ability to see patterns, relationships, spatial orientation, and the connection among diverse pieces of a visual display. Working memory is a measure of short-term memory processing of information whether verbal or visual, emphasizing the brief manipulation of diverse information.

Each of these indexes is expressed as an age-corrected standard score that is scaled to a mean of 100 and a standard deviation of 15. These scores are normally distributed and can be converted to a variety of other metrics if desired.

The SB5 provides three intelligence score composites and five factor indices with a mean of 100 and a Standard deviation of 15. Scores between 90 and 110 are considered average.

	Standard score	Percentile	Conf. interval (95 %)	Descriptive classification
Full scale IQ (FSIQ)	48	0.03	44–56	Delayed
Nonverbal IQ (NVIQ)	62	1	58–70	Below Avg
Verbal IQ (VIQ)	49	0.03	45–59	Below Avg
Factor index scores				
Fluid reasoning (FR)	63	1	57–70	Below Avg
Knowledge (KN)	50	0.05	45–55	Delayed
Quantitative reasoning (QR)	68	2	63–72	Below Avg
Visual spatial (VS)	57	0.14	52–63	Delayed
Working memory (WM)	45	0.02	40–50	Delayed

The above table may be referenced to obtain Keith's performance in each of these areas while the following is a description of each of the factor index scores. Fluid reasoning represents an individual's ability to solve verbal and nonverbal problems and reason inductively and deductively. Knowledge represents the accumulated fund of general information acquired at home, school, work, or in life. Quantitative reasoning reflects facility with numbers and numerical problem solving, whether with word problems or figural relationships. Quantitative reasoning emphasizes problem solving more than mathematical knowledge. Visual-spatial processing reflects the ability to see patterns, relationships, spatial orientation, and the connection among diverse pieces of a visual display. Working memory is a measure of short-term memory processing of information whether verbal or visual, emphasizing the brief manipulation of diverse information.

The SB5 includes ten subtest scores with a mean of 10 and a Standard deviation of 3. Scores between 8 and 12 are considered average. Keith's individual subtest scores were as follows:

Nonverbal tests		Verbal tests	
Fluid reasoning	3	Fluid reasoning	2
Knowledge	2	Knowledge	3
Quant. reasoning	4	Quant. reasoning	3
Visual spatial	1	Visual spatial	2
Working memory	2	Working memory	1

As noted above, Keith's scores were all in the below average to delayed range. Primary interpretative emphasis should be placed upon the full scale scores with secondary placed upon index level scores. It is generally not indicated to interpret at the level of the subtest.

On testing with the SB5, Keith earned a Full Scale IQ of 48. On the SB5, this level of performance falls within the range of scores designated as delayed and exceeded the performance of 0.03 % of individuals at Keith's age. His Verbal IQ (Standard Score = 49; 0.03rd percentile) was in the delayed range and exceeded 0.03 % of individuals Keith's age. Keith's Nonverbal IQ (Standard Score = 62; 1st percentile) was in the delayed range, exceeding 1 % of individuals Keith's age.

Woodcock–Johnson Tests of Achievement-IV (WJ-IV)

The WJ-IV is an achievement test used to measure basic reading, writing, oral language, and mathematics skills. The Reading subtest includes letter and word identification, vocabulary, and comprehension skills. The Writing subtest includes spelling, writing fluency, and simple sentence writing. The Mathematics subtest includes calculation, practical problems, and knowledge of mathematical concepts and vocabulary. Keith obtained the following scores in each of the areas of measurement:

	Standard score	Descriptive percentile	Classification
Broad reading	44	<0.1	Delayed
Letter-word ID	66	1	Delayed
Sentence reading fluency	58	0.3	Delayed
Passage comprehension	37	<0.1	Delayed
Sentence writing fluency	60	0.4	Delayed
Spelling	51	<0.1	Delayed
Broad mathematics	44	<0.1	Delayed
Math facts fluency	57	0.2	Delayed
Applied Problems	64	1	Delayed
Calculation	30	<0.4	Delayed

Standardized achievement test results revealed considerable deficits across all academic domains. Keith will require an intensive, restrictive environment that will focus on functional academic skills.

Bender Visual-Motor Gestalt Test, Second Edition (Bender-II)
The Bender-II measures visual-motor integration skills, or the ability to see and copy figures accurately. A quantitative and qualitative analysis of Keith's drawings suggests that his visual-motor integration abilities (e.g., fine motor skills for paper and pencil tasks) are below average (Copy Standard Score=70; 2nd percentile).

Behavior Assessment System for Children, Second Edition (BASC-2)
The Behavior Assessment System for Children, Second Edition (BASC-2) is an integrated system designed to facilitate the differential diagnosis and classification of a variety of emotional and behavioral conditions in children. It possesses validity scales and several clinical scales, which reflect different dimensions of a child's personality. *T*-scores between 40 and 60 are considered average. Scores greater than 70 (*T*>70) are in the Clinically Significant range and suggest a high level of difficulty. Scores in the At-Risk range (*T*-Score 60–69) identify either a significant problem that may not be severe enough to require formal treatment or a potential of developing a problem that needs careful monitoring. On the Adaptive Scales, scores 30 and below are considered clinically significant while scores between 31 and 39 are considered at-risk.

| | Ms. Lincoln | |
Clinical scales	*T*-Score	Percentile
Hyperactivity	67*	93
Aggression	72**	98
Conduct problems	62*	86
Anxiety	48	47
Depression	74**	98
Somatization	84**	99
Attention problems	62*	86
Learning problems	80**	98
Atypicality	69*	94
Withdrawal	66*	93
Adaptability	41	21
Social skills	52	53
Leadership	39*	19
Study skills	30**	3
Functional communication	21**	2
Externalizing problems	68*	93
Internalizing problems	73**	98
Behavioral symptoms index	73**	98
Adaptive skills	35*	7
School problems	73**	98

*At-risk
**Clinically significant

BASC-2 ratings suggested a clinically significant elevation on the behavioral symptoms, internalizing problems, and school composites with an at risk score on the adaptive skills composite. Specific scales in the clinically significant range include aggression, depression, somatization, learning problems, study skills, and functional communication. BASC-2 results also revealed scores in the at-risk range on the attention, hyperactivity, conduct problems, leadership, atypicality, and withdrawal clinical scales.

Vineland II Adaptive Behavior Scales

The Vineland measures a student's performance of the daily activities necessary for taking care of oneself, socializing, and getting along with others. Ms. Jessie Miller and Jenny Lincoln completed the teacher rating form that assesses Keith's functioning in the areas of Communication (receptive, expressive, and written), Daily Living Skills (personal, academic, school community), and Socialization (Interpersonal relationships, Play and leisure time, coping skills).

Following are the results on the Vineland-II:

	Ms. Miller		Ms. Lincoln	
Domain	Std. Scr	Percentile	Std. Scr	Percentile
Communication	65	1	67	1
Daily Living Skills	80	9	84	14
Socialization	76	5	86	18
Adaptive behavior composite	72	3	77	6

Results indicate that Keith experiences delays in the area of communication (Receptive and expressive). His socialization skills are in the below average/low average range while his Daily Living Skills (e.g., Academic, School Community, Personal) are low average. Keith's Adaptive Behavior Composite scores of 72 (3rd percentile; Ms. Miller) and 77 (6th percentile; Ms. Lincoln) are below average.

Interview Results

Parent Interview (May 6, 2016): Ms. Cher Haley, Keith's mother, was interviewed on May 6, 2016 to ascertain impressions of Keith's progress at school. Ms. Haley noted a positive change in Keith's math ability. She explained that there is much more structure in math and as long as Keith knows what he is dealing with, then he knows what to do. Ms. Haley explained that Keith still struggles, but he has also improved. Ms. Haley indicated that Keith's memory issues stand out. "To be able to remember what word is what is very difficult for him," she noted. His writing is also low. Ms. Haley asked, "if [Keith] has a learning issue that causes him difficulty with remembering words, then how can we expect him to write it?" She continued, "he needs someone assisting him and guiding him so that he can express himself." Ms. Haley indicated that he is doing okay socially, but he tends to get teased by other children since he is beginning to stand out in terms of academics and considering that he is bigger than other children. Ms. Haley noted that it is difficult for him to keep up with other children. He always attempts to participate and raise his hand, but generally does not know the answer. Ms. Haley continued, "it is not that he's having a hard time, it is that the other children are shunning him." She stated that other children tend to call him "dumb" or "stupid." Socially, when outside of school settings he gets along fine. In a school setting he tends to get teased. Behaviorally he's okay. Ms. Haley indicated, "I noticed that his frustration from his learning difference tends to make him angry. He tends to want help. If he's not given the answer, he tends to shut down." She also explained that if Keith has something to look forward to, he will persist without getting upset. Ms. Haley stated that Keith needs more structure than what he is presently receiving. When he does work and it is incorrect, he needs to be corrected; otherwise, he'll actually think it is correct. When he does get things correct on his own then he needs to be praised. She concluded by stating that she does not believe Keith is "mentally retarded." She is concerned that if Keith is placed into a program for children with intellectual disabilities then this will be harmful to Keith's progress. Ms. Haley explained that "Keith may just shut down" if placed in such a program because he will realize that there is something wrong with him.

Student Interview (April 27, 2016): Keith was interviewed to ascertain impressions of his progress at SPS. When asked whether he enjoys SPS Keith stated "yes." When asked what he likes about SPS, Keith stated that he likes homework, reading and recess. Keith was asked what he does best at school and he stated, "listening to the teachers." Keith also stated that he enjoys playing outside. Keith indicated that he does not get into trouble at school. He mentioned that his strengths include math and homework. Keith explained that his needs include homework. Throughout the student interview, Keith was difficult to understand and had difficulty with answering questions posed to him. It was quite apparent that Keith faces considerable communication delays and struggles with answering questions that are abstract.

Teacher Interview (May 4, 2016): Ms. Jenny Lincoln, Keith's second grade teacher, was interviewed regarding Keith's academic, behavioral, emotional, adaptive, and social functioning. Ms. Lincoln first discussed Keith's issue with communication noting that he struggles with both expressing and understanding language. She mentioned that Keith struggles to understand the distinction between friendly and unfriendly intent. She noted that Keith often misinterprets social cues. Ms. Lincoln noted that Keith is both oversensitive and undersensitive to social stimuli. She mentioned that other children sometimes try to provoke Keith. Ms. Lincoln explained that Keith is aware of his own deficit and employs strategies to try to hide them. Some of these strategies can be functional in one way (e.g., get him out of work; have him be a leader at something in school) but maladaptive in another (e.g., alienate him from other children). For instance, Ms. Lincoln commented that Keith attempts to frequently be first in line and will bump into and push other children. Ms. Lincoln noted that Keith tries to engage socially with other children, but other children often have difficulty understanding what he is saying. Ms. Lincoln explained that Keith is a friendly child and knows how to approach a group of children, but struggles with sustaining social contact with them. Ms. Lincoln explained that Keith is very good at emulating other children's behavior, which allows him to blend in with them to some degree. Regarding academics, Ms. Lincoln explained that Keith cannot read or write. She noted that sometimes he struggles with letter recognition and he cannot blend sounds. Ms. Lincoln indicated that Keith knows his one and two digit numbers and can count by fives and tens. Ms. Lincoln explained that Keith is skilled at trying to appear like his peers. She also mentioned that Keith is a friendly child who likes to draw and do art. Ms. Lincoln explained that Keith requires support for difficulties with academics, social progress, and speech.

Teacher Interview (May 6, 2016): Ms. Jessie Miller, Keith's special education teacher, was interviewed regarding Keith's academic, behavioral, emotional, adaptive, and social functioning. Ms. Miller noted that Keith really struggles in school. She explained, "he spends most of his day really trying hard to access the curriculum." Ms. Miller indicated that Keith's teachers also try really hard to assist him. Ms. Miller indicated that Keith's ability to retain and express language is low. Keith is still writing with imaginative spelling which is reminiscent of beginning of kindergarten level. Still, Ms. Miller explained that Keith has worked extremely hard to get where he is. She continued, he gets exhausted even to accomplish this. Ms. Miller noted that Keith can only match about 30 % of the letters to their beginning sounds. He can recognize, mostly, his letters but still gets confused on the "b," the "q," and the "t." He can count to 100 with teacher cues, though he might skip numbers along the way. Ms. Miller indicated that his ability to count to 100 is not consistent. He's about 80 % accurate with that. Ms. Miller stated that keeping track of verbal instructions is difficult for Keith. Ms. Miller was next asked about Keith's social progress. She explained that Keith has a very difficult time reading social situations. For example, Keith does not recognize his role in incidents with other children. He always wants to be first in line, and he'll push other kids and not recognize that this behavior makes children angry. Ms. Miller explained that children are resentful of him pushing to get to the front of the line. Another child will push back and Keith does not recognize why the other child pushed him back. Ms. Miller noted that Keith really wants to connect with other children, but tends to do so in an assertive and aggressive way. Ms. Miller indicated that Keith is a fairly assertive child and getting him to recognize reciprocal (give and take) interaction has been a struggle for him. He is able to emulate other children's behaviors to look fairly typical for his age. This is strength. Ms. Miller indicated that Keith's primary focus is on blending in with other children. She also noted that he is becoming extremely aware of the fact that he is different. As a result, when extra support is offered to him, he does not want it. Ms. Miller explained that this may be a signal to him that he is different. Ms. Miller explained that Keith's needs include comprehension of everyday routines (e.g., classroom; social) and academics across all areas. Ms. Miller indicated that Keith's pace of growth is very slow, and his receptive and expressive language skills are very low. Keith's strengths include his capacity to emulate other children his age, and his strong social motivation which inspires his ability to emulate and engage with other children socially.

Observations

Classroom Observation (May 4, 2016): Keith was observed for 15 min during Ms. Lincoln's class. The class was engaged in a reading workshop activity. Throughout the 15 min observation, Keith did not appear to read a comic book he had selected. Keith talked with another student in his group. He playfully tapped another student. On several occasions, Keith attempted to talk with students in his group, but what he attempted to communicate with them was unintelligible. Toward the end of the class, when Ms. Lincoln rang the chime to signal a need to be quiet, Keith told other children to be quiet thereby violating Ms. Lincoln's directive to be quiet. Impressions of the observation were that Keith was not involved in the reading activity.

Observation during Assessment: Keith eagerly engaged in the assessment process and seemed to enjoy the one-on-one attention he received. He struggled with all tasks but persisted despite his difficulty. The present test results are a valid representation of Keith's abilities.

Conceptualization and Classification

Multiple data sources and methods of assessment inform the conceptualization of Kevin's cognitive, academic, social-emotional, and behavioral functioning include whether he qualifies for special education support. Details in support of these findings are offered below.

Cognitive and Academic Functioning: Keith's present performance on a measure of cognitive ability was in the delayed range (SB5 FSIQ = 48; 0.03 percentile; VIQ = 49, 0.03 percentile; NIQ = 62, 1st percentile). This is consistent with his prior performance (January, 2014) in the delayed range on a measure of cognitive ability (SB5 FSIQ = 50; 0.04 percentile; Verbal IQ = 44; <0.01 percentile; Nonverbal IQ = 74; 4th percentile). Keith's performance on the WJ-IV Achievement was also in the delayed range across all academic areas. When previously assessed in 2014, Keith experienced cognitive delays and functional communication deficits, but his academic skills were in the below/low average range. He also just entered kindergarten and other indicators at that time (e.g., standardized achievement test scores; parental input; socialization skills) suggested that the classification of intellectual disability should be deferred. Keith's present performance in the delayed range on measures of cognitive ability and two adaptive behavior areas (e.g., functional academics and communication) suggest that Keith will qualify, with a reasonable degree of clinical certainty, for a classification of intellectual disability (formerly mental retardation). This classification reflects a revision to the diagnosis from January 2009 where a classification of mental retardation was deferred in favor of a classification of learning disabilities and speech language delay. Keith's present performance in the moderately delayed range on a measure of cognitive ability and academic achievement suggests a need for intensive supports in a more restrictive environment.

Social, Emotional, and Adaptive Functioning: Keith faces considerable difficulty in his communication with other children and adults in the classroom. He also tends to misperceive social stimuli. This results in social skills difficulties. Still, Keith displays areas of strength in his social-emotional and behavioral functioning. He has a capacity to emulate other children's behavior, which helps him to blend in with them. However, when Keith attempts to engage in reciprocal interaction, other children struggle to understand what he is saying. Although Keith can be charming and will often smile at or tease other children in an endearing way, he can be overly assertive, if not aggressive, in his interaction with them. For instance, in his attempt to be first in line, Keith will push others out of his way. This tends to alienate Keith from other children. Keith also struggles with reading and interpreting social cues. And, although he may successfully enter into a conversation or social interaction with other children in the classroom, he struggles to maintain that interaction. Keith will require more intensive social and communication intervention.

Strengths: Background information and interview results indicate that Keith is a friendly child who is good at emulating the behavior of other children which helps him meld in with them. He also has developed strategies that help him hide his academic difficulties. This includes acting like other children when they are engaged in classwork such as pretending to read a book or work on written work. He also understands how to enter into a group of children to engage with them socially. These are all very adaptive social skills.

Summary: Keith experiences delays in cognitive ability, functional academics, and functional communication. These delays are sufficiently severe that Keith will qualify for a classification of intellectual disability.

Summary and Recommendations
Keith faces significant delays in two functional areas: communication and academics. Because of these significant delays, in combination with Keith's delayed performance on a measure of cognitive ability, Keith will require a restrictive environment that can focus on functional academic, communication, socialization, and daily living skills. Keith demonstrates a relative strength in his ability to emulate, and blend in with, other children. However, Keith still faces struggles in the social arena and will require guidance and support for reciprocal interaction and other basic socialization skills. Part of this struggle is related to his inability to communicate at an age-expected level. The other part of this difficulty appears related to Keith's moderate intellectual disability where he struggles with reading and interpreting social cues and situations. Keith displays a strength in his ability to emulate other children's behavior which helps him blend in with them. He experiences delayed communication abilities.

Considering multiple data sources and methods of assessment, Keith will benefit from a more intensive program in a different setting that focuses on functional academic, communication, daily living skills, and social skills. Keith will also benefit from exposure to age-typical peers. The IEP team will convene to discuss additional, specific goals and objectives that will benefit Keith. Meanwhile, the following are a few generalized recommendations for Keith.

1. *Functional Curriculum*: Keith will benefit from greater exposure to a functional academic curriculum that will assist him learn basic reading, writing and mathematics concepts.

2. *Social Skills Support*: Keith will benefit from guidance and support regarding entering into and sustaining social interaction. He will also benefit from appropriate social problem solving skills where he can learn to better read and interpret social cues. Modeling, coaching, and behavioral rehearsal will benefit Keith in the acquisition of appropriate social skills. Peer mediated interventions along with cuing and prompting of acquired social skills will enhance skill performance. Training and practice in diverse settings at school and home will help to generalize and maintain skill acquisition.

3. *Communication*: Keith struggles with oral expression and communicating at an age-expected level. He will benefit from continued support from the speech language pathologist for his communication deficits.

Stefan C. Dombrowski, Ph.D.
Licensed Psychologist (PA and NJ)
Certified School Psychologist (PA and NJ)

References

American Psychiatric Association. (2013). *Diagnostic and statistical manual of mental disorders* (5th ed.). Arlington, VA: Author.
Bergeron, R., Floyd, R. G., & Shands, E. I. (2008). State eligibility guidelines for mental retardation: An update and consideration of part scores and unreliability of IQs. *Education and Training in Developmental Disabilities, 41*, 123–131.
Braden, J. P., & Elliot, S. N. (2003). *Accommodations on the Stanford-Binet Intelligence Scales, Fifth Edition* (Stanford-Binet Intelligence Scales, 5th ed., Assessment Services Bulletin No. 2). Itasca, IL: Riverside.
Kranzler, J. H., & Floyd, R. G. (2013). *Assessing intelligence in children and adolescents: A practical guide*. New York, NY: Guilford.
Martin, R. P., & Dombrowski, S. C. (2008). *Prenatal exposures: Psychological and educational consequences for children*. New York, NY: Springer Science.

Phillips, S. E. (1994). High stakes testing accommodations: Validity versus disabled rights. *Applied Measurement in Education, 7*, 93–120.

Schalock, R. L., Borthwick-Duffy, S. A., Bradley, V. J., Buntinx, W. H. E., Coulter, D. L., Craig, E. M., et al. (2010). *Intellectual disability: Definition, classification, and systems of supports* (11th ed.). Washington, DC: American Association on Intellectual and Developmental Disabilities.

Chapter 15
Other Health Impaired

15.1 Overview

The category of Other Health Impaired (OHI) is unique to IDEA. It is neither in the DSM nor in any other classification taxonomy. OHI encompasses both medical and mental health conditions that are not included under the other IDEA categories. A multidisciplinary team must consider the definition of OHI, in combination with state policies, when making an eligibility decision. OHI is the third most prevalent special education classification comprising approximately 10.6 % of all special education classifications (Scull & Winkler, 2011). This feature makes it an important category for the psychologist in the school to understand.

15.2 Definition

The federal definition of OHI within IDEA is as follows:

Other health impairment means having limited strength, vitality, or alertness, including a heightened alertness to environmental stimuli, that results in limited alertness with respect to the educational environment, that—

(i) Is due to chronic or acute health problems such as asthma, attention deficit disorder or attention deficit hyperactivity disorder, diabetes, epilepsy, a heart condition, hemophilia, lead poisoning, leukemia, nephritis, rheumatic fever, sickle cell anemia, and Tourette syndrome; and
(ii) Adversely affects a child's educational performance. [§300.8(c)(9)]

© Springer Science+Business Media New York 2015   277
S.C. Dombrowski, *Psychoeducational Assessment and Report Writing*,
DOI 10.1007/978-1-4939-1911-6_15

There are numerous disabilities and disorders that may fall under the umbrella of OHI. The federal guidelines expressly list the following but this should not be considered exhaustive:

- ADD and ADHD
- Diabetes
- Epilepsy
- Heart conditions
- Hemophilia
- Lead poisoning
- Leukemia
- Nephritis
- Rheumatic fever
- Sickle cell anemia
- Tourette syndrome

15.3   Identification

The above disabilities are markedly different from one another, making it difficult to furnish a sense of the category other than to state that it is broadly encompassing. The decision to classify a child under OHI should be predicated upon the following two factors experienced by the child:

1. Whether the child experiences limited strength, vitality, or alertness due to chronic health problems.

2. Whether the child's educational performance is negatively affected as a result.

Moreover, there may be additional disabilities and conditions that are not listed within federal guidelines but that may meet criteria for special education classification under this category. The US Department of Education, for instance, mentions the following:

- Fetal alcohol syndrome (FAS)
- Bipolar disorders
- Dysphagia (i.e., difficulty swallowing)
- Other organic neurological disorders

It is important to keep in mind that the existence of one of the above presented conditions does not automatically qualify a child for special education support under OHI. When making a classification decision, an eligibility team must look at other factors (adverse educational impact, state policies, evaluation results) and not just the presence or absence of the condition even if the classification is offered by an outside physician or agency.

15.4   General Guidance Regarding Psychoeducational Assessment of OHI

The assessment of children for classification under OHI is unique to US public school systems. Because it is one of the most prevalent classification categories it should receive increased attention in the literature. Unfortunately, limited guidance is available regarding assessment other than a few legal-based research articles that discuss definitional and legal aspects. When considering eligibility for OHI the psychologist must gather relevant documentation, some of which may require outside professional and medical opinions. One of the more common conditions for which children receive an OHI classification is ADHD.

15.4.1   Attention-Deficit/Hyperactivity Disorder (ADHD)

Children with a definitive DSM classification of ADHD from an outside practitioner or who have attentional issues or impulse control issues within the school, even when lacking an outside diagnosis, may be found eligible for support under OHI if the child suffers from an adverse educational impact. ADHD is a common condition for which students qualify for special education services under OHI. Grice (2002) presents a series of case studies from across the country that established precedent for special education support under this category. In Pennsylvania, for example, a student was found eligible under OHI because his symptoms of ADHD adversely impacted his educational performance. Grice (2002) noted that a similar finding was established in New Hampshire when a hearing officer concluded that a student was unable to control his motor activity, remain seated, persist on tasks, and control generalized disruptive behavior.

The Office of Special Education Programs in the US Department of Education (OSEP) has issued several opinion letters discussing how a child might receive special education support for ADHD under OHI. First, OSEP has asserted that a medical or psychological professional's outside, clinical classification of ADHD does not automatically qualify the child for a classification of OHI. Grice (2002) explained that a school district may choose to require an outside medical or clinical diagnosis, yet the multidisciplinary team must independently determine whether the condition is impairing educational performance. If the school district requires an outside professional's evaluation to be found eligible, then the school district is responsible for paying for that professional to evaluate the child. Ultimately, whether a student qualifies for special education under OHI hinges on the impairment criterion (i.e., adverse educational impact). As an example, consider a student diagnosed with ADHD by his pediatrician or a private practice licensed psychologist. This student has average grades and scores in the average to above average range on all standardized tests but has experienced social problems. The child's social difficulties support the DSM-5 classification of ADHD, but the lack of educational impairment suggests that the child is not eligible for a special education classification of OHI. (This child may qualify, however, for a Section 504 plan, which is discussed in Chap. 16, if the child's social skills deficits impinge upon access to extracurricular activities). Grice (2002) notes that eligibility for special education under OHI is predicated upon an adverse impact upon grades and achievement test scores over time.

Although a child with an outside diagnosis of ADHD may not automatically qualify, a child without an outside diagnosis may qualify for OHI should the child manifest symptoms of inattention, hyperactivity, and impulsivity that adversely impact the child's academic progress (i.e., grades and achievement over time). Because ADHD is one of the most frequent classifications for which students are found eligible under OHI and because IDEA is silent on a framework for classification, the ADHD diagnostic criteria from the DSM-5 may be referenced as a guide for considering whether the symptoms impinge upon academic progress.

Attention-Deficit/Hyperactivity Disorder
(A) A persistent pattern of inattention and/or hyperactivity–impulsivity that interferes with functioning or development, as characterized by (1) and/or (2):

1. *Inattention*: Six (or more) of the following symptoms have persisted for at least 6 months to a degree that is inconsistent with developmental level and that negatively impacts directly on social and academic/occupational activities:
   Note: The symptoms are not solely a manifestation of oppositional behavior, defiance, hostility, or failure to understand tasks or instructions. For older adolescents and adults (age 17 and older), at least five symptoms are required

   (a) Often fails to give close attention to details or makes careless mistakes in schoolwork, at work, or during other activities (e.g., overlooks or misses details, work is inaccurate).
   (b) Often has difficulty sustaining attention in tasks or play activities (e.g., has difficulty remaining focused during lectures, conversations, or lengthy reading).
   (c) Often does not seem to listen when spoken to directly (e.g., mind seems elsewhere, even in the absence of obvious distraction).
   (d) Often does not follow through on instructions and fails to finish schoolwork, chores, or duties in the workplace (e.g., starts tasks but quickly loses focus and is easily sidetracked).
   (e) Often has difficulty organizing tasks and activities (e.g., difficulty managing sequential tasks; difficulty keeping materials and belongings in order; messy, disorganized work; has poor time management; fails to meet deadlines).

(continued)

(continued)

    (f) Often avoids, dislikes, or is reluctant to engage in tasks that require sustained mental effort (e.g., schoolwork or homework; for older adolescents and adults, preparing reports, completing forms, reviewing lengthy papers).

    (g) Often loses things necessary for tasks or activities (e.g., school materials, pencils, books, tools, wallets, keys, paperwork, eyeglasses, mobile telephones).

    (h) Is often easily distracted by extraneous stimuli (for older adolescents and adults, may include unrelated thoughts).

    (i) Is often forgetful in daily activities (e.g., doing chores, running errands; for older adolescents and adults, returning calls, paying bills, keeping appointments).

2. *Hyperactivity and impulsivity*: six or more of the following symptoms have persisted for at least 6 months to a degree that is inconsistent with developmental level and that negatively impacts directly on social and academic/occupational activities:

    Note: The symptoms are not solely a manifestation of oppositional behavior, defiance, hostility, or a failure to understand tasks or instructions. For older adolescents and adults (age 17 and older), at least five symptoms are required.

    (a) Often fidgets with or taps hands or feet or squirms in seat.

    (b) Often leaves seat in situations when remaining seated is expected (e.g., leaves his or her place in the classroom, in the office or other workplace, or in other situations that require remaining in place).

    (c) Often runs about or climbs in situations where it is inappropriate. (*Note*: In adolescents or adults, may be limited to feeling restless).

    (d) Often unable to play or engage in leisure activities quietly.

    (e) Is often "on the go," acting as if "driven by a motor" (e.g., is unable to be or uncomfortable being still for extended time, as in restaurants, meetings; may be experience by others as being restless or difficult to keep up with).

    (f) Often talks excessively.

    (g) Often blurts out an answer before a question has been completed (e.g., completes people's sentences; cannot wait turn in conversation).

    (h) Often has difficulty waiting his or her turn (e.g., while waiting in line).

    (i) Often interrupts or intrudes on others (e.g., butts into conversations, games, or activities; may start using other people's things without asking or receiving permission; for adolescents and adults, may intrude into or take over what others are doing).

(B) Several inattentive or hyperactive-impulsive symptoms were present prior to age 12 years.

(continued)

(continued)

(C) Several inattentive or hyperactive-impulsive symptoms are present in two or more settings (e.g., at home, school, or work; with friends or relatives; in other activities).

(D) There is clear evidence that the symptoms interfere with, or reduce the quality of, social, academic, or occupational functioning

(E) The symptoms do not occur exclusively during the course of schizophrenia or another psychotic disorder and are not better explained by other another mental disorder (e.g., mood disorder, anxiety disorder, dissociative disorder, personality disorder, substance intoxication or withdrawal).

Source: Diagnostic and Statistical Manual of Mental Disorders, Fifth Edition (Copyright 2013). American Psychiatric Association. Pages 59–60.

15.4.2   Other Health Conditions

The admonition regarding outside diagnosis in ADHD also applies to other conditions that might make the child eligible for special education support under OHI. In other words an outside medical or clinical diagnosis is by itself insufficient to qualify a child for an OHI classification. As an example, a child with an outside classification of asthma may be found eligible if his condition limits alertness, vitality, and strength and adversely impacts educational performance. But if the condition does not adversely impact educational performance then the child will not be found eligible for special education support. On the other hand, if a child suffers from diabetes, and the child misses school frequently because of the requirements for medical care or generalized fatigue (i.e., lack of vitality and alertness), then the child could be found eligible. It turns out that any chronic or acute health condition, whether or not noted above, can meet the OHI eligibility criteria if the condition results in limited alertness to the educational environment that adversely impacts educational performance.

When a child is found eligible for special education he or she may be eligible for related services in school. Related services are provided to ensure that the child with a disability under OHI is able to benefit from special education. Two commonly offered related services include medical services and school health/school nurse services (Grice, 2002). Medical services are provided when a child is suspected of having a medically related disability that may result in a child's need for special education. Health services may be found necessary to enable a child with a disability to receive a free and appropriate education as discussed in his individualized education plan. These services are often provided by a school nurse but may be provided by any qualified individual [34 CFR §300.34(c)(13)].

Each state and for that matter each local school district may have specific guidelines related to health impairments and corresponding services. Determined by the IEP team and informed by appropriate medical and other evaluations, health related services to which a child might be found eligible include but are not limited to the following:

- Special feedings
- Administering and/or dispensing medications
- Providing training for all (i.e., teachers, teacher's aides) who serve as caregivers in the school for the child
- Management of a tracheostomy
- Injury prevention in the case of seizure or narcolepsy

15.5   Conclusion

Determining the scope of services under OHI will have to be informed by appropriate medical and related personnel evaluations, but it is still the responsibility of the child's IEP team to decide upon needed related services. The school must then provide these services as part of the child's education program if it is determined that the condition limits the child's access to FAPE and adversely impacts the child's educational progress.

Appendix: Sample Report 1—Qualify Without Outside Diagnosis of ADHD

Psychological Report
Confidential

Name: Tina White   Date of Report: October 18, 2016
Date of Birth: 8/3/2009   Chronological Age: 7 years 2 months
Grade: 2   School: Smith Public School
Name of Examiner: Stefan C. Dombrowski, Ph.D.

Parent Name and Address: Daisy Golden White and Tommie White
                                            Philadelphia, PA

Phone: 567-585-1234

Reason for Referral
Tina struggles with social and behavioral issues at school. was referred for a comprehensive evaluation to determine her present level of functioning and whether she might qualify for specially designed instruction.

Assessment Methods

Reynolds Intellectual Assessment Scale (RIAS)
Woodcock–Johnson Tests of Achievement, Fourth Edition (WJ-IV)
Bender Visual Motor Gestalt, Second Edition (Bender-2)
Behavior Assessment System for Children, Second Edition (BASC-2)

– Ms. Carol Jones (First Grade Teacher)
– *ADHD Rating Scale IV*
– Ms. Carol Jones (First Grade Teacher)
Teacher Interview
– Ms. Carol Jones (First Grade Teacher)
Parent Interview
– Ms. Daisy White (Mother)
Student Interview
– Tina White
Classroom Observations (5/16/16; 5/24/16)
Review of Academic Grade Reports
Review of School Records

Background Information

Tina White is a 7-year-old child in the first grade at the Smith Public School (SPS). Tina received early intervention services but was exited from them during her last year in preschool. Ms. White expressed concern that Tina might still be suffering from the adverse effects of extreme prematurity. Background reports indicate that Tina struggles with attention, distractibility, impulsivity, and loss of focus. She also struggles with conflict resolution and sometimes disregards teacher and classroom rules. Tina's academic performance is considered low in reading comprehension and written expression. Her progress in other core academic areas is reported to be grade appropriate. Teacher reports also indicate concern about Tina's behavioral and social progress.

Prenatal, Perinatal, and Early Developmental History: Tina was born with very low birth weight (1 lb., 6 oz) due to extreme prematurity (26 weeks gestation). She had a 3-month stay in the neonatal intensive care unit. Tina's language was delayed compared to that of her siblings. Ms. Jones noted that Tina faced delays in learning to walk and did not walk until 14 months. All other developmental milestones were attained within normal limits.

Medical: Tina suffered from many ear infections as a child and required ear tubes. Tina wears glasses. Her hearing is within normal limits. She is not currently taking any medications. She is presently under the care of an endocrinologist out of concern that she might be entering puberty early.

Cognitive, Academic, and Language Functioning: Tina struggles with academic subjects that require sustained attention. When given independent work, Tina will start the assignment without reading instructions. This leads to incorrect work and performance below what she is capable of completing when the assignments are structured. Tina is able to fluently decode words and understands basic mathematics facts. However, she struggles with more complex academic activities such as written expression and reading comprehension. When Tina focuses, she is better able to accurately complete classwork. Ms. Jones reports that Tina struggles with homework and is easily frustrated by homework.

Social-Emotional and Behavioral Functioning: Ms. Jones indicates that she is concerned with Tina's social and behavioral functioning. Tina frequently misperceives other children's social cues. She was reported to have pushed a classmate who accidentally bumped into her desk. Tina insisted that the classmate did it on purpose. Tina can be impulsive and likes to be the center of attention in class. Ms. White reports that this is also an issue at home. She is constantly getting into arguments with her siblings over their shared attention with Ms. White.

Strengths: Tina's strengths include potential leadership ability and an interest in doing well. When given the leadership role, Tina rises to the occasion and performs her duties appropriately.

Summary: Tina struggles with academic subjects that require sustained attention. This includes reading comprehension and written expression. Tina also experiences conflict with peers when she misinterprets social cues.

Cognitive and Academic Functioning

Reynolds Intellectual Assessment Scale (RIAS)
Tina was administered the Reynolds Intellectual Assessment Scales (RIAS). The RIAS is an individually administered measure of intellectual functioning normed for individuals between the ages of 3 and 94 years. The RIAS contains several individual tests of intellectual problem solving and reasoning ability that are combined to form a Verbal Intelligence Index (VIX) and a Nonverbal Intelligence Index (NIX). The subtests that compose the VIX assess verbal reasoning ability along with the ability to access and apply prior learning in solving language-related tasks. Although labeled the Verbal Intelligence Index, the VIX is also a reasonable approximation of crystallized intelligence. The NIX comprises subtests that assess nonverbal reasoning and spatial ability. Although labeled the Nonverbal Intelligence Index, the NIX also provides a reasonable approximation of fluid intelligence and spatial ability. These two indexes of intellectual functioning are then combined to form an overall Composite Intelligence Index (CIX). By combining the VIX and the NIX into the CIX, a strong, reliable assessment of general intelligence (g) is obtained. The CIX measures the two most important aspects of general intelligence according to recent theories and research findings: reasoning or fluid abilities and verbal or crystallized abilities.

The RIAS also contains subtests designed to assess verbal memory and nonverbal memory. Depending upon the age of the individual being evaluated, the verbal memory subtest consists of a series of sentences, age-appropriate stories, or both, read aloud to the examinee. The examinee is then asked to recall these sentences or stories as precisely as possible. The nonverbal memory subtest consists of the presentation of pictures of various objects or abstract designs for a period of 5 s. The examinee is then shown a page containing six similar objects or figures and must discern which object or figure has previously been shown. The scores from the verbal memory and nonverbal memory subtests are combined to form a Composite Memory Index (CMX), which provides a strong, reliable assessment of working memory and may also provide indications as to whether or not a more detailed assessment of memory functions may be required. In addition, the high reliability of the verbal and nonverbal memory subtests allows them to be compared directly to each other.

Each of these indexes is expressed as an age-corrected standard score that is scaled to a mean of 100 and a standard deviation of 15. These scores are normally distributed and can be converted to a variety of other metrics if desired.

Following are the results of Tina's performance on the RIAS.

	Composite IQ	Verbal IQ	Nonverbal IQ	Memory index
RIAS index	104	109	98	93
Percentile	61	73	45	32
Confidence interval (95 %)	98–109	102–115	92–103	87–100

On testing with the RIAS, Tina attained a Composite Intelligence Index of 104. On the RIAS, this level of performance falls within the range of scores designated as average and exceeded the performance of 61 % of individuals at Tina's age. Her Verbal IQ (Standard Score = 109; 73rd percentile) was in the average range and exceeded 73 of individuals Tina's age. Tina's Nonverbal IQ (Standard Score = 98; 45th percentile) was in the average range, exceeding 45 % of individuals Tina's age. Tina earned a Composite Memory Index (CMX) of 93, which falls within the average range of working memory skills and exceeds the performance of 32 out of 100 individuals Tina's age.

Woodcock–Johnson Tests of Achievement-IV (WJ-IV)

The WJ-IV is an achievement test used to measure basic reading, writing, and mathematics skills. The Reading composite includes letter and word identification, vocabulary, and comprehension skills. The Writing composite includes spelling, writing fluency, and simple sentence writing. The Mathematics composite includes calculation, practical problems, and knowledge of mathematical concepts and vocabulary.

Tina obtained the following scores in each of the areas of measurement:

	Standard score	Percentile	Descriptive classification
Broad reading	81	11	Low average
Letter-word ID	92	38	Average
Sentence reading fluency	92	38	Average
Passage comprehension	78	7	Below Average
Broad writing	86	20	Low average
Writing samples	77	6	Below average
Sentence writing fluency	81	9	Low average
Spelling	92	27	Average
Broad mathematics	96	48	Average
Math facts fluency	98	49	Average
Applied problems	94	45	Average
Calculation	92	29	Average

Standardized achievement test results revealed low average performance across broad reading and writing clusters. Tina scored in the average range on the broad mathematics clusters. Tina scored in the below average range on the passage comprehension and writing samples subtests.

Bender Visual-Motor Gestalt Test, Second Edition (Bender-II)

The Bender-II measures visual-motor integration skills, or the ability to see and copy figures accurately. A quantitative and qualitative analysis of Tina's drawings suggests that her visual-motor integration abilities (e.g., fine motor skills for paper and pencil tasks) are below average (Copy Standard Score=75; 7th percentile). However, Tina also quickly completed the drawings and was less concerned about her performance on this test.

Social-Emotional and Behavioral Functioning

Behavior Assessment System for Children, Second Edition (BASC-2)

The Behavior Assessment System for Children, Second Edition (BASC-2) is an integrated system designed to facilitate the differential diagnosis and classification of a variety of emotional and behavioral conditions in children. It possesses validity scales and several clinical scales, which reflect different dimensions of a child's personality. T-scores between 40 and 60 are considered average. Scores greater than 70 ($T>70$) are in the Clinically Significant range and suggest a high level of difficulty. Scores in the At-Risk range (T-Score 65–69) identify either a significant problem that may not be severe enough to require formal treatment or a potential of developing a problem that needs careful monitoring. On the Adaptive Scales, scores below 30 are considered clinically significant while scores between 31 and 35 are considered at-risk.

	Ms. Jones	
Clinical scales	T-score	Percentile
Hyperactivity	67*	93
Aggression	74**	98
Conduct problems	71**	97
Anxiety	50	50
Depression	62	88
Somatization	69*	94
Attention problems	62	88
Learning problems	42	23
Atypicality	66*	93
Withdrawal	66*	93
Adaptability	30*	3
Social skills	40	15
Leadership	43	23
Study skills	40	15
Functional communication	49	49
Externalizing problems	72**	98
Internalizing problems	63	89
Behavioral symptoms index	70**	98
Adaptive skills	39*	15
School problems	52	53

*At-risk
**Clinically significant

BASC-2 ratings suggest a clinically significant rating on the overall behavior symptoms index and on the externalizing problems composite. She was rated as at-risk on the adaptive skills composite. Tina was also rated as clinically significant on the aggression and conduct problems scales. She was in the at-risk range on the hyperactivity, somatization, withdrawal, atypicality, and adaptability scales.

ADHD Rating Scale IV
The ADHD Rating Scale IV is a rating scale consisting of ADHD symptoms based on the DSM V diagnostic criteria. In general, scores between the 85th and 93rd percentile are considered above average or "at-risk" for symptom cluster compared to the normative sample. Scores above the 93rd percentile are generally considered clinically significant. Tina received the following scores:

Scale	Teacher percentile	Parent percentile
Hyperactivity/impulsivity	95th (clinically significant)	95th (clinically significant)
Inattention	94th (Clinically significant)	95th (clinically significant)
Combined	97th (Clinically significant)	97th (clinically significant)

Interview Results

Parent Interview (May 16, 2016): Ms. Sharon White was interviewed regarding her impressions of Tina's progress at school. Ms. White explained that Tina is experiencing behavioral issues at school explaining that Tina is "very touchy and tactile" with other children. Ms. White continued, "over the past few weeks, things have gone downhill. I'm getting frequent phone calls." Ms. White indicated that Tina needs constant redirection. She noted that Tina is "very impulsive and does much before thinking." Ms. White explained that this is having an effect on her schoolwork because Tina is being sent out every day and is beginning to dislike school as a result. Ms. White explained that Tina also has a low frustration tolerance and is very easy to agitate. Ms. White noted that Tina was born at 26 weeks weighing 1 lb, 6 oz. Tina had a 3 month stay in the NICU at the Hospital of the University of Pennsylvania. She received early intervention and the gap narrowed. Ms. White explained that in kindergarten, there were no academic issues present, but Tina struggled with social issues and relating to other children. Ms. White stated that Tina's kindergarten report card indicated a wide range of grades. Ms. White stated that she wants to know whether Tina is struggling in any area before it becomes a bigger problem. Ms. White commented on one other medical issue that Tina is facing and noted that this issue is related to her prematurity. Ms. White explained that Tina is under the care of an endocrinologist because she may be entering puberty early. Ms. White noted that Tina's strengths include being a leader and taking pride in doing jobs assigned to her.

Student Interview (May 24, 2016): Tina was interviewed to ascertain impressions of her progress at SPS. Tina indicated that she does not like SPS, noting that "the people at the school are mean." Tina stated that she "hates Mr. Jeff. My grandma came down and cursed him out." Tina was unclear in her description of the incident. Tina was asked about her friendships at school. She stated that she "does not have friends; well, maybe one friend." Tina explained that she prefers to play by herself at home. Tina was next asked about her behavior at school. Tina indicated that she sometimes gets into trouble for no apparent reason. Tina stated that she should not get into trouble at school because she "has not harmed anyone." Tina explained that her strengths/interests include playing card games.

Teacher Interview (May 16, 2016): Ms. Carol Jones, Tina's first grade teacher, was interviewed regarding Tina's academic, behavioral, emotional, and social functioning. Ms. Jones noted that Tina is progressing toward the bottom quarter of the class. She notes that Tina is capable of completing work, but is rarely able to focus. As a result, Tina's academic performance suffers. She explained that Tina is reading at a guided reading of J. Ms. Jones stated that Tina faces difficulties with her behavioral and social progress. She indicated that Tina struggles with social interaction. Ms. Jones stated that Tina tends to misperceive other children's intent and interprets ambiguous and even benign intent as hostile. In turn, Tina tends to overreact, which creates an escalation of the incident. Ms. Jones also explained that Tina pushes in line and prefers to be the center of attention in the classroom. When she does not get it, she sometimes will start pouting. Ms. Jones indicated that Tina tends to be impulsive and will often begin an assignment or answer a question before the directions were offered. Ms. Jones explained that Tina believes she understands what she needs to do and will begin the assignment without fully listening to directions. Ms. Jones explained that Tina's needs include learning how to resolve conflicts and interact with other children in an appropriate way. Tina also needs to improve her listening skills and her tendency to act before thinking.

Observations

Classroom Observation (May 16 and 24, 2016): Tina was observed for 15 min in Ms. Jones's class on two occasions. During the first occasion, Tina was working on an in-class assignment at her desk. She was observed to be on task and following classroom rules. During the second observation, Tina was working in a small group facilitated by Ms. Jones. Ms. Jones was assisting another student on a worksheet. Tina interrupted Ms. Jones during her instruction with another student. Tina was told to wait a few minutes until she was finished with the other student. Tina waited and was furnished with guidance regarding one of the problems. Approximately 7 min into this observation, Tina was asked to report to the Discovery Room where she was tested for reading glasses. Impressions of the observation were that Tina was generally compliant with classroom rules, but was impulsive on one occasion when she sought Ms. Jones' help.

Observation During Assessment: Tina was attentive and compliant during the cognitive assessment. She appeared to enjoy the one on one attention with the examiner. During the achievement portion of the assessment, Tina became inattentive. Several times she asked the examiner if the assessment was almost done. The assessment results are considered a valid representation of Tina's abilities.

Conceptualization and Classification

Multiple data sources and methods of assessment inform the conceptualization of Tina's cognitive, academic, social-emotional, and behavioral functioning including whether she qualifies for special education support. Details in support of these findings are offered below.

Cognitive and Academic Functioning: Tina's present performance on measures of cognitive ability was in the average range (Composite IQ=104; 61st percentile; VIQ=109, 73rd percentile; NIQ=98, 45th percentile). Tina's performance on the WJ-IV Achievement was low average and writing. Tina was average in mathematics. Her attentional difficulties appear to impact her performance on tasks that require sustained attention. For example, Tina scored in the average range on measures of word decoding, spelling and reading fluency, but in the below average range on measures of reading comprehension (passage comprehension) and written expression (writing samples).

Social-Emotional and Behavioral Functioning: Tina struggles with impulsivity, inattentiveness, disorganization, and following directions. She also struggles in her interaction with other children in the classroom. Tina tends to misperceive the intent of others and considers even benign interaction as hostile. On occasion, Tina will disregard teacher and classroom rules, but this is related to not attending to the teacher's request. She will benefit from teacher guidance and support for her social and behavioral difficulties.

Summary: Tina struggles with reading comprehension and written expression as a result of her documented difficulties with inattentiveness, distractibility, and hyperactivity. Tina also experiences difficulty getting along with other children in the classroom.

Summary and Recommendations
Considering multiple data sources and methods of assessment, Tina will qualify for specially designed instruction under a classification of Other Health Impaired since her documented difficulties with Attention-Deficit/Hyperactivity Disorder are adversely impacting her progress in the classroom. The team concludes that specially designed instruction is called for in this case. The following recommendations might benefit her.

1. *Strategies for difficulties with Attention, Distractibility, Hyperactivity, and Loss of Focus*: Background reports indicate that Tina experiences difficulty with attention, impulsivity, distractibility, and loss of focus. As such, the following recommendations might be beneficial for her:

   (a) *Check In, Check Out, and Behavior Report Card*: Tina should have his behavioral expectations reviewed at the beginning of the school day. He should check in with an adult periodically throughout the day to determine whether his goals are being met. At the end of the day, Tina should check out with that same adult and receive a behavior report card that acknowledges his behavioral performance and is sent home to his caregivers.

   (b) *Provision of Directions by Teacher*: When Tina's teachers interact with him, he should be encouraged to repeat and explain instructions to ensure understanding. The provision of directions to Tina will be most effective when the teacher makes eye contact, avoids multiple commands, is clear and to the point, and permits repetition of directions when needed or asked for.

   (c) *Positive Reinforcement and Praise for Successful Task Completion*: Tina's teachers should provide positive reinforcement and immediate feedback for completion of desired behaviors or tasks. Initially, praise and reinforcement should be offered for successful effort on a task or behavior regardless of quality of performance.

   (d) *Time on Task*: Communicate to Tina how long he will need to engage in or pay attention on a particular task. Open ended expectations can be distressing to any child, let alone one with attentional difficulties.

(e) *Prepare Student Discreetly for Transitions*: Furnish Tina with verbal prompts and visual cues that a new activity or task is about to start. This should be accomplished discreetly so as to avoid student embarrassment.

(f) *Recess Time*: Tina should be permitted to participate in recess. Recess should not be a time to complete unfinished classwork or homework.

(g) *Extended Time, Teacher Check In's, Assignment Adjustment, and Frequent Breaks*: Tina should be permitted additional time to complete academic tasks and projects. Tina's teachers should also consider review of classwork as Tina progresses on an assignment or project to assist Tina in avoiding careless mistakes. He may benefit from chunking assignments or assignment reduction. More frequent breaks than what is typical may also reduce careless mistakes and help to maintain focus.

2. *Social Problem Solving Skills*: Tina would benefit from support and guidance regarding conflict resolution with peers. She has a tendency to misperceive the intentions of others which can escalate into a conflict. Social problems solving skills may be taught to her by her teachers as a conflict occurs or within an individual or group counseling session by the school counselor.

3. *Reading Comprehension*: Tina struggles with the comprehension of written text and will benefit from pre-reading and organizational strategies that attempt to improve skills in this area. Following are a few suggestions that will likely benefit Tina:

   (a) Before reading, preview the text by looking at the title and illustrations.
   (b) Encourage the creation of a possible story from the illustrations.
   (c) Make predictions about the story based on story features prior to reading the story.
   (d) During reading, generate questions about the story that are directly related to the text and that require thinking beyond the text.
   (e) After reading, spend time reflecting upon the material and relating it to experiences and events the child has encountered.
   (f) After reading, have Tina engage in the reading material using text summarizing.

4. *Difficulties with Writing*: Tina struggles with expressing her ideas in written form. The following recommendations may be appropriate for her:

   (a) Assist Tina in generating ideas about a topic and then show her how to put the ideas in an outline.
   (b) Demonstrate for Tina outlining principles. Have her practice what you just demonstrated so that she can distinguish between main ideas and supporting ideas.

(c) Assist Tina in creating a paragraph and then show her that that paragraphs require an introduction, a middle, and a conclusion. Require that Tina generate her own paragraph and offer corrective feedback.

(d) Require Tina to proofread her written work and provide corrective feedback when appropriate.

Stefan C. Dombrowski, Ph.D.
Licensed Psychologist (PA and NJ)
Certified School Psychologist (PA and NJ)

References

American Psychiatric Association. (2013). *Diagnostic and statistical manual of mental disorders* (5th ed.). Arlington, VA: Author.

Grice, K. (2002). Eligibility under IDEA for other health impaired children. *School Law Bulletin, 33*, 7–12.

Scull, J., & Winkler, A. M. (2011). *Shifting trends in special education*. Washington, DC: Thomas B. Fordham Institute.

Chapter 16
Miscellaneous IDEA Categories and Section 504

16.1 Overview

This chapter briefly covers several IDEA categories including Visual Impairment, Hearing Impairment, Orthopedic Impairment and Traumatic Brain Injury (TBI). Additionally, it will cover 504 eligibility, offering two sample reports of children deemed eligible under Section 504. The chapter begins with a discussion of Section 504.

16.2 Section 504

The Office for Civil Rights within the US Department of Education oversees and enforces Section 504 in programs and activities that receive Department of Education financial assistance including public school districts, institutions of higher education, and other state and local education agencies (34 C.F.R. Part 104). The Section 504 regulations require a school district to provide a free appropriate public education (FAPE) to each qualified student with a disability who is in the school district's jurisdiction, regardless of the nature or severity of the disability. Under Section 504, FAPE consists of the provision of regular or special education and related aids and services designed to meet the student's individual educational needs as adequately as the needs of nondisabled students are met. Section 504 is distinct from IDEA but has a degree of overlap if a child struggles with learning, cognitive abilities, and certain behavioral and emotional conditions. Slightly broader than IDEA, Section 504 requires that children with a disability be afforded access to extracurricular activities such as sports and band participation. Therefore, a child who struggles with a suspected disability and who may not receive accommodations under IDEA should be considered for Section 504 eligibility.

© Springer Science+Business Media New York 2015
S.C. Dombrowski, *Psychoeducational Assessment and Report Writing*,
DOI 10.1007/978-1-4939-1911-6_16

16.2.1   Definition

Section 504 states that

> No otherwise qualified individual with a disability in the United States, as defined in
> section 705(20) of this title, shall, solely by reason of her or his disability, be excluded
> from the participation in, be denied the benefits of, or be subjected to discrimination
> under any program or activity receiving Federal financial assistance or under any program
> or activity conducted by any Executive agency or by the United States Postal Service
> (29 U.S.C. § 794).

It requires that a local educational agency, vocational agency, or other school
system receiving federal assistance adhere to the strictures of this law.

Section 504 of the Rehabilitation Act of 1973, as amended, 29 U.S.C. 794.

According to section 504 the definition of an impairment includes including
any physical or mental disability that substantially limits one or more of the
following major life activities:

Caring for one's self	Walking	Seeing	Speaking
Breathing	Sleeping Standing	Lifting	Reading
Concentrating	Thinking	Communicating	Working Helping
Eating	Bending Performing	Manual tasks	Learning

Operation of a bodily function (bladder, bowels, endocrine, circulatory, etc.)
Other

The following additional strictures are required:

1. Has a record of such an impairment.
2. Is regarded as having such an impairment.
   34 C.F.R. 104.3 and 42 U.S.C. 12102(4)(a)(2)(A).

A physical or mental impairment is defined as (A) any physiological disorder or
condition, cosmetic disfigurement, or anatomical loss affecting one or more of the
following body systems: neurological; musculoskeletal; special sense organs; respi-
ratory, including speech organs; cardiovascular; reproductive, digestive, genitouri-
nary; hemic and lymphatic; skin; and endocrine; or (B) any mental or psychological
disorder, such as mental retardation, organic brain syndrome, emotional or mental
illness, and specific learning disabilities (34 C.F.R. 104.3).

16.2.2   Identification and Psychoeducational Assessment

The identification for Section 504 services must be based upon an evaluation and conducted by a team of individuals knowledgeable about the student. Section 504 plans are generally the responsibility of general education while IDEA falls under the auspices of special education. The threshold for qualification is an impairment in a major life function. The child does not need to have a disability for eligibility for a 504 plan.

The determination of whether an impairment substantially limits a major life activity is to be made as if a child is not using what are called mitigating measures. Mitigating measures are defined as follows:

(A) Medication, medical supplies, equipment, or appliances, low-vision devices (which do not include ordinary eyeglasses or contact lenses), prosthetics including limbs and devices, hearing aids and cochlear implants or other implantable hearing devices, mobility devices, or oxygen therapy equipment and supplies;
(B) Use of assistive technology;
(C) Reasonable accommodations or auxiliary aids or services; or
(D) Learned behavioral or adaptive neurological modifications. 42 U.S.C. 12102(4)(a)(4)(E)(i).

Many students, but not all, who qualify for a classification under IDEA may also meet eligibility requirements under Section 504. In other situations, a student may not meet eligibility requirements under IDEA but may qualify for a Section 504 plan. The determination for eligibility is made on a case-by-case basis. If the impairment involves a major life activity such as learning, reading, concentrating, thinking, speaking or communicating, then the team should consider referring the student for a full evaluation to determine eligibility under IDEA. As with the IDEA evaluation process, a periodic reevaluation of the 504 plan is required. Some school districts may choose to review at 3 year intervals or more frequently as needed.

16.2.3   Conclusion

Section 504 was reinvigorated with the 2009 amendment and increasingly school districts will be required to consider the regulations in their provision of FAPE to students. A comprehensive guide that is available free of charge off the Internet may be downloaded from the following site:http://doe.sd.gov/oess/documents/sped_section504_Guidelines.pdf

This document offers additional information regarding Section 504 including detailed forms for school districts to remain compliant with Section 504 regulations.

16.3   Traumatic Brain Injury (TBI)

16.3.1   Overview

The term traumatic brain injury (TBI) encompasses injuries to the head that result in total or partial disability that adversely affects a child's educational performance. More than one million children sustain a TBI annually resulting in approximately 150,000 hospitalizations and 5,000 deaths (Langlois, Rutland-Brown, & Thomas, 2005). Glang, Tyler, Pearson, Todis, and Morvant (2004) estimate more than 130,000 children with TBI have functional limitations significant enough to receive special education services yet less than 20 % of those children receive such support under the TBI category. The lack of school psychologists' training in and understanding of TBI has been cited for the low rate of classification of TBI (Hooper, 2006). The incomplete understanding of TBI has an additional problem. It hampers recovery through inappropriate educational and interventional planning.

16.3.2   Definition

Traumatic brain injury means an acquired injury to the brain caused by an external physical force, resulting in total or partial functional disability or psychosocial impairment, or both, that adversely affects a child's educational performance. Traumatic brain injury applies to open or closed head injuries resulting in impairments in one or more areas, such as cognition; language; memory; attention; reasoning; abstract thinking; judgment; problem-solving; sensory, perceptual, and motor abilities; psychosocial behavior; physical functions; information processing; and speech. Traumatic brain injury does not apply to brain injuries that are congenital or degenerative, or to brain injuries induced by birth trauma. [34 Code of Federal Regulations §300.8(c)(12)].

16.3.3   Correlates of TBI

The sequelae of brain injury can vary depending upon location and severity of injury. Children who experience a brain injury may face physical, cognitive, behavioral, and social-emotional difficulties. The following chart is illustrative of possible sequelae, but it is not intended to be exhaustive.

Possible Sequelae of Traumatic Brain Injury

Physical symptoms	Cognitive	Social-emotional/behavior
Problems speaking	Short-term memory	Mood
Seeing and hearing	Long-term memory	Anxiety
Headaches and fatigue	Concentration and attention	Aggression
Muscle contraction/tightening	Slow processing	Depression
Writing and drawing	Ordering and sequencing	Restless
Balancing and walking	Judgment	Limited emotional control
Partial or full paralysis		

The complications from brain injury can range from mild to severe. There is often a gradient relationship between severity of brain injury and outcome, with moderate to severe brain injuries associated with more negative sequelae (Yeates & Taylor, 2006). Early intervention following a concussion or brain injury is critically important and can mitigate adverse outcomes. There are specific head injury protocols that need to be assiduously followed. These protocols often recommend rest for the child and avoidance of overstimulating activities (e.g., video games; no late nights) and athletic activities (e.g., soccer, bicycle riding) that can increase risk for additional head injury. It is the subsequent head injuries following a concussion that pose grave risk for permanent brain injury. The school psychologist is an important point of contact as she helps students transition and reintegrate back to school. The school psychologist can also monitor recovery and remain vigilant for possible future manifestation of problems as sequelae may develop over a period of days, months and years following injury (Gfroerer, Wade, & Wu, 2008; Yeates & Taylor, 2006). In fact, sequelae may remain dormant for an extended time period only to manifest at a later point. As the child develops, teachers and other school professionals may notice new problems as prior brain injury may interfere with acquisition of new skills. Parents and educators may misattribute this difficulty to a learning disability or another other IDEA classification category when it was related to the prior brain injury.

16.3.4 Guidance Regarding Psychoeducational Assessment

The assessment and evaluation of traumatic brain injury will require a multifaceted approach from a team of professionals, some of whom reside outside of the educational setting. This may include physicians, neurologists, rehabilitation counselors, occupational therapists, physical therapists, and neuropsychologists. The school psychologist will also be involved in reviewing the information furnished by the outside professionals, undertaking a traditional psychoeducational evaluation, and continuously monitoring the child's progress toward recovery including whether the child will manifest later sequelae. It is important to keep in mind that children who experience head injury may experience symptoms months to years later (Telzrow, 1991). School psychologists and other school professionals will have to remain vigilant for this occurrence. A neuropsychological evaluation, if it has not been conducted, may be an important adjunct to the psychoeducational evaluation. Neuropsychology had its origins in and evolved from the understanding of head injury so it is particularly well-suited for the evaluation of TBI.

16.3.5   Conclusion

School psychologists may be ill-prepared to evaluate, work with, and monitor students with TBI (Hooper, 2006). Additional education may be necessary. This is important because the cognitive, academic, behavioral, social-emotional, and adaptive difficulties following a head injury may not manifest until months or years later. A multidisciplinary team approach that includes outside medical specialists, occupational therapists, physical therapists, and neuropsychologists may be necessary.

16.4   Visual Impairment/Blindness

16.4.1   Overview

School psychologists will not be in the position to diagnose a visual impairment. This is beyond the scope of their expertise and within the realm of the ophthalmologist, a medical doctor who specializes in the diagnosis and treatment of disorders of the eye. However, the psychologist, as part of a multidisciplinary team, will be responsible for determining whether the visual issue is creating an adverse impact on educational functioning and which accommodations the child might need. The school psychologist may be in the position to assess the child's cognitive and academic abilities via norm referenced instruments. However, rigid adherence to standardized protocol may be inappropriate. Only the auditory aspects of a test of cognitive ability or achievement may be able to be administered to some youth with visual impairments.

16.4.2   Definition

Visual impairment including blindness means an impairment in vision that, even with correction, adversely affects a child's educational performance. The term includes both partial sight and blindness [§300.8(c)(13)].

The more commonly recognized visual impairments include near-sightedness and far-sightedness. However, there are additional visual impairments of which psychologists and other school professionals should be aware:

Strabismus—the eyes look in different directions and do not focus simultaneously on a single point.
Congenital cataracts—the lens of the eye becomes cloudy.
Retinopathy of prematurity—A condition of prematurity where the retina has not developed sufficiently to accommodate light.
Retinitis pigmentosa—A heritable disease that slowly destroys the retina.
Coloboma—A section of the structure of the eye is missing.
Optic nerve hypoplasia—An optic nerve condition that impacts depth perception, sensitivity to light, and visual acuity.
Cortical visual impairment (CVI)—Damage to the visual cortex that results in an impairment to vision. The eyes are intact.
Adapted from National Dissemination Center for Children with Disabilities (NICHCY) (2012). *Disability Fact Sheet#13. Visual impairments, including blindness.* NICHCY: Washington, DC.

Keep in mind that the term blindness does not necessarily mean that the individual cannot see anything at all. A child who is legally blind may have partial sight and be able to see light, colors and objects.

16.4.3   Identification and Psychoeducational Assessment Considerations

The identification of a visual impairment or blindness occurs outside the school setting by an ophthalmologist or optometrist. This information is then reviewed by a school multidisciplinary team to determine appropriate educational planning. Within the school setting, additional evaluation procedures are undertaken including those by the school psychologist. A teacher of students who are visually impaired and the orientation and mobility specialist will likely undertake a functional vision assessment (FVA) and a learning media assessment (LMA). The FVA evaluates the best way to present material to a child to accommodate their vision. The LMA discusses which learning and literacy media (e.g., reading and writing) is appropriate for supporting a child's learning. An expanded core curriculum assessment may also be undertaken. The expanded core curriculum assessment determines the child's needs to be successful in school and in postgraduate pursuits. There is often overlap among the types of assessment. Finally, the school psychologist may administer a revised battery of assessment instruments, depending upon the level of visual impairment, in an attempt to determine cognitive and academic functioning.

The following offers a general overview of the components of the FVA, LMA and expanded core curriculum needs assessment that is undertaken by various professionals in the school:

Functional vision assessment	Learning media assessment	Expanded core curr. assessment
– Review of eye-care professional reports	– Reading, writing, and listening skills	– Orientation and mobility
– Interviews with parents, teachers, and students	– Readability of materials	– Social interaction
– Student observations	– Functional vision	– Independent living
– Appearance of the eyes	– Reading level of students	– Recreation and leisure
– Visual reflexes	– Availability of materials	– Career education
– Visual response to light	– Environments	– Assistive technology
– Visual response to objects	– Print size assessment	– Sensory efficiency
– Muscle imbalance and eye preference	– Near and distance reading and writing	– Self-determination
– Functional peripheral and central fields		– Compensatory/functional academic skills including communication modes (top priority)
– Color and contrast discrimination		
– Light sensitivity and preference		
– Depth perception		
– Developmental and visual perception screening		
– Near acuity and discrimination		
– Identification of common objects		
– Behavioral abnormalities		
– Distance acuity and discrimination		
– Oculomotor behaviors (fixation, convergence, tracing, tracking, scanning, shifting gaze)		

Adapted and reprinted with permission from Steciw (2012)

Each of these evaluations requires specialized training and knowledge. Additional resources are available on these topics and provide more in-depth information than the generalized guidance provided above (See Bradley-Johnson & Morgan, 2008).

Most school psychologists may not be trained or experienced in evaluating children with visual impairments. This makes it extremely critical to collaborate throughout the process with specialists in visual assessment. School psychologists may need to learn how to present test items to blind or visually impaired children while respecting the child's personal space, communication methods, and any additional needs including environmental.

Degree of vision loss will impact the type of evaluation that may be conducted. For example, if there is complete vision loss, then the attempted administration of nonverbal (i.e., performance related subtests such as block design) will be inappropriate. The clinician should attempt to use tests or subtests that can be made accessible to the child. It will be necessary to use clinical judgment when deciding whether to continue to administer items with visual stimuli. If the items or the instrument is modified in any way, then the instrument should be interpreted qualitatively. Let's consider the use of an IQ test. The verbal portion may be administered to yield a verbal IQ. When visual-spatial portions of tests are administered in most cases the score should not be reported as this can inappropriately depress the full scale score and subsequently be misinterpreted and misused by other professionals. Instead, visual-spatial portions of a test should be used qualitatively in an effort to gather additional information about a child's capacity in this area.

16.4.4   Conclusion

Children with visual impairments need to learn the same subjects and academic skills that children in the general education curriculum learn. They must also learn additional skills that are distinct to visual impairments including how to safely and independently move around their environment, use whatever residual vision they have, read and write in Braille, and use assistive technologies. The overall evaluation of the child with visual impairment or blindness including that aspect conducted by the school psychologist should help to determine how to best furnish educational and adaptive accommodations.

16.5   Hearing Loss and Deafness

16.5.1   Overview

The school psychologist is unlikely to be involved in the actual determination of whether a child has a hearing impairment. This will be determined by an otolaryngologist and audiologist who have specialized training regarding disorders of the ear.

The school psychologist will be involved in the determination of whether the child's hearing impairment is having an impact on educational performance. As part of this process, the psychologist may administer a battery of tests to better understand the child's present level of functioning. This may include IQ tests, achievement tests and additional norm-referenced instruments as appropriate.

Depending upon the child's hearing capacity the psychologist will need to enlist the help of an expert in sign language. This individual should be instructed in the approach to standardized testing and told to avoid coaching and other inappropriate standardized test behavior. For instance, acknowledging correctness or wrongness of a response (unless otherwise specified in the standardized directions), coaching, and giving additional chances or guesses is clearly inappropriate. Individuals with deafness or a hearing impairment may struggle relative to age typical peers particularly with language based topics (Bradley-Johnson & Morgan, 2008). This is a result of their disability and should not be misconstrued as having lower cognitive capacity.

16.5.2   Definition

Hearing impairment means an impairment in hearing, whether permanent or fluctuating, that adversely affects a child's educational performance but that is not included under the definition of deafness in this section.

Deafness means a hearing impairment that is so severe that the child is impaired in processing linguistic information through hearing, with or without amplification that adversely affects a child's educational performance.

16.5.3   Degree of Hearing Loss

Hearing loss is classified by the amount of acuity loss measured in decibels (dB). The following chart depicts the level of hearing loss and a degree of insight into accommodations that will be necessary.

Mild (16–40 dB): Soft noises may not be heard. Speech may be difficult to hear in loud environment. Background noises may interfere with detection of speech unless hearing aids and an FM amplification system is used.

Moderate (41–70 dB): Amplification becomes critically important without which class discussion and conversation is missed. The tone, pitch, and quality of a child's speech may also be impacted. Speech therapy may be required.

Severe (71–90 dB): Full time amplification will be necessary. The child may not understand speech (if the speech loss was before language acquisition) or there may be significant difficulties with speech, writing, and language skills. An interpreter may be necessary as will a hearing aide.

Profound (90+dB): Amplification such as hearing aids may not work. Vision will be the primary modality for learning and communication. The child may need placement in a special program and exposure to deaf culture.

16.5.4   Identification and Psychoeducational Assessment Considerations

Students may enter the school system with an outside, documented hearing loss. If not, professionals within the school district sometimes refer a child for an audiological evaluation when hearing difficulties are suspected. For a child to obtain services and to assist with educational planning, a written report from an outside professional will be required. Individuals involved in the identification of hearing impairment include but are not limited to a physician, an audiologist, a speech language therapist, and American Sign Language/Deaf studies teacher, and a school psychologist.

School psychologists who may be involved in the evaluation of children who are deaf or hard of hearing must recognize limits of competence and seek consultation where appropriate. The evaluation of a child with a hearing impairment entails greater understanding of numerous factors including proper use of interpreters, proper selection of assessment instruments (e.g., the UNIT), and understanding of the deaf culture. Optimally, a school psychologist who understands sign language or who can communicate in the student's communication mode should be used to conduct the evaluation. When unavailable, the school psychologist should enlist the assistance of an interpreter. The interpreter should have experience with the psychoeducational assessment process. If not, the psychologist is responsible for training the interpreter in the nuances of standardized administration procedures and how to serve in an adjunctive capacity with respect to the evaluation process.

16.5.5   Conclusion

The evaluation of children who are deaf or hard of hearing requires a highly specialized skill set. Multiple professionals including a physician, an audiologist, a speech-language pathologist, a teacher versed in ASL and a school psychologist may be involved in determining eligibility for hearing impairment/deafness. Outside documentation from an audiological specialist (e.g., physician, audiologist) will be a necessary, but insufficient aspect of eligibility. Additional needed information may include norm-referenced and informal assessment to determine whether and where the hearing impairment is having an adverse educational impact. For this purpose, the school psychologist will play a role. An interpreter may be a necessary participant in the eligibility identification process unless the school psychologist is versed in communication modes (e.g., ASL) familiar to the child. Children who are found eligible under the category hearing impaired or deaf will require specially designed services and accommodations which may include an amplification system, services from an interpreter, captioning for oral media, introduction to the deaf culture, preferential seating to assist with lip reading, and a notetaker.

16.6 Orthopedic Impairment

16.6.1 Overview

Orthopedic impairments are experienced by 0.12 % (approximately 54,000) of all students attending kindergarten through 12th grade (Skull & Winkler, 2011). Orthopedic impairments have varied etiology. Causes of orthopedic impairment range from congenital (i.e., existing at birth) anomalies to accidents and injuries. Congenital causes include cerebral palsy, osteogenesis imperfecta, joint deformity, and muscular dystrophy. Other causes include premature birth, motor vehicle accidents and sports related injuries. The need for accommodation often varies based upon the severity of the orthopedic impairment. Some children wear braces, prosthetics and orthotic devices while others will require a walker or wheelchair for mobility. Children with severe disabilities sometimes have a concomitant orthopedic impairment requiring a multiple disabilities classification.

16.6.2 Definition

Orthopedic impairment means a severe orthopedic impairment that adversely affects a child's educational performance. The term includes impairments caused by a congenital anomaly, impairments caused by disease (e.g., poliomyelitis, bone tuberculosis), and impairments from other causes (e.g., cerebral palsy, amputations, and fractures or burns that cause contractures).

Specific examples of more prevalent orthopedic impairments are as follows:

Spina bifida—A birth defect resulting from an incomplete closure of the spinal column.

Scoliosis—Curvature of the spine with no known etiology that causes shoulders and hips appear uneven.

Cerebral Palsy—Injury to the brain that often occurs during the prenatal and perinatal period resulting in too tight or loose muscles. Mobility is either mildly impaired or severely impaired.

Muscular Dystrophy—A genetic disease that is progressive in nature resulting in muscle weakness and rapid deterioration.

16.6.3   Psychoeducational Assessment Considerations

Most children with orthopedic impairments enter school with documentation of a physical disability that makes them eligible for an orthopedic impairment classification. A smaller subset will be overlooked and will be suspected as having a disability within a school setting when school personnel notice signs of poor coordination, awkward gait, frequent accidents, or complaints of pain. When an orthopedic impairment is suspected by the school, then the child should be referred for a medical evaluation by a physician with specialized training in that area. The school will be responsible, in part, to assess how the orthopedic impairment affects the child's ability to learn in the school setting. Additional assessment considerations include transportation to and from school, mobility within the school including how to get to and from classes, how to fulfill required physical education curricula, and social, emotional, and behavior issues that might result from the orthopedic impairment. Professionals undertaking the assessment may include a speech-language pathologist, a physical therapist and an occupational therapist to evaluate and make recommendations regarding speech, fine motor and gross motor skills deficits including need for adaptive equipment. A psychologist will be responsible for evaluating the child's cognitive, academic, adaptive, social, emotional, behavioral, and physical needs.

16.6.4   Conclusion

The symptoms and characteristics of children with orthopedic impairments are varied. No two orthopedic impairments are alike making it difficult to extrapolate symptom characteristics from one to the next. One child may be paralyzed from the waist down while another child may be able to walk but with a gait. Other children may be unable to use writing tools or turn pages in a book. Still, other children may have concomitant speech impairments. A comprehensive evaluation from multiple professionals will determine what types of symptoms to expect and what accommodations will be necessary to support the child's functioning in the school.

Appendix: Section 504 Report Example

Psychological Report
Confidential

Name: Billy Smith   Date of Report: February 7, 2016
Date of Birth: 10/21/07   Chronological Age: 8 years 3 months
Grade: 2   School: Smith Public School
Name of Examiner: Stefan C. Dombrowski, Ph.D.

Parent Name and Address: Patty Smith
                             1234 Briar Cliff Lane
                             Philadelphia, PA, 19138

Phone: 609-585-1234

Reason for Referral:

Billy was referred for a comprehensive evaluation following concerns about his progress in the classroom. This evaluation was conducted to determine Billy's present level of functioning and recommendations that may be appropriate for him.

Assessment Methods and Sources of Data
Reynolds Intellectual Assessment Scales (RIAS)
Woodcock–Johnson Test of Achievement—Fourth Edition (WJ-IV)
Bender Visual Motor Gestalt, Second Edition (Bender-2)
Behavior Assessment System for Children, Second Edition (BASC-2)

– Ms. Cynthia Pleasant
ADHD Rating Scale IV
– Ms. Cynthia Pleasant (Second Grade Teacher)
– Ms. Patty Smith (Grandmother)
Teacher Interview
– Ms. Cynthia Pleasant (Second Grade Teacher)
Parent Interview
– Ms. Patty Smith (Grandmother)
Student Interview
– Billy Smith

Review of Lower School Discipline Report
Review of TSS Worker Intake Report
Classroom Observations (1/31/16)
Review of School Records

Background Information and Developmental History
Billy Smith is an 8-year-old second grade student at Smith Public School (SPS). He has experienced considerable behavioral difficulties including aggression (both verbal and physical) toward other students, oppositionality, rule noncompliance, and disregard of teacher requests. Billy will require continued structure and support for his behavioral and social difficulties. He will not qualify for a special education classification due to solid academic progress.

Prenatal, Perinatal, and Early Developmental History: Ms. Smith noted that Billy was born at full term. All Billy's developmental milestones were attained within normal limits and met all his early developmental milestones.

Medical: Billy has been diagnosed with Attention-Deficit/Hyperactivity Disorder, Combined Type (ADHD; 314.01) and Disruptive Behavior Disorder (312.91). Billy takes Concerta (27 mg) and Tenex for the management of his behavioral symptoms. He has been assigned a TSS worker and a behavior specialist coordinator. Billy has no other medical concerns at this time. His hearing and vision are intact. Billy has neither experienced a head injury nor a major infection.

Cognitive, Academic, and Language Functioning: Billy progress in the curriculum is at grade expected levels despite several suspensions and behavioral incidents that may begin to interfere with his progress.

Social-Emotional and Behavioral Functioning: Billy struggles with impulsivity, hyperactivity, and inattentiveness. Billy receives behavioral support from both a Behavior Specialist Coordinator and a TSS worker. Billy has a few friends at school, but tends to alienate himself from them because of his impulsive style and tendency to physically aggress. Billy also seeks to do what he wants, as he pleases, which gets him into trouble at school.

Strengths: Billy's strengths include solid cognitive ability and being a sweet, kind child.

Summary: Billy has deficits in the social-emotional and behavioral areas. He does not have any current academic concerns and is performing at a grade expected level in the curriculum.

Cognitive and Academic Functioning

Reynolds Intellectual Assessment Scale (RIAS)

Billy was administered the Reynolds Intellectual Assessment Scales (RIAS). The RIAS is an individually administered measure of intellectual functioning normed for individuals between the ages of 3 and 94 years. The RIAS contains several individual tests of intellectual problem solving and reasoning ability that are combined to form a Verbal Intelligence Index (VIX) and a Nonverbal Intelligence Index (NIX). The subtests that compose the VIX assess verbal reasoning ability along with the ability to access and apply prior learning in solving language-related tasks. Although labeled the Verbal Intelligence Index, the VIX is also a reasonable approximation of crystallized intelligence. The NIX comprises subtests that assess nonverbal reasoning and spatial ability. Although labeled the Nonverbal Intelligence Index, the NIX also provides a reasonable approximation of fluid intelligence and spatial ability. These two indexes of intellectual functioning are then combined to form an overall Composite Intelligence Index (CIX). By combining the VIX and the NIX into the CIX, a strong, reliable assessment of general intelligence *(g)* is obtained. The CIX measures the two most important aspects of general intelligence according to recent theories and research findings: reasoning or fluid abilities and verbal or crystallized abilities.

The RIAS also contains subtests designed to assess verbal memory and nonverbal memory. Depending upon the age of the individual being evaluated, the verbal memory subtest consists of a series of sentences, age-appropriate stories, or both, read aloud to the examinee. The examinee is then asked to recall these sentences or stories as precisely as possible. The nonverbal memory subtest consists of the presentation of pictures of various objects or abstract designs for a period of 5 s. The examinee is then shown a page containing six similar objects or figures and must discern which object or figure has previously been shown. The scores from the verbal memory and nonverbal memory subtests are combined to form a Composite Memory Index (CMX), which provides a strong, reliable assessment of working memory and may also provide indications as to whether or not a more detailed assessment of memory functions may be required. In addition, the high reliability of the verbal and nonverbal memory subtests allows them to be compared directly to each other.

Each of these indexes is expressed as an age-corrected standard score that is scaled to a mean of 100 and a standard deviation of 15. These scores are normally distributed and can be converted to a variety of other metrics if desired.

Following are the results of Billy's performance on the RIAS.

	Composite IQ	Verbal IQ	Nonverbal IQ	Memory index
RIAS index	96	98	96	92
Percentile	39th	45th	39th	30th
Confidence interval (95 %)	92–100	91–105	92–106	87–100

On testing with the RIAS, Billy attained a Composite Intelligence Index of 82. On the RIAS, this level of performance falls within the range of scores designated as below average and exceeds the performance of 12 % of individuals at Billy's age. Billy attained a Verbal Intelligence Index of 98 (45th percentile), which exceeds 45 % of individuals Billy's age. His Nonverbal IQ was 96 (39th percentile). Billy attained a Composite Memory Index (CMX) of 92, which falls within the average range of working memory skills and exceeds the performance of 30 out of 100 individuals Billy's age.

Woodcock–Johnson Tests of Achievement-IV (WJ-IV)

The WJ-IV is an achievement test used to measure basic reading, writing, oral language, and mathematics skills. The Reading subtest includes letter and word identification, vocabulary, and comprehension skills. The Writing subtest includes spelling, writing fluency, and simple sentence writing. The Mathematics subtest includes calculation, practical problems, and knowledge of mathematical concepts and vocabulary.

Billy obtained the following scores in each of the areas of measurement:

	Standard	Confidence	Descriptive	
	Score	Percentile	Interval (95 %)	Classification
Broad reading	91	27	86–94	Average
Letter-word ID	93	32	88–98	Average
Passage comprehension	90	25	82–98	Average
Sentence reading fluency	97	42	86–108	Average
Broad mathematics	87	21	80–93	Low average
Calculation	84	14	72–95	Low average
Math facts fluency	90	24	83–96	Average
Applied problems	92	29	84–99	Average
Broad written language	92	29	85–99	Average
Spelling	92	30	85–100	Average
Sentence writing fluency	99	48	86–112	Average
Writing samples	90	25	80–100	Average

Standardized achievement results revealed low average mathematics skills with average performance in reading, and writing.

Bender Visual-Motor Gestalt Test, Second Edition (Bender-II)

The Bender-II measures visual-motor integration skills, or the ability to see and copy figures accurately. A quantitative and qualitative analysis of Billy's drawings suggests that his visual-motor integration abilities (e.g., fine motor skills for paper and pencil tasks) are average (Copy Standard Score = 100; 50th percentile).

Social-Emotional and Behavioral Functioning

Behavior Assessment System for Children, Second Edition (BASC-2)
The Behavior Assessment System for Children, Second Edition (BASC-2) is an integrated system designed to facilitate the differential diagnosis and classification of a variety of emotional and behavioral conditions in children. It possesses validity scales and several clinical scales, which reflect different dimensions of a child's personality. Scores in the Clinically Significant range (*T*-Score >70) suggest a high level of difficulty. Scores in the At-Risk range (*T*-Score 65–69) identify either a significant problem that may not be severe enough to require formal treatment or a potential of developing a problem that needs careful monitoring. On the Adaptive Scales, scores below 30 are considered clinically significant while scores between 31 and 40 are considered at-risk.

Ms. Pleasant

Clinical scales	*T*-Score	Percentile
Hyperactivity	69*	94
Aggression	94**	99
Conduct problems	86**	98
Anxiety	42	22
Depression	50	50
Somatization	47	48
Attention problems	72**	86
Learning problems	44	32
Atypicality	46	35
Withdrawal	63	86
Adaptability	39*	10
Social skills	38*	10
Leadership	44	32
Study skills	38*	10
Functional communication	49	49
Externalizing problems	85**	98
Internalizing problems	45	35
Behavioral symptoms index	68*	93
Adaptive skills	40	20
School problems	53	62

*At-risk
**Clinically significant

BASC-2 ratings suggested clinically significant elevations across the externalizing composite with an at-risk rating on the behavioral symptoms index. BASC-2 ratings suggest a clinically significant elevation on the aggression, inattention and conduct problems scales with an at-risk rating on the hyperactivity scale, adaptability, and social skills scales.

ADHD Rating Scale IV

The ADHD Rating Scale IV is a rating scale consisting of ADHD symptoms based on the DSM V diagnostic criteria. In general, scores between the 85th and 93rd percentile are considered above average or "at-risk" for symptom cluster compared to the normative sample. Scores above the 93rd percentile are generally considered clinically significant. Billy received the following scores:

Scale	Teacher Percentile	Parent Percentile
Hyperactivity/impulsivity	95th (clinically significant)	95th (clinically significant)
Inattention	94th (clinically significant)	97th (clinically significant)
Combined	97th (clinically significant)	98th (clinically significant)

Interview Results

Parent Interview (February 7, 2016): Ms. Patty Smith, Billy's grandmother, was interviewed to ascertain her impressions of Billy's cognitive, academic, social, and behavioral progress. Ms. Smith explained, "I have a concern because Billy has ADHD." She noted that she has had Billy since 18 months. Ms. Smith noted that Billy's mother is also back in his life (since 2007). Commenting on Billy's behavior, Ms. Smith explained that Billy will do what he wants to do. She noted that he likes to be in control and needs structure, support, and clear expectations. Ms. Smith explained that if provided, Billy will comply "but if you turn your back he'll do what he wants." As an example, she indicated that Billy took a pack of gum from school without asking because other kids had gum on the bus and he wanted it. Ms. Smith explained that at home, Billy listens and reads. She expressed that he wants to be older than what he is and this can put him into bad situations. Ms. Smith noted that without structure, Billy struggles. She explained that Billy has a behavior specialist coordinator and a TSS worker. Commenting on Billy's social progress, Ms. Smith indicated that "he wants everybody to be his friend, but when they're not he can be a bully and become upset." She explained that Billy struggles with boundaries when making new friends. Ms. Smith noted, "he does not realize that he cannot jump in someone's face and then all of sudden become their friends." She also explained that we had to teach him how to work as a team, noting that Billy always wants to be first. Ms. Smith noted that "academically, Billy is okay. But I'm concerned about his behavior and how it takes away from his education. I want him to have the best and wonder if a more structured school would be better for him." Ms. Smith indicated that Billy's areas of strength include being sweet, kind, and bright. His areas of need include attention, social skills, following directions, and following classroom rules particularly during times transition times.

Student Interview (February 1, 2016): Billy was interviewed to ascertain impressions of his progress at SPS. Billy indicated that he likes SPS. He stated that he likes everything about SPS. Billy said that he does well in school in every subject. Billy then indicated that he does well with mathematics and reading but only "sometimes good with writing." Billy noted that he sometimes gets into trouble at school and described in precise detail what he needs to do. Billy noted that he needs to treat his friends more kindly and must learn how to deal with people that are mean to him. Billy stated that he generally only gets into trouble when he stands up for his friends when they are picked on. Billy explained that his interests include playing with video games and with his cousins. Billy also indicated that he enjoys basketball, baseball, and football.

Teacher Interview (January 6, 2016): Ms. Cynthia Pleasant, Billy's 3rd grade teacher was interviewed regarding Billy's academic, behavioral, social, and emotional functioning. Ms. Pleasant expressed that Billy's greatest issue is behavioral and that he is generally on-target academically. Ms. Pleasant noted that Billy has a tendency to physically aggress. She explained that he punches other children, kicks, slaps, and one time has been observed to choke another child. Ms. Pleasant noted that Billy engages in inappropriate behavior. For instance, he once yelled out that one student had sex with another student. Ms. Pleasant noted that Billy becomes interested in a girl at school and then tends to say inappropriate things to that girl. Ms. Pleasant indicated that his conflicts in the classroom are generally with other girls. Ms. Pleasant mentioned that Billy had a TSS worker (part-time) in kindergarten, but Billy did not have one in first grade because his behavior tended to appear only during transitions and not during class time last year. Ms. Pleasant explained that this year, Billy has been caught engaging in inappropriate behavior but he has been somewhat sneaky about it. Ms. Pleasant explained that Billy struggles with peer interaction as a result of his interpersonal style. She noted that some children in the class are turned off by him. Others just tolerate his behavior. Ms. Pleasant mentioned that Billy is generally involved in a conflict whenever there is free play or a group activity. Ms. Pleasant stated that Billy is at or slightly above grade level academically. She explained that his strengths include knowing what he is supposed to do and his display of good behavior earlier in the year. Ms. Pleasant noted that Billy's needs include greater interpersonal skills to manage conflicts. She also mentioned that Billy tends to test boundaries with adults and classroom rules. She explained that over the past 2 months, Billy's behavior has deteriorated.

Observations

Classroom Observation (January 31, 2016): Billy was observed in Ms. Cynthia Pleasant's class for 20 min. The initial part of the observation occurred during silent reading time. Billy had gone to the bathroom and returned approximately 5 min later. Billy required prompting on two occasions to return to class as soon as he finished using the bathroom. Upon returning to class, Billy approached his new TSS worker. The two greeted each other and then Billy was instructed to go over to his group to begin a group activity. Billy worked within a small group for the next 10 min. He required several redirections to remain on task. Impressions of the observation were that Billy required considerable structure and support to sustain his attention on the activity.

Observation during Assessment: Billy was active and impulsive throughout the testing session. He required considerable structure and support to sustain his attention on the testing session. At times, Billy would attempt to peer over the administration book to see what the examiner was doing. He also asked on numerous occasions when the testing session would be completed. With considerable prompting, structure and support, Billy was able to complete the testing. The results are considered to be a valid indication of his abilities.

Conceptualization and Classification

Multiple data sources and methods of assessment inform the conceptualization of Billy's cognitive, academic, social-emotional, and behavioral functioning include whether he qualifies for special education support. Details in support of these findings are offered below.

Cognitive and Academic Functioning: Billy's performance on measures of cognitive ability was in the average range (RIAS Composite IQ=96; 39th percentile) with an average verbal intelligence index (Std. Score=98; 45th percentile) and non-verbal intelligence index (Std. Score=96; 39th percentile). Billy's performance on the WJ-IV was in the average range in reading and writing with a low average range on the mathematics composite. Billy is presently performing at or slightly above second grade level standards in the classroom setting.

Social-Emotional Functioning: Billy is a child who experiences considerable behavioral difficulties at school. He has an outside diagnosis of Attention-Deficit/Hyperactivity Disorder, Combined Type (ADHD; 314.01) and Disruptive Behavior Disorder (312.91). Billy takes Concerta (27 mg) and Tenex for the management of his behavioral symptoms. He has been assigned a TSS worker and a behavior specialist coordinator. Billy has been suspended, written up or sent to CARES on numerous occasions for behaviors that include hitting, kicking, rough housing, fighting, slapping, bullying, and pinching other students. He has also received discipline reports for other behaviors including destroying property of others, inappropriate touching, disregard of school rules, lying, and using inappropriate behavior. Background reports reveal that Billy faces difficulties with attention, impulsivity, hyperactivity, rule compliance, aggression toward others, and social skills. The end result has been consistent need for structure and behavioral support. Despite Billy's behavioral and social difficulties, his academic attainment across both standardized achievement and classroom measures suggests grade appropriate progress. As a result, a special education classification is not appropriate at this time. Instead, Billy may benefit from a Section 504 plan for his behavioral and social difficulties.

Summary: Billy is performing at grade expected levels in the classroom. He faces behavioral and social difficulties at school for which he has received a TSS worker and a behavior specialist coordinator. Although Billy faces behavioral and social difficulties at school, these difficulties do not appear to be impairing his educational progress.

Conclusions and Recommendations

Billy Smith is a child who is experiencing considerable behavioral and social difficulties at school. His academic progress is at grade expected levels. Considering
Billy's performance on measures of achievement, cognitive ability and behavior,
combined with actual classroom performance, academic grade reports, parent interviews, behavior observations, and teacher interviews, Billy is not eligible for special
education support. However, he will benefit from a Section 504 plan. The following
might benefit Billy.

1. *Individual Counseling and Behavioral Support*: Billy will benefit from counseling
   and behavioral support for the following difficulties:

   (a) Boundary awareness.
   (b) Low frustration tolerance.
   (c) Oppositionality and rule noncompliance.
   (d) Social skills difficulties including aggression toward other students.
   (e) Being disrespectful to adults in the classroom.
   (f) Impulsivity, hyperactivity, and inattentiveness (see below).

2. *Strategies for difficulties with Attention, Distractibility, and Loss of Focus*:
   Background reports indicate that Billy experiences difficulty with attention,
   impulsivity and distractibility. As such, the following recommendations might be
   beneficial for him:

   (A) *Check In, Check Out, and Behavior Report Card:* Billy should have his
       behavioral expectations reviewed at the beginning of the school day. He
       should check in with an adult periodically throughout the day to determine
       whether his goals are being met. At the end of the day, Billy should check
       out with that same adult and receive a behavior report card that acknowledges
       his behavioral performance and is sent home to his caregivers.

   (B) *Provision of Directions by Teacher:* When Billy's teachers interact with him,
       he should be encouraged to repeat and explain instructions to ensure under-
       standing. The provision of directions to Billy will be most effective when the
       teacher makes eye contact, avoids multiple commands, is clear and to the
       point, and permits repetition of directions when needed or asked for.

   (C) *Positive Reinforcement and Praise for Successful Task Completion:* Billy's
       teachers should provide positive reinforcement and immediate feedback for
       completion of desired behaviors or tasks. Initially, praise and reinforcement
       should be offered for successful effort on a task or behavior regardless of
       quality of performance.

   (D) *Time on Task*: Communicate to Billy how long he will need to engage in or pay
       attention on a particular task. Open ended expectations can be distressing to
       any child, let alone one with attentional difficulties.

   (E) *Prepare Student Discreetly for Transitions*: Furnish Billy with verbal
       prompts and visual cues that a new activity or task is about to start. This
       should be accomplished discreetly so as to avoid student embarrassment.

(F) *Recess Time*: Billy should be permitted to participate in recess. Recess should not be a time to complete unfinished classwork or homework.

(G) *Extended Time, Teacher Check In's, Assignment Adjustment, and Frequent Breaks*: Billy should be permitted additional time to complete academic tasks and projects. Billy's teachers should also consider review of classwork as Billy progresses on an assignment or project to assist Billy in avoiding careless mistakes. He may benefit from chunking assignments or assignment reduction. More frequent breaks than what is typical may also reduce careless mistakes and help to maintain focus.

3. *Psychotropic Medication Compliance and Monitoring*: Billy will benefit from continued compliance with his physician-determined medication plan. Since he recently changed medication from Ritalin to Concerta, it might be beneficial for Ms. Smith to consult with Billy's physician regarding a monitoring plan to determine the effectiveness of his medication.

Stefan C. Dombrowski, Ph.D.
Licensed Psychologist
Certified School Psychologist

References

Bradley-Johnson, S., & Morgan, S. K. (2008). *Psychoeducational assessment of students who are visually impaired or blind: Infancy through high school* (3rd ed.). Houston, TX: Region IV Educational Service Center.

Glang, A., Tyler, J., Pearson, S., Todis, B., & Morvant, M. (2004). Improving educational services for students with TBI through statewide consulting teams. *Neurorehabilitation, 19*, 219–231.

Gfroerer, S. D., Wade, S. L., & Wu, M. (2008). Parent perceptions of school-based support for students with traumatic brain injuries. *Brain Injury, 22*, 649–656.

Hooper, S. R. (2006). Myths and misconceptions about traumatic brain injury: Endorsements by school psychologists. *Exceptionality, 14*, 171–182.

Langlois, J. A., Rutland-Brown, W., & Thomas, K. E. (2005). The incidence of traumatic brain injury among children in the United States: Differences by race. *Journal of Head Trauma Rehabilitation, 20*, 229–238.

National Dissemination Center for Children with Disabilities (NICHCY) (2012). *Disability Fact Sheet #13. Visual impairments, including blindness*. NICHCY: Washington, DC.

Skull, J., & Winkler, A. M. (2011). *Shifting trends in education*. New York: Thomas Fordham Institute.

Steciw, M. (2012, April 5). Essential assessment for students with visual impairment. Functional vision assessment. Webinar presented on April 5, 2012 at Pennsylvania Training and Technical Assistance Network (PaTTan).

Telzrow, C. F. (1991). The school psychologist's perspective on testing students with traumatic head injury. *Journal of Head Trauma Rehabilitation, 6*, 23.

Yeates, K. O., & Taylor, H. G. (2006). Behavior problems in school and their educational correlates among children with traumatic brain injury. *Exceptionality, 14*, 141–154.

Part IV
Oral Reporting and Miscellaneous Topics in Psychoeducational Assessment and Report Writing

Chapter 17
Culturally and Linguistically Diverse Learners

17.1 Overview

The degree of cultural and linguistic diversity in this country is large. Approximately 8 % of school aged children in the USA are limited in English proficiency (LEP) and would be considered English Language Learners (ELL). The heterogeneity among LEP is remarkable with over 400 different languages of which nearly three quarters speaks some dialect of Spanish (Rhodes, Ochoa, & Ortiz, 2005). The problem of accurately assessing culturally and linguistically diverse individuals has haunted the practice of psychological assessment within the USA for over a century and well before the infamous *Larry P v. Riles* case. The Larry P case led to the decade's long avoidance of IQ tests in the state of California with African-American students. However, the misattribution of individual traits has plagued the field since at least the turn of the twentieth century. Woodworth, a prominent personality scale author, categorized various groups of Europeans according to stereotyped characteristics. For instance, Woodworth (1916) noted that Europeans who were blonde generally fared better in most endeavors in life. He also how those of a Slavic origin were prone to patience and humbleness while those from western Europe were haughty and aggressive. Continuing through the first and second World Wars, the IQ testing movement described Mediterranean and eastern European cultures as having inferior intellectual capacity while Scandinavian and northern European countries were thought to have superior intellect (Kamphaus, 2005). Of course, IQ tests during those periods were sufficiently culturally bound and biased to lead to misrepresentation of vast cultural groups. This legacy persisted through the early 1970s when IQ tests were judged to be biased against minority groups such as African-Americans to the extent that such tests where no longer permitted for use with such groups in the state of California.

© Springer Science+Business Media New York 2015   321
S.C. Dombrowski, *Psychoeducational Assessment and Report Writing*,
DOI 10.1007/978-1-4939-1911-6_17

17.2 Psychoeducational Assessment Considerations

Contemporary psychometrics has resolved many of these concerns, but even contemporary instruments may continue to suffer from a degree of bias as the instruments arc constructed and therefore encapsulated within a distinct cultural context. Most assessment instruments used in the USA and Canada are constructed within a distinct cultural milieu and normed entirely in English. As a result, there may be linguistic and cultural confounds that render these instruments less valid and reliable for the purpose of assessment of individuals from diverse linguistic and cultural backgrounds. The problems with such instruments are not resolved with the use of interpreters, the translation of the instrument into the child's native language, or with the use of instruments that claim to be culturally free (e.g., UNIT). This represents an improvement upon the blanket use of an instrument without regard for linguistic or cultural heritage, but problems still persist.

Accordingly, Rhodes et al. (2005) contend that conclusions derived from many psychoeducational assessments are based on approaches that may be haphazard and biased because they do not account for cultural and linguistic factors within the assessment process. There are three factors that need to be considered because they have been found to bias the assessment process (Rhodes et al. 2005):

1. The cultural content that is embedded within a given instrument.
2. The linguistic demands imposed by the assessment instrument.
3. The lack of, or poor, representation within the normative sample of individuals from diverse backgrounds.

For instance, research shows that even nonverbal instruments such as the UNIT may not be language free (e.g., DeThorne & Watkins, 2006). This chapter does not capture all of the demands of assessment with linguistically and culturally diverse children. There are resources for more in-depth discussion (e.g., Clinton, 2014; Rhodes et al., 2005). This section's discussion is only intended to highlight the critical need for competency when evaluating a child with LEP or from a diverse cultural background and to offer generalized guidance for the psychoeducational assessment process.

17.2.1 General Concepts

The following generalized guidance is offered with the understanding that it is incumbent upon all school psychologists to undergo training in the assessment of students from diverse linguistic and cultural backgrounds.

Translations, Translators, and Interpreters. The availability of trained translators and interpreters is a problem faced by school districts throughout the USA. When hiring an interpreter (for orally provided information) or a translator (for written information) the individual should be fluent in English and the student's native language. The individual should also receive training in educational and psychological terminology. The nuances of the assessment process will need to be discussed with the translator/interpreter. For instance, the individual should avoid a dual relationship (i.e., being a relative of the child being evaluated) and should not become emotionally involved in the outcome. The requirement to assiduously adhere to standardized assessment (e.g., no coaching, no hints, follow standardized directions) should be conveyed to the interpreter. The translator and interpreter should also be able to maintain confidentiality. When the psychologist and other school personnel speak, these individuals should address the caregiver and not the interpreter. The use of translators and interpreters may seem like a panacea for assessment bias, but it still carries problems. Written or oral translations miss linguistic and cultural nuance and the resulting evaluation results may not accurately represent the child's abilities. Translations of English-normed instruments may yield a norm referenced score that may not be valid and reliable depending upon the degree of congruency between the student's native language and English. But the information furnished by the instrument may be of value so it is important to weigh the limitations with the information that may be ascertained from the instrument. Similarly, translators and interpreters must be trained in educational and psychological terminology as well as the nuances of standardized assessment. A translator and interpreter should be used with parents when discussing the psychoeducational assessment process, informed consent, limits to confidentiality, the completed report and the IEP.

Use of Nonverbal Assessment Instruments. Although nonverbal instruments such as the UNIT may be furnish a degree of language free assessment, they still are culturally bound and linguistically loaded (DeThorne & Watkins, 2006; Swisher, Plante, & Lowell, 1994). These limitations must be recognized when evaluating students. Still, they may well represent the best way to date to obtain a norm-referenced account of nonverbal intellectual capacity.

Assess the Role of Language. Extensive background information on the student's language history, primary language, and language preference must be explored. As the child enters school age and begins extensive exposure to English, the child may begin to lose primary language skills. Thus, assessment in the child's primary language, while well intended, may give an inaccurate portrait of the child's functioning.

Use a variety of functional assessment instruments in addition to norm referenced instruments. This may include performance-based measures, curriculum-based measures, portfolios, and observational data. As mentioned, norm-referenced instruments may lack sufficient reliability and validity so additional sources of data should be referenced when making a decision about a child's functioning.

Entertain the possibility that a child has a disability. The evaluation team may conclude that a child has a learning, behavioral, or intellectual ability but only after ruling out language and cultural factors. When arriving at a classification of a disability, the methods and procedures that are used should measure whether the child has a disability rather than the child's English language skill. IDEA includes this provision to protect children from culturally and linguistically diverse backgrounds from receiving an inaccurate classification. As an example, a child's cultural background may impact his or her behavior or response set in a way that is not readily understood by teachers or other school personnel. Or a child from a linguistically diverse background may not understand directions, words on a test, or idiomatic expressions and may incorrectly answer the question. Accordingly, the child may mistakenly appear to have a leaning or intellectual disability or to have a hearing or communication problem. After ruling out cultural and linguistic factors it will be important to entertain the possibility that a child from a linguistically or culturally diverse background has a disability.

17.2.2   Nondiscriminatory Assessment of Culturally and Linguistically Diverse Students

The two major classification systems (e.g., IDEA and DSM) used to classify children both require the assessment of linguistic and cultural factors before arriving at a classification decision. When considering a student for special education eligibility, IDEA established the following guidelines that apply to culturally and linguistically diverse students and those who are proficient English speakers from the dominant culture.

Evaluation Procedures

"... (c) Other evaluation procedures. Each public agency must ensure that—

(1) Assessments and other evaluation materials used to assess a child under this part—

    i. Are selected and administered so as not to be discriminatory on a racial or cultural basis;

    ii. Are provided and administered in the child's native language or other mode of communication and in the form most likely to yield accurate information on what the child knows and can do academically, developmentally, and functionally, unless it is clearly not feasible to so provide or administer..."

34 CFR § 300.304 Evaluation procedures, (c) (1) (i) (ii)

17.2.3   Additional Considerations

When contemplating a classification the psychologist will need to consider several factors. This includes ascertaining whether the problems exist in the student's first language, whether the problems persist across settings (e.g., home, school, classroom), and whether the student is learning at the same rate of other children with LEP. Other considerations include whether the student has learned to read in his or her native language and whether any cultural considerations are impacting progress.

17.3   Conclusion

Consideration of cultural and linguistic factors is necessary to avoid misclassification. Psychologists will need additional training and consultation in this area and should be mindful of the limits to their competency. The field has made strides in the assessment of culturally and linguistically diverse students but must remain vigilant about evidence-based practices. This chapter furnishes a generalized overview of psychoeducational assessment issues. The reader is directed to additional, specialized resources on this topic.

References

Clinton, A. (2014). *Assessing bilingual children in context: An integrated approach*. Washington, D. C: American Psychological Association.

DeThorne, L. S., & Watkins, R. V. (2006). Language abilities and nonverbal IQ in children with language impairment: Inconsistency across measures. *Clinical Linguistics & Phonetics, 20*(9), 641–658.

Kamphaus, R. W. (2005). *Clinical assessment of child and adolescent intelligence*. New York: Springer.

Rhodes, R., Ochoa, S. H., & Ortiz, S. O. (2005). *Assessment of culturally and linguistically diverse students: A practical guide*. New York: The Guilford Press.

Swisher, L., Plante, E., & Lowell, S. (1994). Nonlinguistic deficits of children with language disorders complicates the interpretation of their nonverbal IQ scores. *Language, Speech and Hearing Services in Schools, 25*, 235–240.

Woodworth, R. S. (1916). Comparative psychology of races. *Psychological Bulletin, 13*, 388–397.

Chapter 18
Oral Reporting

18.1 Overview

The purpose of the feedback conference is to review findings with the multidisciplinary team and caregivers. This will include a discussion of the approach to evaluation, a discussion of the report's findings, and then a presentation of the recommendations. Throughout the report conference the psychologist will permit time to address any questions the caregiver might have.

18.2 Format and Meeting Participants

There are two general ways in which to structure report conferences: (1) private conference between psychologist and caregivers or (2) team approach which is spearheaded by the psychologist or some other member of the multidisciplinary team. The first approach to feedback conferences has the psychologist and the caregiver separately discuss the report. This approach is sometimes taken in the schools as the psychologist may be able to more appropriately convey sensitive information in a more private setting. It is also the clinic-based approach taken within a private agency or university clinic. When this approach is taken within the schools, after the feedback conference, the psychologist and the caregivers will convene the IEP or Section 504 meeting, if there is need, and proceed to a discussion of the IEP or 504 plan.

The second approach has the psychologist furnish feedback to parents in front of all the multidisciplinary team members. Many school districts choose this approach as it conveys the perspective that the report and its conclusions were predicated upon a team decision-making process. It also permits participation from the team's participants who might have additional perspective regarding the child. Participants within the report conference may include the student's teachers, the caregivers, instructional aides, administrators such as the director of special education or the

© Springer Science+Business Media New York 2015   327
S.C. Dombrowski, *Psychoeducational Assessment and Report Writing*,
DOI 10.1007/978-1-4939-1911-6_18

principal, and sometimes even the child. Additional participants who may attend a meeting include a special education advocate, an outside therapist or psychologist, and an attorney. Conferences formatted in this fashion often have one person (i.e., psychologist, special education teacher, case manager) facilitate the meeting and ensure that all attendees are able to participate. The psychologist will still be responsible for discussing a significant portion of the report. However, there are elements such as classroom performance, behavior, or how services will look in the classroom that are best be clarified by additional personnel.

18.3 General Framework for Feedback Conferences

In the majority of report conferences it is the psychologist who will be responsible for discussing the report. The following general framework will help students learn this often complex process. The structure is presented below followed by a more detailed discussion of each component.

1. Starting the Conference.
2. Provide a Very Brief Description of Evaluation Process.
3. Present strength-based assessment results and then classification decision.
4. Address any question or concerns.
5. Discuss each Section of the Report.
6. Integrate findings.
7. Discuss recommendations.

18.3.1 How to Start the Conference

When the caregivers were initially interviewed the process of rapport building began. During the interview phase of the evaluation process you should have discussed the aims and scope of the evaluation including what information you were gathering, what is to be expected from the evaluation, and when the evaluation might be completed. Since it may have been some time since the psychologist last corresponded with the caregiver(s) the psychologist should engage briefly with them. This is not the time, however, for protracted or affected attempts at connecting with the caregiver(s). Caregiver(s) may be quite anxious and want to get started with hearing your perspective (and that of the multidisciplinary team if you are in a US public school setting) regarding eligibility and services to which the child might be entitled.

Example

Psychologist: Hello Mrs. Smith. It is good to see you again. I am glad we are able to discuss Johnny's report. How have things been since we last spoke?

Mrs. Smith: It is good to see you too. Things have been just about the same. Johnny still struggles with reading and writing.

18.3.2 Brief Description of Evaluation Process

Although you may have discussed with the caregiver(s) the information you were gathering and the approach to evaluation you were undertaking, you should review the process you used to conduct the evaluation. Since much of this information, even when discussed in a straightforward manner, will seem quite technical, you should revisit the process you used to arrive at your conclusions and recommendations.

Example

Psychologist: I see. Johnny is still struggling with reading and writing. Well. Let's jump right in and get started with a review of Johnny's report.

Mrs. Smith: Very good.

Psychologist: As we had discussed previously when we last spoke I was responsible for conducting the evaluation of Johnny. As part of that process I used multiple methods of assessment and gathered information on his progress in several areas including how he is doing academically, cognitively, behaviorally and socially. As part of this process I gathered input from you, his teachers and from standardized testing. I also observed Johnny in his classes.

18.3.3 Presentation of Strengths-Based Assessment and Then the Classification Conclusion

Following the discussion of the evaluation process should be a discussion of the positive aspects of the child. The focus of the report conference will be on the child's struggles and the accommodations for those struggles, so it will be important to begin with a brief discussion of the results of your strength-based assessment. After presenting this information immediately move to a discussion of the classification conclusion and whether the child is eligible for support. Many caregivers may be anxious and not hear anything else you might say up until that point.

Example

Psychologist: Please allow me to discuss Johnny's strengths. Numerous sources of evaluation data revealed that he is a kind, compassionate and well-liked child. He also is an exceptional athlete and quite motivated to learn mathematics. These qualities are important to highlight. Now I would like to move to the classification decision. Based upon the comprehensive evaluation. Johnny will qualify for special education support under a classification of learning disabilities.

18.3.4 Address Any Questions or Concerns

Once you present your classification decision, then this is a logical place to address any questions or concerns that the caregiver might have. The caregiver may have several reactions ranging from agreement and relief to denial and anger. At this point it may be appropriate to inquire with caregivers about their initial perspective regarding the classification decision and any other concerns or questions they might have.

Example

Psychologist: Do you have any thoughts, concerns or questions about this classification?
Mrs. Smith: I always suspected Johnny had something going on. His older brother never struggled the way he did, so this makes sense.
Psychologist: I am glad this makes sense. Shortly, we will discuss recommendations that will hopefully improve Johnny's reading and writing, but first I would like to review some of the details of the report including how the classification decision was arrived at by the team. Is this okay with you?
Mrs. Smith: Yes it is.

18.3.5   Discuss Each Section of the Report

After the classification decision is offered and any questions or concerns addressed you should delve into each section of the report. Be cautious, however, about getting too technical unless the caregiver asks for additional technical details. For instance, it is less appropriate to discuss the intricacies of confidence intervals and the standard error of measurement. Granted, these are important concepts but they may be too technical for the average caregiver. Instead, comment in general how the child is doing in the major domains: cognitive, academic, behavior, social-emotional, and adaptive.

18.3.5.1   Cognitive and Academic

When reviewing standard scores, it is best to avoid presenting too much technical information unless it is asked for. There are two approaches that may be taken when presenting standardized cognitive and academic information. One approach has the psychologist present an annotated depiction of the bell curve and discuss where the child falls on the curve. This requires the psychologist to note various points on the curve (e.g., average, below average, above average) and discuss where the child being evaluated falls on the curve. The danger in this presentation is that it can be overly difficult to understand for some caregivers. A second option is to discuss the child's performance more linearly noting that percentiles range from approximately 1 to 99. Explain that the average falls somewhere between the 25th and the 75th percentile and then place the child on the percentile continuum. Take a child who scores at the 60th percentile as an example. Indicate to the caregiver that the child scored at the 60th percentile which means that she scored greater than 60 of 100 children her age. You could even state if we line up 100 children of your child's age then your child would be number 60 out of 100. After discussing norm-referenced scores move to a discussion of curriculum-based assessment results, grade reports and teacher impressions of academic progress.

Example

Psychologist: Please allow me to begin with a discussion of Johnny's cognitive and academic performance on standardized testing. Johnny scored in the average range, at the 75 percentile, on a measure of cognitive ability. He struggled on a measure of academic achievement—the WIAT-III—in the areas of reading and writing where he scored in the 6th and 8th percentiles, respectively. This means that if we place Johnny next to 100 of his peers, he scored higher than 75 on the IQ test and higher than 6 and 8 of children his age on a measure of reading and writing. He also struggled on a measure of phonological awareness (the CTOPP-2) scoring at the 9th percentile. Johnny's difficulties with these achievement tasks is consistent with teacher and parent reports where Johnny faces significant difficulty with activities involving reading and writing. Does this make sense?

Caregiver: Um. Yes. His difficulties make sense to me, but I don't know what you mean by phonological awareness.

Psychologist: Okay. Good question. Phonological awareness represents Johnny's ability to connect the sounds that words make to the words themselves. It helps him to decode or sound out words. Johnny has difficulty with these tasks—sounding out words and decoding them. It is a reason why he struggles with reading so much. For Johnny to fluently read and therefore comprehend what he has read, he must quickly and efficiently decode words. He struggles with his word attack skills and so this is interfering with his ability to quickly read and understand what he has read. Does that make sense?

Caregiver: Yes. I think so.

18.3.5.2   Social-Emotional and Behavioral

The threshold for discussion with social, emotional, and behavior instruments is generally the average, at-risk, and clinically significant range. Discuss standardized test results and reconcile with observations, background information, and teacher reports.

Psychologist: Okay. Let's move on to a discussion of Johnny's progress in the behavioral and social-emotional arena. Johnny was described by his teachers and rated on the BASC-2 as a well-adjusted child. He sometimes loses focus easily but this occurs during reading instruction and not mathematics. He is helpful to the class and a good friend to several students in the class. Other than his occasional loss of focus during reading instruction, there do not appear to be any additional concerns.

Caregiver: Do you think Johnny's loss of focus is related to his difficulty with reading?

Psychologist: It is certainly possible that this is the case, but we have to be cautious about making such a definite statement. Still, since he does not lose focus when other academic subjects are being discussed, it seems like a possible explanation. We will continue to monitor his behavior in this area to see whether the supports that he will receive will help.

18.3.6   Integrate Findings

Here is where you put it all together. It need not be a long synthetical discussion but it should tie your results together so that you move into the recommendation and intervention planning phase. When caregivers ask for more elaborate discussion of the information then it is appropriate to take the time to discuss that information.

Example

Psychologist: Based upon multiple methods of assessment and sources of data including standardized assessment, review of grade reports, medical records, interview results, observations, all supported by clinical judgment, Johnny qualifies for specially designed instruction under a classification of learning disabilities. His tendency to lose focus during reading will continue to be monitored. Johnny is otherwise described as a well-adjusted and well-liked child with several friends who seeks to help others.

Caregiver: Yes. That makes sense. Do you think he will overcome his learning disability?

Psychologist: The scientific evidence suggests that learning disabilities are a life-long condition. This does not mean that Johnny will not be successful and cannot learn. He will learn strategies that will help him learn. I would imagine you have numerous thoughts going through your head, some of which may be scary for you.

Caregiver: Yes! The world is a tough place and I want Johnny to be successful. I'm concerned that he won't do well in high school and beyond and then not be able to make it.

Psychologist: These are very valid concerns. But I think that Johnny will be able to learn and it is our hope that he will understand how to make adjustments to his learning style that will help him. No one can predict the future, but I think that Johnny is a bright child and this bodes well for his future success. Keep in mind that there is a difference between a learning disability and an intellectual disability. Johnny does not have an intellectual disability.

Caregiver: Uh. When I went to school, if one received a special education classification, then we never saw the child anymore. He was placed in a separate class in a separate building.

Psychologist: No. This will not happen with Johnny and it would be inappropriate. Our school embraces an inclusive philosophy and most of Johnny's additional support will take place right in the classroom. Does this make sense?

Caregiver: I think so.

Psychologist: Well. Ms. Anne can describe more fully the look and feel of Johnny's services. She will also be discussing the components of his IEP. I think some of your concerns will be addressed further by Ms. Anne.

Caregiver: Okay. Thank you.

18.3.7 Discuss Recommendations

Within this section, you will discuss your recommendations for the child. If presenting the feedback in a school setting, this should flow into a discussion of the IEP or Section 504 plan (if the child is found eligible).

Example

Psychologist: As we discussed, Johnny struggles with reading and writing. Let's please turn to the recommendations section of the report and review the recommendations that are indicated for Johnny. More specific intervention recommendations are offered within Johnny's IEP and the team will move to a discussion of the IEP following a discussion of the recommendations that are deemed appropriate for him.

Mother: Great.

Psychologist: [The psychologist would proceed to discuss recommendations].

18.4   Case Examples

There is no replacement for practicing the provision of feedback with caregivers and a multidisciplinary team. The discussion of a few case examples cannot capture all of the varied scenarios faced by psychologists, but they will give a sense of the process.

18.4.1   Case Example 1: The Unexpected Response

This is an example of a case that involved a third grade child who scored in the gifted range on measures of academic achievement (reading, writing, and mathematics). He was the highest in his grade in all academic areas. His score on a measure of cognitive ability was approximately 108. His mother, a highly involved parent, referred the child for an evaluation to see whether he qualified for special education support because he would sometime lose focus, have poor handwriting, and was somewhat clumsy. Upon completing the evaluation, it seemed as if this would be a smooth conference with the provision of positive results. In reality, the conference was unexpectedly antagonistic.

Psychologist: Good Morning Ms. Smith. Thank you for coming to this meeting to discuss the results of Sammy. It is good to speak with you again.

Mother: Thank you.

Psychologist: As I mentioned to you previously, I conducted a comprehensive evaluation of Sammy looking at his progress across multiple domains including cognitive ability, academic achievement, behavior, social, and emotional.

Please allow me to begin with a discussion of Sammy's numerous strengths. He excels in all academic areas and is in the highest reading and math groups in his grade. He is also a very thoughtful child who reaches out to and supports others in need. It was a genuine pleasure getting to know Sammy. Because Sammy is one of the highest achievers in his grade, and scored in the gifted range on measures of academic achievement he will not be eligible for special education support. What are your thoughts about this finding?

Mother: I disagree. My sister who is a special education attorney with A, B & C law firm read through your report and indicated it was poor. She expressed that it was disorganized and the cognitive ability instrument that you used is not commonly used to evaluate children who might be gifted. She also said that you also use achievement instruments that are old and outdated. Thus, I dismiss this report and its findings and feel that it is inaccurate.

Psychologist: I am sorry that you feel that the report and the procedures used to arrive at the conclusions are inappropriate. What is it that you thought you would have expected to see?

Mother: I am surprised that Sammy was not classified with a learning disability or some other classification so that he can obtain services. He struggles with his handwriting and loses attention easily. I think he needs special education support. I am also surprised that he did not score in the gifted range on the IQ test. My sister questions the reliability and validity of the IQ test you used to evaluate Sammy. She mentioned that it is not commonly used for gifted testing and she said that you should have used instead the Stanford–Binet 5.

Psychologist: I can understand why think that Sammy might be eligible for special education support. It is difficult to watch such a bright child struggle with writing out his responses when he has so much to convey. It must also be frustrating when you work with him to see him tune out and lose focus.

Mother: Yes. But this does not change the fact that he needs support for those difficulties and I want that support provided through an IEP.

Psychologist: Please allow me to explain why Sammy was not found eligible and then perhaps brainstorm with the team to come up with a plan to support Sammy's struggles with handwriting and loss of focus.

Mother: Okay.

Psychologist: I can assure you that the instruments used within the report and the evaluation itself was comprehensive. One of the requirements for special education eligibility is to determine whether a condition experienced by the child adversely impacts educational performance. Sammy's scored in the gifted range (i.e., higher than 130 or at the 98th to 99th percentile) on all academic achievement tests. He is also considered to be at the highest level in his class across all subjects. Because he is one of the highest students in his class we could not make a case that his condition is adversely affecting his educational performance. This does not mean that we will not attempt to provide accommodations for his difficulties. We will. It is just that he will not be eligible for special education support for those difficulties. Does this make sense to you?

Caregiver: Yes. It makes sense but it still does not address the issue of using an inappropriate IQ test for giftedness testing.

Psychologist: Please allow me to assure you that the IQ test used is a valid and reliable measure of cognitive ability. It is the newest IQ test available and therefore may not be as widely known. But rest assured that it is valid and reliable for the purpose of ascertaining an IQ test score.

Caregiver: Okay. I will convey that information to my sister. She had serious reservations about the test and even about your report.

Psychologist: I think now is the time to move to a discussion of the recommendations that I have for Sammy. Although he did not qualify for special education support, he still would benefit from recommendations for his occasional attentional lapses and his handwriting difficulties.

…The psychologist goes on to discuss the case…

18.4.2   Case 2: The Caregiver in Denial

The following case represents a caregiver who is not quite ready to acknowledge the possibility that her son has an autism spectrum classification. The son was in kindergarten and struggled with the core symptoms of ASD.

Psychologist: Good Morning Ms. Jones. Thank you for coming to this meeting to discuss the results of Jackie. It is a pleasure to meet with you in person.

Mother: Thank you. Same here.

Psychologist: As I mentioned to you previously, I conducted a comprehensive evaluation of Jackie looking at her progress across multiple domains including cognitive ability, academic achievement, behavior, social, and emotional.

Please allow me to start with a discussion of Jackie's strengths and then move to my conclusion. It was a genuine please being able to evaluate Jackie. She is an incredible artist who produces creative drawings. She also has an outstanding capacity to spell and really understands how to navigate the Windows operating system. However, Jackie struggles with communication, socialization and other behaviors suggest that she will qualify for special education support under a classification of autism. The evaluation results indicate that Jackie has high functioning autism spectrum disorder.

What are your thoughts about this classification?

Caregiver: I completely disagree with you. My sister works at the Center for Autism in Smithville, USA and she does not see autism in Jackie. She thinks it is more a learning disability combined with a speech issue and attention deficit disorder.

Psychologist: Please allow me to explain how the classification decision was arrived upon. Ms. Jones, as mentioned when we spoke, I conducted a comprehensive evaluation of Jackie's functioning looking at her cognitive, academic, social, emotional, behavioral, and adaptive functioning. Although Jackie's cognitive ability is approximately in the average range, she struggles with socializing and communicating at an age expected manner. For instance she rarely makes eye contact when spoken too and often has her back turned to others while they attempt to engage her in conversation. When asked a question, Jackie tends to furnish tangential responses or switch the conversation to a topic preferred by her. Jackie also spends a significant amount to time playing in the sand tray. When redirected she will engage briefly in the requested activity, but then return to the sand tray moments later. Jackie also becomes upset when the classroom routine is changed. For instance, when her teacher is absent or when the class is abbreviated, Jackie becomes distressed and starts flicking her fingers. All these characteristics suggest that she meets criteria for an autism spectrum classification.

Does this make sense?

Mother: I understand what you are saying but I think that she is young and will outgrow many of these social issues. I know that my husband was shy as a child and struggled socially, but he does not have autism. I think that kids these days tend to be classified with autism much more than they should. My sister agrees and thinks that Jackie just has a communication issue, a speech issue, and ADHD.

Psychologist: I respect your perspective. At this point I would encourage you to take some time to consider what we have discussed at this conference. If you agree then we can move forward with an IEP.

Mother: I would like to consider my options. Would it be possible to get a second opinion?

Psychologist: Yes. You are entitled to a second opinion. Please let us know and we can furnish you with a list of individuals who are qualified to conduct independent educational evaluations or you can furnish a few names of appropriately qualified individuals.

18.4.3 Case 3: The Appreciative Caregiver

In this third example the case that will be presented is of a child who qualifies for special education via the IDEA category OHI. The caregivers have been concerned about the child's ability to focus and complete schoolwork.

Psychologist: Good Morning Mr. and Mrs. King. Thank you for coming to this meeting to discuss the results of Jamal. It is good to speak with you again and a real pleasure to meet you in person.

Parents: Thank you. It is nice to finally meet you in person too.

Psychologist: As I mentioned to you previously, I conducted a comprehensive evaluation of Jamal looking at his progress across multiple domains including cognitive ability, academic achievement, behavior, social, and emotional.

Please allow me to begin with a discussion of Jamal's numerous strengths. Jamal's mathematical abilities are quite high. He is particularly good at geometry. He also is an outstanding artist. Jamal's teachers indicated that he is a charming child who has many friends. It was a genuine pleasure getting to know Jamal. The results of the evaluation suggest that Jamal will be eligible for special education support under a classification of Other Health Impairment. Multiple methods of assessment and sources of data suggest that his attention related difficulties are negatively impacting his academic performance particularly in reading and writing. What are your thoughts about this finding?

Parents: We definitely agree and feel as if this report describes Jamal really well. It is right on target. And, thank you for pointing out Jamal's positives. We have heard so much this year about how he is not paying attention and how poorly he is doing. It is getting difficult to hear this over and over. So, what does this mean for Jamal?

Psychologist: I am glad you feel that the report accurately portrays Jamal. Since you agree with the findings, the next steps will be to briefly discuss some of the details of the report and then move to a discussion of the report's recommendations.

Parents: Okay. That sounds great.

...Psychologist and parents discuss additional details and then move to the recommendations and the IEP.

18.5   General Oral Reporting Guidelines

The guidelines for report writing may also be applicable for oral conference reporting. Here are a few general suggestions that should be considered when involved with an oral report conference.

18.5.1   Facilitate the Meeting and Engage All Appropriate Participants

If you are discussing the child's progress in the classroom with the classroom teacher and other school professionals (e.g., teacher's aide) present then ask the teacher or the aide to furnish his or her impression of the child's functioning. A first hand accounting of perspective is superior than having it furnished second hand.

18.5.2   Team Decision

Emphasize that although you wrote the report the conclusions are the result of multiple perspectives, methods of assessment, and a collaborative decision-making process that involves caregiver.

18.5.3 Avoid Pedantic Psychobabble

Speak to parents in direct terms using accessible language. Speak parsimoniously avoiding big words and pedantic psychobabble. This is discussed more fully in Chapter 19 under report writing but is also applicable when orally conveying results to caregivers and teachers.

18.5.4 Expect the Unexpected

As sample case 1 above illustrates when you think that the report conference will go smoothly, it may not. You may anticipate a difficult report conference only to have it go smoothly. You may expect a smooth conference to have it turn out to be difficult.

18.5.5 Pressure or Negotiation for a Classification

Caregivers may wish to receive service for their children but may seek to receive a different diagnostic label, one that they perceive is less pejorative (i.e., LD instead of autism). Do not amend your classification decision for this reason or for any other reason that is not supported by your evaluation results. This is not only unethical but also illegal.

18.5.6 Be Empathetic but Maintain Boundaries

This is a corollary of the above recommendation. You will need to empathize with caregivers, but be cautious to maintain boundaries. Psychologists tend to be kind people who hope to help and please. New psychologists, under certain circumstances, will need to balance the need to be empathetic and the need to establish appropriate boundaries.

18.5.7 Be Prepared

Rehearse what you will say and be well prepared for the conference.

18.5.8 Be Direct but Gentle

Do not avoid difficult questions or issues. Similarly, be cautious about being brutally blunt in your communication.

18.5.9 Speak Slowly and Permit Time for Caregivers to Process Information and Ask Questions

You will be furnishing a lot of technical information loaded with potentially emotional content. Caregivers will need time to process this information so you should speak slowly. Caregivers may also require clarification questions and the psychologist should anticipate and ask whether there are any questions.

18.6 Conclusion

Within this chapter you have been furnished with a general framework for how to structure and guide the oral feedback meeting. Like report writing the discussion of the written report requires complex cognitive skills and can be challenging to the beginning psychologist. The guidelines offered within this chapter should help furnish guidance on the process. However, a chapter on the topic can never supplant experience with the practice (and art) of oral reporting. But it is a good start.

Chapter 19
Special Issues in Psychoeducational Assessment and Report Writing

19.1 Overview

This chapter offers guidance on important topics in assessment and report writing and comprises two sections. The first section discusses professional and ethical issues in psychoeducational assessment and report writing. The second section covers general assessment and report writing issues.

19.2 Applicable General Ethical Principles and Test Standards

When working with children, whether conducting psychoeducational assessments, engaging in behavioral intervention or facilitating psychotherapy, psychologists must engage in practices that are consistent with ethical codes and professional standards. There are several bodies of work that provide ethical and professional guidance for the school or clinical child psychologist in the psychoeducational assessment of children and adolescents. This includes the *Standards for Educational and Psychological Testing* (AERA, APA, & NCME, 1999), the National Association of School Psychologists (NASP) Principles for Professional Ethics (2010), and the American Psychological Association's (APA) Ethical Principles of Psychologists (2010). The APA and NASP ethical guidelines are available in download for free. The Test Standards may be purchased for a fee. Presented first within this chapter are general ethical principles from APA and NASP along with applicable guidance from the *Standards for Educational and Psychological Testing* (1999). This is by no means a comprehensive coverage of all test standards and ethical issues related to psychoeducational assessment, report writing and oral reporting. Instead, it serves to highlight salient issues faced by child psychologists working with children in an assessment setting. The reader is referred to the original ethical guidelines, test standards, and textbooks on ethical issues in psychology for more comprehensive information.

© Springer Science+Business Media New York 2015   339
S.C. Dombrowski, *Psychoeducational Assessment and Report Writing*,
DOI 10.1007/978-1-4939-1911-6_19

19.2.1   Beneficence and Nonmaleficence

Both APA and NASP ethical codes require that psychologists avoid doing any harm and engage in practices that strive to benefit those with whom they work (i.e., APA Principle A: Beneficence and Nonmaleficence; NASP Standard I Professional Competence and Responsibility). The APA's Principle A: Beneficence and Nonmaleficence indicates that "Psychologists strive to benefit those with whom they work and take care to do no harm" (APA, 2010, p. 3). The NASP Principles for Professional Ethics (2010) Principle II, Professional Competence and Responsibility, requires that "beneficence, or responsible caring, means that the school psychologist acts to benefit others" (p. 6). This has relevance for the psychoeducational assessment process. The process itself should work toward the betterment of the child. As an example, Dombrowski and Gischlar (2014) contend that the IQ-Achievement discrepancy approach conflicts with this general principle and should be avoided because of the potential for misdiagnosis and therefore harm to children who are assessed using this diagnostic algorithm. A second example might be the use of culturally loaded assessment instruments for students who are non-English speakers. Both assessment practices, under certain conditions, may conflict with APA's/NASP's ethical mandate to "do no harm."

19.2.2   Respect for Rights and Dignity of Individuals

APA and NASP both hold that psychologist's must respect the rights and dignity of those with whom they come in contact. APA's general principle of respecting people's rights and dignity and NASP's Theme I related to respecting the dignity and rights of all individuals undergirds the need to understand and respect sociocultural and individual differences including linguistic, gender, sexual, socioeconomic, racial, and religious. These principles also establish the basis for discussing the purpose of the evaluation with the child at the onset of the evaluation process and debriefing the child at the end. To the degree possible, you should obtain child assent by explaining the purpose of the evaluation to the child. The practice of using culturally loaded assessment instruments (or assessment instruments that are inappropriate for their purpose) may also conflict with the general principle of respect for the rights and dignity of the individual.

19.2.3   Competence

Both APA (APA 2.01 Boundaries of Competence; 2.03 Maintaining Competence) and NASP (Theme II) require that psychologists practice within the boundaries of their competence. Implicit in this standard is the need to avoid engaging in practices (i.e., knowing the boundaries of your competence) for which you are ill-prepared or under-qualified. For instance, you should not assert that you are a neuropsychologist unless you have undertaken specialized predoctoral and postdoctoral training in that area. Additionally, you should be cautious about claiming capacity to engage in couples therapy without specific training. When representing your credentials, do not present credentials [i.e., John Doe, Ph.D. (ABD) or Susan Smith, Ed.S. Candidate] that are misleading to the public.

The standard of competence also serves another purpose. It encourages psychologists to engage in continuing education and monitor the proficiency of their skill set regardless of whether their state requires it. This would suggest that psychologists have a responsibility to keep current with research and seek new training opportunities. In the same way that it would be ill-advised to use a physician who graduated in 1975 with no further training to diagnose and treat a child, it would also be ill-advised to use a school or clinical child psychologist who does not stay current with the research literature and professional knowledge base when evaluating and treating children.

19.2.4   Engage in Empirically Validated Practices

Both APA and NASP require that psychologists engage in evaluation practices that have an empirical basis. The APA code of ethics indicates in 2.04 Bases for Scientific and Professional Judgments that a "psychologist's work is based upon established scientific and professional knowledge of the discipline" (p. 5). The NASP code of ethics requires psychologists to "…use scientific knowledge from psychology and education to help clients…" (NASP 2010 Code of Ethics, p. 6). The NASP 2010 code of ethics in Standard II.3.2 speaks in more detail to this issue by directing psychologists to "use assessment techniques and practices that the profession considers to be responsible, research-based practice" (p. 7). Psychologists are encouraged to reflect upon the use of identification and intervention practices in consideration of these ethical strictures to use empirically validated practices. The Standards for Educational and Psychological Testing (1999) developed jointly by the American Educational Research Association (AERA), the American Psychological Association (APA), and the National Council on Measurement in Education (NCME) (AERA, APA, & NCME, 1999) also speak to the need to engage in evidence-based practices. The Standards indicate the need for assessment models and instruments to have appropriate reliability and validity. Practitioners and researchers alike are required to determine the validity and reliability of any assessment method prior to its use (AERA, APA, & NCME, 1999). Standards 4.19 and 4.20 discuss responsible test use and recommend caution when interpretation involves using one or more cut scores and requires that empirical evidence of the cut score's validity be provided. Standard 13.7 recommends that multiple sources of information and data are considered when making placement decisions that portend to have a major impact on students. The implication is that the use of clinical judgment might be necessary when making a classification decision instead of the rigid application of a diagnostic heuristic that display less than acceptable validity and reliability.

19.2.5 Conflict Between the Law and Ethical Standards

Most of the time, the laws governing the practice of psychology are consistent with ethical standards. There are times, however, when the law conflicts with ethical strictures. An important ethical stricture from NASP's and APA's codes require a psychologist to adhere to a higher standard of care than the law requires when the law potentially conflicts with ethical obligations. The NASP (2010) Principles for Professional Ethics, for instance, generally require "a more stringent standard of conduct than law, and in those situations in which both apply, school psychologists are expected to adhere to the Principles." (p. 2). The APA code of ethics has a similar ethical requirement.

19.2.6 Confidentiality and Maintenance of Records

Psychologists are required to hold information in confidence. This applies not only to information revealed during a counseling session but also to information collected during a psychoeducational evaluation. Psychologists should therefore be circumspect when discussing confidential psychoeducational assessment information inside the school (e.g., teacher's lounge) or outside the school. Related to this, teachers and other school personnel often have access to student records including psychological reports. Because of the potential for misuse and misunderstanding, I recommend that test protocols and psychoeducational reports are kept in a different location and file from other educational records. This will help to preserve confidentiality, maintain test security, and limit unsupervised access by untrained individuals.

Reports and summaries should be kept for 5 years past the student's enrollment in a particular school (Canter, 2001) before they are discarded. This should be considered generalized guidance and specific state guidelines and school district policy needs to be referenced as there is considerably more legal and ethical nuance.

19.2.7 Limits to Confidence

There are generally three situations under which psychologists are legally obligated to break their confidentiality requirement. This includes when the psychologist (1) suspects maltreatment; (2) determines that the client is a danger to himself; and (3) encounters a scenario where the client threatens to harm other individuals. When one of these three scenarios is encountered, then the psychologist is legally and ethically required to take protective action by contacting child protective services, law enforcement or caregivers depending upon the circumstances. The reader is referred to Dombrowski, Ahia, and McQuillan (2003) for detailed guidance regarding mandated child abuse reporting in a school setting. Jacobs et al.'s work is recommended for more in-depth coverage regarding dangerousness to self or others including a discussion of the Tarasoff decision.

19.2.8 Consent for Assessment

Signed written consent is required prior to beginning the evaluation. Do not under any circumstances begin an individualized evaluation without obtaining written consent from the legal guardian who may or may not be the biological parent. Also, be sure that you have custodial (i.e., legal guardian) written consent before speaking with the non-custodial parent. Sometimes a parent or caregiver will be listed in the school records as having permission to pick up a child from school. You may even see this caregiver frequently involved in the child's life. This parent or caregiver may not have authority to give consent to evaluate.

19.2.9 Consent to Share Records

Do not, under any circumstances, share a report with another professional including a doctor, attorney, or outside service provider without a written release to do so. There may be times when you receive a written request from an attorney requesting records regarding the child. This may seem rather official and be presented in language "demanding" your provision of any and all records pertaining to a child. Do not release any information to the attorney, whether or not they have been retained by the legal guardian, unless the legal guardian furnishes signed written consent or unless you receive a court order from a judge.

19.2.10 Report Security

Consistent with the duty to protect confidential information, any reports sent via email should be encrypted with a password or protected by some other encryption method. This will help to prevent unintended viewing of the records. Similarly, any draft reports need to be shredded so that confidential information is protected.

19.2.11   Release of Test Protocols

Based upon an appeals decision by the 9th district court, California school districts are now distributing copies of test protocols to parents without violating federal copyright law (Canter, 2005). Canter (2005) recommends that "when a parent makes a legitimate request to review or have a copy of a test protocol, be sure to provide accompanying information about the nature and limitations of the test procedure and how the results are used." Canter (2005) also recommends that an appropriate multidisciplinary team member should review the information with the caregiver including the importance of test security so that future administration of the instrument is not compromised.

There is sure to be continued controversy and litigation regarding this practice. Certain circuit courts' decisions should not necessarily be considered precedent-setting due to the high frequency of overturning of such decision made by those courts. It turns out that the 9th Circuit Court is notorious for being one of the most overturned circuits of all time with nearly three of four decisions overturned by the Supreme Court. Furthermore, this decision ruled on whether copyright laws could be used to deny parents copies of a protocol, but it did not rule on whether other reasons could be used to deny parents. It is anticipated that we will see additional guidance on this ruling in the years to come perhaps even from the Supreme Court.

19.2.12   Maintenance of Records

Because of the potential for misuse and misunderstanding, I recommend that test protocols are kept in a different location and file from other educational records. This will preserve confidentiality, maintain test security, and limit unsupervised access by untrained individuals.

19.3   General Assessment and Report Writing Principles

The following section offers generalized guidance and report writing tips that will be useful to practicing school and clinical child psychologists.

19.3.1   Avoid the Use of Age and Grade Equivalent Scores

The reporting and presentation of grade and age equivalent scores should be avoided. Grade and age equivalent scores are not based upon equal metrics making them difficult to interpret and potentially misleading. For instance, let's consider grade equivalent (GE) scores. GE scores give the impression that they are linked to the curriculum, but this is incorrect. Grade equivalent (and age equivalent) scores are norm-referenced, not criterion referenced, and reflect median level performance relative to the standardization population (Reynolds, 1981). Take a child who is in fifth grade and scores at a 12th grade equivalent level. This child is clearly advanced but the child is not on the same level as a 12th grader who is taking calculus. Conversely, consider a fifth grader who is reading at a first grade equivalent level. This individual is not reading at a guided level F—the approximate first quarter first graded guided reading level—but is much higher and at a level M. As a further example, consider the aforementioned fifth grade child where the median GE is a 5th grade equivalency. An eighth grade level might be akin to one standard deviation above the mean (i.e., standard score of 115) while an 11th grade level could be a score of just four items higher (i.e., a standard score of 119)! What is the explanation for this specious scaling metric? Age and grade based scores are not based upon equal intervals and are therefore exceedingly problematic for interpretation. The presentation and use of grade or age equivalent scores could lead to erroneous interpretive practices and therefore should be avoided.

19.3.2   *Know Points on the Normal Curve*

Psychologists should seek to thoroughly understand the distribution of points along the normal curve. A psychologist's level of competence will be questioned if the psychologist cannot immediately recognize the interchangeability of points on the curve such as the 50th percentile, 84th percentile, 97.5th percentile among others. Psychologists should know by heart the percentile rank equivalency of major points along the normal curve of both T-scores and standard scores. This includes one, two, and three standard deviations above and below the mean. You should also understand the percentile range of a T-score associated with an at-risk (e.g., $T=60$ or 65) or clinically significant (e.g., 70 or higher) score.

19.3.3   *Evidence-Based Test Use and Interpretation*

I have seen over the years psychologists making statements about a child's functioning that lacks any linkage to the empirical evidence. Here are a few instances:

1. *Singular reliance on a test to make a classification decision.* For instance the reliance on the Draw-a-Person test to classify emotional disturbance is inappropriate. The literature is clear in indicating the problems with use of a singular assessment instrument, let alone one based upon a drawing with limited psychometric properties, to conceptualize and classify a child (Frick, Barry, & Kamphaus, 2010). A second example is the use of an IQ test as a means to

classify a child with autism spectrum. Poor performance on the comprehension section of the WISC—IV should not be construed to mean that a child has low social comprehension (Watkins, Glutting, & Youngstrom, 2005).

2. *Overreliance on narrow-band measures for classification decisions.* For example, selected narrow band measures of ED and autism spectrum lack adequate psychometric support. Even though many instruments report a norm-referenced score these instruments should not be afforded a greater degree of credibility than a qualitative assessment. The instrument's technical properties should be sound. Floyd and Bose (2003) conducted a review of ED instruments and found that they should only cautiously be used, if at all, because of poor technical properties.

3. *Caution about subtest interpretation.* Selected textbooks have devoted countless pages to interpretation of subtests from the Wechsler scales and other instruments. Empirical evidence from the literature on reliable subtest variance (McDermott, Fantuzzo, & Glutting, 1990) and structural validity (Canivez, 2013; Dombrowski & Watkins, 2013) suggest that this may not be good empirical practice. Although the technical manuals of most IQ tests and subsequent independent CFA studies support the interpretation of IQ tests at the level of the subtest and index, other studies, primarily using EFA techniques, suggest that this is inappropriate. This literature base indicates that the greatest amount of variance resides at the full scale level. Intuitively it might make sense to assume that a subtest that has memory items actually measures memory but the item itself may only represent a small amount of the variance tested. The debate is sure to continue as well-regarded researchers on both sides of the debate provide reasoned arguments. Kranzler and Floyd (2013) offer an empirically guided approach to intelligence test interpretation known as the KISS model. This represents a reasoned approach to intelligence test interpretation to which psychologists might consider adhering.

4. *Disregard of Psychometric g*: It is inappropriate to disregard the full scale IQ score when there is a large and statistically significant difference between various indices (i.e., SB5 Verbal-Nonverbal) or when there is a high degree of subtest scatter. This may be common practice among practitioners and advocated by some well-regarded academicians, but it is a practice that is in opposition with the empirical literature. For instance, if we find a large split between the SB5 verbal and nonverbal scale it would be inappropriate to dismiss the full scale IQ score in favor of interpretation of two distinct IQ scores.

19.3.4 Avoid the Discrepancy Approach

The discrepancy is codified into state statute and federal code, but it has been abandoned by the DSM-5 and criticized severely in the empirical literature. For that reason, the discrepancy approach, in its varied iterations, should be avoided. Please see numerous articles and books on this topic (e.g., Brueggeman, 2014; Dombrowski & Gischlar, 2014; Dombrowski, Kamphaus & Reynolds, 2004). I suggest alternative procedures be employed including that recommended by the Joint Committee on Learning Disabilities. Ideally, those procedures may use some form of problem-solving process. This may include RtI but there may also be scientifically based alternative models. Regardless of what is chosen it is recommended that a comprehensive evaluation be employed to rule out additional issues that may have a bearing on the child including intellectual, emotional, or behavioral issues.

19.3.5   Adhere to Standardized Directions

Standardized test procedures are established for a reason. They ensure consistency in administration and therefore the reliability and validity of the instrument. For instance, school psychologists trained in Dothan, Alabama, Davis, California, or Lawrenceville, NJ will administer the instruments in the same way as school psychologists trained in Williamsburg, VA, Storrs, Connecticut or Athens, Georgia. If you do decide to deviate from the standardized administration procedures, the do not report a standard score or at a minimum discuss the rationale for deviating and offer a caveat about using the derived standard score.

19.3.6   Report Test Scores, But Do Not Overemphasize Numbers

I have seen reports that merely indicate that a child scored in the average, below average, or above average range without displaying the test scores in the body of the report or at the end of the report. This is poor practice. On the other hand, do not be overcome by the tendency to hyper emphasize numbers at the expense of understanding and conceptualizing the child's functioning. It is easy to get lost in the details and spend too much time focusing on specific index or even subtest scores and miss the big picture.

19.3.7   Fully Complete Test Protocols

Ensure that test protocols are fully completed. For instance, do not just place a check mark in the test item from the comprehension section of the WISC-V if the child answered correctly. Instead, ensure that the WISC-V item is fully written out. If your test protocols are ever reviewed in some type of hearing then your credibility as a psychologist will be harmed if you took shortcuts.

19.3.8   Pressure or Negotiation for a Classification

There may be tacit or direct pressure placed upon psychologists to offer a classification other than for what the child qualified. This may occur when a school district fears that the classification decision may lead to an out-of-district placement and the placement will impact other programs at the school. For instance, in some smaller school districts with limited resources, the placement of a child in a $100,000 out-of-district placement could lead to the elimination of an art or music program. Despite the poor funding structure of special education in the United States it is the responsibility of the school psychologist to offer a classification for which the child qualifies regardless of the impact on the broader school system. Conversely, parents may attempt to influence the classification decision-making process by attempting to negotiate a classification. I have encountered situations where parents seek to receive services for a child, but wish to have what they perceive as a more benign classification label (i.e., speech-language or LD instead of Autism; OHI instead of ED). The acquiescence to these pressures is not only unethical but it is also illegal. Thus, avoid offering a classification other than that which is appropriate and that which has been supported through a comprehensive evaluation.

19.3.9   No Classification, Now What?

Children are referred for a comprehensive psychoeducational evaluation because of a problem he or she might be facing. At times, and despite the child's difficulties in one of the domains of functioning, the child will not be found eligible for special education services. In these situations, the psychologist still has an obligation to assist the teacher with ideas for supporting the child in the general education setting.

19.3.10   Use of New Instruments

Graduate students, newly credentialed psychologists and even experienced psychologists must ensure that they have inspected and understand an instrument's technical properties including norming, reliability, and validity. For instance, I recall one instrument that was normed in a single college town in Virginia but was being used nationwide as a measure of caregiver stress. The use of this instrument within an urban, lower SES setting would be inappropriate. Here is where your basic course in tests and measurements comes to fore.

Kamphaus (In press) offers a series of questions to consider when evaluating a new intelligence test (p. 176). Many of these questions are also appropriate for any assessment instrument that is being considered by the psychologist and are therefore presented below as a guide to ensure competent understanding of the instrument:

1. Is the premise of the test reasonable? Is its theory based on some supportive citations of previous research?
2. Are the test development goals clearly delineated?
3. Are the manuals complete including topics ranging from theory to interpretation of the results?
4. Are administration and scoring guidelines complete and easy to follow?
5. Are the test materials attractive to children? Are they sturdy and practical?
6. Are all of the items derivatives of those on other tests? Are some new?
7. Were the items subjected to judgmental bias reviews so as to not be offensive to test users or takers?
8. Is the test easy to administer so that the examiner can focus on the child's behavior during testing?
9. Is there evidence of content validity? Were content experts consulted? Does the item content seem consistent with theory?
10. Were statistical item bias studies undertaken?
11. Was the test norming sample collected recently?
12. Does the norming sample closely match the stratification statistics selected? Was there some measure of SES used for stratification?
13. Are the internal consistency and stability coefficients high—above .90 for the composite?
14. Is there evidence of good factorial, predictive and concurrent validity?
15. Are several derived scores offered, such as standard scores and percentile ranks in order to enhance interpretation?
16. Are interpretative tables for determining intraindividual strengths and weaknesses offered?
17. Are the scaling methods (i.e., norm-development procedures) described in detail?
18. Have early reviews been favorable or optimistic?
19. Is the test appropriate for the population of children that is served? For example, does it have extended norms for children with exceptionalities?

19.3.11 Old Versus New Instruments

There is not a particular ethical standard that addresses this issue clearly, but Dombrowski (2003, 2004) and Oakland (2003) first discussed this issue in regard to newly revised IQ tests. Dombrowski (2003, 2004) suggested a standard of 1 year to move to a new instrument after it has been developed. Kranzler and Floyd (2013) suggested an approximate 2 year time period when moving to a new instrument. All authors discuss the need for thoughtful investigation of a new instrument, particularly an IQ test, when it arrives. Several years later Lichtenstein (2010) continued this discussion and suggested flexibility rather than a rigid time period. Oakland (2003) and Lichtenstein (2010) recommend advise against establishing a transition time frame. These authors leave the decision up to the individual psychologist. I still maintain that a standard of approximately 1 year is sufficient to transition to a new assessment instrument. This may be perceived as too short, but it will allow time for external review of the technical properties of the new instrument. For instance, the Boros *Mental Measurement Yearbook* conducts reviews of most instruments. Keep in mind, however, that there are only a few measurement researchers with the expertise to look behind the veil and rigorously scrutinize an instrument's psychometric properties. These researchers often have other obligations and research interests that preclude the possibility of a review of all instruments of interest to the field. Take, as an example, the Woodcock–Johnson Test of Cognitive Abilities, Third Edition. It was not until 1 year prior to the release of the fourth edition of this instrument that its internal structure was called to question (Dombrowski, 2013; Dombrowski, 2014; Dombrowski & Watkins, 2013). Of course, there should be flexibility depending upon the instrument under scrutiny and there may be exceptions to this 1 year rule but the field should consider an end game for transitioning to a new instrument. Otherwise, practitioners may continue to use an instrument years after the new one has arrived. For all the reasons discussed above, the one year transition period seems appropriate.

19.3.12 Consider Culture and Language

When evaluating a child, numerous books (e.g., Rhodes, Ochoa, & Ortiz, 2005) and handbooks (Clinton, 2014) are available that discuss the need to evaluate a child's cultural background and language proficiency as part of the evaluation process. Psychologists have an ethical and professional responsibility to assess these areas. Without a thorough investigation of cultural factors the psychologist could easily misdiagnose the child. In turn this may result in harm to the child, a situation that is in opposition with the overarching ethical principle undergirding both APA and NASP ethical codes. Similarly, a child's language capacity should be evaluated appropriately particularly when that child is an English Language Learner. This may entail evaluation of the child's proficiency in both English and the language to which the child was exposed prior to school entry. For additional insight please see Chap. 16 and additional resources on the topic.

19.4 Conclusion

There are numerous challenges to writing effective psychoeducational reports. The process is often highly nuanced and requires the synthesis of multiple sources of data from many different methods of assessment. This chapter furnished guidance regarding the ethical, professional, and legal aspects of report writing. It will help the graduate student in school and clinical child psychology to better understand this complex process.

References

American Educational Research Association (AERA), American Psychological Association (APA), & National Council on Measurement in Education (NCME). (1999). *Standards for educational and psychological testing*. Washington, DC: American Educational Research Association.

Brueggeman, A. E. (2014). *Diagnostic assessment of learning disabilities in childhood*. New York: Springer.

Canivez, G. L. (2013). Psychometric versus actuarial interpretation of intelligence and related aptitude batteries. In D. H. Saklofske, C. R. Reynolds, & V. L. Schwean (Eds.), *The oxford handbook of child psychological assessments* (pp. 84–112). New York: Oxford University Press.

Canter, A. (2001). Test protocols part II: Storage and disposal. Communiqué, 30. Retrieved on June 3, 2014 from http://www.nasponline.org/publications/cq/cq301protocolsII.aspx.

Canter, A. (2005). Test protocols and parent's rights—to copies?. Communiqué, 34. Retrieved on June 3, 2014 from http://www.nasponline.org/publications/cq/cq341protocols.aspx.

Carlson, J. C. Hansen, N. R. Kuncel, S. P. Reise, & M. C. Rodriguez (Eds.), APA handbook of testing and assessment in psychology, Vol. 2: Testing and assessment in clinical and counseling psychology (pp. 35–50). Washington, DC. American Psychological Association.

Clinton, A. (2014). *Assessing bilingual children in context: An integrated approach*. Washington, DC: American Psychological Association.

Dombrowski, S. C. (2003). Ethical standards and best practices in using newly revised intelligence tests. *Communiqué, 32*(1), 12.

Dombrowski, S. (2004). To WISC-III or not to WISC-III, that is the question: A rejoinder to Thomas Oakland. *Communiqué, 32*(3), 15–16.

Dombrowski, S. C. (2013). Investigating the structure of the WJ-III at school age. *School Psychology Quarterly, 28*, 154–169.

Dombrowski, S. C. (2014). Exploratory bifactor analysis of the WJ-III cognitive in adulthood via the Schmid–Leiman procedure. *Journal of Psychoeducational Assessment, 32*, 330–341. doi:10.1177/0734282913508243.

Dombrowski, S. C., Ahia, C. E., & McQuillan, K. (2003). Protecting children through mandated child abuse reporting. *The Educational Forum, 67*(2), 76–85.

Dombrowski, S. C., & Gischlar, K. L. (2014). Ethical and empirical considerations in the identification of learning disabilities. *Journal of Applied School Psychology, 30*, 68–82.

Dombrowski, S. C., Kamphaus, R. W., & Reynolds, C. R. (2004). After the demise of the discrepancy: Proposed learning disabilities diagnostic criteria. *Professional Psychology: Research and Practice, 35*, 364–372.

Dombrowski, S. C., & Watkins, M. W. (2013). Exploratory and higher order factor analysis of the WJ-III full test battery: A school-aged analysis. *Psychological Assessment, 25*, 442–455.

Floyd, R. B., & Bose, J. B. (2003). Behavior rating scales for the assessment of emotional disturbance: A critical review of measurement characteristics. *Journal of Psychoeducational
Assessment, 21*, 43–78.

Frick, P. J., Barry, C. T., & Kamphaus, R. W. (2010). *Clinical assessment of children's personality
and behavior* (3rd ed.). New York: Springer.

Kamphaus, R. W. (in press). *Clinical assessment of child and adolescent intelligence* (3rd ed.).
Springer: New York.

Kranzler, J. A., & Floyd, R. G. (2013). *Assessing intelligence in children and adolescents: A practical guide*. New York: Guilford Press.

Lichtenstein, R. (2010). How soon must you switch to a new test? Communiqué, 38. Retrieved on
April 23, 2014 from http://www.nasponline.org/publications/cq/index.aspx?vol=38&issue=8.

McDermott, P. A., Fantuzzo, J. W., & Glutting, J. J. (1990). Just say no to subtest analysis: A critique on Wechsler theory and practice. *Journal of Psychoeducational Assessment, 8*, 290–302.

Oakland, T. (2003). Standards for using revised tests: A different opinion. *Communiqué, 32*(3),
10–11.

Reynolds, C. R. (1981). The fallacy of "two years below grade level for age" as a diagnostic criterion for reading disorders. *Journal of School Psychology, 19*, 350–358.

Rhodes, R., Ochoa, S. H., & Ortiz, S. O. (2005). *Assessment of culturally and linguistically diverse
students: A practical guide*. New York: The Guilford Press.

Watkins, M. W., Glutting, J. J., & Youngstrom, E. A. (2005). Issues in subtest profile analysis. In
D. P. Flanagan & P. L. Harrison (Eds.), *Contemporary intellectual assessment: Theories, tests,
and issues* (2nd ed., pp. 251–268). NY: Guilford.

Index

CPSIA information can be obtained at www.ICGtesting.com
Printed in the USA
LVOW01*0741100815

449509LV00004B/9/P